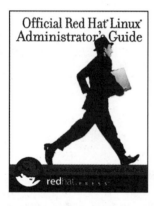

Red Hat® Linux® Internet Server

Red Hat® Linux®
Internet Server

Paul G. Sery and Jay Beale

Wiley Publishing, Inc.

Red Hat® Linux® Internet Server

Published by
Wiley Publishing, Inc.
10475 Crosspoint Boulevard
Indianapolis, IN 46256
www.wiley.com.

Copyright © 2003 by Wiley Publishing, Inc., Indianapolis, Indiana

Published by Wiley Publishing, Inc., Indianapolis, Indiana

Published simultaneously in Canada

Library of Congress Control Number: 2001093383

ISBN: 0-7645-4788-7

Manufactured in the United States of America

10 9 8 7 6 5 4 3 2 1

1B/RU/RR/QS/IN

Ⓦ Wiley Publishing, Inc. is a trademark of Wiley Publishing, Inc.

Credits

ACQUISITIONS EDITOR
Debra Williams Cauley

PROJECT EDITOR
Valerie Haynes Perry

TECHNICAL EDITOR
Jason Luster

RED HAT REVIEWER
Joshua Jensen

RED HAT PRESS LIAISONS
Chris Grams, Manager of Marketing
Services
Lorien Golaski

SPECIAL RED HAT ASSISTANCE
Kathleen Langhi
Jonathan Opps
Jeremy Hogan
Mark Cox

COPY EDITOR
Tamara Castleman

EDITORIAL MANAGER
Mary Beth Wakefield

VICE PRESIDENT AND EXECUTIVE
GROUP PUBLISHER
Richard Swadley

VICE PRESIDENT AND EXECUTIVE
PUBLISHER
Bob Ipsen

VICE PRESIDENT AND PUBLISHER
Joseph B. Wikert

EDITORIAL DIRECTOR
Mary Bednarek

PROJECT COORDINATORS
Jennifer Bingham
Dale White

GRAPHICS AND PRODUCTION
SPECIALISTS
Karl Brandt
Jackie Nicholas
Jeremey Unger

QUALITY CONTROL TECHNICIANS
John Greenough
Andy Hollandbeck
Susan Moritz

PERMISSIONS EDITOR
Laura Moss

MEDIA DEVELOPMENT SPECIALIST
Travis Silvers

PROOFREADING AND INDEXING
TECHBOOKS Production Services

About the Authors

Paul G. Sery is a computer systems engineer employed by Sandia National Laboratories in Albuquerque, NM, USA. He is a member of the Computer Support Unit, Special Projects, which specializes in managing and troubleshooting UNIX and Linux systems.

When he is not beating his head against systems administration problems, he and his wife Lidia enjoy riding their tandem through the Rio Grande valley. They also enjoy traveling throughout Mexico. Paul is the author of *LINUX Network Toolkit* (IDG Books Worldwide, 2000) and the coauthor of several other books. He has a bachelors degree in Electrical Engineering from the University of New Mexico.

Jay Beale is the lead consultant for JJB Security Consulting and Training, and lead developer of Bastille Linux. He is the author of a number of articles on Linux/Unix security and wrote the Center for Internet Security's system auditing tool for Solaris, Linux and HP-UX, and their benchmark document for Linux.

Contributors

Russell C. Pavlicek is the Open Source columnist for *Info World Magazine*. He is a consultant with Linux Professional Solutions and frequent speaker about Open Source technology.

Peter C. Norton has been administering and programming with Linux andUnix since 1993. He is an independant consultant who has worked forStarmedia Networks, TheStreet.com, VA Linux Professional Services among others. Peter is an officer of the New York Linux User Group, nylug.org.

Preface

The book you hold now, *Red Hat Linux Internet Server*, is an insider's guide to understanding and deploying Red Hat Linux. If you are new to e-business, or if you are responsible for your company's B2B initiatives, this book is everything you need to master this emerging standard. Starting with Red Hat Linux fundamentals, Red Hat Linux OASIS committee members Paul G. Sery and Jay Beale provide a unique blend of e-business insight and representative Red Hat Linux deployment scenarios based on real-world implementations. Not just an overview of the standard, *Red Hat Linux Internet Server* is exactly what you need to understand how Red Hat Linux affects the business-to-business domain and impacts your business and customers.

This book is aimed at the experienced computer user who wants to provide network services to a LAN and/or the Internet. The book describes how to construct secure basic and advanced services using the popular and powerful Red Hat Linux distribution. Sample networks are designed to serve as the basis for all of the examples throughout the book. By the time you finish reading it, you should be able to construct Red Hat Linux servers that can run your home or company network.

How This Book Is Organized

This book is divided into five parts and four appendices. The parts organize topics in order to help you create and manage increasingly advanced servers. The first part describes the foundation technologies necessary for creating networks and networking services. The next two parts introduce more complex services. One part is devoted to managing your network servers and the final one shows you how to secure your systems. The appendices provide helpful information such as how use an old-style telephone dial-up connection.

Part 1: Building a Linux Network

This part introduces networking concepts and examples that are used throughout the book. The TCP/IP protocols and the Red Hat network configuration utilities are described in order to provide the reader with a foundation to work from. Next, two example networks are designed to provide a platform for all succeeding examples throughout the book. The new and popular DSL and cable broadband technologies are also introduced in order to provide a full-time and reasonably fast method to get an Internet connection. The final chapter describes how to use stateful packet filters to create a gateway firewall.

Part II: Building a World Wide Web Server

There are several network services that are the bread and butter of the Internet. This part describes how to create the ubiquitous Web and streaming media servers. Additional instructions show how to connect the Web server to a database and use a secure SSL connection. The Open Source Icecast server shows how to provide network audio streams.

Part III: Providing Basic Internet Services

This part shows how to construct several systems that provide basic network services. Chapters describe how to create systems such as the Domain Name Server (DNS), Sendmail, File Transfer Protocol (FTP) and Samba. These services are hardly exciting but form the foundation of both LANs and the Internet.

Part IV: Managing Your Linux Servers

This part focuses on making your servers more reliable. Chapter 13 describes how to back up machines automatically over a network. Systematically making backups is the most important administrative process you can perform; it provides both security and reliability to your network. Chapter 14 looks at several technologies that you can use to increase the reliability of individual servers. One of the simple systems you can use is software based RAID where you use multiple disks to decrease the danger of losing data. You learn how to create fail-over servers so that a backup server will take over from a primary server when it fails.

Part V: Increasing Security

This part begins by describing basic server security concepts including threats to security, how to identify attackers and how to defend your server. You learn basic secure system administration practices, how to use standardized configurations, and how to apply all security fixes to your operating system components. Then you learn how to harden a system manually, and receive an introduction to Bastille Linux. The final chapters describe using a Network-based IDS (intrusion-detection system) as an integrated part of an overall defense strategy, and explain system logging as an effective measure in maintaining system security.

Conventions Used in This Book

You don't have to learn any new conventions to read this book.

- ◆ When you are asked to enter a command, you need to press the Enter or the Return key after you type the command at your command prompt.

- ◆ A monospaced font is used to denote configuration or code segment

- ◆ Text in italic needs tobe replaced with relevant information

Watch for these icons that occasionally highlight paragraphs:

 The Note icon indicates that something needs a bit more explanation.

 The Tip icon tells you something that is likely to save you some time and effort.

 The cross-reference icon tells you that you can find additional information in another chapter.

Acknowledgments

Many people worked very hard over a long period of time to produce this book. Debra Williams Cauley was absolutely essential for driving this project through many rapids and cross-currents to its completion. Without her patience and fortitude the book would not have been possible. Special thanks go to Russell Pavlicek and Peter C. Norton for writing the Postfix chapter. We also greatly appreciate the Linux expertise that Josh Jensen and Mark Cox at Red Hat provided. Valerie Perry, Jason Luster, and Tamara Castleman also provided us with a great deal of editorial and technical help.

Contents at a Glance

Contents

Part I

Building a Linux Network

Chapter 1

Introducing the Example Networks

IN THIS CHAPTER

◆ Introducing the sample networks

◆ Explaining server functions

◆ Adding subnets to both networks

THIS BOOK IS WRITTEN to provide you with a road map for creating one or more Red Hat Internet Servers. The design process can be as simple as installing Red Hat's Server class on a PC and connecting it to a network. Red Hat simplifies the process of creating common Internet services such as Web pages, Samba file sharing, and NFS servers. If you're only interested in providing simple Web pages on a local area network (LAN), then Red Hat's default services, combined with a broadband Internet connection like DSL or cable modems, may be all you need.

However, if you want to securely provide more than basic services on a simple network, then the design process becomes more difficult. You have to consider where you're going to place the server (or servers) within an existing network or how you're going to build a new network. You can configure each service in many different ways, but you have to ensure that those configurations work with other services and servers. And since the Internet is increasingly used by hackers to launch attacks, you must fully and completely integrate security into the design.

We believe that giving overall descriptions of each subject and then providing concrete examples is an effective way to learn. This chapter serves as the basis for the book by creating two network designs. One network is simple and the other more complex. The two examples bracket a large percentage of real-world networks.

Introducing the Sample Networks

You can configure networks in a nearly infinite number of ways, although most networks boil down to a few basic pieces. For instance, the most common network in use today is a very simple network consisting of a modem connecting a single computer to an Internet Service Provider (ISP) – and, thus, the Internet. On the other end of the spectrum, large organizations typically maintain multiple subnets within individual buildings to create LANs. The LANs are then interconnected

3

within a campus setting to create a wide area network (WAN), and finally virtual networks are created across the Internet to connect the WANs.

You can create many network configurations in between the two extremes. In this book, we concentrate on two topologies that many small to medium-sized organizations commonly use. These two networks create the basis for all of the examples we use throughout this book, which we describe in some detail in this chapter. That way, you get an overview of our philosophy, and we avoid confusion later on.

The example networks are called the *Direct Connect to Internet* (DCI), which is designed for the smallest company or home office, and *Demilitarized Zone to Internet* (DMZI), which is designed for small or medium-sized organizations. The former is this book's own convention but the latter incorporates the commonly used DMZ acronym to – hopefully – create a name that you can easily remember.

Direct Connect to Internet (DCI)

The DCI network design is very simple to construct. It connects a Red Hat Internet server directly to the Internet via an ISP. In our example, you have the option of connecting the server to an internal, private network.

Figure 1-1 depicts the DCI model.

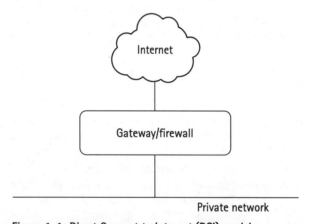

Figure 1-1: Direct Connect to Internet (DCI) model

Our DCI network, which anchors the low end of our network examples, has the following advantages:

◆ Low cost.

◆ Simple to configure.

◆ Simple to manage.

◆ Easy to provide Intranet services to private network.

It has the following disadvantages:

◆ More difficult than the DMZI network to provide services to the Internet.

◆ More exposure of private network to the Internet.

DMZ to Internet (DMZI)

Our second network example expands the DCI to provide more functionality and security. The private network is connected to an external network through a Gateway/Router. The external network is connected to the Internet through a DSL modem (or a cable modem) and provides services to the outside world. The external network is commonly referred to as a Demilitarized Zone (DMZ) and is not protected as heavily as the private network. The Gateway/Router also functions as a firewall and protects the private network from the Internet. Separating the two networks allows us to provide services to the Internet while protecting our private network. Figure 1-2 shows the DMZI configuration.

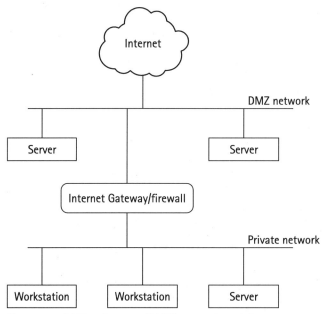

Figure 1-2: DMZ to Internet (DMZI) network model

Note that we made some compromises with the DMZ network to reduce costs. Many real-world DMZ configurations are protected by dedicated firewalls. We've chosen to place that function directly on the servers themselves by taking advantage of the fact that Red Hat pre-bundles the iptables software on their Linux distribution. These machines use the same *iptables/Netfilter* (iptables/Netfilter is a stateful IP packet filtering system that enables you to create a firewall on any Linux computer) system that the firewall/router uses.

The DMZ network firewall protection is configured as follows:

A DSL modem is used as a simple firewall instead of a dedicated one. We use a Cisco 675 DSL modem in our examples to provide stateless *IP packet filtering* and *Network Address Translation (NAT)*. IP packet filtering permits you to limit access based on IP addresses and ports. NAT effectively limits most packets from being routed into your network. Chapter 4 provides a description of how IP packet filtering and NAT work, as well as instructions for protecting these networks. Packet filtering and NAT provides significant protection for the DMZ network without affecting its ability to provide services to the Internet.

The DMZ servers are protected. The iptables IP packet filters are installed directly on the DMZ servers. The rule sets that determine which packets are allowed into each machine are tailored for those machines. This is actually better than the traditional method of providing a single firewall for the entire DMZ network because this method allows fewer packets into each machine than the traditional method does.

The private network uses a dedicated Red Hat Linux computer as its firewall and router. Providing the private network with a higher level of protection is essential because it typically houses more valuable information. Because the DMZ's nature is to provide services and information to the outside world, you must make it more accessible.

The DMZI has the following advantages:

- ◆ Allows you to easily provide Internet services.
- ◆ Allows you to easily provide Intranet services to private network.
- ◆ Offers less exposure to the Internet.

This network has the following disadvantages:

- ◆ More expensive to operate than the DCI.
- ◆ More configurations to make than the DCI. You must configure each server on the DMZ with its own internal firewall (packet filtering with iptables).
- ◆ More management.

Explaining Server Functions

The following sections explain how the services we describe in this book are going to be distributed across the two networks, as well as places you can efficiently install these services. Of course, these are only suggestions, but we've found them to work well. Here are the services, along with their basic description:

◆ **Web:** Chapter 6 provides instructions for configuring an Apache Web server. Apache is the most widely used Web server on the Internet and is included in the Red Hat Linux distribution.

◆ **Database (connected to the Web server):** You can produce dynamic Web services by attaching a database to your Apache server. Chapter 7 introduces the concept of providing information to Apache via a MySQL database and the PERL scripting language.

◆ **RealServer:** Streaming multimedia productions over the Internet is one of the functions that you can serve from a Linux computer. Chapter 8 shows how to create a simple RealServer on a Red Hat Linux server.

◆ **Domain Name Service (DNS):** It is important to provide DNS to your private network as well as the Internet. Chapter 9 describes how to set up DNS.

◆ **E-mail (sendmail/SMTP):** E-mail delivery is one of the core functions of the Internet. We describe how to set up a Simple Mail Transport Protocol (SMTP) system in Chapter 10; we expand on the straightforward, initial system and create a more secure version.

◆ **FTP:** Transporting files from one machine to another is an important use of the Internet. Chapter 11 describes how to create a File Transport Protocol (FTP) server.

◆ **Samba:** Sharing files and directories over your private network greatly enhances the productivity of your users. Samba provides the ability for both Microsoft Windows and Linux computers to share information. Chapter 12 shows how to configure a Samba server.

Determining how many services to place on individual machines is a difficult engineering decision. You have to balance the need for security with the ease of maintenance and economy. From a security perspective, one service per machine is best. Security is tightly tied to simplicity; simple configurations increase security for a couple of reasons:

◆ **First, fewer processes running means fewer potential vulnerabilities and fewer opportunities for the bad guys:** If a machine is running five services and one of them is exploited, then all five are compromised. Your company can probably survive relatively unscathed if your anonymous FTP server is compromised. However, your company will face far more resounding problems if your Web server is defaced because someone cracks your anonymous FTP server. Keeping the services separate helps prevent a chain of disasters.

◆ **Second, recognizing a problem is easier when only a few processes are running:** If you have pages and pages of processes running on a server, identifying an out-of-the-ordinary pattern becomes very difficult. Less "noise" means better security.

In reality, you don't always have the resources to create an ideal — or even reasonable — environment. The average home office and small company often neither has nor wants to spend the resources to optimize their security environment. Larger organizations have the resources but often choose not to allocate them, leaving the computer systems' engineer to allocate scarce resources as best as possible. This book identifies the idealized environment and then provides you with two network designs in an effort to provide enough choices so that you can more readily interpolate to your own best solution.

Using virtual Linux machines to provide dedicated servers

We'd like to offer an intriguing alternative to using individual computers for each service. Instead of using a physical machine (PM) you can use a virtual one. You can find both commercial and open source systems that create virtual computers within physical ones. By creating virtual servers, you can run individual services on individual computers.

Here's how the process works:

1. Install the virtual machine (VM) software on an adequately configured computer. Typically, the VM runs best on at least 64 MB of memory. The VM server should have at least 64 MB times the number of VMs you intend to run, plus enough memory for its own operating system. To run a single VM you want at least 128 MB (64 MB plus 64 MB), 192 MB for two VMs, and so on. Allocate 2 GB of disk space for each VM.

2. Install Red Hat Linux on the VM just as you would on a physical computer. Install a minimal Red Hat Linux system. For instance, in order to keep the whole server simple, avoid installing X Window System.

3. Configure the Red Hat Linux networking. We describe the general-purpose configuration process in Chapter 4. However, one simple modification is necessary — you need to configure the VM network interface connector (NIC) in bridged mode. Doing so allows you to use the PM's NIC as a bridge to the VM; the PM NIC appears to be the VM's NIC. (A network bridge transports all IP packets from one of the interfaces to the other. A bridge performs an error check but, unlike a router, doesn't examine IP addresses.)

4. Configure the VM for its intended service. For instance, install Apache to create a Web server and configure it as desired. The configuration process for a VM is no different than that of a PM.

After you configure the VM and its service (or services), it appears as a server on your network and provides the same functionality as if it was on a PM. As long as its host is adequately powerful, it should perform well.

Don't place heavily used services, such as an e-commerce business, on a VM. The extra overhead of the VM will use too much of the host's resources and you should dedicate as many computers as necessary to run your business. However, low volume services, such as Web servers intended for informational use within an organization should work very well. Anonymous FTP, low usage Web pages, and even DNS services are good candidates.

VMs appear to be a good investment from a security viewpoint, too. Not only do they allow the frugal organization to save money, but they also provide the following advantages over dedicated PMs:

◆ **You can manage multiple VM machines from a single login session on the PM:** Though not a big advantage, whenever a system administrator can save time on simple drudgery related tasks, more time is available for security monitoring.

◆ **If an intruder finds and exploits a vulnerability, only the VM process on the PM is compromised:** The VM process exists in user space on the PM and possesses no special privilege. However, if the same exploit occurs on a PM, then that entire computer is compromised. A compromised VM process can, of course, be used to launch attacks but it poses less of a threat than a defeated PM. This assumption is still being debated within the industry, however, it is our opinion that a compromised VM process poses less danger than a compromised PM.

You may want to use the commercial vmware system sold by VMware, Inc. to provide DMZ services. Vmware is available on a 30-day trial basis from www.vmware.com. An open source VM system is available from www.plex86.com. It wasn't operational for the Linux 2.4 kernel as of this writing. It is reported to work well for the 2.2 kernel, but we have no direct experience with it.

Understanding the DC1 configuration

The network topology in Figure 1-1 shows a simple, "flat" private network connected to the Internet through a Red Hat Linux server. The server acts as the private network's gateway to the Internet. The server routes packets coming from the private network with destined for addresses not on that network.

Figure 1-3 shows a private network of the DCI model in more detail.

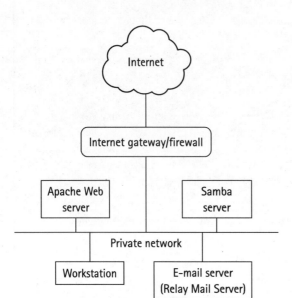

Figure 1–3: An example DCI network

The DCI network example shows several servers and a workstation attached to the private network. The gateway/firewall must be modified to permit external connections to each server if you want to provide services to the Internet. For instance, port 80 must be opened to the Apache Web server. Opening holes in the firewall decreases the security of the private network. The workstation is made more vulnerable, for instance, if the Web server is compromised.

Introducing the DMZ configuration

Adding a DMZ network to the DCI network provides two benefits: additional security and flexibility. Security is enhanced by moving Internet services from the private network. You gain flexibility because you can make services available to the public while maintaining the security of your private network.

Figure 1-4 shows the DMZ portion of our example DMZ network in more detail. The DMZ network places the Internet servers on the DMZ network. The DMZ network is more open than the private network. The DSL (or cable) modem provides basic packet filtering but allows connections to each of the services provided by the DMZ. In this example, connections can be made to the Web, ftp and e-mail servers. The private network is protected much more heavily than the DMZ; our Gateway/firewall example in Chapter 4 only permits Secure Shell (SSH) to enter from the outside (and SSH is not allowed directly through). Adding a DMZ network maintains high security while still providing Internet services.

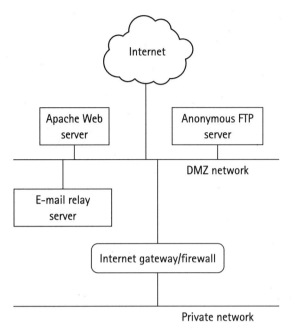

Figure 1-4: An example DMZ network

Adding Subnets to Both Networks

You can expand both of the example networks in this chapter with additional subnets. You can configure these subnets in numerous ways. We'll focus on two basic configurations. However, please be aware that you can add sub-networks to the private network of both the DCI and DMZ. Figure 1-5 shows two possible configurations.

This network uses separate routers to connect the engineering and marketing subnetworks to the gateway/firewall. The gateway/firewall can be a dual-homed Linux server or a dedicated device. The same is true for the subnetwork routers. This configuration is flexible but requires more devices (the individual routers) than the one shown in Figure 1-6.

This configuration requires a multi-homed gateway/firewall. A Linux-based gateway/firewall requires three Ethernet NICs for instance. This configuration requires less hardware than the previous one because the routing is done in the gateway/firewall. The gateway/firewall requires more configuration, however, and it is not as flexible as the one shown in Figure 1-5.

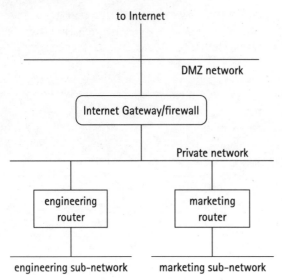

Figure 1-5: Adding additional subnets via individual routers

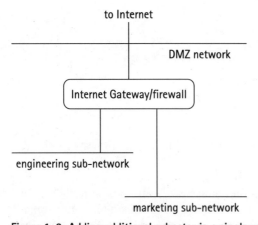

Figure 1-6: Adding additional subnets via a single router

Summary

This book shows how to use Red Hat Linux as a platform to provide Internet services. Before we start constructing Internet services we need a platform from which to operate. This chapter builds the platform by outlining two model networks that we use throughout the rest of the book. The network models are called the Direct Connect to the Internet (DCI) and DMZ to the Internet (DMZI).

The DCI model is simple to construct and operate. The private network is connected directly to the Internet. The Gateway/firewall is the only protection from the Internet and, therefore, the DCI model is relatively insecure. We recommend the DCI model for those who do not need to provide Internet services (for instance, if you only need to provide Web service to your private network), who want to experiment with building Red Hat Linux Internet servers, or who can't afford the security provided by the DMZI network.

The DMZI network is more complicated and secure than the DCI. It uses a separate network called the DMZ to insulate the private network from the Internet. Machines on the DMZ provide Internet services. The extra security requires more equipment and configuration than the DCI. We encourage anyone who provides production Internet services to use this model.

The two models we describe in this chapter set the stage for the rest of the book. Each chapter that deals with a specific service starts by describing the basic operation of the service. The chapter then provides one or more examples of the service. The examples are based on the DCI and DMZI network models described here. Using these models allows us to provide step-by-step instructions for configuring the service. Providing concrete examples, in our opinion, is the best way to learn a new system.

Chapter 2

Configuring Red Hat Linux Networking

IN THIS CHAPTER

- ◆ Introducing the Internet Protocol (IP)
- ◆ Explaining network layer protocols (IP Routing)
- ◆ Examining the physical link protocols (Ethernet Frames)
- ◆ Describing the layout of a Red Hat Linux (RHL) system
- ◆ Configuring one or more NICs

THIS CHAPTER DESCRIBES how to configure Red Hat Linux networking. Network configuration involves telling the operating system what equipment to use, its address (or how it should get its address), and where to go to find information about other computers, such as their addresses. You use specific tools to insert information into configuration files.

You can use several GNU is Not UNIX (GNU) command-line and Graphical User Interface (GUI) tools to manually configure Linux networking. Red Hat also produces and provides tools to aid in the process. Both types of tools have their advantages, which we describe in this chapter.

Configuring a Red Hat Linux workstation is a straightforward process for anyone familiar with IP networking; Red Hat's graphical networking utilities ask you for the networking parameters, such as the IP address, but otherwise hide the details. However, when you want a more complex networking configuration, such as an Internet gateway, then a deeper knowledge of Red Hat's network configuration is useful and often necessary.

Finally, this chapter describes what networking tools are available and how to use them. We describe sample configurations and provide detailed information about supporting network related files and scripts. Before jumping into describing Red Hat's networking structure, we want to introduce the networking protocols that make the Internet and most of the world's private networks possible.

Introducing the Internet Protocol

The Internet universe is based on the Internet Protocol (IP). IP is actually the conglomeration of separate protocols, each designed to perform a specific function. The term IP often refers to an address (as in IP address). An IP address is most often shown as four decimal numbers, 192.168.1.1 or 216.184.13.99, for example. However, IP more generally means the superset of protocols that makes the Internet function and is often referred to as Transport Control Protocol/Internet Protocol (TCP/IP).

When we use the word internet (with the "i" in lower case) we mean the set of protocols, such as TCP, UDP, ICMP, Telnet, FTP, and so on that provide the technical basis for interconnecting computers and other network devices. Using the word Internet, with the capital "I", we're referring to the worldwide collection of interconnected computers that share information and resources. This distinction helps our discussion of both subjects.

Networking and the OSI network model

The International Standards Organization (ISO) has developed the Open Systems Interconnect (OSI) networking model. This model logically separates higher- and lower-level networking functions into seven layers. Understanding the logical layers helps you follow the flow of information from one network device to another. IP packets carry information across the Internet (from one private network to another). Figure 2-1 reduces the model to four layers for simplicity.

Application Layer	HTTP, SSH, Telnet, FTP, SMB, etc.
Transport Layer	TCP, UDP, ICMP
Network Layer	IP
Physical/Data Link Layer	Device drivers (Ethernet) and media (wiring)

Figure 2-1: The seven-layer OSI networking model, reconfigured as four layers

The four-layer interpretation of the OSI networking model has the following layers:

◆ **Application:** The Application layer deals with high-level protocols, including SMB, NFS, FTP, SNTP, DNS, SNMP, and Telnet. Application programs that rely on these protocols access them directly. For example, the ftp program speaks the FTP protocol. If you write one of these programs, this layer concerns you.

◆ **Transport:** The Transport layer includes the Transmission Control Protocol (TCP), the User Datagram Protocol (UDP), and the Internet Control Message Protocol (ICMP). The Application layer protocols depend on these protocols to ensure that the packets they produce get to their destination reliably. By "reliably," we mean that either sooner or later (depending on the protocol) each packet either is or isn't acknowledged, and the Transport layer protocol informs the Application layer as to each packet's status.

◆ **Network:** The Network layer contains the Internet Protocol (IP), which deals with how to get each packet to its destination. It's responsible for encapsulating the higher-level packets (that is, a TCP or UDP packet) in an IP packet, which includes the destination and source addresses, the type of protocol, and several other chunks of information. If a packet is destined for a location outside of its LAN, routers down the line interpret this stuff and make their best guess on where and how to forward the packet.

◆ **Physical/Data Link:** The Physical/Data Link layer deals with the physical media, such as the cable and the electrical bits that come into and out of the network adapter. (Note: If your only network connection is a PPP or SLIP link, you can think of that link as your network adapter.) In an Ethernet adapter, the circuits on the adapter know how to interpret the electrical signals coming out of the demodulator – the actual wire conducts radio frequency (RF) signals – and then turn them into binary bits. From there, the bits are compared to the permanent Ethernet MAC (Medium-Access Control) address; when they match, they're forwarded to the Network layer.

To summarize, the OSI model logically breaks up the path (in the form of packets) that information takes in going from one computer to another as well as within the computer. The abstraction in this model enables you to ignore the messy details that need to occur for whatever process you need to create or use. Regardless of the level on which you're working, this model enables you to understand how your LAN (as well as the entire Internet) functions.

The following sections describe the lower three layers of the simple OSI model. We're skipping the Application layer because it's not of interest when studying how networking works – it simply makes use of the underlying protocols.

Introducing the Transport layer protocols

The Transport layer in the OSI model contains the protocols that the Application layer uses. These protocols take care of the bookkeeping necessary to ensure the proper and timely delivery of information to and from applications. The following list describes the function of each protocol:

◆ **Transmission Control Protocol (TCP):** This protocol is called a connection-oriented protocol because it makes sure that when the intended host receives each packet, it acknowledges the packet immediately and in sequence.

◆ **UDP:** A connectionless protocol, UDP doesn't guarantee that a packet will reach its destination. The application is responsible for doing that. UDP is simpler than TCP, uses fewer resources, and is more efficient. Thus, systems like DNS use UDP because name queries don't require synchronous responses.

The UNIX/Linux ports (sometimes referred to as Sockets) work at the Transport layer. You can connect to the TCP port 25 with Telnet, for example, and the *sendmail* daemon, which was monitoring port 25, will talk to you. The Linux operating system provides this abstraction to ease the process of writing interprocess and internetwork communication.

Explaining Network Layer Protocols (IP Routing)

The Network layer protocol is responsible for delivering information from one network to another. IP dictates the addressing scheme used to route packets from point A to point B. The addressing system uses the ubiquitous four octet decimal address familiar to all network administrators and many civilians. IP routing works as follows:

1. **You click on a URL, Telnet to your ISP, or send an e-mail:** The application that takes your request sends its communication request to the Linux kernel (we're being vague here for the sake of brevity). The Linux kernel creates a Transport layer TCP or UDP packet and then passes it to the Network layer and creates an IP packet.

   Part of the process of creating an IP packet included the process of converting a URL or other address into a numerical one. The kernel sends out a name service request and receives (hopefully) the corresponding numeric address. It then inserts that address into the IP packet header as the destination address; it uses its own address as the local address part of the header. The type of service for which the packet is intended determines the port number that is inserted into the IP header. The kernel generates a random number above 1024 to use as the source port.

2. **The kernel sends the new IP packet onto the local network:** Next, the packet is sent to a local router – for this book, that router is typically an Internet gateway. Each router that encounters the packet relays it to the next best router. (The "next best" router is determined by the protocol that the router uses, but describing those protocols is beyond the scope of this book.)

3. **The packet reaches the router serving the destination host:** At that point, the router encapsulates the packet in an Ethernet frame (or whatever the physical protocol requires, such as ATM, FDDI, and so on). The next section describes how the Ethernet frame works.

4. **ICMP:** The most simple of the Network layer protocols, ICMP is an auxiliary protocol used for troubleshooting and maintenance. For instance, PING uses ICMP. This protocol is only interested in the delivery of simple payloads that are primarily used for testing and troubleshooting networks.

Examining the Physical Link Protocols (Ethernet Frames)

The Physical Link layer (typically Ethernet) protocol is used to deliver IP packets to their final destination. When two computers are communicating across sub-networks or the Internet, IP packets are used to encapsulate TCP and UDP packets. The IP packets are routed from one network to another until they land on the sub-network where the destination network device is physically attached; the routing is based on the source and destination IP address contained in the IP header. After the IP packet is routed to the final destination sub-network, it must be delivered to the physical device. That process is accomplished by encapsulating the IP packet in an Ethernet frame (or packet).

Unlike an IP packet, the Ethernet frame doesn't contain IP addresses, ports, or other information in its header. Instead, it uses the hardware address of the destination network device's Ethernet NIC (network interface card). Every Ethernet device in the world has (or, at least, should have) a unique address set by the manufacturer. The hardware (also referred to as the machine, or MAC) address consists of six hexadecimal numbers, such as 00:05:5D:F1:03:C4.

The local router that controls the sub-network where the IP packet is destined encapsulates it within an Ethernet frame. The destination network device reads the first several bytes of every Ethernet frame that it sees. If the Ethernet frame address matches the network device's Ethernet MAC address, then the NIC reads in the rest of the frame. The NIC sends the Ethernet frame to the Linux kernel. The kernel extracts the IP packet from the Ethernet Frame.

Looking at the Network Layout of a Red Hat Linux System

Red Hat Linux (RHL) uses a number of programs, scripts, and files to store information about and configure its networking system. RHL stores these entities, which perform various functions, in several directories. This section describes the files, their locations, and their function.

Important network configuration files

Knowing the locations of the configuration files and scripts is important because these files contain the information that the system uses to initialize network interfaces and routes during boot time. You can also use these files and scripts to manually perform the same tasks.

THE /ETC DIRECTORY

This ubiquitous directory stores most of the Linux operating system's (and many applications') configuration information. The /etc directory and its subdirectories store information about the network name, NICs, routes, and name resolution. The following list describes those files:

◆ hosts: Contains the IP addresses, fully qualified machine name and aliases of your loopback, and local machine NIC(s). It optionally includes any additional machine IP addresses and names that you want to include.

The following lines are found in the /etc/hosts file from our server chivas (name server, e-mail server).

```
# Do not remove the following line, or various programs
# that require network functionality will fail.
127.0.0.1       localhost.localdomain    localhost
192.168.1.250   chivas.paunchy.net       chivas
```

You find both the logical loopback's and the host's own addresses here. The loopback address is only used internally by the Linux kernel and doesn't refer to a physical interface; some applications, as well as the Linux kernel, use this interface for communication. The physical Ethernet interface is given the IP address of 192.168.1.250. The computer's host name is chivas.paunchy.net and you can also refer to it by the alias chivas.

The above /etc/hosts file shows a minimal configuration. You can put all or some of the hosts located on your private network, or accessed frequently from other networks, in the file. However, we use and recommend sticking with the minimal configuration and letting your domain name service (DNS) take care of assigning addresses to names, which simplifies your overall LAN management. Keeping a sparse /etc/hosts file ensures that it won't become outdated as you modify your DNS.

◆ **resolv.conf:** This file contains the host's domain name, name server address (or addresses), and search domains. The information tells the Linux computer where to find the DNS server(s) and what domain names to use.

The following sample resolv.conf file is used for our example private network:

```
domain paunchy.net
search paunchy.net
nameserver 192.168.1.250
nameserver 198.59.115.2
```

The first line tells the host's networking system that it belongs to the *paunchy.net* domain. Don't confuse the term domain used here with the one that Microsoft uses. Microsoft's use of the term refers to their method for accessing computer resources within logical domains. The term here means the name of the network (paunchy.net). The DNS appends the domain name to the host name to create a Fully Qualified Domain Name (FQDN), such as chivas plus paunchy.net equals *chivas.paunchy.net*. You can then resolve the FQDN to the IP address 192.168.1.250.

◆ **modules.conf:** Configuration files control the modules loaded at boot time. For instance, the following example shows a server with two NICs and subsequently two entries in the /etc/modules.conf file:

```
alias eth0 3c59x
alias eth1 eepro100
```

The first line directs Linux — via the kernel thread kmod — to load the 3c59x.o module and assign it to the first NIC — eth0. The second line loads the eepro100.o module for the second — eth1 — NIC.

You can manually modify the modules.conf file or use the Red Hat Network Configuration utility to do so. The kudzu process will also detect new hardware and update the modules.conf file during the start up process.

◆ **nsswitch.conf:** This configuration file tells Linux where to find networking and other system information, such as host names. For instance, if you want your computer to look in the /etc/hosts file before using DNS, then you use this file to do so.

The default Red Hat Linux nsswitch.conf configures host name resolution as follows:

```
hosts:      files nisplus dns
```

This sequence tells Linux to look in the /etc/hosts table first when looking for a name. If Linux doesn't find the name, then it uses nisplus and finally dns to find the information.

◆ **sysctl.conf:** This contains kernel-level network configuration information. You find flags that turn IP forwarding on or off, IP defragmentation, and source route verification in this file. The sysctl program uses this information to modify the kernel. Here is the default /etc/sysctl.conf file:

```
# Disables packet forwarding
net.ipv4.ip_forward = 0
# Enables source route verification
net.ipv4.conf.all.rp_filter = 1
# Disables the magic-sysrq key
kernel.sysrq = 0
```

For example, if you want to create a Linux Internet gateway, modify the first parameter as follows:

```
net.ipv4.ip_forward = 1
```

Run the command sysctl –p as root and IP forwarding will be turned on.

THE /ETC/RC.D/INIT.D/NETWORK DIRECTORY

This script starts and stops the networking functions on a Linux box; it can also provide the status and other information about networking on the machine. The soft links, (they are a type of Linux file that essentially act like pointers) /etc/rc.d/rc3.d/S10network (Linux running in non-graphical mode) and /etc/rc.d/rc5.d/S10network (graphical mode) point to the /etc/rc.d/init.d/network script. The system uses these pointers to turn networking on when you boot the computer.

The script uses the information stored in /etc/sysconfig/network and the files in /etc/sysconfig/network-scripts directory to start, stop, and display the status of the Red Hat Linux network. We're omitting the details of the script for the sake of brevity.

THE /ETC/SYSCONFIG/NETWORK DIRECTORY

This file contains the hostname, default route IP address, the gateway device (NIC), and IP forwarding flag (although this flag doesn't actually change that function anymore). The scripts in /etc/sysconfig/network-scripts use this information when configuring the computer's networking.

THE /ETC/SYSCONFIG/NETWORK-SCRIPTS DIRECTORY

This directory contains the scripts used to control Red Hat Linux networking. The scripts like `ifcfg-eht0` contain information specific to a particular interface. The `network-function` script contains subroutines used by the control scripts. Scripts like `ifup`, `ifdown` and `ifup-routes` control the state of the network interfaces.

- ◆ **ifup and ifdown:** These scripts use the information contained in files such as `ifcfg-lo`, `ifcfg-eth0`, and so on to turn the appropriate interfaces on and off.

- ◆ **ifcfg-lo:** Contains information about your loopback interface. `ifup` and `ifdown` use this script to turn the loopback interface on and off.

- ◆ **ifcfg-eth0:** Contains the configuration information, including the IP address, about your first Ethernet adapter. ifup and ifdown use this script to turn the device on and off.

- ◆ **ifcfg-eth1, ifcfg-eth2, . . . :** Contains the configuration information, including the IP address, about your second, and any additional Ethernet adapters. ifup and ifdown use this script to turn the device on and off.

- ◆ **ifup-ppp and ifdown-ppp:** Contains information about the Point-to-Point Protocol (PPP) device and is used by the ifup and ifdown scripts to turn PPP on and off. PPP is generally used to connect a computer and/or network to an ISP over analog telephone connections. (Some ADSL devices use PPP to connect to an ISP; however, they use their own internal PPP configuration to establish a connection.)

- ◆ **ifup-routes:** Contains configuration information about any network routes in addition to the default gateway (that information is stored in the `/etc/sysconfig/network` file). ifup and ifdown use this script to turn your routes on and off.

- ◆ **network-functions:** This script contains general-purpose network information and control functions (the functions returning network interface and routing information). The other scripts in this directory use the network-functions script.

The `/etc/sysconfig/static-routes` file is used to configure individual, static routes. Normally, one generic route is created for each network interface. For instance, a route is created to the 192.168.1.0 subnetwork for the eth0 NIC when that interface is activated. However, you may need to create specific routes (static) if your machine is connected to multiple subnetworks. The static-routes file is used to store additional routes.

Important applications and scripts

Linux networking uses a number of tools and configuration files. When used together, you can gain information about a system's configuration and operation and then solve almost any problem. The following programs are used to configure and display information about networking devices:

- ◆ arp/rarp
- ◆ ifconfig
- ◆ netstat
- ◆ redhat-config-network-cmd/redhat-config-network-druid
- ◆ nmap
- ◆ ping
- ◆ route
- ◆ sysctl
- ◆ tcpdump
- ◆ usernetctl
- ◆ modprobe

These tools, which aren't terribly complicated to learn or use, are the essential items that knowledgeable administrators must keep in their toolbox. The following sections describe each tool briefly.

arp/rarp

Linux keeps a list of MAC and IP addresses of local network devices with which it has had communications. The list is stored in an Address Resolution Protocol (ARP) table. You use the arp command both to display and manipulate the cache. Running the arp command returns results similar to the following:

```
Address          HWtype  HWaddress          Flags Mask      Iface
192.168.1.254    ether   00:50:BA:DE:25:35  C               eth0
192.168.1.12     ether   00:05:5D:F1:03:C4  C               eth0
```

In this example, Linux has cached ARP information about two machines with which it recently had communications. The IP address is associated with the network type, Hardware (MAC) address, and an interface.

ifconfig

The ifconfig utility sets the IP address, netmask, and other parameters on a NIC. It can also display information about a NIC. A non-root user can use this utility to display information, but you must be root to set any NIC parameters. You should use the `ifup` and `ifdown` scripts, rather than ifconfig to configure your network interface however.

`ifconfig` uses the following syntax:

```
ifconfig interface [aftype] options | address ...
```

`ifconfig` can set the following parameters:

◆ **Display all network interfaces.** When no options are given, `ifconfig` displays information about all configured interfaces including the logical loopback device. If the interface parameter is included, then information about that device is shown.

◆ **eth0.** The interface on a Linux is almost always an Ethernet device such `eth0`, but can be another class of devices, such as a Token Ring interface `tr0` (Token Rings provide a communication protocol like Ethernet does. Token Ring systems competed with Ethernet a decade ago but have steadily lost popularity.) The first device always has a zero (0) appended to the device type (`eth0`); the zero is incremented to a one (1) (`eth1`) for the second device and so on.

◆ **The aftype parameter refers to the address family (protocol) that the interface uses.** TCP/IP is the default. Options include the next generation (version 6) internet protocol `IPv6`, amateur packet radio `ax25`, Appletalk phase 2 `ddp`, and Novell's IP somewhat compatible `IPX`. (We use TCP/IP exclusively in this book, but mention the others for completeness.)

◆ **Many available options can be set.** Those that are used for performance tuning find less use with passing time. In the past, networking hardware and operating systems were less sophisticated and required more hand-tuning. Evolutionary improvements have made networking more reliable and fast.

Other options provide functional capabilities that the systems we describe in this book generally don't use. You can use the following options with ifconfig, however, we strongly advise that you use the ifup and ifdown scripts to turn a network interface on and off:

■ **up/down:** These two options turn the interface on and off. They're useful when you're troubleshooting a device and want to see the affect of a change.

- **promisc:** This toggles promiscuous mode on and off. When in promiscuous mode, the interface passes all the network packets it encounters up to the higher-level network layers. Promiscuous mode permits your computer to operate as a network sniffer. Network sniffing refers to the process of listening to all the network traffic that a network device is exposed to. Sniffing can be used to troubleshoot network problems and eavesdrop on other people's communication.

  Be careful when using this mode. Many organizations consider a NIC set in promiscuous mode to be evidence of a hacker.

netstat

The netstat program displays information about routing tables, interface statistics, and masquerading connections, which is valuable for debugging networking problems. (You can also use this command to gain information about other network connections.)

nmap

This program belongs in the class of utilities known as *port mappers*. nmap transmits packets in various tortured states to a target (or targets) and examines their return packets. The responding packets are collected and analyzed by nmap to determine information about the machine.

ping

ping is a simple — and very useful — program that sends out ICMP packets and listens for responses. For instance, if you want to find out whether another computer (with the IP of 192.168.1.101) is active on a network, run the command:

```
ping 192.168.1.101
```

The following code shows a typical response:

```
PING atlas.paunchy.net (192.168.1.101) from 192.168.1.10 : 56(84) bytes of data.
64 bytes from puma.paunchy.net (192.168.1.101): icmp_seq=0 ttl=255 time=78 use c
64 bytes from puma.paunchy.net (192.168.1.101): icmp_seq=1 ttl=255 time=73 use c
64 bytes from puma.paunchy.net (192.168.1.101): icmp_seq=2 ttl=255 time=63 use c
...
```

This example ping session shows that the computer at the address 192.168.1.101 is alive and active.

If you don't get a response from a ping, the computer may be turned off, disconnected from a network, improperly configured, and so on.

Chapter 5 describes some basic troubleshooting techniques that use ping.

redhat-config-network-druid/
redhat-config-network-cmd

Red Hat has created a Network Configuration utility called redhat-config-network-druid and redhat-config-network-cmd. (The druid version refers to the graphical version of the utility while cmd is a command-line version.) The utility can configure any network device from the Ethernet adapters to modems. You access Network Configuration druid from the GNOME panel by clicking the Main Menu→System Tools→Network Configuration buttons. The utility is self-explanatory and a system administrator should have no difficulty learning and using it.

route

The route program configures, removes, and displays routes. When using this command to create or modify a route, use the following syntax:

```
route [-v]  [-A  family] add [-net|-host] target [netmask
            Nm] [gw Gw] [metric N] [mss M] [window W] [irtt  I]
            [reject] [mod] [dyn] [reinstate] [[dev] If]
```

Many of the options shown above are only used in specialized cases, so we don't discuss them here. We find the following options useful:

◆ **add [-net|-host]:** Adds either a sub-network address (for instance, 192.168.1.0) or a specific host address (192.168.1.1), respectively. Typically, you use the network address to create a default route, such as to the Internet.

The command **route add –net default gw 192.168.1.254**, for instance, sets up a route that catches all IP packets that don't match any specific routes, as shown below. The –net default special case is used frequently to create a route that directs packets destined to go outside the local subnet to the Internet. We use this function to direct packets from our private network to our Internet gateway.

```
Destination Gateway Genmask     Flags Metric Ref Use Iface
default     192.168.1.254 0.0.0.0 UG   0      0      0 eth0
```

◆ **target:** The target is the IP address of the add option's destination. In the example from the preceding bullet, the target is all unmatched IP addresses (the default target). The target parameter describes the local sub-network address when setting up the route to a local subnet or host. For instance, you need to tell Linux how to route packets destined for the local sub-network. The command **route add –host 192.168.1.0** accomplishes that task and sets up a route as follows:

```
Destination Gateway Genmask      Flags Metric Ref Use Iface
192.168.1.0 *        255.255.255.0 U     0      0     0 eth0
```

Occasionally, you need to create a route to a specific host. In that case, use the –host option. For instance, the command **route add –host 192.168.32.1 gw 192.168.1.254** creates a route that directs all traffic destined for the host 192.168.32.1 through the network device with the address of 192.168.1.254.

◆ **gw GW:** This option sets up the destination of a gateway (to another network). The example in the first bullet sets up a route pointing to the address 192.168.1.254. Throughout this book, we use the highest address of a class C network as our gateway.

◆ **dev:** The device option configures a route to use a device as its destination. When setting up a local route, for instance, designating the NIC as the destination is convenient: **route add –net 192.168.1.0 dev eth0.** This route directs all IP packets with the destination address of 192.168.1.X to go out through the first Ethernet NIC.

The route command can be used to delete an existing route. The syntax used to delete an existing route looks like the following:

```
route  [-v]  [-A  family]  del [-net|-host] target [gw Gw]
              [netmask Nm] [metric N] [[dev] If]
```

The options work the same as we just described except that you use them to delete existing routes. For instance, enter the following command to delete the default route:

```
route del -net default
```

These are the options and parameters most often used in conjunction with the route command. Consult the route man page for information about the other options. (Run the command **man route** to look at the man page.)

sysctl

sysctl configures and displays kernel parameters found in the /proc/sys directory. sysctl can set or reset networking functions, such as IP forwarding, IP defragmentation, and source route checking. You can do all of the sysctl controlled functions manually or automatically by editing the /etc/sysctl.conf file.

The sysctl –a command displays all system parameters. For instance, if you want to see every parameter related to IP forwarding, run the following command:

```
sysctl -a | grep forward
```

The following output is for a computer with two Ethernet interfaces (our Internet gateway).

```
net.ipv4.conf.eth0.mc_forwarding = 0
net.ipv4.conf.eth0.forwarding = 0
net.ipv4.conf.eth1.mc_forwarding = 0
net.ipv4.conf.eth1.forwarding = 0
net.ipv4.conf.lo.mc_forwarding = 0
net.ipv4.conf.lo.forwarding = 0
net.ipv4.conf.default.mc_forwarding = 0
net.ipv4.conf.default.forwarding = 0
net.ipv4.conf.all.mc_forwarding = 0
net.ipv4.conf.all.forwarding = 0
net.ipv4.ip_forward = 0
```

Most of these parameters deal with forwarding related to individual interfaces. If you're using your RHL computer as a router or Internet gateway, then turn forwarding on. In that case, you're interested in the **net.ipv4.ip_forward** parameter.

For instance, you can turn on forwarding on the appropriate parameters, such as both of the Ethernet interfaces, by entering the following command (don't put any spaces around the equal sign):

```
sysctl -w net.ipv4.ip_forward=1
```

Everything you can do with sysctl you can also do manually. For instance, enter the command **cat /proc/sys/net/ipv4/ip_forward** if you want to display the status of IP forwarding. To change a parameter, you must send a binary value (0 or 1) to it, such as **echo "1" > /proc/sys/net/ipv4/ip_ forward**.

tcpdump

You use tcpdump to examine the headers of IP, other protocols, and packets. You can analyze your network by looking at the source and destination addresses and ports of packets traversing your network. This function is particularly useful when trying to figure out why a firewall isn't working properly.

modprobe

You can compile device drivers directly into the Linux kernel. However, the common method of supporting devices is to use *loadable modules*. A loadable module is a piece of compiled, but unlinked code (or object) that interfaces the device with the Linux kernel. Linux has advanced to the point where it is rarely necessary to manually load/unload modules. However, you can use the modprobe utility if you do need to load a module.

You can use the modprobe command to manually load modules at any time. Modprobe uses the following syntax:

```
modprobe  [  -adnqv  ] [ -C config ] module [ symbol=value ... ]
```

Please consult the man page for the details of the flags. If, for instance, you want to load the module for a 3c509 Ethernet interface, run the following command:

```
modprobe 3c509
```

Modprobe takes care of finding and loading the module /lib/modules/2.4.2-2/ kernel/drivers/net/3c509.o. After loading, the Linux kernel can immediately use the device; you don't have to reboot the computer to activate a module.

The *lsmod* program lists all loaded modules. *rmmod* removes, or unloads, loaded modules.

Configuring One or More NICs

We describe how to configure networking on a Red Hat Linux computer in this section. The examples correspond to the configurations necessary to create the private network models (DCI and DMZ) we introduced in Chapter 1. (These examples are used throughout the remainder of this book.)

This section is intended to give a consistent configuration for all examples we describe in this book.

Example 1: Configuring a single NIC

This example configures a Red Hat Linux computer to connect to a private network. The network (or subnet) is routed to a single Internet gateway. Figure 2-2 shows an example of a Red Hat Linux host (workstation or server), connected to the private network (192.168.1.0) that needs its single Ethernet interface (eth0) and its routing table configured. This example pertains to both the DCI and DMZ configuration because both models depend on an identically configured Internet gateway.

The following two sections describe how to configure basic Red Hat Linux networking manually and graphically.

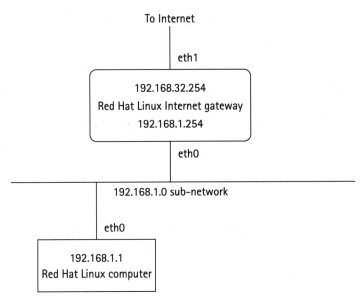

To Internet

eth1

192.168.32.254
Red Hat Linux Internet gateway
192.168.1.254

eth0

192.168.1.0 sub-network

eth0

192.168.1.1
Red Hat Linux computer

Figure 2-2: A Red Hat Linux host with a single Ethernet device

MANUALLY CONFIGURING NON-PERSISTENT NETWORKING (SINGLE NIC)

Knowing how to manually configure networking (and other system) functions is important for two reasons. First, Linux servers are often created as minimalist systems without the X Window System installed (which is the model we use in this book). Minimalist systems provide the highest performance and most secure servers possible. You must, therefore, be able to use non-graphical tools. Second, as a system administrator, you need to understand a server as completely as possible. Using manual tools forces you to learn the underlying networking systems to a greater degree than graphical ones do.

In this example, we're configuring the Red Hat Linux server chivas with the address of 192.168.1.250. This machine is our private network's DNS and send-mail/imap server.

Perform the following steps to set up non-persistent Linux networking. The following steps configure the NIC and routes that work until the next time that you reboot the computer or restart networking with the /etc/init.d/network script.

1. Log in as root.

2. Clear out any existing interface configurations, but don't remove the loopback interface (127.0.0.1).

   ```
   ifconfig eth0 down
   ```

3. Clear out any existing routes except for lo.

```
route del -net 192.168.1.0
route del default
```

4. Add the first, and only, Ethernet interface *eth0*.

```
ifconfig eth0 192.168.1.1
```

If necessary, add the loopback interface: **ifconfig lo 127.0.0.1**.

5. Add a route to the local subnet 192.168.1.0.

```
route add -net 192.168.1.0 dev eth0
```

6. Add a default route to the Internet gateway.

```
route add -net default gw 192.168.1.254
```

7. For network security, make sure that you turn off IP forwarding.

```
sysctl -w net.ipv4.ip_forward=0
```

8. Edit the /etc/resolv.conf file to contain the information.

```
search paunchy.net
nameserver 192.168.1.250
```

These are the parameters we use in our network examples. You can use your own parameters if you're using another nameserver and domain name.

9. Edit the /etc/nsswitch.conf file and remove all references to nisplus and nis. (You can do so, when running vi, by using the substitution :g/nisplus/s// and :g/nis/s//.)

10. You can look at the network interfaces by running the ifconfig without parameters. The following interface information displays:

```
eth0  Link encap:Ethernet  HWaddr 00:E0:29:53:F8:3E
inet addr:192.168.1.250  Bcast:192.168.1.255
Mask:255.255.255.0
      UP BROADCAST RUNNING MULTICAST  MTU:1500  Metric:1
      RX packets:6843 errors:0 dropped:0 overruns:0 frame:0
      TX packets:7388 errors:0 dropped:0 overruns:0 carrier:0
      collisions:447 txqueuelen:100
      Interrupt:9 Base address:0x3000

lo    Link encap:Local Loopback
      inet addr:127.0.0.1  Mask:255.0.0.0
      UP LOOPBACK RUNNING  MTU:16436  Metric:1
      RX packets:2664 errors:0 dropped:0 overruns:0 frame:0
```

```
TX packets:2264 errors:0 dropped:0 overruns:0 carrier:0
collisions:0 txqueuelen:0
```

11. And, of course, you can look at the routing table by running the route
command:

```
Kernel IP routing table
Destination   Gateway      Genmask       Flags Metric Ref Use Iface
192.168.1.0   *            255.255.255.0 U      0     0   0 eth0
127.0.0.0     *            255.0.0.0     U      0     0   0 lo
default       192.168.1.254 0.0.0.0      UG     0     0   0 eth0
```

Note the difference between the local subnet and default routes. The former makes use of the device option; all traffic with a destination address
of the local subnet 192.168.1.0 is simply directed to the Ethernet interface
eth0. However, you must give the latter the Internet gateway's IP address.
When an IP packet with a destination address unmatched by a specific
route appears, the routing table directs it to the default gateway
192.168.1.254 via eth0.

That is the complete process. The only caveat is when the kernel can't determine
which loadable module the NIC requires. In that situation, you may need to complete the process manually. In that case, please consult the section "Troubleshooting
Linux Networking" in Chapter 5 for more assistance.

TIP   The Red Hat Linux process allows you to configure networking during the
installation process. The steps described here perform the same function.

MANUALLY CONFIGURING PERSISTENT NETWORKING (SINGLE NIC)
The configuration process described in the previous section was non-persistent.
After you reboot the machine or run the /etc/rc.d/init.d/network restart script,
the networking parameters revert to another state. Using that system is adequate
when learning about Red Hat Linux networking. However, you should definitely
use persistent networking when constructing a server.

You can construct a persistent network configuration by modifying several Red
Hat Linux networking configuration files. The following instructions describe how
to create a persistent network as follows:

1. Change your computer's network name. For instance, modify the
/etc/sysconfig/network to change the name to *chivas* as follows:

```
HOSTNAME=chivas
```

2. Edit the `/etc/sysconfig/network-scripts/ifcfg-eth0` to look as follows:

```
DEVICE=eth0
BOOTPROTO=static
BROADCAST=192.168.1.255
IPADDR=192.168.1.250
NETMASK=255.255.255.0
NETWORK=192.168.1.0
ONBOOT=yes
```

The `/etc/rc.d/init.d/network` script uses this information to set up the first Ethernet interface, as in Step 4 of the preceding numbered list.

3. Edit the `/etc/sysconfig/network` file to contain the following information:

```
NETWORKING=yes
HOSTNAME=chivas.paunchy.net
GATEWAY=192.168.1.254
GATEWAYDEV=eth0
```

The `/etc/rc.d/init.d/network` script uses this information to set up the default route.

4. Edit the `/etc/sysctl.conf` file and make sure that the IP forwarding is turned off.

```
net.ipv4.ip_forward = 0
```

5. Configure the name resolution configuration file `/etc/resolv.conf` as in Step 8 in the preceding section.

6. Configure the `/etc/nsswitch.conf` file exactly as in Step 9 in the preceding section.

7. Run the Red Hat Linux network start/stop script.

```
/etc/rc.d/init.d/network restart
```

8. Check that the NIC has been set up correctly. Step 9 in the preceding section describes the process and shows what the results should look like.

9. Check that the routing table has been configured correctly, as we describe in Step 11 in the preceding section.

These steps should ensure that the Red Hat Linux computer they are run on gets a consistent network configuration. If you encounter any problems, please consult the section "Troubleshooting Linux Networking" in Chapter 5 for further assistance.

USING GUI-BASED TOOLS

We leave the use of graphical network configuration tools to your discretion. Such tools are useful and, in some cases, powerful. However, we believe it is necessary to learn and use the manually configured methods if one wants to understand the essence of Red Hat Linux networking. You can use the information described in this chapter when using graphical tools.

Example 2: Configuring dual NICs (dual homed)

The preceding example is useful for configuring Red Hat Linux generic workstations and servers. Machines that don't perform routing functions generally require only a single NIC. Computers that are intended to serve as firewalls, routers, and gateways require more configuration.

This section describes how to configure a Red Hat Linux computer with two NICs. We expand the process described in the preceding section to add an additional NIC and the appropriate routes.

MANUALLY CONFIGURING NON-PERSISTENT NETWORKING (DUAL HOMED)

Routers, gateways, and firewalls typically use two NICs (devices with more than two interfaces are used in many situations but are beyond the scope of this book). In the case of our Internet gateway, shown in Figure 2-2, one NIC connects to the private network and the other to the DSL modem (DCI model) or the DMZ network (DMZI model). This configuration is referred to as a *dual-homed gateway.*

In this example, we're configuring the Red Hat Linux server *atlas* with the address of 192.168.1.254. This machine is our private network's Internet gateway and firewall.

The configuration is the same as described in the previous examples except that we're working with two devices, and you need an extra route. The job is the same as in the previous section (non-persistent) with a few changes.

Configuring the non-persistent example requires that you change Steps 2, 4, 5, and 7 as follows:

◆ **Step 2:** Clear out any existing interface configurations.

```
ifconfig down eth0
ifconfig down eth1
```

◆ **Step 4:** Add the extra interface.

```
ifconfig eth0 192.168.1.254
ifconfig eth1 192.168.32.254
```

◆ **Step 5:** Add another route for the 192.168.32.0 network.

```
route add -net 192.168.1.0 dev eth0
route add -net 192.168.32.0 dev eth1
```

◆ **Step 7:** Turn on forwarding by editing /etc/sysctl.conf to include the following line:

```
net.ipv4.ip_forward = 1
```

Put the change into effect.

```
sysctl -p
```

When you check the configuration, you see the extra NIC and local route.

MANUALLY CONFIGURING PERSISTENT NETWORKING (DUAL HOMED)

The configuration is the same as described in the previous examples except that you're working with two devices, and you need an extra route. The job is the same as in the previous section with a few changes.

In this example, you need to change Steps 2, 3, and 4 as follows:

- ◆ **Step 2:** This step is split into two parts:

  - ■ Edit `/etc/sysconfig/network-scripts/ifcfg-eth0` as follows:

```
DEVICE=eth0
BOOTPROTO=static
BROADCAST=192.168.1.255
IPADDR=192.168.1.254
NETMASK=255.255.255.0
NETWORK=192.168.1.0
ONBOOT=yes
```

  - ■ Copy the `/etc/sysconfig/network-scripts/ifcfg-eth0` to `/etc/sysconfig/network-scripts/ifcft-eth1`. Edit the `ifcfg-eth1` script to look as follows:

```
DEVICE=eth1
BOOTPROTO=static
BROADCAST=192.168.32.255
IPADDR=192.168.32.254
NETMASK=255.255.255.0
NETWORK=192.168.32.0
ONBOOT=yes
```

- ◆ **Step 3:** Edit the `/etc/sysconfig/network` file to contain the following information:

```
NETWORKING=yes
HOSTNAME=chivas.paunchy.net
GATEWAY=192.168.32.254
GATEWAYDEV=eth1
```

- ◆ **Step 4:** Edit the `/etc/sysctl.conf` file and make sure that you turn on IP forwarding.

```
net.ipv4.ip_forward = 1
```

These changes configure the networking necessary to create the networking infrastructure for the Internet gateway and firewall that we use in this book. Use these processes to configure any Red Hat Linux computer that requires connection on two networks.

Example 3: Configuring a Red Hat Linux router

The network configuration we describe in Example 2 is designed for an Internet gateway and firewall. However, you can easily use that configuration to route between two or more sub-networks within a private network. This section describes the general configuration necessary to create a router.

Dividing a private network into multiple sub-networks is often useful and sometimes necessary. When an organization grows beyond a small home office, it should make use of multiple sub-networks. Dividing a private network along functional lines, such as engineering, marketing, financial, and so on, is a logical choice, providing security and better performance. Keeping financial records limited to the financial types – engineering documents among engineers, and so forth – enhances security. Dividing network traffic onto separate sub-networks increases performance, because each segment handles fewer packets.

The following sections describe two different models for routing two or more sub-networks onto a common network. This model makes use of the single Internet gateway, DNS, and e-mail servers that we've placed onto a single sub-network.

USING MULTIPLE DUAL-HOMED RED HAT LINUX ROUTERS

This model uses multiple dual-homed routers to connect sub-networks to the backbone sub-network. Each sub-network requires individual Red Hat Linux based routers. Figure 2-3 shows such a configuration.

Here, router A connects subnet A to the backbone sub-network; router B does the same for subnet B. If you have a third sub-network (subnet C), then create router C, and so on. This model is conceptually simple to create and maintain.

Use the network configuration we describe in Example 2. For router A, change Steps 2 and 3 as follows:

◆ **Step 2:** This step is split into two parts:

■ **Edit** `/etc/sysconfig/network-scripts/ifcfg-eth0` as follows:

```
DEVICE=eth0
BOOTPROTO=static
BROADCAST=192.168.2.255
IPADDR=192.168.2.254
NETMASK=255.255.255.0
NETWORK=192.168.2.0
ONBOOT=yes
```

- Copy the /etc/sysconfig/network-scripts/ifcfg-eth0 to /etc/
  sysconfig/network-scripts/ifcft-eth1. Edit ifcfg-eth1 as follows:

```
DEVICE=eth1
BOOTPROTO=static
BROADCAST=192.168.1.255
IPADDR=192.168.1.240
NETMASK=255.255.255.0
NETWORK=192.168.1.0
ONBOOT=yes
```

◆ **Step 3:** Edit /etc/sysconfig/network to contain the following information:

```
NETWORKING=yes
HOSTNAME=routera.paunchy.net
GATEWAY=192.168.1.254
GATEWAYDEV=eth1
```

Change Step 2 to configure router B. Use the following information:

◆ **Step 2:** This step is split into two parts:

- Edit /etc/sysconfig/network-scripts/ifcfg-eth0 as follows:

```
DEVICE=eth0
BOOTPROTO=static
BROADCAST=192.168.3.255
IPADDR=192.168.3.254
NETMASK=255.255.255.0
NETWORK=192.168.3.0
ONBOOT=yes
```

- Copy the /etc/sysconfig/network-scripts/ifcfg-eth0 to
  /etc/sysconfig/network-scripts/ifcft-eth1. Edit ifcfg-eth1
  as follows:

```
DEVICE=eth1
BOOTPROTO=static
BROADCAST=192.168.1.255
IPADDR=192.168.1.241
NETMASK=255.255.255.0
NETWORK=192.168.1.0
ONBOOT=yes
```

- Edit /etc/sysconfig/network to contain the following information:

```
NETWORKING=yes
HOSTNAME=routerb.paunchy.net
GATEWAY=192.168.1.254
GATEWAYDEV=eth1
```

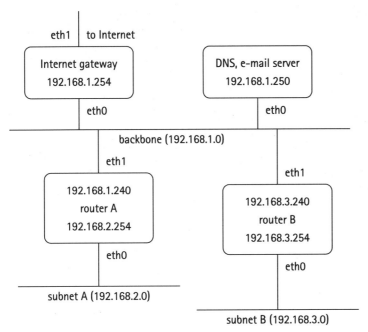

Figure 2-3: Routing between two sub-networks

On its surface, this model appears to be expensive to create. However, you can use inexpensive PCs to create each router. Even older 486 boxes configured with 64 MB of memory, should be able to handle 100-megabit (Mb) equipment and, of course, Red Hat Linux is very inexpensive. (Definitely run such equipment without graphics.)

USING A SINGLE MULTIPLE-HOMED RED HAT LINUX ROUTER

You can configure a single Red Hat Linux computer with three or more NICs if you don't want to create and maintain multiple routers. This section describes the process. Figure 2-4 shows a multi-homed router serving three sub-networks.

Use the network configuration we describe in Example 2. Change Steps 2 and 3 as follows:

◆ Step 2: This step is split into three parts:

■ Edit /etc/sysconfig/network-scripts/ifcfg-eth0 as follows:

```
DEVICE=eth0
BOOTPROTO=static
BROADCAST=192.168.2.255
IPADDR=192.168.2.254
NETMASK=255.255.255.0
NETWORK=192.168.2.0
ONBOOT=yes
```

■ Copy the /etc/sysconfig/network-scripts/ifcfg-eth0 to /etc/
sysconfig/network-scripts/ifcft-eth1. Edit ifcfg-eth1 as follows:

```
DEVICE=eth1
BOOTPROTO=static
BROADCAST=192.168.3.255
IPADDR=192.168.3.254
NETMASK=255.255.255.0
NETWORK=192.168.3.0
ONBOOT=yes
```

■ Copy the /etc/sysconfig/network-scripts/ifcfg-eth0 to /etc/
sysconfig/network-scripts/ifcft-eth2. Edit ifcfg-eth2 as follows:

```
DEVICE=eth2
BOOTPROTO=static
BROADCAST=192.168.1.255
IPADDR=192.168.1.240
NETMASK=255.255.255.0
NETWORK=192.168.1.0
ONBOOT=yes
```

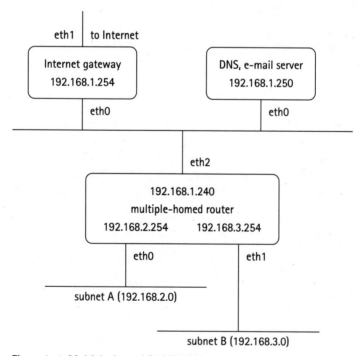

Figure 2-4: Multiple-homed Red Hat Linux router

◆ **Step 3:** **Edit** `/etc/sysconfig/network` to contain the following information:

```
NETWORKING=yes
HOSTNAME=router.paunchy.net
GATEWAY=192.168.1.254
GATEWAYDEV=eth1
```

Complete this process, and you have a multiple-homed Red Hat Linux router.

Summary

This chapter outlined the structure of Red Hat Linux networking. Red Hat Linux makes use of numerous configuration files, scripts, and utilities to make its network work. We described the scripts and files in this chapter to give you an overview of their location and function.

We also described several network examples in this chapter to create a basis for subsequent examples given later in this book. The first two examples described how to configure single and dual network interfaces. The first example described the configuration used for all Red Hat Linux servers and workstations. The second showed the process necessary for configuring our Internet gateway/router.

The final two examples illustrate how to configure a Red Hat Linux computer as a router between two sub-networks. The former uses a simple dual-homed configuration, and the latter uses a multiple-homed router. The dual-homed example requires using a separate machine for each routed sub-network, but the second machine can handle several sub-networks at once.

Chapter 3

Connecting to the Internet via DSL

IN THIS CHAPTER

◆ Introducing DSL technology

◆ Understanding DSL terminology

◆ Creating your DSL Internet connection

◆ Basic troubleshooting tips

BROADBAND INTERNET CONNECTIONS have recently become available in most areas of the United States. *Broadband* refers to high-speed, reliable, and constant connections. The regional Bell and other communication companies market broadband connections to consumers and businesses in the form of Digital Subscriber Loop (DSL) technology; DSL is sometimes called Digital Subscriber Line. Cable TV companies provide competitive broadband service oriented toward consumers.

Until recently, the only high-speed Internet connections available was T1/Frame Relay (or the higher-speed T3), which only larger business could generally afford. The cost differential between DSL service and a T1 circuit is enormous. (Fractional T1 are competitive, but at the cost of speed.) Consumer and small-business oriented broadband in the form of Asymmetrical DSL (ADSL) tends to cost less than $100 per month. Single-line DSL (SDSL) provides higher speeds at only slightly higher prices. Full T1 costs into the $1000 to $2000 per month region, while fractional T1 runs from $100 per month and up.

The price/performance ratio of DSL and cable is outstanding. These broadband services provide individuals and businesses both small and large with high-speed Internet access. Both systems are economical and fast growing. Cable systems tend to provide higher-speed access to the Internet than ADSL systems at this time. However, the family of DSL variants provides more options to consumers and businesses alike. You can use products such as SDSL if you need to provide high-speed access to customers accessing your Internet services.

Because DSL offers high-speed, full-duplex Internet connections, we describe the important aspects of DSL technology in this chapter, and give you some real-world examples, as well. We then go on to describe installing and configuring an ADSL connection.

43

Introducing DSL Technology

DSL technology is designed to use the existing analog telephone infrastructure for high-speed digital transmission. The world already has a huge installed base of Plain Old Telephone System (POTS) wiring. The infrastructure is constructed with unshielded twisted-pair copper wire pairs that are called loops, lines, and/or circuits. The circuits connect a very high percentage of the world's structures to telephone companies' facilities — the United States alone has hundreds of millions of loops as does Europe and much of Asia. This infrastructure makes it possible to economically provide broadband communication to the majority of the U.S. and many other countries.

Actually, the vast majority of Internet users already use the telephone infrastructure via the ubiquitous modem. Modems convert digital signals that computers generate into analog signals that the POTS infrastructure can handle. The combination provides functional access to the Internet but at slow speeds. For economic reasons, the POTS network is designed to provide only enough bandwidth — 4 Kilohertz (KHz) — to distinguish one human voice from another. Today's modems perform several encoding tricks to force up to 56 kilobits per second (Kbps) through that skinny 4 KHz pipe. However, that speed is about all that can be forced through, and it's inadequate for today's average computer user. (The long latency involved in waiting for the Telco connection and ISP authentication is also a major factor that make analog modems unsatisfactory.)

DSL uses frequencies in the Megahertz (MHz) range. You can transmit much more information when you use higher frequencies. The problem is, however, that the unshielded copper wire in use today has higher impedance at higher frequency and quickly attenuates the signal that DSL uses. (The POTS infrastructure also has problems related to corrosion, voice coils, mismatched wire gauges, and cross talk with adjacent lines, all of which decrease the circuit's throughput.)

 Much of the information that comprises the human voice exists at frequencies between 300 Hz and 3300 Hz (cycles per second). That frequency range contains enough information to distinguish one person's voice from. (Singing, however, requires higher frequencies.) The original telephone networks made use of this fact and deliberately limited the bandwidth to save money. That was not a bad idea in 1930 or 1970 but not in 2002.

Fortunately, the emergence of inexpensive Digital Signal Processing (DSP) electronics in the past decade has made it possible to overcome many of the problems the existing copper wire infrastructure presents. DSP is used to increase the signal-to-noise ratio and cancel out echoes introduced by cross talk between the bundled copper wire pairs.

TIP You often hear the term *last mile* in discussion about bringing broadband communications to consumers. The term refers to the short physical distance between the digital communication networks that comprise most of the Internet and the people and organizations that make use of the Internet; in other words, the distance between the broadband service provider and your home or office. The short distance is actually very difficult and expensive to bridge because the service providers have to make so many connections. Technologies such as DSL, cable TV, frame relay, and so on, use the existing POTS infrastructure to solve the problem.

DSL provides high-speed Internet connections by electronically converting the digital signal that represents an Ethernet frame into another form that can be transmitted over the POTS network. ADSL modems, for instance, convert the Ethernet signal into a Discrete Multi-Tone modulation (DMT) signal at the end-user connection to the Telco POTS. The DMT signal propagates across the POTS circuit to the nearest Central Office (CO). A DSL Access Multiplexer (DSLAM) at the CO converts the DMT signal into an ATM packet. The ATM packet is inserted into the DSL provider's ATM (or in a few cases a Frame Relay) network, and delivered to the DSL subscriber's ISP. The ISP inserts the packet into the Internet and from there it is routed onto its final destination. The reverse process is performed on IP packets destined for the DSL subscriber.

From your perspective, your LAN doesn't "see" the DSL connection. The connection between you and your DSL provider works at the physical and link layers described in Chapter 2. Your IP packets exist at the Network level, which is responsible for routing packets from one network device to another (routers, hosts, servers, printers, and so on). Therefore, when machines on your LAN generate packets that are destined for the Internet, the IP packets get routed to your Internet gateway/firewall first, and then go through the DSL connection to your ISP. Your DSL connection creates a high-speed, point-to-point connection to your ISP.

After the DSL modem converts Ethernet to DMT, the signal propagates across the copper wire to the nearest CO. The CO uses a DSLAM to convert the DMT signal back into ATM. The ATM packets get routed to your ISP, which is connected to the DSL provider's ATM backbone network. The ISP converts the ATM packets back into the original IP form. The IP packets are then routed to the Internet and their final destination.

TIP A CO is typically the building where your local telephone company terminates its POTS connections; however, a CO can also be a small structure or
cabinet housing a DSLAM and/or other equipment. Smaller COs are becoming a popular way to provide digital service to neighborhoods, office com-
plexes, and even individual buildings.

Actually, the IP packets transmitted across a DSL connection are encapsulated
with the Point-to-Point Protocol (PPP). Designed to support IP connections made
across serial connections, PPP has been used for years to encapsulate IP packets
sent across dial-up connections. IP is designed for bus structure of a network and
doesn't work on a serial connection without assistance. ADSL modems, for
instance, make use of PPP over ATM and occasionally PPP over Ethernet connections, which are referred to as PPPoA and PPPoE, respectively (and PPPoX collec-
tively). PPPoX is responsible for establishing a logical connection between your
LAN and ISP; the DSL signal carries the PPPoX packets. Figure 3-1 shows how DSL
works between your networked host and the ISP.

Comparing DSL, cable, and T1/Frame Relay

Cable TV companies were among the first to introduce consumer-oriented broadband
Internet connections. They recognized that they could piggyback computer networks
onto their cable infrastructure. Combining digital information with traditional
television is a good match because 1) it provides immediate additional value to
customers, and 2) it provides the promise of video-on-demand in the future.

Initially, cable TV franchises used their coaxial copper cabling to transmit digital data.
Some companies were also experimenting with fibre optic systems that were ideal for
transmitting digital information. Over time, cable TV companies have become major
broadband providers.

Cable modems are used to connect individual customers to digital networks. The
modems are similar in function to DSL modems. Cable modems modulate/demodulate
the Ethernet signal into another form for transmission across the cable network.

Internet cable and DSL are competitive in both price and performance. Consumer
cable probably provides higher performance than ADSL (consumer DSL) right now.
Both cost the same and both offer asymmetrical data rates. Single-line DSL (SDSL) has
the advantage of offering symmetrical data rates, but we aren't aware of any
symmetrical cable systems. Most individuals and small businesses are well served by
either cable or ADSL. Larger businesses that need to provide customers with adequate
Internet access probably need to use ADSL, though.

T1 connections provide the same functionality as DSL and Cable but differ in the technology used. From a functional perspective, T1 refers to a constant digital data connection at 1.54 Mbps; you can rent a fractional T1 connection that provides various fractions of the 1.54 Mbps speed. Technically, a T1 circuit is a Time Division Multiplexer (TDM) digital circuit that uses two twisted-pair wires. A T1 circuit uses 24 time slots, called DS0, of 64 Kbps each. T1 circuits are often connected to the Telco's Frame Relay network to provide a virtual, point-to-point network connection. If the end point is an ISP, then a T1 provides a high-speed connection to the Internet.

T1 connections, like DSL and Cable, are point-to-point from the customer premises to the local CO. Data, whether IP or other protocols, are modulated/demodulated in a device called a CSU/DSU (Channel Service Unit/Data Service Unit). The CSU/DSU is connected to the CO via the same copper lines that DSL and POTS use. After the signal arrives in the CO, it's routed into the telephone company's Frame Relay and/or ATM networks and delivered to the subscribed ISP.

T1 connections provide a range of speeds similar to DSL. The traditional advantage that T1 offers over DSL is quality of service (QOS). Telephone companies provide their customers with Service Level Agreements (SLA) that guarantee a high level of availability. The QOS is purchased at a premium. T1 connections are generally an order of magnitude more expensive than consumer and business DSL. However, the gap is closing rapidly as technology advances and DSL becomes more popular. Technological advances such as end-to-end ATM networks provide increasing QOS because ATM has built-in QOS (TCP/IP does not). DSL's popularity is proving to businesses that its price-to-performance advantage doesn't outweigh reliability.

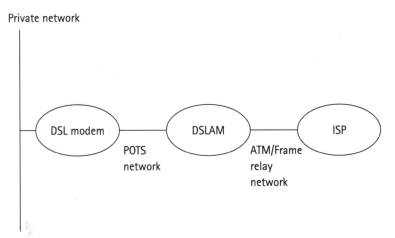

Figure 3-1: Diagramming a DSL connection with the OSI networking model

That, in a nutshell, is the essence of DSL (although a full description requires many more details). Your DSL modem converts (modulates) your network's Ethernet frames using the DMT protocol. The DSL modem sends the converted signal across the POTS infrastructure to a DSLAM to be converted into ATM, or sometimes Frame Relay, and inserted into the Telco's ATM or Frame Relay network. The IP packets, which are originally contained within Ethernet frames, are encapsulated in PPPoA for the traversal of the DSL connection (the PPPoA packets ride on the DMT signal). Once the DMT signal hits the DSLAM, it is converted into ATM and routed to your ISP, which is connected to the Telco's ATM network. The original IP packet is retrieved from the ATM packet and your ISP routes your IP packets to the Internet. Figure 3-2 shows a logical diagram of the DSL topology.

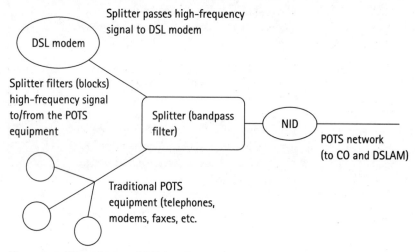

Figure 3-2: The end-to-end DSL topology

From a technical perspective, the term DSL really means the connection that's made between the end user's modem at one end and the provider's DSLAM at the other end.

Understanding DSL Terminology

The main components that make DSL possible are conceptually straightforward: You connect a DSL modem to one end of a pair of copper wires and your DSL provider connects their equipment to the other end. The equipment on both ends converts digital information from one type of electrical signal (Ethernet) into another (DMP or CAP). The signals are transmitted between the equipment and converted as necessary. The IP packets that emerge on the DSL provider's end are sent to your ISP and the Internet.

Although the concept is simple, the details are more complex. In order to under-stand all of the parts that comprise the ubiquitous telephone system that's used to provide DSL service, you first need to understand a large number of acronyms and their definitions. The following sections define the acronyms and terms related to DSL technology.

General terms

The following list provides an explanation for the most widely used DSL terms.

◆ **ATM (Asynchronous Transfer Mode):** ATM is used for much of the Internet's backbone by encapsulating most of the Internet's IP traffic. (ATM is also extensively used to transport non-IP based information, such as voice and video.) ATM uses the virtual circuit concept so that it can provide quality of service (QOS) to each circuit. The ATM packet header contains QOS information that it uses to govern the transport of IP pack-ets. ATM speed ranges from 155 Mbps up to 2 Gbps.

◆ **Bridged/DHCP:** The DSL modem acts as a bridge to the ISP network. A *bridge* is a device where all packets showing up at the first network inter-face are transmitted to the second one, and vice versa. Error detection is performed on a bridge and corrupt packets aren't transmitted. On a DSL bridging modem, the packets arriving at the LAN interface are transmitted to the WAN interface and vice versa, but no routing is performed. This process is analogous to an Ethernet hub broadcasting the packets received on one port to all other ports. DHCP (Dynamic Host Configuration Protocol) is used to provide the client DSL modem with a temporary IP address.

◆ **Baby Bells:** *See* Regional Bell Operating Company.

◆ **CO (Central Office):** The line that runs from your building terminates at your telephone company's nearest CO. The CO is typically a building that houses the DSLAM that provides your DSL service. A CO can also be a simple enclosure in or near your neighborhood that holds the same type of equipment. The CO may house DSL equipment from third party CLECs.

◆ **CLEC (Competitive Local Exchange Carrier):** DCLEC refers to Digital CLEC or Data CLEC. United States law requires that the Baby Bells lease portions of their infrastructure to competitors. CLECs are companies leas-ing the infrastructure for services, such as long distance voice communi-cations. DCLECs use the infrastructure to provide data communications, such as DSL.

◆ **CPE (Customer Premise Equipment or Customer Provided Equipment):** CPE refers to the wide range of telephone-related equipment, such as tele-phones, modems, and terminals, available today.

◆ **CSU/DSU (Channel Service Unit/Data Service Unit):** The CSU/DSU is a device that connects a T1 subscriber's network to the Telco's CO.

◆ **DSL provider:** We use this term to refer to your DCLEC.

◆ **DSL transmission methods:** The following methods are used to modulate the transmitted signal between the DSL modem and DSLAM. Recall that the Ethernet signal carries (or transmits) IP packets on your private LAN; Ethernet uses Carrier Sense Multiple Access/with Collision Detection (CSMA/CD) modulation. In order to transmit the information across the POTS line to the DSLAM, DSL modems convert the Ethernet signal that the LAN connection uses to one of the following forms:

  ■ **CAP (Carrierless Amplitude Phase):** CAP modulation is a proprietary ADSL encoding method. It has effectively been superseded by, and is incompatible with, DMT.

  ■ **DMT (Discrete Multi-Tone):** DMT modulation is a standard DSL line-encoding format. Most ADSL modems use DMT to modulate/demodulate the electrical signal that represents the digital data stream your private network uses.

  ■ **Quadrate Amplitude Modulation (QAM):** QAM combines amplitude modulation and phase shift keying.

  ■ **2B1Q (2 Binary 1 Quaternary):** 2B1Q is the encoding method used for T1 and SDLS connections.

◆ **DSLAM (Digital Subscriber Loop Access Multiplexer):** The key to the entire DSL technology, DSLAM is the device to which your DSL modem electrically connects. One side of the DSLAM is connected to the POTS network. The other end is connected to both the phone company's PSTN network and a high-speed ATM or Frame Relay backbone.

On the POTS side, the DSLAM separates the analog voice from the digital DSL signals. The DSLAM directs the voice signal into the Telco's PSTN network and the DSL signal into either an ATM or Frame Relay network. The DSL subscriber IP packets are routed to the appropriate ISP, which is connected to the ATM or Frame Relay backbone.

◆ **DSL modem:** The device that most DSL providers require you to use to connect to their DSLAM. Modern DSL modems perform three functions: 1) using DMT, modulate and demodulate the signal to and from the DSLAM, 2) perform PPPoX encapsulation of the IP packets for transport across the wire, and 3) perform NAT (Network Address Translation) on the IP connections to and from the ISP.

◆ **Frame Relay (FR):** Frame Relay is a high-speed communications technology that hundreds of networks throughout the world use to connect LAN, SNA, Internet, and even voice applications. FR was designed in the 1960s to provide AT&T with the ability to internally exchange information. FR was so successful that AT&T turned it into a commercial service. ATM is currently replaying FR in many applications.

◆ **Line (or telephone line):** Line is often used as a synonym for the twisted-pair of copper wires that forms the backbone of the world's POTS networks. For instance, the term phone line describes the wires that connect a telephone set to the telephone company's local equipment. Of course, line can also refer to the logical connection between two phone sets that allows people to have a conversation. However, in this book's context, we use line to mean the physical connection consisting of unshielded, twisted copper wire loop.

◆ **Loop:** Loop is synonymous for line or telephone line.

◆ **ILEC (Incumbent Local Exchange Carrier):** ILEC refers to the existing Telco. By law, ILECs must lease their infrastructure to the CLECs and DCLECs. We refer to ILECs, CLECs, and DCLECs generically as DSL providers in this book.

◆ **NID (Network Interface Device):** NID is the box (or housing) connected to your building that contains the Telco POTS wiring on one end and your wires on the other. The Telco is responsible for the wiring up to the NID.

◆ **Phone Company:** *See* Regional Bell Operating Company.

◆ **PPPoA (PPP over ATM):** DSL is a point-to-point connection and lends itself to the use of PPP. The PPP protocol encapsulates IP packets over a point-to-point serial DSL connection. Some ISPs have infrastructure built around the ATM protocol (ATM divides all information into 48 bit packets). PPPoA streamlines operations for ATM-based ISPs.

PPPoA modems establish ISP connections by supplying a username and password. Once the connection is authenticated, all IP packets destined for the Internet are encapsulated into ATM packets and transmitted to the ISP. That is, IP packets with external destination addresses that show up on the modem's LAN interface destination addresses.

Most DSL modems use PPPoA to encapsulate IP packets for transmission across the POTS network to the DSLAM at the CO. This is done because the DSL to DSLAM connection is a point-to-point connection and lends itself to the PPP protocol.

◆ **PPPoE (PPP over Ethernet):** Many ISPs use PPP, which is used to connect TCP/IP clients over dialup modem connections, because their infrastructure is already built around it. PPPoE and PPPoA are cost effective protocols for ISPs to use.

◆ **POTS (Plain Old Telephone Service):** POTS is the term used to describe all analog telephone systems that use twisted-pair copper wires to connect to a PSTN.

◆ **PSTN (Public Switched Telephone Network):** This is the network that effectively connects one telephone device to another. When you dial your phone, a connection is made to your telephone company through the copper wire attached to your phone. The telephone company computers interpret the number that you dial and a circuit is set up to the destination telephone.

The circuit is a logical one. The phone company digitizes the input (voices) on each end and packetizes the information. Those packets, or frames in Telco terminology, are routed through the PSTN to the CO closest to the destination phone. The digital packets are converted back into analog form so that the destination telephone can use them. (Some installations, such as large organizations that have digital phone systems, can accept the digital data directly.)

◆ **Regional Bell operating company:** AT&T was broken into seven telephone companies that service mutually exclusive regions of the United States. They're also called Telcos, Baby Bells, Regional Bells or just "the telephone company."

◆ **RJ11:** RJ11 is the ubiquitous telephone jack that POTS devices plug into. RJ11 connectors plug into RJ11 jacks and have between two to six wires. RJ11 jacks look similar to RJ45 jacks that are used to connect Ethernet (10baseT) devices. RJ45 uses eight wires (PCMCIA uses 4 wires).

◆ **Telephone Company:** *See* Regional Bell Operating Company.

◆ **Telco:** *See* Regional Bell operating company.

◆ **Twisted-pair:** *See* Line.

◆ **Upstream/Downstream:** These terms refer to the direction of data flowing through the DSL modem. Upstream refers to data traveling from your DSL modem to your ISP. Downstream, as you may guess, is data flowing in the opposite direction.

Types of DSL service

This section lists the various types of DSL available. Most locales will only have access to two or three of these services.

◆ **ADSL (Asymmetrical DSL):** ADSL uses a single twisted-pair POTS line. ADSL's upstream and downstream speeds are different. Individual consumers use the Internet to browse the Web more than any other function. Browsing inherently involves downloading data far more often than uploading information. Therefore, the DSL provider can minimize their infrastructure and costs by taking advantage of the their customers' usage patterns and provide them with lower-cost, but effectively high-speed, service.

The maximum ADSL speed is 8 Mbps, but it's usually limited to less due to the POTS infrastructure limitations. The DLECS also limit upstream to lower speeds than downstream to make more efficient use of the infrastructure and deliver lower prices to their consumers.

◆ **G.Lite:** Also known as Universal DSL and splitterless ADSL, G.Lite is a low-speed version of ADSL that doesn't require filtering out the POTS signal. It provides up to 1.5 Mbps downstream and 512 Kbps upstream. G.Lite is DMT incompatible, so it requires a modem different than the ADSL modems in use today.

◆ **HDSL (High bit-rate DSL):** HDSL is a symmetrical protocol with both upstream and downstream speeds being equal. You can use HDSL as a substitute for T1 connections because it provides the same data rates of 1.544 Mb/s. (HDSL also provides the same rate of up to 2.048 Mb/s as E1 connections do in Europe.) This technology uses two loops (4 wires) and works up to roughly 6,000 feet; it requires repeaters to go up to a maximum of 12,000 feet.

◆ **HDSL2 (High Bit-rate DSL 2):** HDSL2 provides the same specifications as HDSL but works over a single twisted-pair connection.

◆ **IDSL (ISDN Digital Subscriber Loop):** IDSL is the successor to the current ISDN technology. It uses the same line encoding (2B1Q) as ISDN and SDSL. Unlike ISDN, IDSL requires only a single line. IDSL is mostly used to provide DSL service in areas where the more popular forms, such as ADSL and SDSL, aren't available. IDSL is capable of providing upstream and downstream rates of 144 Kbps.

◆ **SDSL (Single-line DSL):** SDSL is commonly called *Symmetric DSL* because SDSL upstream and downstream speeds are the same. SDSL is a two-wire version of HDSL. Businesses use SDSL because they need to upload information for customers. SDSL requires only a single pair of copper wires (Early DSL required two pairs.) SDSL supports T1/E1 up to 11,000 feet (3,667 meters).

◆ **VDSL (Very high bit rate DSL):** VDSL provides up to 50 Mb/s over distances up to 1,500 meters on short loops, such as from fiber to the curb. In most cases, VDSL lines are served from neighborhood cabinets that link to a CO via optical fiber. VDSL is particularly useful for campus environments — universities and business parks, for example. VDSL is currently being introduced in market trials to deliver video services over existing phone lines. You can also configure VDSL in symmetric mode.

◆ **xDSL:** xDSL is a generic term for all of the DSL flavors.

TIP All of the DSL flavors are *full duplex*. Full-duplex connections are capable of simultaneously transmitting data in both directions.

Creating Your DSL Internet Connection

You need to connect your DSL modem to your DSL service provider after you obtain a broadband provider and ISP. The line from your NID to the DSLAM at the CO is a direct connection. Therefore, the connection process involves first connecting the DSL modem to your POTS wiring, which itself is connected to your NID. Next, you need to configure the DSL modem to connect to your ISP.

Obtaining a DSL Internet connection

You must obtain both DSL and ISP services to make your broadband connection. Some companies, notably Regional Bells, can provide both services. However, in our case, we preferred our ISP and were fortunate to retain them when purchasing our DSL service.

The DSL provider market is currently very fluid. DLECs are finding it difficult to remain profitable for a variety of reasons. Analyze the DSL service providers in your area carefully before choosing one, and remember that longevity is as important as price. For better or worse, the Regional Bells are more likely to provide long-term service than many of their competitors. Keep in mind that one advantage of ADSL service is that you often don't have to sign a service contract, so you can reasonably switch providers if you're unsatisfied with the service.

You must select an ISP after you choose a DSL provider. Selecting an ISP is as much about personal preference as it is about price.

Physically connecting your DSL modem

Connecting your DSL modem to your POTS wiring is basically a straightforward process. Describing how to make the wiring connections is just about impossible with the myriad options available, but we can give you the basic considerations you need to take into account.

This section describes issues involved in connecting your DSL modem to your building's POTS wiring. (Your DSL provider may insist on installing the equipment, particularly if you're using SDSL equipment because it requires a separate line.)

There are three types of wiring configurations:

◆ **Dedicated line:** Several types of DSL, such as SDSL and IDSL, require the use of separate twisted-wire pairs.

◆ **Shared line with splitter:** ADSL, for instance, can co-exist with a POTS voice signal. However, the DSL modem and CPE devices, such as telephones, can't handle each other's signals. (Note: Non-CPE equipment, such as a closely placed halogen light, can interfere with ADSL modems.)

A *splitter* is a band pass filter that separates the DSL and CPE signals at the customer's NID. Using a splitter requires that the DSL line be on a separate circuit from the POTS equipment; therefore, all CPE equipment remains on a single circuit separate from the DSL modem. The splitter keeps the DSL signal from entering the POTS circuit and the POTS signal from the DSL circuit. However, both signals are allowed to pass through the line to the DSLAM.

Figure 3-3 shows the splitter configuration.

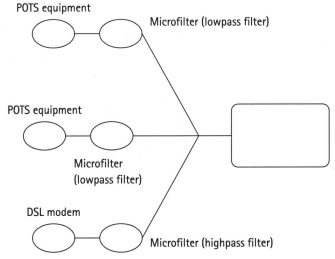

Figure 3-3: POTS with a splitter connection

◆ **Shared line with filters:** The alternative to placing a splitter between the POTS and DSL equipment is to use individual filters to separate the POTS devices from the DSL signal, which is called a *splitterless* configuration. Splitterless configurations install microfilters between POTS devices and their RJ11 jacks to prevent the DSL signal from interfering with the CPE device.

The splitterless configuration is easier to use than the splitter configuration because microfilters are easier to install than a splitter (they plug into your wall jacks but a splitter must be installed at the NID). However, the splitterless topology doesn't provide as good a signal separation. It's generally adequate if the POTS line provides a good connection to the DSLAM. However, if the line is marginal, then using the splitter is a better option.

Determine the type of wiring configuration best suited to your DSL service. Make the connections and proceed to the next section.

Configuring your DSL provider's equipment

Writing explicit configuration examples is always problematic. The DSL world is still young and we're not convinced that any in-fact standards have emerged. Chances are that our instructions won't match your equipment.

However, we're at least using fairly common equipment. The Baby Bells, such as Qwest, are the leaders in providing DSL circuits, so a significant percentage of DSL users use this equipment. Our Cisco 675 DSL modem/router is Qwest's recommended equipment. If you're using different equipment, then our instructions should still be useful in outlining the general process of configuring a DSL connection.

COMMUNICATING WITH THE CISCO MODEM

You need to configure your Linux computer before connecting to the Cisco 675 DSL modem for the first time. The modem comes with management software that runs on Windows computers but not, of course, Linux computers; Linux is still not considered by all manufactures even though it comprises a large market – be sure to inform manufactures that you purchase their equipment. The modem comes with two other configuration vehicles however: a direct serial (RS232) connection and Telnet.

You can't use the Telnet method until you configure the Cisco DSL modem to allow it. So, at least initially, you must use the serial line method, which is actually fortuitous from a security viewpoint because the serial method is less vulnerable to hacks than the Telnet. You can tighten the Cisco's Telnet configuration to be reasonably secured, but it's always vulnerable to misconfigurations. For instance, you must set the device's password and prohibit Telnet connections from the Internet. Serial line connections are completely private and can not be sniffed. We use serial connections exclusively in our examples.

The following list describes how to configure a Cisco 675 DSL modem.

1. Connect the blue port management (RS232 serial cable with a 9 pin DB9 female connector) between the computer and the Cisco 675 DSL modem. We use the server Atlas as the computer in this example.

2. Log in as root on your Internet gateway/firewall.

3. Install the minicom terminal emulator package if it hasn't been already. If minicom has not been installed, then download and install it from Red Hat's anonymous FTP site: `ftp.redhat.com`.

   ```
   mount /mnt/cdrom
   rpm -ivh /mnt/cdrom/dsl/minicom*
   ```

4. Create the default minicom configuration file.

   ```
   minicom -s
   ```

5. Run the program.

```
minicom
```

6. A warning is displayed about not running minicom as root. If you wish, login as a regular user before using minicom.

7. The initial minicom screen is displayed.

```
Welcome to minicom 1.83.1

OPTIONS: History Buffer, F-key Macros, Search History Buffer,
I18n
Compiled on Feb 23 2001, 07:31:40.

Press CTRL-A Z for help on special keys
```

8. Press the Ctrl+A and then Z to enter the configuration menu. Change the communication device from /dev/modem to /dev/ttyS0 (or the serial device that is appropriate to your system (/dev/ttyS1, /dev/ttyS2 or /dev/ttyS3).

9. Change the communication parameters to a speed of 9600, 8 bits, and no parity. Turn off hardware and software flow control if necessary.

10. Connect to the Cisco DSL modem by pressing the return key. The first time that you connect to the modem you should see the following prompt:

```
User Access Verification
Password:
```

11. No password is set yet, so just press the Enter key. The Cisco Broadband Operating System (cbos) prompt should appear.

```
cbos>
```

You have successfully configured the serial connection to the Cisco DSL modem. The next steps involve setting up the Cisco 675 to access your ISP via its DSL connection.

CONFIGURING THE CISCO ADSL MODEM
The following steps describe how to configure an ADSL modem. We use an ADSL modem here because it's the most common DSL device available today. The process of configuring an SDSL modem differs in details, but the process is similar because both systems require the configuration of LAN and WAN network interfaces and PPP parameters.

The following process involves setting up your authentication, routing, and NAT. You must first configure the ADSL modem with its own passwords and other information.

TIP If you want to reconfigure your DSL modem from scratch, then enter the **set nvram erase**, **write**, and **reboot** commands before proceeding with these instructions. Running those commands effectively returns your Cisco 675 DSL modem to its factory default settings.

1. You must set your modem's passwords once you're connected via the serial connection. The Cisco 675 uses both a regular (non-privileged) password called *exec*, and an administrative password, called *enable*. Only the administrative user can set passwords, so enter the following command to enter enable mode:

   ```
   enable
   ```

2. No enable password is set, so press the Enter key when prompted for the password. The cbos> prompt changes to cbos# with the pound sign (#) indicating that you're in enable mode.

3. Enter the following command at cbos> prompt to set the exec password:

   ```
   set password exec iamnotanumber
   ```

   iamnotanumber is just an example password. Enter a password of your choice in place of that example.

4. Set the enable password by using the following command:

   ```
   set password enable iamanumber
   ```

   Once again, substitute your own password for iamanumber. Make sure that the exec and enable passwords are different.

5. The system doesn't remember any parameter you change until you write it to non-volatile ram (nvram). Save the passwords that you just set by running the following command:

   ```
   write
   ```

   You can look at the values stored in nvram by running **show nvram**, which should show the values (the password values are hashed) that you just saved.

   ```
   [[ CBOS = Section Start ]]
   NSOS Root Password = a_lsbgegr
   NSOS Enable Password = a_lsbgegr
   ```

6. Configure the DSL modem's Ethernet interface so that it can communicate with the Internet gateway/firewall Atlas.

   ```
   set interface eth0 address 192.168.32.1 netmask 255.255.255.0
   ```

(Setting the netmask is optional because cbos correctly interprets the 192.168.32 as a class C network. We show it here just in case you're using another address space, such as 10.0.1.)

7. Now set up your ISP's PPP connection parameters. Start by entering your PPP login name and password. The DSL modem uses the wan0-0 (the first WAN) interface for the PPP connect. In this case, our ISP uses an e-mail address as the login name. Your ISP may use another convention.

```
set ppp wan0-0 login iwantdsl@myisp.com
set ppp wan0-0 password givemedslplease
```

Substitute your own values in place of our sample e-mail address and password.

8. Set up the modem's default route.

```
set ppp wan0-0 ipcp 0.0.0.0
```

9. Tell the modem to go through the default route for DNS.

```
set ppp wan0-0 dns 0.0.0.0
set dhcp server enabled
```

10. Disable Telnet connections so that no one can find and exploit a weakness in the device's Telnet server.

```
set telnet disabled
```

11. Finally, enable NAT.

```
set nat enabled
```

The Cisco 675 DSL modem now automatically converts the source addresses and ports of outgoing connections to its external (wan0-0) interface.

12. Save the changes to nvram.

```
write
```

13. You can examine the parameters again by displaying the nvram contents. The command **show nvram** should provide the following information:

```
[[ CBOS = Section Start ]]
NSOS Root Password = a_lsbgegr
NSOS Enable Password = a_lsbgegr
NSOS Remote Restart = enabled
[[ PPP Device Driver = Section Start ]]
PPP Port User Name = 00, iwantdsl@myisp.com
PPP Port User Password = 00, givmedslplease
PPP Port Option = 00, IPCP,IP Address,3,Auto,Negotiation Not
Required,Negotiabl0
```

```
PPP Port Option = 00, IPCP,Primary DNS
Server,129,Auto,Negotiation Not Required0
PPP Port Option = 00, IPCP,Secondary DNS
Server,131,Auto,Negotiation Not Requir0
[[ IP Routing = Section Start ]]
IP Port Address = 00, 192.168.32.1
IP NAT = enabled
[[ DHCP = Section Start ]]
DHCP Server = enabled
DHCP Relay = disabled
[[ Telnet = Section Start ]]
Telnet = disabled
```

Note that your ISP password is shown in plain text, which is one reason why protecting your DSL modem is essential — we use a dedicated serial connection to configure the device.

14. Reboot the modem to put all the changes into effect.

```
reboot
```

15. The Wan LED indicator should start blinking after you reboot the modem, indicating that the device is attempting to connect to the ISP's router on the other side of the DSL connection. If the connection is established and authenticated, then the light turns to a constant on state. If the connection isn't established, then consult the troubleshooting section at the end of this chapter.

Many early DSL modems were bridges rather than routers. Bridges pass IP packets from one interface to another without checking addresses; rather they perform error checking and reject corrupted packets. If you happen to find an ISP that still uses bridging instead of routing, you have to configure your modem appropriately. In that case, skip the PPP and NAT configuration steps and replace them with the necessary steps. In all likelihood, the ISP will recommend and/or supply a bridging modem with the appropriate instructions.

CONFIGURATION SUMMARY

This section reviews the basic DSL modem configuration issues. These are the macro configuration steps that should be relevant to most DSL modems. Combining the following items with the previous detailed instructions should help you to configure a non-Cisco device:

◆ Connect the modem in order to configure it.

◆ Set up the modem user and administrative passwords.

- ◆ Set up the ISP/DSL connection account name and password.

- ◆ Configure the modem's internal (private) network interface.

- ◆ Configure the modem's PPP settings.

- ◆ Configure the modem's NAT settings.

- ◆ Save the settings to non-volatile memory and reboot.

POST CONFIGURATION ISSUES

After you obtain basic DSL connectivity, you may want to allow external connections through it. The process involves configuring the DSL modem/router to provide the correct NAT mappings that allow certain connections in from the Internet. Some DSL modems permit packet filtering similar in function to iptables. (Most, if not all, consumer DSL modems don't provide stateful filtering, but that situation will likely change with time. Stateful filtering determines whether to pass or block IP packets based on whether they belong to an existing connection or not.)

We again use the Cisco 675 to perform the straightforward address translation process.

1. Determine what machine(s) you want to provide services to the outside world. In our example we use a machine connected to the DMZ (cancun) with an address of 192.168.32.251. In the case of a DCL configuration, the Internet gateway/router performs as the platform.

2. Provide Internet access to sendmail (port 25), Secure Shell (port 22), and Web services (port 80).

3. Login to the router as the administrator.

4. Add the NAT mappings to permit the DSL modem/router to pass through sendmail, ssh, and httpd packets to cancun, which is a computer on our DMZ network.

   ```
   set nat entry add 192.168.32.251 25 tcp
   set nat entry add 192.168.32.251 22 tcp
   set nat entry add 192.168.32.251 80 tcp
   ```

   If you want to direct HTTP traffic to another machine, 192.168.32.253, for instance, then change the last entry to **set nat entry add 192.168.32.253 80 tcp**. Programming the DSL modem's NAT settings provides a great deal of flexibility.

5. Write the settings to nvram.

   ```
   write
   ```

6. Display the new NAT mappings by entering the command **show nat**. The output looks similar to the following:

```
NAT is currently enabled
Inside Global Address set to 216.184.14.13
Inside Local          Inside Global  Timer Flags  Protocol
192.168.32.251:  22  216.184.14.13:  22  0  0x41   tcp
192.168.32.251:  25  216.184.14.13:  25  0  0x41   tcp
192.168.32.251:  80  216.184.14.13:  80  0  0x41   tcp
192.168.32.254: 2293  216.184.14.13:10190 8613 0x146  tcp
192.168.32.254: 2296  216.184.14.13:10193 8565  x146 tcp
```

The first three lines in the table are the NAT entries that we just made. The inside local address corresponds to the machine that we want packets arriving from the Internet that are addressed to the ports 22, 25 and 80; their destination addresses will be that of our external wan0-0 address, which is 216.184.14.13. The NAT maps those destination addresses to the ones that we set above.

The last two NAT settings are dynamic ones set up by the modem itself. They correspond to outgoing connections arriving from the Internet gateway/router atlas.

7. Test the new configuration by trying to connect to any of the three services from the Internet. If the server is operating correctly, you'll connect to the services.

Several Web sites can test your DSL modem's speed. The following site sends data to and from your modem and measure the speed. Please note that the routers that lie between your DSL modem and the testing site affect the test's accuracy.

www.dslreports.com/information/kb

Basic Troubleshooting Hints

The problem with troubleshooting DSL is that many problems are outside of your direct reach. Telcos and ISPs account for much of the activity that takes place when using DSL, and you have to deal with them indirectly through phone calls, e-mail, and so on. This section concentrates on the problems that you can affect. DSL problems that you can deal with directly are "local" DSL problems or issues; "remote" problems occur outside your premises. If you're having difficulty getting your DSL system to work and have exhausted local troubleshooting methods, then contact your DSL and/or ISP providers. The following areas are examples of local DSL problems:

- ◆ DSL wiring problems
- ◆ DSL modem configuration problems

◆ DSL modem syncing problems

Remote DSL problems fall into the following categories:

◆ DSL provider configuration problems

◆ POTS wiring problems

◆ ISP configuration problems

We describe possible solutions to each problem category below.

Your DSL modem must synchronize with the DSLAM in order to establish a link. The syncing process starts when you connect the modem to the POTS RJ11 and power it up. The green SYNC light starts to blink and then turns a constant green when the synchronization completes and the link is established. If the sync process fails and the light never turns green, then you need to look at several possible problems.

 Always exercise great caution when working with any electrical device. POTS wiring carries 32 volts, which shouldn't be life-threatening on contact, but may be dangerous given certain situations. And, your POTS wires may be in contact with a 120-volt source. If in doubt, hire a professional.

The following items describe some of the problems common to first-time DSL installation. These items are geared towards finding a problem before you ever establish service.

◆ **Contact your DSL provider desk if your DSL modem doesn't sync.** DSL service is still relatively new and many DSL providers haven't streamlined all of their communications and procedures. Check with your provider's help desk to verify that your connection exists and is configured properly. DSL providers should be able to perform tests on your line to verify that you have a good (or at least marginal) electrical connection.

Your DSL provider can also inform you if they have equipment failure, such as a broken DSLAM, on their end.

◆ **Check your internal – home or office wiring – if your modem syncs intermittently.** Make sure that you've placed splitterless microfilters on all of your analog telephone equipment if you use a splitterless system. Otherwise, if you are using a splitter type configuration, check the splitter-wiring at the NID. (Check that the wiring in your NID is solidly connected).

If you suspect that your building's internal POTS wiring is at fault, then consider connecting directly to your NID. Most NIDS have an RJ11 jack to which you can connect directly. Record the color-coding on the wires and temporarily disconnect the building's internal POTS connection from the NID. Take your DSL modem to the NID and connect the WAN port to the NID RJ11 jack. You may need to lug an extension cord to the NID to power the modem. Connecting directly to the NID and disconnecting the POTS circuit eliminates any internal wiring problems. Make your test and then reconnect the wires.

If you discover a problem with the wiring, then use your best judgment to fix the situation. Any number of potential imperfections can cause such problems: old, corroded wires or connectors and interference form RF sources, such as halogen lights, Ham radios, and so on. Older, slower POTS devices, such as telephones, will often continue working with degraded wiring because they function at low frequencies. DSL circuits however, have no margin for error and are good devices for detecting bad wiring.

◆ **Disconnect all POTS devices such as telephones and faxes if you're using a splitterless DSL system:** Try to get a sync when you establish a "clean" environment.

◆ **Check the cable between the DSL modem and wall jack:** Test the cable by using it to connect a telephone and listening for a dial tone. Don't use the splitterless microfilter on the cable if you're doing that type of test, just in case the filter is defective.

◆ **Check your PPP configuration:** Make sure that the username and password match the values your ISP provided.

If you're experiencing problems after you establish DSL service, try the following:

◆ **Check the power to your DSL modem:** If power is available, then cycle it once or twice.

◆ **Try connecting to the modem from the LAN (Telnet) or the serial management port (minicom):** If you can communicate with the device, then the WAN connection is most likely not the problem. Check the following items before assuming that the modem has failed:

■ **Check the modem's PPP configuration:** Make sure that the username and password match the values your ISP provided.

■ **Look for RF sources if you experience intermittent failures or degraded connection speeds:** Halogen lights, Ham radios, or even AM/FM radios in the modem's vicinity can cause interference problems.

■ **Try connecting directly to the NID if you suspect an intermittent problem is due to bad wiring.** Bad internal POTS wiring can also cause intermittent problems, such as degraded service. Connecting directly to the NID requires that you either transport your DSL modem and at least one computer to NID; you recreate a mini-network near the NID so that you bypass your structure's internal wiring. Alternatively, you can string a cable from your DSL modem to the NID. The latter method should be used with caution because it can potentially give you an electric shock if the cable should somehow come into contact with an exposed electrical wire.

- **Reduce your local circuit's impedance to decrease the effective distance to the CO.** Being at the outer edge of DSL service can cause intermittent syncing problems. Your signal might be adequate under good environmental conditions but high humidity, strong winds, and so on can affect the POTS wiring between your structure and the CO. Converting from splitterless microfilters to a splitter system helps, as well.

- **Contact your DSL provider for further assistance when you've exhausted all remedies:** You may also have to covert to another technology like a cable modem or a T1 circuit, which is also limited by the distance to the CO.

 We describe and recommend the use of stand-alone DSL modems in this book. Standalone modems are guaranteed to work because they use Ethernet LAN connections and don't require any special drivers to work. If you use an internal PCI card or USB DSL modem, then you must verify that you have Linux drivers to make it work.

Summary

This chapter introduced the technology of broadband Internet connections. We concentrated on using Asymmetrical Digital Subscriber Loop (ADSL) as a cost-effective, broadband connection system.

We described the basic function of ADSL, as well as the process that converts a digital signal into a form that can be transmitted across ordinary telephone wires. Definitions and descriptions were given to the many terms and acronyms that DSL and telephone technology use. We also gave you an example of configuring an ADSL modem, and we discussed troubleshooting techniques.

The following topics were covered in this chapter:

- ◆ **Introducing the concept of broadband Internet:** The ubiquitous analog modem still dominates the Internet's consumer and small business sides. As their prices drop, technologies such as DSL and cable TV networks are quickly becoming available to the public. Broadband connections now present an avenue for those who want high-speed, continuous Internet connections. Anyone who wants to create an Internet-based server must consider using such technologies.

◆ **Introducing DSL technology:** The basic concept of DSL is very simple: transmit high-speed, digital information across common telephone lines from the customer's location to the Telco's CO. The Telco's infrastructure is capable of transporting data in the megabit range. Technology has reached the point where DSL modems are available at consumer prices and the Telco's have invested enough in equipment to make high-speed communication possible.

◆ **Describing how an IP packet is delivered to the Internet via DSL:** Although the concept of DSL is quite simple, the implementation is less so. A number of processes must occur to make DSL possible. We endeavored to describe the process from end-to-end.

◆ **Comparing cable TV-based Internet connections with DSL and T1/Frame Relay:** Traditional broadband technology, such as T1/Frame Relay, is being challenged by new ones like DSL and cable TV networks. We introduced T1 and cable so you can compare the technologies.

◆ **Configuring an ADSL modem to connect with an ISP:** We provided a concrete example of how to configure an ADSL connection, by showing you how to configure the popular Cisco 675 DSL modem. The example should be useful to you even if you don't use this system because other equipment will use a similar process.

◆ **Troubleshooting common DSL problems:** Installing and configuring a DSL can be tricky. We outlined some of the common problems that you may encounter and gave you their solutions.

Chapter 4

Building a Firewall

IN THIS CHAPTER

◆ Introducing firewalls

◆ Building the firewall

◆ Allowing external connections via Secure Shell

◆ Managing your firewall

IT IS ESSENTIAL to protect your servers and workstations from mischief once you connect your private network to the Internet. The Internet is an outstanding tool for many different functions but it also provides the perfect medium for hackers and other anti-social types to gain access to and possibly hurt or destroy your network. Building a firewall is your first line of defense against the bad guys.

This chapter describes the basics of firewall construction. We describe the difference between an application level (sometimes called proxy) and a packet filtering firewalls. This chapter shows how to construct stateful packet filtering firewalls and then modify them to act as a hybrid application/packet filtering firewall. We show you how to tailor your firewall to your own needs by showing different configurations.

Introducing Firewalls

A *firewall* is a network device configured to prevent unauthorized access on an individual computer or network. For the purposes of this book, a firewall is a Linux computer set up to protect the private network we're building.

This book uses somewhat different terminology than what you find in the technical literature on the subject. We refer to the local network with which we've been working as the private network rather than local area network (LAN). We call the Red Hat Linux-based firewall the firewall server; in other circles that machine is often called a screening router or bastion host. We do use the term DMZ to the semi-open network that sits between the firewall server and the Internet.

Firewalls come in two primary flavors: filtering and proxy. Filtering firewalls look at each IP packet and decide whether to pass or reject the packets based on a set of rules that you determine; they work at the Open Systems Interconnection (OSI) Network layer. Proxy — also called application — firewalls act as an intermediary between a program client and its server by replicating the communication and performing other security functions. They work at the OSI Application layer.

Please see the section Networking and the OSI Network Model in Chapter 2 for more information.

We construct a hybrid firewall in this chapter that uses both IP filtering and a proxy in order to take advantage of both systems. We can do so because we're constructing the private network to make use of the Internet but not provide services to it. Therefore, we can construct the firewall like a diode, allowing connections to the Internet to be made from the inside out, but not the other way.

Packet filtering firewalls

Packet filtering firewalls work by examining every TCP, UDP, and ICMP packet that pass through their interfaces (the Ethernet interfaces and logical loopback interface, for example). The source and destination IP addresses plus the source and destination port numbers are compared against a set of rules by the Linux kernel. The rules tell the kernel whether the packet is permitted to pass through the firewall or is blocked. IP filters work at the Network layer of the OSI model described in Chapter 2.

Filtering firewalls are relatively easy to configure and use. All you have to do is determine what type of connections (based on port numbers) to allow into and out of the firewall and then write the corresponding rules. After the rules are in place, no extra steps are necessary to access the services those rules allow. If the rules permit port 23 (Telnet) through, then you can establish Telnet connections. As you'll see in the next section, the same doesn't hold true for proxy firewalls.

IP filtering systems are bundled with Red Hat Linux. Combined with the ease of installation and writing rules, they're straightforward to use. IP filters are also efficient because having the Linux kernel examine IP packet headers doesn't create much overhead — an Intel 486 based firewall server can readily handle a medium-sized network containing dozens of computers.

The problem with IP filters, however, is that they can't see the forest for the trees. IP filters are very good at determining whether individual packets meet the specified rules, but they can't "see" the big picture: whether any given stream of packets are intended for valid purposes or are part of an attack. For instance, the filter rules may allow Telnet packets through, but an attacker who knows a valid password can use Telnet to break into your system. The filter only sees the IP header information and has no mechanism for validating beyond that.

IP filters can still form the basis for a very good firewall. After introducing the IP filter counterpart — Proxy firewalls — in the next section, we'll configure our filters in such a way as to combine the best of both systems. The resulting firewall is good for a large number of circumstances.

Proxy firewalls

Proxy firewalls work at the OSI Application level. Unlike IP filters, they require authentication of the application attempting entry before allowing a connection to be established. For instance, a proxy firewall requires you to enter a password before allowing a Telnet connection to be completed. Proxy firewalls are based on the idea of looking at the forest and not the trees.

TIP Using one-time passwords makes gaining access to your system very difficult for unauthorized users.

The problem with proxy firewalls is that they're relatively difficult to set up and inconvenient to use. They're also somewhat more inefficient, and are vulnerable to software bugs and new attack methods. Configuration is more difficult because each application that you want to proxy requires its own configuration.

Proxy firewalls are also somewhat vulnerable to new attacks because only the proxy's own programming can fix any attack that finds an opening. For instance, when Denial of Service (DoS) attacks first appeared, you had to reprogram any proxy that fell victim to them. (Filtering firewalls, although not immune to new attacks, can readily be reprogrammed to simply deny the IP packets that carry that attack.) The fact that a proxy firewall is often sitting out on the Internet means that potentially everyone on the Internet can pound away at your firewall. The more attempts made on your firewall, the higher the probability that an attacker will find a weak spot.

Don't assume that proxy firewalls are inadequate for the job, we only point out the potential hazards for completeness. We don't use pure proxy firewalls in this book because the filters described here work well when a network only (or mostly) accesses the Internet and usually doesn't allow anyone to come in.

Hybrid firewalls

This book assumes a networking model where most, if not all, of your Internet traffic is outward bound to the Internet. This model is true of many organizations today where they house networks of people browsing, e-mailing, and interacting with the Internet, but only provide a small number of services to the Internet. Individual proxies are provided for the services provided to the Internet.

This book uses a hybrid firewall designed to minimize your work while maximizing your safety. Once you're protected, you have a window of time to learn security more fully and make decisions on how much additional protection you need. You may very well never require anything more than what we describe here.

Understanding IP NAT or masquerading

Using IP Network Address Translation (NAT), also known as IP masquerading, is an elegant method for attaching your network to the Internet. IP masquerading converts an IP source address into another address. In this example, the source addresses of packets originating from within the private network get converted into the source address of the Internet connection (via ISP) on the Linux gateway/firewall. Once on the Internet, they all appear to be coming from a single machine, no matter what computer on the private network you're using.

If you use NAT, then you don't need any official registration to allow your network to access the Internet. Without masquerading, you have to obtain IP addresses for your network from an ISP. Using NAT conserves the quickly diminishing pool of IP addresses, too.

IP masquerading also provides the advantage of hiding your network behind a single address. Anyone trying to probe or attack your private network has to go through your single (and typically dynamic) address. Because IP masquerading is in effect a one-way street, most (if not all) attacks on your networked computers die on the vine. Packets originating outside the firewall don't exist in the NAT state table and can't obtain a destination address/port number on the private network; they'll never find their way onto the private network, although they can contact the server doing the translation can. (Note that the only route that's configured on the Internet gateway atlas is the default route to the broadband Internet connection. Returning masqueraded packets get shunted back into the private network via iptables, which is described the section Introducing Stateful Packet Filters (iptables/Netfilter) later in this chapter. Incoming, non-masqueraded packets have no route to the private network.)

One of the few ways for a probe or attack to get a foothold is to seize an existing connection. However, even if that's possible, the packets have to be part of an existing connection originating from the private network. The packets will be treated as return packets and should never be able to start a new connection. NAT ultimately makes your firewall safer than it is without it.

The last line in the `ipfilter.rules` script, in the section "Building a Working Filter," describes the masquerading rule for the paunchy.net network. IP masquerading converts one IP address into another IP address. That translation permits one or more computers to masquerade as a single IP address.

A little more happens during masquerading than just the source address translation. The source port also gets converted to another port. Recall that the TCP/IP protocols make use of both IP addresses and ports. Ports are used to separate network communication between different applications. For instance, the standard Hypertext Transport Protocol (HTTP) uses port 80 by default. If you look at the `/etc/services` file, then you see all of the standard applications and protocols along with their ports; the ports below 1024 are referred to as *well-known ports*. During masquerading, the port gets changed to a number above 1024. This process allows the iptables software to de-masquerade the returning, masqueraded packets back to their original locations.

When there's a response to a masqueraded packet, the reverse translation is performed. The returning packets have their destination IP address converted back to the originating IP address, and the destination port is also converted back to the original port number.

Understanding how a packet flows through the Internet

Following a packet around the network is a useful tool for understanding how this whole process works. This section describes how a single packet originates from your browser, goes through the private network to the Internet gateway, and then on to its final destination. The following steps assume that you're running Mozilla on a Linux workstation, named veracruz, on a private network.

1. From Mozilla enter the location of either of our (hey, it's our book) Web pages: www.mylinuxbooks.com or www.mostwanted.com.

2. Mozilla sends a gethostbyname (a Linux function call) request to the Linux TCP/IP stack. The stack sends a request to the DNS server specified in the */etc/resolv.conf* file, which on our example network is 192.168.1.250.

3. The local DNS server in our example, chivas, is authoritative for the domain paunchy.net but not for either mylinuxbooks.com or most-wanted.com. It cannot resolve the request so it consults the */var/named/named.ca* file. That file contains the addresses of the root servers that can resolve domain names registered with InterNIC.

4. Chivas sends a domain name request to one of the root name servers. One of them responds with the address of the authoritative name server for that domain — mylinuxbooks.com or mostwanted.com.

5. Chivas sends its request to the appropriate name server. That name server then sends back the requested machine's IP address — in this case either www.mylinuxbooks.com or www.mostwanted.com.

6. Chivas sends the numeric IP address to veracruz. With the address in hand, the Linux kernel encapsulates the TCP packet in an IP packet by adding an IP header to the TCP packet.

7. The Linux kernel consults its own routing table, shown below, and decides to send the IP packet to the local default gateway, which is atlas (192.168.1.254). The Linux kernel broadcasts an Address Resolution Protocol (ARP) request to the local sub-network and atlas responds by sending its Multiple Access Computers (MAC) address to veracruz (if the kernel has recently communicated with atlas, it skips this step and caches the address).

```
Destination     Gateway           Genmask         Flags   MSS
Window  irtt Iface
192.168.1.0     *                 255.255.255.0 U         40 0
0 eth0
127.0.0.0       *                 255.0.0.0       U       40 0
0 lo
default         atlas.paunchy.net 0.0.0.0         UG      40 0
0 eth0
```

8. Linux encapsulates the IP packet in an Ethernet frame and sends it out on the network (onto the *wire* in geek speak).

9. The Ethernet frame arrives at atlas's `eth0` network interface. Atlas decodes the first few packets of the frame and determines that the MAC address matches its own. It passes the frame up through its own stack. After decoding the IP header, atlas determines that the packet is destined for an external network and sends it to its own default route.

10. The iptables system determines that the packet matches its ACCEPT rule, which tells the kernel to allow the packet to pass through, (`iptables -p OUTPUT -a ACCEPT --dport ...`) and allows it to pass. It also matches a masquerading rule that converts every packet from the private network to the address of the default route NIC – `192.168.32.1`.

11. As part of the masquerading process, the packet's IP header is "mangled" and given the source address of `192.168.32.254`. From there the packet is encapsulated in an Ethernet frame and sent onto the DMZ sub-network.

12. The broadband interface (a Cisco 675 DSL modem in our example) intercepts the packet; we have named the DSL modem dsl. dsl determines that the packet is destined for the Internet and forwards it to its own default address. The packet is once again masqueraded, but this time the IP address of our ISP is assigned to the DSL modem – in this case, `216.184.14.13`.

13. The packet inherits the ISP's source IP address. The packet now has a valid, and thus routable, IP address and is routed through the ISP. The ISP determines the appropriate downstream router to which to send the packet. The packet is subsequently sent from router to router, a process not surprisingly called routing.

14. The packet finally finds its way to the intended Web server. The operating system on the Web server processes the packet and generates the second packet of the three-way TCP handshake. The Web server and packet go through the entire process described in the preceding steps, except that the DNS lookup isn't necessary.

15. The return packet is routed back to our Cisco 675 DSL modem and is de-masqueraded. On entry, the packet has the destination address of the ISP side of the DSL connection – `216.184.14.13`. The DSL modem recognizes that address and port from the state table it maintains; the state table is the list of connections that the kernel maintains that makes it possible to determine whether a packet belongs to an existing connection. It replaces that information with the original address and port number.

16. The return packet is routed back to atlas. After de-masquerading the packet again, the state table recognizes it as the second part of the three-way TCP handshake started by the original connection's original first packet.

17. The packet is sent back to veracruz. The Linux kernel generates the handshake's third packet. The packet repeats the process we've just described. When the packet arrives at the Web server, the TCP connection is established.

18. Packets from both the Web client and the server are then sent back and forth. The packets follow the same process as described here, except they no longer posses the handshake attributes.

This complicated, yet elegant, dance takes place across the Internet billions of times per day and is the Internet's technical essence.

Introducing stateful IP packet filters (Netfilter/iptables)

Stateful packet filtering is the most important security-related advancement that the 2.4 Linux kernel has created. The ability to examine a packet's state permits very tight control over what packets the firewall passes or rejects without impacting the functionality of the network it protects. Stateful filtering allows you to create an IP filtering-based firewall that is much more powerful than previously possible.

Stateful packet filters can determine whether or not a packet belongs to an existing TCP connection. Packets belonging to an existing connection are less likely to be hazardous. For instance, if we design a filter that only allows outgoing TCP connections (Telnet, FTP, http, SSH, and so on), then a stateful filter only allows the return packets to pass back through. It won't allow any TCP packets originating from the outside to pass through.

You can manipulate packets originating externally to look like they belong to an existing connection. Older Linux IP filters, such as ipchains and ipfwadm, could be tricked into allowing such packets to pass through because they were unable to check the state of existing connections, creating the potential for hackers to gain a foothold. Netfilter/iptables solves that problem and increases the security of your firewall and network.

Netfilter/iptables introduces stateful packet filtering to the Linux world. There are two parts to the Linux stateful packet filter: Netfilter and iptables. Netfilter is the kernel level system that makes the decision whether to allow a packet to pass from one network interface to another. The iptables work in user space and creates the rules that Netfilter works from. We use the term iptables generically when referring to the overall stateful packet filtering system. Otherwise, we use the term Netfilter/iptables to describe the processes working in the kernel space and iptables to describe the user interface.

State checking works as follows:

1. An application starts a TCP connection that must pass through the firewall to an external network. If, for instance, you're running Mozilla and click on an external link, Mozilla creates the packet at the Application layer and sends it to the Linux TCP/IP stack.

2. Linux creates an IP packet by attaching an IP header to the TCP packet at the Transport layer. The original TCP packet becomes the IP packet's *payload*, or data segment. Linux inserts the critical IP address and port information into the IP header as follows:

   - The remote server's destination address is discovered (recall the gethostbyname function) and inserted into the IP header.

   - The destination port – in this example port 80 – is already known and is inserted into the header.

   - The source address is also known and is folded into the header.

   - Linux generates a source port number. This number is called an *ephemeral port* because it changes each time a new TCP connection is established. Its value is randomly generated and has a value greater than 1024 and less than 65535. The TCP/IP protocol guarantees that all TCP connections are always unique by using different ephemeral port values.

3. After the IP packet is created, it's sent to the Network layer where it's encapsulated into an Ethernet frame. The Ethernet frame is sent out onto the wire – the networking media – and in this case, is destined for our Internet gateway/firewall.

4. The first packet arrives at the firewall and is checked against the rule set. If the packet matches an ACCEPT rule, it's allowed to pass through. As part of the process, the kernel saves the destination and source address, the destination and source port, and also several of the IP header flags.

   The TCP protocol uses what is called a three-way handshake to start a connection. The first packet of a TCP connection has its SYN bit set. The second part of the handshake sends a packet that has its SYN and ACK bits set. The final packet sends a packet with just its SYN bit set.

   The IP protocol makes use of ports to assure that each connection is unique. Recall that when starting a connection, the IP header contains information about the source and destination addresses. The header also stores the source and destination port numbers. The destination port is usually set to values below 1024 that are called well-known ports. Well-known ports correspond to well-known services, such as HTTP (port 80), Telnet (port 23), FTP (port 21), SSH (port 22), and so on. (You can violate this convention if you like, but doing so only causes confusion).

   The source port, however, is set to values above 1024. Those values are (or at least should be) set randomly and are called ephemeral ports. The fact that they're set to random values allows all TCP connections to be distinguishable between each other. If you start a dozen Web connections, for example, then each has a different ephemeral source port, even though each one's destination port is set to 80.

These conventions allow Netfilter/iptables to perform stateful inspections. Netfilter/iptables uses the combination of unique source ports and IP header flags to perform its checks.

5. The packet is routed to its destination.

6. The packet arrives at its destination and the server processes it. In this example, the Web server sends the first response packet back to your browser. The packet has both its SYN and ACK bits set, plus the destination port is set to the ephemeral port.

7. The firewall sees the return packet. It examines the header information and checks it against its state table. The destination port (originally the source port) and SYN/ACK flags match up against the original packet's state and it's allowed to pass.

8. The browser sends the final installment of the three-way TCP handshake to complete the TCP connection. The firewall checks that packet, plus all succeeding packets, against the rule set and state table. All packets with the correct state that also match the ACCEPT rules are allowed to pass.

INTRODUCING THE DEFAULT IPTABLES CHAINS

The iptables have three built-in chains: INPUT, OUTPUT, and FORWARD. These chains are designed to act on packets coming into, leaving from, and passing between the computer's network interfaces. Following is a summary of the default chains functions:

◆ INPUT: The INPUT chain acts on packets coming into the computer's network interface or interfaces. This chain must accept packets before they can encounter the computer's internal processes (for instance, the Secure Shell daemon, which accepts encrypted interactive connections), or be examined by the FORWARD chain.

◆ OUTPUT: In a departure from they way it worked in ipchains and ipfwadm, the OUTPUT chain only interacts with packets originating from within a computer going out to one of its interfaces. (On the ipchain and ipfwadm filtering systems, OUTPUT controlled packets leaving from a computer's interfaces, no matter where they originated.) Processes running on the computer must now create the packets.

◆ FORWARD: The FORWARD chain examines packets that enter on one interface and are routed to another. The forwarding process is essential for gateway routers.

Figure 4-1 shows how packets interact with the default chains.

UDP Packets

The UDP protocol doesn't allow for complete stateful checking. The UDP header doesn't store enough information, such as TCP port and sequence numbers or SYN/ACK flags, for a filter to completely check for state. Fortunately, iptables approximates UDP state and can effectively filter out most harmful packets. iptables accomplishes semi-stateful filtering by assuming that the only valid response to a DNS query is a DNS response from the server that the originating UDP packet was sent to. Send a UPD DNS query to server X and only X should respond with a DNS answer.

The assumption that iptables makes to approximate state can theoretically be taken advantage of by a hacker. Conceivably, a hacker can monitor the DNS queries and responses and sneak an erroneous response packet through the filter because there is no way for the filter to completely distinguish one DNS response packet from another — DNS packets that have the same source/destination addresses and ports look the same to the filter. You should realize that iptables can make your network safer, but not completely safe.

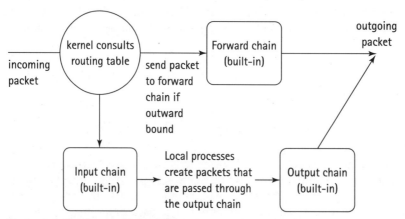

Figure 4-1: The three built-in chains

You can also create your own custom chains that make use of the primary chains. Creating custom chains allows you to create complex rule sets that are also readily maintainable so that you can group decision making into logical clusters.

Building a custom chain is straightforward. The following rule builds a custom chain called newchain:

```
iptables -N newchain
```

You can modify the newchain to suit your needs. For instance, the following command sets up a newchain that accepts incoming TCP packets on the first Ethernet interface destined for the Secure Shell daemon.

```
iptables -A newchain -p TCP -i eth0 --dport 22
```

IPTABLES MODES, PARAMETERS, AND OPTIONS
The following is a summary of frequently used iptables commands:

- ◆ -A appends one or more rules to a chain.

- ◆ -D deletes one or more rules from a chain.

- ◆ -E renames a chain.

- ◆ -F flushes a chain; all rules are lost.

- ◆ -I inserts a rule into a chain.

- ◆ -L lists the rules in a chain.

- ◆ -N creates a new chain.

- ◆ -P sets a policy for a chain.

- ◆ -R replaces a rule from a chain.

- ◆ -X deletes a chain

Please consult the iptables man page for more information (`iptables --help` will display the same information too).

Here are some of the more frequently used `iptables` parameters:

- ◆ `-d (--destination) [!] address[/mask]`: Sets the destination address of the rule you're configuring. Every IP packet has a destination address, as well as a corresponding destination port. When Netfilter identifies a packet with a destination address and/or port that matches an iptables rule, the packet is passed through the filter.

- ◆ `[!] -f, --fragment`: Tells the rule to work on the initial packet's second and subsequent fragments. IP packets are often split into fragments while traversing the Internet; however, you should configure the Linux kernel to reconstruct fragments.

- ◆ `-i (in-interface) [!] name`: Sets filtering rules for an individual, or type of, input interface. This option only affects packets entering the specified network interface.

- ◆ `-j (--jump) target`: Sets the destination for the packet to jump to when the packet matches the rule. For instance, if a packet matches a rule and the parameter `-j ACCEPT` is set, then the packet is sent to the `ACCEPT` target, which means that the packet will be allowed to pass through the filter onto its destination.

◆ `-o (out-interface) [!] name`: Sets filtering rules for an individual, or type of, output interface. This option only affects packets leaving the specified network interface.

◆ `-p (--protocol) [!] protocol`: Set the protocol (for instance, tcp, udp, or icmp) for the rule or packet to check. The rules in a chain only apply to packets that match the protocols. You can find the available protocols in the */etc/protocols* file.

◆ `-s (--source) [!] address[/mask]`: Sets the source address of the rule you're configuring. Every IP packet has a source address as well as a corresponding source port. When Netfilter identifies a packet with a source address and/or port that matches a Netfilter/iptables rule, the packet is passed through the filter.

The state module options are as follows: You set the connection states to which packets are matched packets against by using the `--state state` option. The states are NEW, ESTABLISHED, INVALID, and RELATED. The NEW option refers to packets that are establishing a new connection – for instance, the first SYN packet in a TCP connection's three-way handshake. The ESTABLISHED option matches all packets belonging to an existing connection. The INVALID parameter matches packets that don't belong to any known connection. Finally, the RELATED option refers to packets belonging to a connection that works with another connection; the FTP data connection must make use of the RELATED option. For instance, the ftp-data connection for which the ftp connection calls is related to the ftp connection.

Finally, here are some of the most commonly used iptables options:

◆ `-b`: Forces a rule to work in both directions. For example, in the previous steps, you can replace the two rules for the UDP protocol with one rule. You can't use this option if you want to limit incoming packets with the SYN (! -y) parameter.

◆ `-h`: Display iptables options and parameters.

◆ `-n`: Sets the numeric output mode and displays IP numbers instead of names.

◆ `-v`: Sets the verbose mode. If you use this option with the `-L` list command, you get a display with more information about each chain.

◆ `! -y`: Only allows packets with their SYN bit set through. You typically use this option to limit network traffic to only the return packets of existing, outgoing connections.

Building the Firewall

So far we've described in general how firewalls determine the fate of the IP packets with which they interact. The process isn't terribly complicated, but to really understand it, you have to put the theory into practice. This section describes how to consolidate the theory into real firewalls. We construct a firewall that protects both the DCI and DMZ network models we described in Chapter 1. We can design a single firewall because both models utilize a single Internet gateway.

We start by constructing the firewall function like a diode, the common electron device that allows current to flow in only one direction. The firewall allows only outgoing connections in order to maximize security. IP filters work very well in this configuration. For providing Internet services, however, a diode-like firewall is only a starting point. We'll add rules that allow certain incoming connections, and we'll utilize Web proxies to protect the Web server.

We use Open Secure Shell (OpenSSH) to provide the incoming connectivity. The beauty of OpenSSH is that it provides not only direct, interactive connections – similar in function to Telnet and FTP – but it also forwards any port you want. Its default configuration automatically forwards X (X Window System), for instance. By making use of OpenSSH, we can effectively create a proxy firewall that completes our hybrid firewall configuration.

Protecting the networks with a simple rule set

Both of the network models, described in Chapter 1 – DCI and DMZ –, gain access to the Internet through a broadband network device (a Cisco 675 DSL modem, in our example). The differences between the models don't affect the way the Internet gateway/firewall acts. The private network in both models sees the Internet gateway as just that, a gateway.

Therefore, you configure the gateway/firewall identically for both models. This section describes how to configure a simple rule set that will provide adequate protection for the private network. (Please take note that if you configure a DMZ network – as in the DMZ model – the firewall described here doesn't provide any protection for it because the firewall protects only the private network. Instead, we create customized packet filters on the DMZ servers. Those filters act as host-based firewalls and act as a firewall for the computer – host – that they are configured on.)

Figure 4-2 shows the Internet gateway/firewall protecting the private network from the outside world. This configuration is valid for both the DCI and DMZ network models. Atlas acts as the Internet gateway and firewall.

The initial firewall configuration is set as follows:

◆ **Deny all incoming, outgoing, and forwarded packets:** That policy creates a perfect firewall and never allows a hacker any access to your network. Unfortunately, the same policy also prevents your network from using the Internet. Keep in mind that this is just the starting point. We'll judiciously poke holes through the firewall to allow functionality, but by starting with an opaque firewall, we won't accidentally create an unintended hole.

♦ **Allow all outgoing TCP connections:** We allow all TCP connections – Web, Telnet, SSH, etc. – to go out. Our firewall acts analogously like a diode that allows current to go out but not back in.

♦ **Allow the return packets of outgoing TCP connections back in through the firewall:** The state of the return packets is checked (thanks to the 2.4 kernel's powerful new Netfilter/iptables tool) to verify that they belong to the outgoing connection.

Before Netfilter/iptables, we had to approximate the ability to check state by setting the rules to only allow packets that had their SYN and ACK bits set. We could further synch down the firewall by only allowing certain outgoing TCP connections – such as Telnet, FTP, http, and SSH – and their return packets; the idea being that we were at least preventing SYN/ACK packets directed to some unused port from passing through. That slightly narrowed the window of opportunity presented to hackers, but it was far from being able to check state. Now, with stateful filtering, we can be nearly certain that the TCP packets returning through our firewall aren't malicious, giving us much greater confidence in our firewall.

♦ **Allow outgoing UDP connections to specific name servers on port 53, but only allow incoming DNS packets to our internal name server chivas:** Our firewall is set to allow very specific DNS packets through, however, and that greatly reduces the window of opportunity for malicious hackers. However, we can construct UDP packets to pass in through our firewall. As long as the DNS server (the named daemon on chivas – 192.168.1.250) doesn't have a bug or hasn't been replaced by a Trojan, the malicious DNS packets shouldn't affect our network. Still, continually updating important software when possible is essential because of the ever-present possibility that a hacker will find and exploit a vulnerability.

♦ **Create rules to allow the kernel to forward packets from one network interface to another as appropriate:** Packets originating on the private network that are addressed to the Internet need to be forwarded from the internal to the external interface – from eth0 to eth1 in our examples. Their return packets need to be sent back in the opposite direction. The trick is to write the rules so that all connections get forwarded out of the gateway but only their return packets get forwarded back in. Stateful filtering makes this task straightforward.

♦ **Load the necessary Netfilter modules and proxies:** The kernel modules allow the Linux kernel to implement the filtering rules. Proxies for applications such as FTP allow protocols that require unusual connections to function. For instance, by default, FTP requires that an incoming connection be made back in through the firewall in order to function correctly. The proxies take care of that process.

◆ **Turn on IP forwarding in the kernel:** That process isn't part of the Netfilter/iptables system, so you have to carry it out separately.

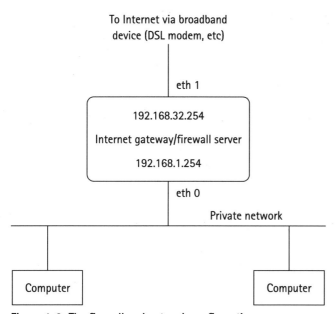

To Internet via broadband
device (DSL modem, etc)

eth 1

192.168.32.254

Internet gateway/firewall server

192.168.1.254

eth 0

Private network

Computer   Computer

Figure 4-2: The firewall and network configuration

BUILDING THE BASIC FIREWALL

This section describes how to build the IP filtering rules on the Internet gateway/firewall. We use the Red Hat Linux computer atlas as the firewall in this example.

1. Log in to the Internet gateway/firewall server — atlas — as root.

2. Reconnect to your ISP. Recall that we instructed you to disconnect your broadband Internet connection in Chapter 3. You're completely vulnerable to the hostile Internet environment until you create a firewall.

3. Check that your ISP connection is working:

```
ping yourisp
```

4. The Red Hat Linux computer must be able to forward packets from one interface to another in order to act as a gateway. We want the gateway to automatically configure itself as a gateway, so modify the */etc/sysctl.conf* file to include the following line:

```
net.ipv4.ip_forward = 1
```

Set IP forwarding by running the sysctl program:

```
sysctl -p
```

You can verify IP forwarding by examining the /proc file system:

```
cat /proc/sys/net/ipv4/ip_forward
```

It should return a value of 1.

5. After you take care of the preliminaries, proceed to configure iptables. Start by resetting the chain policies and removing any existing rules:

```
iptables --policy INPUT ACCEPT
iptables --policy OUTPUT ACCEPT
iptables --policy FORWARD ACCEPT

iptables --flush
iptables --flush -t nat
```

6. List all the filtering rules:

```
iptables -L
```

The following results appear:

```
Chain INPUT (policy ACCEPT)
target     prot opt source              destination

Chain FORWARD (policy ACCEPT)
target     prot opt source              destination

Chain OUTPUT (policy ACCEPT)
target     prot opt source              destination
```

The output shows that no input, output, or forwarding rules are set and that the default policy is to accept any IP packet to come into or out of your network. Your system is completely open.

7. Set up the base filter policies to deny all network traffic:

```
iptables --policy INPUT    DROP
iptables --policy OUTPUT   DROP
iptables --policy FORWARD ACCEPT
```

These rules set the firewall's basic policy. The output, input, and forwarding chains on atlas are set to deny any packets passing in any direction. At this point, you have a very safe, very impractical firewall.

You can deny passage of a packet in two ways with Netfilter/iptables. iptables uses the DROP and REJECT methods to prevent a packet from passing. The difference between the two methods is that DROP stops the packet without telling anyone, while REJECT sends an Internet Control Message Protocol (ICMP) message to the sender stating that the packet has been denied passage. We use the DROP method in order to deny the wily hacker as much information as possible. For instance, if we use the REJECT method, then a port scanner such as nmap is informed that our firewall exists via the ICMP packet that the firewall generates. Dropping packets rather than rejecting them eliminates any response from being generated by the firewall and minimizes the information that a scanner gains about the firewall.

8. Allow all internal network traffic on the loopback interface:

```
iptables -A OUTPUT -j ACCEPT -o lo
iptables -A INPUT  -j ACCEPT -i lo
```

9. Configure the outgoing TCP rule. This rule affects only traffic originating on the server — atlas, in this case — itself:

```
iptables -A OUTPUT -j ACCEPT -o eth1 -p tcp -m state --state
ESTABLISHED,NEW
```

   ◆ We don't specify either the source or destination address. When you don't specify any addresses, iptables defaults to allow all addresses. We'll specify explicit addresses in later rule sets in order to tighten security. However, we want to simplify the rules here as much as possible to facilitate the learning process.

   ◆ The –j ACCEPT parameter tells iptables to jump to the ACCEPT state, which allows any packet that matches the rest of the rule to be accepted and pass through the filter.

   ◆ The –o eth1 option specifies the second — at least, in our case — Ethernet interface. It also specifies that the interface is outgoing; the –i parameter indicates an incoming interface.

   ◆ The –p tcp parameter tells iptables to apply this rule to all TCP packets.

   ◆ The –m state option informs iptables to use the state checking module.

   ◆ Finally, the –state ESTABLISHED,NEW parameter specifies what states are to be checked. The ESTABLISHED flag matches packets belonging to an existing TCP connection. The NEW flag specifies the first packet attempting to create a new TCP connection. This rule specifies that packets belonging to both new and established TCP connection will be passed out through the eth1 Ethernet interface.

10. Allow packets into the two interfaces. The first rule below accepts all traffic from the private network arriving at the private network interface. The second rule examines the state of each packet arriving at the external network interface. Packets that belong to existing TCP connections are allowed to pass.

```
iptables -A INPUT -i eth0 -p -s $PRIV -j ACCEPT
iptables -A INPUT -i eth1 -p -m state --state
ESTABLISHED,RELATED -j ACCEPT
```

11. Configure the rules to forward packets from one network interface to the other.

```
iptables -A FORWARD -i eth0 -j ACCEPT
iptables -A FORWARD -i eth1 -m state -state
ESTABLISHED,RELATED -j ACCEPT
```

The first rule accepts all packets originating from the private network interface – eth0. Those packets are forwarded to the external network interface – eth1. The second rule examines each packet arriving at the external network interface – eth1. Those packets are forwarded to the internal network interface – eth0 – if they belong to an existing connection.

12. The final step requires the establishment of the NAT rule. First, load the iptables NAT module and then create the NAT rule:

```
modprobe iptables_nat
iptables -A POSTROUTING -t nat -o eth1 -j SNAT --to
192.168.32.254
```

In this rule, the –t nat parameter tells iptables to use the NAT table to translate the packets that it encounters. The –A POSTROUTING tells the iptables to apply the specified table translation as the packets are about to be sent out. The rule is set to act on packets going out the external network interface – –o eth1. The –j SNAT option sets the network address translation to act on the source address and the -to 192.168.32.254 changes the source address of each packet to 192.168.32.254.

Packets matching this rule have their source address changed to the IP address of the firewall's external network interface. Those packets appear to the Internet as though they originate from the firewall server, which is atlas in our example. Figure 4-3 shows how packets interact with the NAT rules.

EXAMINING THE RULES

These rules create a simple, but quite effective, firewall. Enter the following command to see the status of your IP filters:

```
iptables -L
```

The rules you just created are displayed as follows:

```
Chain INPUT (policy DROP)
target     prot opt source           destination
ACCEPT     all  --  anywhere         anywhere
ACCEPT     tcp  --  anywhere         anywhere        state ESTABLISHED
ACCEPT     udp  --  anywhere         anywhere        udp spt:domain

Chain FORWARD (policy ACCEPT)
target     prot opt source           destination

Chain OUTPUT (policy DROP)
target     prot opt source           destination
ACCEPT     all  --  anywhere         anywhere
ACCEPT     tcp  --  anywhere         anywhere        state NEW,ESTABLISHED
ACCEPT     udp  --  anywhere         anywhere        udp dpt:domain
```

The first input and output rules are for the loopback interface (lo). The second rule works on TCP packets, and the last for UDP packets. The forwarding rule is necessary because the Red Hat Linux box is configured as a router and must forward packets from one interface to the other.

These rules are organized into a script called fw.simpl that you can download from http://www.wiley.com/compbooks/sery.

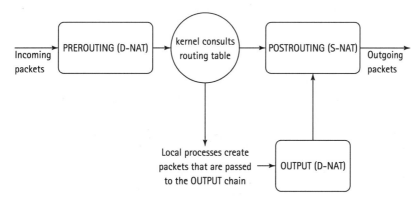

Figure 4–3: The network address translation diagram

AUTOMATING YOUR FIREWALL

Red Hat provides a script for saving your iptables rules to a script. Once you are satisfied that your firewall is working you use the iptables-save script to save the rules to the /etc/sysconfig/iptables file. Once you've saved the filtering rules you can use the /etc/init.d/iptables service script to control the firewall. You can use the iptables service script to manually start, stop, restart, and display status of the firewall; Red Hat Linux uses the iptables service script to automatically start/stop the firewall at boot and reboot time.

The following instructions describe the process saving the firewall rules and then starting/stopping them.

1. Log in to the Internet gateway/firewall server — atlas — as root.

2. Build the firewall as described in the previous section.

3. Run the following command.

   ```
   iptables-save > /etc/sysconfig/iptables
   ```

4. Use the iptables service script to start the firewall.

   ```
   /etc/init.d/iptables start
   ```

5. You can reset — turn off — the firewall as follows:

   ```
   /etc/init.d/iptables stop
   ```

6. If you modify the firewall, you can make the changes take effect by restarting the firewall.

   ```
   /etc/init.d/iptables restart
   ```

   You can also display the firewall status with the following command.

   ```
   /etc/init.d/iptables status
   ```

Using the iptables-save utility makes the creation and modification of iptables-based firewalls simple. The iptables service script simplifies controlling the firewall and ensures that the firewall will start whenever your system is booted.

Tightening the firewall with custom chains

We expand the basic firewall here by using custom chains, which help deal with the increasing complexity, and filtering specific services (ports). We also expand the TCP rules to act on specific addresses and ports.

TIP Creating more specific rules reduces the window of opportunity for potential hackers. Using custom chains allows you to create complex rule sets that are reasonably easy to understand and maintain.

The basic rule set doesn't check anything other than the state of TCP connections. The more complex rule set specifies what TCP ports can be used as well as the connections' source address.

Creating specific rules to handle individual connection reduces which ports a hacker can try to utilize. For instance, if someone is able to introduce a Trojan onto your firewall and/or network, then she can use the general-purpose outgoing TCP rule against you. Not all exploits work directly from the outside-in.

For instance, some Trojans connect to their masters from the inside-out. Those Trojans can then either transmit information to the outside world or gain their interactive instructions from the machine that controls them. By limiting outgoing connections we limit potential Trojans somewhat. Of course, a Trojan can make use of a port, such as http (80), that we allow through the firewall. We can't build a perfect firewall, but using a more involved rule set does help. We preach defense in-depth (also known as a layered defense). We can incrementally increase our system's security wherever possible, and we do so here.

BUILDING THE MODIFIED FIREWALL

The modified firewall breaks the outgoing TCP rule into several specific ones. The new rules are dedicated to particular services, such as HTTP, ssh, Telnet, and FTP. We create custom chains to better organize the rules:

1. Log in to the Internet gateway/firewall atlas as root.

2. Reconnect to your ISP. (Recall that we instructed you to disconnect your broadband Internet connection in Chapter 3 because you're completely vulnerable to the hostile Internet environment until you create a firewall.)

3. Check that your ISP connection is working:

```
ping yourisp
```

Carry out the following instructions from your Linux server's console. The rules initially shut off all network communication. If you are working on atlas remotely, then your remote session will freeze when you set up the initial rules. You can run the fw.reset script, which you can download from http://www.wiley.com/compbooks/sery.

4. The Red Hat Linux computer must be able to forward packets from one interface to another in order to act as a gateway. We want the gateway to automatically configure itself as a gateway, so modify the */etc/sysctl.conf* file to include the following line:

```
net.ipv4.ip_forward = 1
```

Set IP forwarding by running the sysctl program:

```
sysctl -p
```

You can verify IP forwarding by examining the */proc* file system.

```
cat /proc/sys/net/ipv4/ip_forward
```

It should return a value of 1.

5. After you take care of the preliminaries, proceed to configure iptables. Start by resetting the chain policies and removing any existing rules:

```
iptables -policy INPUT ACCEPT
iptables -policy OUTPUT ACCEPT
iptables -policy FORWARD ACCEPT

iptables --flush INPUT
iptables --flush OUTPUT
iptables --flush FORWARD
```

6. List all the filtering rules:

```
iptables -L
```

If you haven't configured any filtering rules yet, the following results should appear:

```
Chain INPUT (policy ACCEPT)
target     prot opt source              destination

Chain FORWARD (policy ACCEPT)
target     prot opt source              destination

Chain OUTPUT (policy ACCEPT)
target     prot opt source              destination
```

The results show that no input, output, or forwarding rules are set and that the default policy is to accept any IP packet to come into or out of your network. Your system is completely open.

7. Your filter is set in a known state. You can proceed to setup your default filter policy to deny all network traffic.

```
iptables --policy INPUT   DROP
iptables --policy OUTPUT  DROP
iptables --policy FORWARD DROP
```

8. Allow all internal network traffic on the loopback interface.

```
iptables -A OUTPUT -j ACCEPT -o lo
iptables -A INPUT  -j ACCEPT -i lo
```

9. We're designing a Linux computer to act as an Internet gateway and firewall. The gateway function requires a machine with an internal and external network interface. Recall that our filtering firewall acts like a diode, allowing packets to go out to the Internet and their return packets to come back in. Therefore, we're going to create two custom chains to deal with packets arriving from the private and external network interfaces.

10. Create a chain – priv – to handle traffic arriving from the private network. This chain passes return packets of existing connections, incoming SSH packets addressed to the firewall, and FTP, SSH, and HTTP packets destined for the Internet. The INPUT chain rules, described below, direct packets to this chain:

```
iptables -N priv
iptables -A priv -m state --state ESTABLISHED,RELATED -j
ACCEPT
iptables -A priv -p TCP -s $PRIV --dport 22 -d 192.168.1.254
-j ACCEPT
iptables -A priv -p TCP -d 0/0 --dport 21   -j ACCEPT
iptables -A priv -p TCP -d 0/0 --dport 22   -j ACCEPT
iptables -A priv -p TCP -d 0/0 --dport 80   -j ACCEPT
iptables -A priv -p TCP -d 0/0 --dport 8080 -j ACCEPT
```

11. Create a chain – ext – to handle traffic arriving from the DMZ (if used) and external network traffic. This chain drops all packets with source addresses from the private and DMZ networks because 1) the former are spoofed addresses, and 2) by policy, we don't allow traffic originating on the DMZ to enter into the private network. The chain accepts packets from existing connections and addressed to the Internet.

```
iptables -N ext
iptables -A ext -s 192.168.32.0/24 -j DROP
iptables -A ext -s 192.168.1.0/24  -j DROP
iptables -A ext -s 0/0 -dport 1024:65535 -j ACCEPT
iptables -A ext -s 0/0 -d 192.168.32.254 -j ACCEPT
```

12. Now configure the INPUT chain to direct packets to the custom priv and ext chains.

```
iptables -A INPUT -i eth0 -j priv
iptables -A INPUT -i eth1 -j DROP
```

13. Modify the FORWARD chain to create the gateway function. Packets from new or existing connections from the internal network interface are routed – forwarded – to the external interface. Netfilter only permits forwarding of packets from existing connections coming from the external network interface. Netfilter logs unmatched packets that meet certain threshold parameters.

```
iptables -A FORWARD -i eth0 -m state --state
NEW,ESTABLISHED,RELATED -j ACCEPT
iptables -A FORWARD -i eth1 -m state --state
ESTABLISHED,RELATED -j ACCEPT
iptables -A FORWARD -m limit --limit 5/minute --limit-burst 5
-j LOG --log-level
  DEBUG
```

14. Next, establish the NAT rule. First, load the iptables NAT module, and then create the NAT rule:

```
modprobe iptables_nat
iptables -A POSTROUTING -t nat -o eth1 -j SNAT --to
192.168.32.254
```

This rule sets the NAT to act on the source address and the -to 192.168.32.254 changes each packet's source address to 192.168.32.254.

15. Your Linux server acts as an Internet gateway/firewall after you install the rules from Steps 9 through 13.

16. Configure the OUTPUT chain to allow packets originating from the firewall server to go to the private network and the Internet.

```
iptables -A OUTPUT -o eth0 -d $PRIV -j ACCEPT
iptables -A OUTPUT -o eth1 -m state --state
NEW,ESTABLISHED,RELATED -j ACCEPT
```

EXAMINING THE SIMPLE FIREWALL RULES
These rules create a simple, but quite effective, firewall. Enter the following command to see the status of the IP filters. (Note that the –v option shows additional information about the network interfaces.)

```
iptables -L -v
```

The rules you just created are displayed as shown below. (The first two columns, which display the number of packets and bytes that have passed through the rule, are deleted to enhance formatting for sake of clarity; otherwise one line will be carried over onto the next, which makes it difficult to read.)

```
Chain INPUT (policy DROP 1 packets, 52 bytes)
target prot opt in  out   source        destination

ACCEPT all  --  lo   *    0.0.0.0/0    0.0.0.0/0
priv   all  --  eth0 *    0.0.0.0/0    0.0.0.0/0
ext    all  --  eth1 *    0.0.0.0/0    0.0.0.0/0


Chain FORWARD (policy DROP 0 packets, 0 bytes)
```

```
target prot opt in     out  source     destination

ACCEPT all  -- eth0   *   0.0.0.0/0   0.0.0.0/0 state NEW,RELATED,ESTABLISHED
ACCEPT all  -- eth1   *   0.0.0.0/0   0.0.0.0/0 state RELATED,ESTABLISHED
LOG    all  -- *      *   0.0.0.0/0   0.0.0.0/0 limit: avg 5/min burst 5 LOG
flags 0 level 7

Chain OUTPUT (policy DROP 0 packets, 0 bytes)
target prot opt in out    source     destination

ACCEPT all  -- * lo     0.0.0.0/0   0.0.0.0/0
ACCEPT all  -- * eth0   0.0.0.0/0   192.168.1.0/24
ACCEPT all  -- * eth1   0.0.0.0/0   0.0.0.0/0  state NEW,RELATED,ESTABLISHED

Chain ext (1 references)
target prot opt in  out   source      destination

DROP   all  -- *    *    192.168.32.0/24    0.0.0.0/0
DROP   all  -- *    *    192.168.1.0/24     0.0.0.0/0
ACCEPT all  -- *    *    0.0.0.0/0   192.168.32.254

Chain priv (1 references)
target     prot opt in   out    source         destination

ACCEPT all  -- *    *    0.0.0.0/0      0.0.0.0/0 state RELATED,ESTABLISHED
ACCEPT tcp  -- *    *    192.168.1.0/24 192.168.1.254  tcp dpt:22
ACCEPT tcp  -- *    *    0.0.0.0/0      0.0.0.0/0 tcp dpt:21
ACCEPT tcp  -- *    *    0.0.0.0/0      0.0.0.0/0 tcp dpt:22
ACCEPT tcp  -- *    *    0.0.0.0/0      0.0.0.0/0 tcp dpt:80
ACCEPT tcp  -- *    *    0.0.0.0/0      0.0.0.0/0 tcp dpt:8080
ACCEPT udp  -- *    *    0.0.0.0/0      0.0.0.0/0 udp dpt:53
```

The INPUT and OUTPUT chains allow all loopback — lo — traffic to pass. The INPUT rule directs all other traffic to the priv and ext chains. The FORWARD chain passes all traffic that meets the state requirement. The custom chain rules are set up just as we described in the preceding steps.

The neat thing about the custom chains is that you can modify them very easily. For instance, if you want to allow Telnet traffic to go out from the private network, just add the following rule to the priv chain:

```
iptables -A priv -p TCP -d 0/0 --dport 23   -j ACCEPT
```

With a carefully set up default policy, you can be confident that rules you add, like the one above, will work as desired. Modifying your rule sets is more difficult without custom chains.

TIP   Display the NAT rule by running the command **iptables –L –t nat**.
```
Chain PREROUTING (policy ACCEPT)
target prot opt source       destination

Chain POSTROUTING (policy ACCEPT)
target prot opt source       destination
SNAT    all  --  0.0.0.0/0    0.0.0.0/0 to:192.168.32.254

Chain OUTPUT (policy ACCEPT)
target      prot opt source   destination
```
The POSTROUTING chain modifies the source addresses of all matching packets to the firewall's external IP address — 192.168.32.254.

These rules are organized into a script called `fw.full` that you can download from `http://www.wiley.com/compbooks/sery`.

Allowing External Connections via Secure Shell

So far, our firewall allows only outgoing connections. This configuration is very secure until you start modifying the rule set to allow external access. If you don't need incoming connections, then this configuration adequately guards your private network, and you can skip this section. However, if you want to provide access through your firewall from the outside world, then you need a proxy firewall. Proxy firewalls work at the Application level in order to authenticate individual connections, such as a Telnet connection. IP filters work at the Network level and can only inspect the state of individual packets, which don't contain enough information to authenticate each connection. Therefore, you must augment IP filtering firewalls to provide adequate security.

Proxy firewalls are available for Linux. The most well-known, freely available ones are the TIS Toolkit (`www.fwtk.org/fwtk`) and SOCKS (`www.socks.nec.com`) firewalls. Unfortunately, the latest version of the TIS Toolkit is from February 1998 and apparently isn't being maintained. SOCKS is kept more up to date but the last verified version of Red Hat is 6.0. Neither of the freely available proxy firewalls encrypt their connections. Even though connections must be authenticated, the passwords can be sniffed. Security is enhanced by using expensive, one-time passwords (you can use the freely available S/Key one-time password system, but it's not supported or updated either), but the communications remain unencrypted even then. Therefore, both systems have serious drawbacks.

We use OpenSSH as an inexpensive and effective substitute for the traditional proxy firewall. OpenSSH provides fully encrypted connections and a combined host/user authentication system. OpenSSH also has the ability to forward any port (for instance, X), thus providing the ability to act as an encrypted proxy. We describe these abilities in more detail below:

 TIP OpenSSH is the open source version of the commercial Secure Shell (SSH). The OpenSSH designers have rewritten all proprietary subroutines under the Open Source license.

- **Provides interactive shell sessions over an encrypted channel:** You log in to a remote system, running OpenSSH, and obtain an interactive shell (just as you would by Telnet or rsh) to log into the computer. The difference is that OpenSSH encrypts your session's packets. (OpenSSH was designed to replace programs like rsh.) OpenSSH also provides a non-interactive method called Secure Copy (scp) for copying files from machine to machine. Unlike FTP, Secure Copy isn't interactive, but with practice, you'll find scp functional enough to almost replace it. Secure FTP is interactive and will be included with the OpenSSH package in the future.

- **Forwards any port within an OpenSSH session:** OpenSSH allows you to piggyback any TCP protocol within an SSH session. By default, it forwards X11, and you can configure it to forward any port. This powerful feature will satisfy many, if not most, of the needs previously met by traditional proxy firewalls. For instance, if you want to login to a server on the private network and display an X window, OpenSSH provides the functionality to do so.

- **Provides both host and user authentication by passing encryption keys:** By default, OpenSSH authenticates via the traditional Linux MD5 hash password system. However, OpenSSH can be configured to use public and private keys to authenticate not only the user, but also the host. The OpenSSH client can be sure of each other's identities as well as the user. As long as the calling user and host private keys aren't compromised, then total authentication is assured.

OpenSSH doesn't provide a true proxy, such as the TIS Toolkit firewall. The true proxy firewall authenticates a connection request and then rewrites each packet of that connection from the external to internal network interface. Once the connection is established, it's transparent to the user.

Although SSH doesn't operate as a classic proxy, it can provide a similar protection level when you use it correctly. We construct our hybrid system as follows:

♦ **Configure a Linux box to accept SSH logins:** This machine is placed on the DMZ, so it's accessible from the Internet. Users log in to it via SSH and then complete their connections to private network via SSH again — two separate logins. The intermediate SSH Linux box is a simple, but effective proxy firewall.

Note that the DMZ SSH server is configured to act only as an SSH server. The SSH server is configured to accept key-based authentication; it runs no other services, or daemons. The SSH server uses its own tight, IP filter rule set that only allows incoming SSH packets from the Internet.

♦ Create an IP filter rule on the firewall to allow SSH packets from the SSH server to pass through to the private network.

♦ Configure OpenSSH on each of the private network's machines to allow only public/private key-based logins.

♦ Create the public/private keys on the remote machines that will be used as platforms to enter the private network. That is, anyone who is able to access the internal, private network from the Internet must possess the correct keys.

This model is only moderately labor intensive. As the systems administrator, you must maintain login accounts on the SSH server for the users who need external access. You can't use labor saving devices, such as NIS, because it's insecure for this application, you don't want to modify the firewall to allow its use, and your must configure SSH to use key public key authentication, which doesn't use the password file. Figure 4-4 shows the SSH server model.

To further enhance security, configure SSH to use a one-time password system. You can do so by using the freely available S/Key system, which generates a one-time key on the user's computer. Although many organizations still use S/Key, it hasn't been updated in a long time, making its long-term viability uncertain. SecureID, an even more secure system, relies on a credit-card sized token generator, which generates a one-time number after you enter your personal identification number (PIN). If your PIN matches the PIN that the server generates, then you're allowed entry. If at all possible, we recommend using SecureID or a similar system as the safest method for authenticating users.

Configuring the SSH server

This section describes how to use OpenSSH to enhance your firewall and network security. Please note that the configuration we describe here works only with the

DMZ network model. You can modify this configuration for the DCI network by placing the SSH server on the private network and modifying the firewall to pass SSH packets through to it. Though not as safe as the DMZ configuration, it's a reasonable compromise.

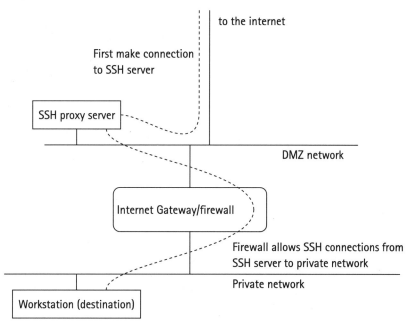

Figure 4-4: The SSH pseudo proxy

Red Hat Linux distributions 7.0 and above include OpenSSH. The following instructions describe how to install and configure the SSH server, pumas.

1. Log in as root on the SSH server – pumas – and install OpenSSH. You need to install OpenSSH on the machines that you'll be using on the private network and outside the firewall.

   ```
   rpm -ivh /mnt/cdrom/RedHat/RPMS/openssh*
   ```

   RPM installs several OpenSSH packages including the server and client.

2. Modify the following parameters in the /etc/ssh/sshd_config file:

   ```
   PermitRootLogin no
   PasswordAuthentication no
   ```

   The first parameter prevents anyone from logging in directly as root. This is a good practice because then you have a log of uses of the su command to change to the root user. Therefore, a hacker has to break/find/guess/steal two passwords instead of one.

The second option prevents using a password to log in. Instead of using passwords that can be broken/lost/guessed/stolen, we're going to use public/private keys to authenticate both our users and their hosts.

3. Log in on atlas, the firewall/gateway server, as a user who will be permitted access to the server and/or the private network.

   ```
   su - pablo
   ```

4. Generate the user's public/private keys.

   ```
   ssh-keygen
   ```

5. Enter a long and complicated phrase, including non-alphanumeric characters, when prompted. Pick a phrase like "home of the brave" and distort it in some way: h0m30fdabr@v3. The pass phrase is used to encrypt your private key, so protecting it well is absolutely critical. (If someone is able to break into your computer account where your private key is stored, the pass phrase helps prevent that key from being used against you.) We're basing much of the firewall's integrity on keeping these keys secret, and that depends on the pass phrase. Choose well.

6. Copy your public key – identity.pub – to the *authorized_keys* file in your home directory on the SSH server (for instance, /home/pablo/.ssh/authorized_keys). Do so as secretively as possible, even though it is a called a public key, by using scp or sftp to copy it across.

7. Try logging in. If all is successful, then you're prompted for your pass phrase. Enter it and you're logged into the SSH server. From there, you can use OpenSSH to connect to your private network machines.

   When you enter your pass phrase, your private key on your local machine is decrypted. The private key is never transmitted from your machine. However, the public key is passed to the SSH server, which uses it to generate a challenge. The private key verifies that challenge on the local machine.

TIP   The SSH server is a potential candidate for running on a virtual machine. If you run an SSH server on a virtual machine on the DMZ, you don't have to use a dedicated computer. The SSH server runs in user space as a single process. You tighten security to the maximum on the virtual machine and even if it's hacked, the compromised machine is only a user process. This method isn't foolproof, but if you don't have the resources to purchase separate machines, then it's a reasonable alternative.

Creating a firewall (or other server) on a virtual machine

We mentioned in Chapter 1 that you can create entire servers on a virtual machine. Two packages create, or emulate, a computer within a computer. Plex86 is the open source project and VMware is a commercial one.

We create a virtual PC with VMware and then install Red Hat Linux on the PC. We use Red Hat Linux installation CD-ROMs to install the operating system in exactly the same way as on a physical PC. Once installed, the virtual Linux server works the same as a traditional one.

The virtual Linux box uses a virtual Ethernet interface. The virtual interface operates through the physical NIC, which is used as a *bridge* for the virtual NIC. Bridges transmit all Ethernet frames after performing error checking, so the virtual NIC sees all the same frames as the physical one — before they're passed through the physical Linux server's IP filters. The physical Ethernet NIC operates effectively as a hub, and you effectively create a virtual LAN!

The virtual PC also sees all the frames that the physical PC does. You need to create a firewall for the virtual PC in the same way that you do for the physical one. You can, however, make the physical PC impervious to all network traffic. For instance, if you intend to manage the physical PC from its console or a serial connection, then its IP filtering rules will consist of nothing more than default policy drop rules. We've implemented this very cool concept. Time will tell whether we run into any show-stopping gotchas. With that caveat in mind, the use of virtual servers will provide cost and management benefits. The best security policy is generally to create a single server for a single service. Thus, you run a Web server exclusively on a single box and don't clutter it with other services, such as DNS. Most shops can't even consider such a thing, but the virtual machine concept makes it possible.

The other possible benefit, from the security viewpoint, is that the virtual machine runs — or should run — as a regular user process. If the virtual server is broken into, the host machine shouldn't be affected any more severely than if the virtual server were another physical box on the local network. The user process has some access to the host machine but not much. The virtual server should be easier to deal with after you discover an intrusion because the administrator can suspend or kill it. Please be aware that although we're using this concept, it's in the early stages of investigation and may still turn out to have serious problems.

You must, of course, install OpenSSH on other machines. You need to install OpenSSH on any machine on which you intend to use it. Configure the OpenSSH server and client on your private net's machines and the OpenSSH client on those outside on the Internet.

Modifying the firewall server (atlas) to allow SSH

Modifying the firewall to allow SSH connections is a two-step process. You create one rule to allow SSH packets from the SSH server into the private network and another to masquerade the connections so that the source IP address gets routed through the firewall. The masquerade rule obviates the need to create a specific route on the firewall server for incoming connections — the packet's source address is changed from the DMZ sub-network to the private network and, thus, is routed by the private network route.

The filtering rules on atlas to allow incoming SSH connections are shown here:

```
iptables -A INPUT -j ACCEPT -i eth1 -p tcp -m state --state ESTABLISHED,NEW \
-s 192.168.32.251 --sport 22 -d 192.168.32.0/24 --dport 22

iptables -t nat -A POSTROUTING -j MASQUERADE -o eth0
```

The first rule permits SSH (port 22) packets from the SSH server pumas to pass through the firewall server atlas into the private network.

Managing Your Firewall

Maintaining a firewall requires more work than simply designing the IP filter rule sets. The following maintenance and observation tips aren't definitive, but they'll get you pointed in the right direction. Firewall management, like every other aspect of computer security, is a moving target.

- ◆ **Work with your management to create a process for developing effective policy:** Your policy drives your administrative process, so it should define your responsibilities, who's going to work on the firewall, and what kind of access the firewall is going to provide to the private network. The policy should also cover how you're going to handle incidents and disaster recovery. An effective policy statement is no longer than a few pages — otherwise, nobody will read and digest it — so many details are left to the systems administrator's discretion.

- ◆ **Conduct regular backups of your firewall server, as well as your other servers:** Keep backup copies of some backups at another location. What backups you keep off-site ultimately depends on what information you absolutely need to recover from a disaster, such as fire or flood.

- ◆ **Minimize your firewall server installation:** You only need a few Red Hat Linux systems — the base system, Netfilter/iptables, and so on. When building the Linux server to use as your firewall, you should use Red Hat's minimal installation option. If you're using a computer with more than the minimum packages, then removing the unnecessary packages is best.

Removing unneeded packages reduces the potential number of vulnerabilities that hackers can exploit, so remove the compilers such as gcc, the NFS, autofs, rpc packages, and the X Window system if installed.

◆ **Use Tripwire as a simple, effective host-based intrusion detection system (IDS):** Configure Tripwire to record system configuration and the firewall configuration files that shouldn't change (except when you, the systems administrator, update the system or modify the firewall). Tripwire helps you identify security compromises in the case of a break-in.

◆ **Run the Snort IDS on your firewall server:** Snort looks for known intrusion fingerprints. Snort can, for instance, detect the nmap stealth scans that are so prevalent on the Internet. Snort provides you with information about what scans and exploits that may be running against you. That information helps you to better monitor suspicious activities.

◆ **Monitor your log files:** Logs provide information about what's happening to your firewall.

◆ **Use scanning programs to test your firewall:** Systems such as nmap and nessus provide an outsider's view of your firewall. The first part of the cracking process involves obtaining information about your system, and tools like nmap can obtain that information.

Summary

This chapter describes how to set up a firewall to protect your private network from the worst of the Internet. The Netfilter/iptables system serves as the heart of the firewall. It provides IP filtering that offers excellent protection for your private network. When combined with monitoring and testing tools, you can maintain the firewall to provide maximum protection at a reasonable cost.

Topics covered in this chapter include the following:

◆ **IP filtering and proxy firewalls:** We briefly discussed the advantages of each and gave the reasoning for using a hybrid firewall.

◆ **IP packet journey across the Internet:** We described this process to help you understand how the process works, an essential component to understanding how firewalls function.

◆ **State checking:** The new Linux 2.4 kernel introduces the ability to check the state of each packet that passes through the iptables-based firewall. Checking state allows you to create much tighter firewalls.

◆ **The iptables system:** We explained this system's basic functions and gave you a simple example.

◆ **IP filtering firewall configuration:** We described a basic set of iptables rules that function as a basic firewall.

◆ **Configuring a more detailed IP filtering rule set:** We gave you specific rules for accessing popular services, such as http, Telnet, ssh, and so on. Specifying specific services reduces the chances that hackers can utilize Trojans from within your private network and provides tighter administrative control of which services users can access.

◆ **External access to the private network is provided via Secure Shell:** OpenSSH is open source software and allows you to provide encrypted access to your network from the Internet. OpenSSH also utilizes public-key authentication of both user and host. No passwords need cross the Internet, and you can authenticate the originating host.

Chapter 5

Introducing Basic Troubleshooting

IN THIS CHAPTER

- ◆ Troubleshooting with the fault tree
- ◆ Diagnosing Red Hat Linux networking problems
- ◆ Diagnosing DSL problems
- ◆ Diagnosing IP filtering firewall problems
- ◆ Investigating troubleshooting tools and resources

COMPUTERS ARE COMPLEX SYSTEMS, and complex systems break or are misconfigured, so troubleshooting is the one constant of computer system management. Still, you can take steps to minimize the difficulty of fixing systems when they break.

Troubleshooting is more an art than a science – some people can see a problem and its solution better than others, especially if they know a particular system well – although some fairly simple science does come into play. You must deal with any problem in a systematic fashion by identifying the problem and then systematically eliminating each possible cause, working from the simple to the complex, until you solve the problem.

The first chapters guided you through the process of configuring Red Hat Linux networking, connecting to the Internet via a DSL connection, and protecting your network with a firewall. The systems and subsystems necessary to perform those functions create a highly complex system. Those subsystems include the following:

- ◆ **The server hardware:** Disks, memory, interface cards, network wires, power strips, and so on.

- ◆ **The server software:** Linux operating system's networking software and the scripts used to control it; GNU – Gnu is Not Unix (a recursive acronym) – utilities, such as ifconfig, route, and so on.

- ◆ **The Internet protocols:** Transmission Control Protocol (TCP), User Datagram Protocol (UDP), Internet Control Message Protocol (ICMP), and Internet Protocol (IP).

◆ **Your Internet connections:** Your broadband connection, such as DSL, digital cable, satellite, T1 modem, and/or router, plus the "last mile" connection from your provider. Please see the section Introducing DSL Technology in Chapter 3 for an explanation of "last mile."

◆ **The firewall software:** ipchains and iptables, plus the scripts that run them.

A large number of processes and hardware/software subsystems need to work together in precisely the right way to allow your customers to browse your Web site. If one subsystem isn't working, then the browsing doesn't occur.

When something goes wrong with the network, the best way to fix the problem is to pinpoint the exact cause of the problem, eliminating each possible cause, one by one. This chapter is here to help you with that process by describing a simple, but effective, way to identify and fix a problem.

Troubleshooting with the Fault Tree

To fix a problem, you first have to identify its cause, which is often difficult on complex computer systems. You can simplify the process by modeling the problem.

One method of modeling problems is the *fault tree*. In a fault tree, the inverted trunk represents the problem, and each branch represents a potential cause of the problem. This conceptual model simplifies the process of finding the solution. For instance, what do you do if you can't browse the Internet from a workstation on your private network? If you're new to networks, this problem may seem impossible. However, you can find the answer by breaking the problem down into small, more easily understandable parts.

Figure 5-1 shows the fault tree of the possible answers to the problem. The first branch on the left involves problems with the physical connections on your private network: Are the network cables connected correctly? Do you have a break in a cable? Have you configured your network adapter(s) properly? The second branch deals with your network's dual-homed Internet gateway: Have you installed the network interfaces and cabling correctly? Are the dual routes set up properly? Have you checked your firewall rules and network address translation (NAT)? Finally, your Internet connection (we use DSL as the broadband example in this book) must be working before you can connect to the Internet.

Each sub-branch deals with the specifics of the more general problem. For example, if the problem relates to the physical connection, you can trace the problem to one of several causes: no adapter, a misconfigured adapter, a break in the wire, a faulty connector, or no connector at all. Or, if the problem involves the network configuration, you know that the cause can be only one of a few things. By using the fault tree, you can break any problem down into simpler problems and eventually locate the root cause.

Your goal in troubleshooting problems with your network is first to identify the problem, and then choose an approach. Before proceeding with an example, take inventory of the problem solving tools available to you.

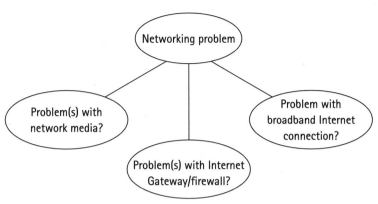

Figure 5-1: Troubleshooting by using the fault tree

 See Chapter 2 for discussions of problem solving tools and configuration files.

Troubleshooting Linux Networking

If the network on your Linux computer isn't working, use the following sections as a simple fault tree that you can follow to troubleshoot your network. The troubleshooter isn't comprehensive, but it does cover some of the typical problems that you're likely to encounter.

You can take several steps to check your network for problems. The following sections identify common problem areas to check. Over time, you'll find that these areas account for most of the problems you see.

Is the power turned on?

First, verify that you've turned on the power. Sounds simple, but hey, sometimes the simplest things go wrong. (This is the problem we're best able to solve.)

Has your network cabling been compromised?

Compromised network cables are a simple, but common, problem. Cables get walked on, pulled, crimped, and generally abused. Checking cables is generally limited to visual inspection, although you can sometimes find a break by running your fingers along the line. Keeping extra cables on hand is a good, time-saving idea; cables are expensive, low-technology devices, but your network absolutely depends on them.

Using ancient technology – Thinnet

Thinnet is topologically a bus structure. In other words, each computer on a Thinnet cable is electrically connected to all the other computers in the network. Each computer sees all the network traffic on that cable. If any part of that bus is compromised, all traffic ceases. For example, disconnecting the terminator at either end of the cable ends all communication. The best way to troubleshoot that type of problem is to start at one end and work your way down the line. Try to get just two computers connected, then three, and eventually you'll find the fault.

To determine whether your Thinnet network cable has been compromised, you have to address the following issues:

◆ Make sure that the BNC (Bayonet Nut Connector) connectors are securely attached.

◆ Look at the interface between the coaxial cable and the BNC connector to make sure that they are in good physical contact: Sometimes, the cable can pull out a little bit, so the little pin in the center of the cable doesn't make contact with the other end of the BNC connector.

◆ Look at the cable itself and make sure that it hasn't been cut or crushed.

◆ Test the continuity of both the center conductor and the outer shield conductor if you have an ohmmeter: Make sure that the cable isn't attached to anything.

◆ Make sure that the center conductor isn't short-circuited (touching) the shield: The shield is the thin, braided metal wire immediately under the outer insulation.

◆ Make sure that each end of the cable has a 50ohm terminator attached to it: You must terminate a Thinnet or else it won't work (just as it won't work if the cable is broken) because the radio frequency (RF) signal reflects from the unterminated end and interferes with the incoming signals.

Try substituting a cable that you know is good. The idea is to eliminate as many segments that you're unsure about as possible. If you have just two computers in close proximity and you suspect a problem with the cable you're using, all you can do is try another cable. If the computers are far apart and rely on several segments or a long cable, try moving them close together and using one short segment. If you have three or more computers, try getting just two of them working together. Then try adding another one. Proceed until you find the faulty segment.

Is your network switch or hub configured correctly?

Defective switches and hubs are another simple, but common, cause of networking problems. Modern, unmanaged switches and hubs are inexpensive and simple to use. Very little can go wrong with these devices, but do check the following three things:

- Make sure that the power is turned on.

- Make sure that the network cables are properly seated.

- **Make sure that the uplink switch is properly set:** You use the uplink function to connect multiple switches or hubs together. When the uplink is set, you can connect one device to another by using a cable connected to the appropriate ports. (Check the documentation and labels to determine which ports to use.) Make sure that you turn the uplink switch off if you don't want to use this feature.

Is your network adapter configured correctly?

Sometimes a startup script is misconfigured and the startup screen goes by but you don't see an error message. Login as Root, and from the shell prompt enter the command:

```
ifconfig
```

On your Internet gateway/firewall, you should see a listing of three interfaces, as shown in Listing 5-1; you only see two interfaces on a non-routing workstation or server. The program *ifconfig* tells the Linux kernel that you have a network adapter, and gives it an IP address and network mask, which is the first step in connecting your Linux box to your network.

Listing 5-1: Network interfaces listed

```
[root@chivas /]# ifconfig
eth0      Link encap:Ethernet  HWaddr 00:50:BA:DE:25:35
          inet addr:192.168.1.254  Bcast:192.168.1.255  Mask:255.255.255.0
          UP BROADCAST RUNNING MULTICAST  MTU:1500  Metric:1
          RX packets:1188585 errors:0 dropped:0 overruns:0 frame:0
          TX packets:1373096 errors:0 dropped:0 overruns:0 carrier:0
          collisions:16985 txqueuelen:100
          Interrupt:12 Base address:0xe400

eth1      Link encap:Ethernet  HWaddr 00:50:DA:0F:CE:C2
          inet addr:192.168.32.254  Bcast:192.168.32.255  Mask:255.255.255.0
          UP BROADCAST RUNNING MULTICAST  MTU:1500  Metric:1
          RX packets:474206 errors:0 dropped:0 overruns:0 frame:0
          TX packets:414452 errors:0 dropped:0 overruns:0 carrier:0
          collisions:7 txqueuelen:100
          Interrupt:10 Base address:0xe000

lo        Link encap:Local Loopback
          inet addr:127.0.0.1  Mask:255.0.0.0
```

Continued

Listing 5-1 *(Continued)*

```
UP LOOPBACK RUNNING  MTU:3924  Metric:1
RX packets:10 errors:0 dropped:0 overruns:0 frame:0
TX packets:10 errors:0 dropped:0 overruns:0 carrier:0
collisions:0 txqueuelen:0
```

If you don't see the line containing lo, which is the loopback interface, or eth0, which is your network adapter, then your physical network connections haven't been set up correctly. The loopback interface isn't a physical device; it's used for the network software's internal workings. It must be present for the network adapter to be configured.

If the loopback interface isn't present, enter the following command:

```
ifconfig lo 127.0.0.1
```

If the network interface is absent, enter the following command:

```
ifconfig eth0 192.168.1.254
```

Or, for the second interface (in the case of a dual-homed gateway) use the command:

```
ifconfig eth1 192.168.32.254
```

Because you're working with a class C network address, ifconfig automatically defaults to the 255.255.255.0 netmask.

Note that ifconfig is useful for displaying network information and interactively troubleshooting NIC problems. However, ifconfig should not be used to regularly configure network interfaces. Once you have debugged a problem you should configure the network control files found in the /etc/sysconfig and /etc/sysconfig/network-script directories (for instance ifcfg-eth0) and then use the ifup and ifdown scripts to operate your network interfaces. Chapter 2 describes how to use the networking scripts.

 You shouldn't have a non-standard netmask such as 255.255.255.252 (standard netmasks are 255.255.255.0, 255.255.0.0 and 255.0.0.0), but if you do, enter the following command: **ifconfig eth0 192.168.1.254 netmask 255.255.255.252**

Enter **ifconfig**, and your network adapter should display correctly. If it doesn't, examine the manual page on ifconfig.

If you're still having problems, look at the Linux startup information by running the following command:

```
dmesg | grep -i eth
```

The information that was displayed during the boot process appears. Look for your Ethernet NIC, which should appear after the following "Adding Swap" line:

```
eth0: RealTek RTL-8029 found at 0xe400, IRQ 12, 00:50:BA:DE:25:35.
eth1: 3Com 3cSOHO100-TX Hurricane at 0xe000,  00:50:da:0f:ce:c2, IRQ 10
device eth0 entered promiscuous mode
```

If you don't see your Ethernet adapter, then you may have a hardware problem. Check your adapter. Reseat it and see whether it works. If not, then you probably need a new NIC.

If you do see the NIC, then look inside the Linux kernel and see which devices it has. You can examine files in the /proc directory. The /proc directory is a logical, not a physical file system, whose files contain process and system information. The *pci* file contains detailed information about all PCI bus devices (the Peripheral Component Interconnect/Interface (PCI) is the de facto PC standard). Enter the following command to display any Ethernet device information:

```
grep -i eth /proc/pci
```

You should see information about your network adapter (or adapters) similar to the following:

```
Ethernet controller: 3Com Unknown device (rev 48).
Ethernet controller: Realtek 8029 (rev 0).
```

If no devices show up in this file, then Linux doesn't have the correct device drivers loaded, the cards are defective, or they don't exist. Linux frequently has problems working with Plug 'n Play (PnP) NICs, so if your NIC is PnP compatible, that may be your problem.

Try configuring your Ethernet NIC again. If it still doesn't run, then you need to get more information about the NIC. You may have an interrupt or address conflict. Look first at the list of interrupts and then at the Input/Output (IO) addresses of all the devices that the kernel knows about by entering the following commands:

```
cat /proc/interrupts
cat /proc/ioports
```

The IO address is the actual location in memory where the microprocessor (that is, your Pentium or 486 chip) accesses the device, such as the network adapter. The interrupt is a way to stop the microprocessor from whatever it's doing so that it can process the information that's arrived at the device sending the interrupt. Thus, when we stop to save this text, our Windows computer sends this new information to my Linux server. The Ethernet adapter sends packets containing this text and the Ethernet adapter on the Linux side collects a bunch of packets and then sends an interrupt to the processor. Linux picks up on what is happening and directs the information to Samba, which takes care of saving the data in the correct file.

Listing 5-2 shows both the interrupts and the IO addresses.

Listing 5-2: Linux interrupts listed

```
[root@chivas /proc]# cat /proc/interrupts
  0:     378425    timer
  1:       1120    keyboard
  2:          0    cascade
 10:      16077    3c509
 13:          1    math error
 14:      63652 +  ide0

[root@chivas /proc]# cat /proc/ioports
0000-001f : dma1
0020-003f : pic1
0040-005f : timer
0060-006f : keyboard
0080-009f : dma page reg
00a0-00bf : pic2
00c0-00df : dma2
00f0-00ff : npu
01f0-01f7 : ide0
0300-030f : 3c509
03c0-03df : vga+
03f0-03f5 : floppy
03f6-03f6 : ide0
03f7-03f7 : floppy DIR
```

Look for your network adapter. In our case, it's the 3c509. We don't have any conflicts, or we wouldn't be writing this page, because our server would be dead in the water. If you do have a conflict, you have to reconfigure the adapter. Run your Ethernet NIC configuration program and set the adapter's parameters in its EEP-ROM. Older adapters may have jumpers or little switches called Dual In-line Pin (DIP) (also known as Dual In-line Package) switches to set. If you think you need to do so, remember to write down all the other devices' interrupts and IO addresses so you don't end up conflicting with something else.

You also may be using a kernel that doesn't have networking installed. (This problem is unlikely in the newer versions of Red Hat because the kernel thread *kmod* automatically loads networking (and other) modules on demand. However, looking at these files in order to gain an understanding of how Linux works is worthwhile.) Display the networking devices by entering the following command:

```
cat /proc/net/dev
```

Listing 5-3 shows that the kernel is configured for loopback and an Ethernet NIC (eth0). Linux uses the loopback interface only for internal networking. You want to see the Ethernet interface. If you don't see it, your network adapter may be unsupported, defective, or misconfigured. By default, Red Hat installs and automatically loads kernel modules, as they're needed (assuming they're available). You can look back at the results of your boot process by using the dmesg command. If you get a message that says delaying eth0 configuration, then most likely, either Linux was unable to load the network adapter module or the adapter isn't working.

Listing 5-3: Linux kernel network configuration

```
[root@chivas net]# cat /proc/net/dev
Inter-|   Receive                    |  Transmit
 face |packets errs drop fifo frame|packets errs drop fifo colls carrier
   lo:    116    0    0    0    0     116    0    0    0     0    0
 eth0:  16292   19   19   23   19    7245    0    0    0    54    0
```

The next step is to make sure that your network routing configured correctly. Look at your routing table by entering the following command:

```
netstat -r -n
```

A listing like the one shown in Listing 5-4 should appear.

Listing 5-4: Routing table displayed

```
Kernel IP routing table
Destination      Gateway      Genmask         Flags   MSS  Iface
192.168.1.0      0.0.0.0      255.255.255.0   U       1500 eth0
127.0.0.0        0.0.0.0      255.0.0.0       U       3584 lo
```

Note the following definitions:

◆ *Destination* is the location (IP address) to which you want to send packets.

◆ *Gateway* is the address (computer or router) where the packets need to be sent so that they can find their way to their destination. In the case where the destination is the local network, then the 0.0.0.0 means "no gateway."

◆ *Genmask* separates the parts of the IP address that are used for the network address from the host number.

◆ *Flags* are used to indicate things like *U* for up and *G* for gateway.

◆ *MSS* refers to the maximum Ethernet frame size in bytes.

◆ *Iface* refers to the network interface.

You must have a route to the loopback interface (also referred to as *lo*), which is the 127.0.0.0 address.

If you're missing either or both parameters, you must set them. To set the loop-back device, which must be set for your internal networking to work, enter the following command:

```
route add -net 127.0.0.0 netmask 255.0.0.0
```

To set the route for the network adapter and your local network, enter the following command:

```
route add -net 192.168.1.0 netmask 255.255.255.0 dev eth0
```

Run **netstat -r -n** to see your routing table. You should see entries for the loop-back and the Ethernet, as shown in Listing 5-4.

If you don't see a route to your network interface, try repeating the preceding steps. You may have to delete a route. To delete a route, enter the following command:

```
route del -net 192.168.1.0 netmask 255.255.255.0
```

If the network adapter is configured correctly and the routing is correct, check the network. The best way to do so is to ping the loopback interface first and then the other computer. Enter the following command, let it run for a few seconds (one ping occurs per second), and stop it by pressing Ctrl+C:

```
ping 127.0.0.1
```

You should see a response like the one shown in Listing 5-5.

Listing 5-5: Ping the loopback interface

```
PING 127.0.0.1 (127.0.0.1) from 127.0.0.1 : 56(84) bytes of data.
64 bytes from 127.0.0.1: icmp_seq=0 ttl=255 time=253 usec
64 bytes from 127.0.0.1: icmp_seq=1 ttl=255 time=95 usec
64 bytes from 127.0.0.1: icmp_seq=2 ttl=255 time=92 usec
64 bytes from 127.0.0.1: icmp_seq=3 ttl=255 time=97 usec

--- 127.0.0.1 ping statistics ---
4 packets transmitted, 4 packets received, 0% packet loss
round-trip min/avg/max/mdev = 0.092/0.134/0.253/0.069 ms
```

Each line shows the number of bytes returned from the loopback interface, the sequence, and the round-trip time. The last lines are the summary, which shows whether any packets didn't make the trip. If you don't see any returned packet, something's wrong with your setup, and you should review the steps outlined in the preceding paragraphs.

```
ping 192.168.1.254
```

You should see a response like the one shown in Listing 5-6:

Listing 5-6: Ping the gateway

```
PING 192.168.1.254 (192.168.1.254) from 192.168.1.250 : 56(84) bytes
of data.
64 bytes from 192.168.1.254: icmp_seq=0 ttl=255 time=1.053 msec
64 bytes from 192.168.1.254: icmp_seq=1 ttl=255 time=447 usec
64 bytes from 192.168.1.254: icmp_seq=2 ttl=255 time=431 usec

--- 192.168.1.254 ping statistics ---
3 packets transmitted, 3 packets received, 0% packet loss
round-trip min/avg/max/mdev = 0.431/0.643/1.053/0.290 ms
```

If you get a continuous stream of returned packets and the packet loss is zero or very near zero, your network is working. If not, the problem may be in the Linux computer. Review the troubleshooting steps we described in this chapter. (Note: The ICMP is taking about one full millisecond (ms) longer to travel to our Windows box than to the loopback device because the loopback is completely internal to the Linux box.)

Troubleshooting Your DSL Connection

The previous section dealt with fixing problems occurring on your private or DMZ network. This section looks at getting your external connection working. This book assumes a DSL connection, so we'll focus on some common DSL problems. However, unlike Linux, DSL has no de facto configuration standards, so we're not going to describe the debugging process in general terms. (We offered explicit debugging information for the Cisco 675 DSL modem in Chapter 3 for those who happen to be using that equipment.)

You've just signed up for an inexpensive broadband connection that'll provide an order of magnitude speed improvement over a modem for a few bucks a month. Better yet, your Internet connection will be on full-time.

Your equipment's in place and everything's ready, but you don't have a connection. What's wrong? Using the fault tree again, here's a list of the possible problems:

◆ Your DSL modem/router isn't properly configured.

◆ Your DSL provider isn't configured properly.

◆ Your ISP isn't configured properly.

The following sections describe each of the major problem areas in more detail.

Checking your DSL modem/router configuration

Check the following points if you think your DSL provider and ISP are set up correctly:

◆ Make sure that your modem/router is powered up.

◆ Check that the cables are properly connected.

◆ Check that your internal network is configured correctly.

◆ Check that your external WAN connection is configured properly.

◆ Check that your routes are configured correctly.

◆ Check that your NAT is configured correctly, if applicable.

CHECK YOUR DSL DEVICE POWER
Of all the possible problems, this one is the most basic and the easiest to check and fix. Checking power may sound trivial, but doing so is actually quite useful. Simple oversights do occur.
Most DSL modem and/or routers have an LED indicating power. If lit, then the device is powered. If not, check the power cord and power outlet.

CHECK YOUR CABLES
The next step is to check your network cables. This simple check may just be your most effective step. Network cables get stepped on, pulled, yanked, and just generally abused, so they become disconnected quite easily.
Use your best judgment when conducting this simple step. Look for frayed cables and connectors, loose connectors, and so on. You can also use the link status light as an indicator that a cable is good: if it's on, then the cable is okay, if off, then the cable (or NIC) is suspect.

Verifying that a cable is intact can be problematic. For instance, if you don't have link status on your DSL modem/router/bridge and/or switch/hub, then the problem can be with your cable, your NIC, or both. A bad cable, NIC, or switch/hub all prevent the link status light from turning on.

CHECK YOUR INTERNET NETWORK CONFIGURATION
When you're reasonably sure that your cables are good, you can use your internal network (private network) to check the DSL device. Using either of the network

models from Chapter 1 — Direct Connect to WAN (DCWAN) or a DMZ — should allow you to communicate with the DSL device.

The device that connects to your DSL device must be configured correctly. For instance, if the NIC on your gateway is configured incorrectly, then you can't communicate with the DSL device.

Use the steps described in the first section — Troubleshooting with the Fault Tree — of this chapter to check and troubleshoot your gateway.

Checking your DSL provider configuration

If your DSL connection to the Internet still isn't working after you've verified that your private network connections and configurations are okay, then you need to check that your DSL provider is providing service as they promised.

This process can be the most time consuming and frustrating of all. DSL is still a relatively young service, if not technology, in many places, so the service providers often don't have a single process for fixing problems. Be aware that being shuffled between several telephone numbers and departments isn't unusual.

With the wide range of equipment and DSL services, an in-depth discussion is beyond the scope of this book, so we describe the following DSL troubleshooting tips in general terms. (If you use an ADSL Cisco 675 DSL modem, you can revisit the detailed discussion in Chapter 3.)

- ◆ **Check your DSL line quality:** Some DSL devices can show the quality and strength of DSL connections. For instance the Cisco 675 WAN link status light is steady when the signal is above a minimum level and blinks when below.

- ◆ **Re-check your DSL device configuration:** If you have an ADSL connection, then go through the instructions described in Chapter 3. (Use the instructions as a general guideline if you're not using the same equipment described in that chapter). You can, and should, reexamine the instructions your DSL provider supplies.

- ◆ **Keep notes:** If you have to talk to more than one person — and you most likely will — then you need to keep track of to whom you spoke, when you had the conversation, and what you discussed. That way, you avoid the frustration of not being able to remember what things were promised or suggested after the third or fourth phone call.

- ◆ **Make a diagram of your DSL/gateway network:** Doing so helps you understand how the various parts fit together. Your best bet is to think in terms of packets coming in and going out from the DSL device.

- ◆ **Check your routes and/or NAT configuration:** Any diagrams you've made will come in useful during this step. Examine the routes and NAT entries to see if you've left out any that are necessary. For instance, if you want your DSL modem to allow connections to your Web server but don't have a NAT entry to do so, your Web server will not work.

TIP   We describe DSL but not Cable Internet connections here for the sake of brevity. Cable Internet connections are good alternative to DSL and may be the better choice depending on your location. You can find more comparative information at: `http://www.epinions.com/cmd-review-60CE-57F88B0-3818C85B-bd4`

Checking your ISP configuration

Because the DSL connection provides the pathway to your ISP, your DSL service has to be working before you can check your ISP connection to the Internet. The following list describes what ISP related systems must be working before your DSL connection will work.

◆ Has your DSL provider coordinated with your ISP?

◆ Has your ISP turned on your account?

◆ Is your ISP using the same protocols as your DSL device?

◆ Have you entered the correct login user name and password?

Troubleshooting Your Firewall/Gateway

After your DSL connection to your ISP is working correctly, you still may encounter communication problems. If you can communicate within your private network and you're confident that your DSL connection is working, then you may have a problem with your firewall.

The following list outlines possible problems that your firewall may cause:

◆ Are the dual Ethernet interfaces on your gateway working properly?

◆ Are the routes on your gateway configured correctly?

◆ Are the proper kernel modules installed?

◆ Is your firewall script properly configured?

◆ Are you using the correct test? For instance, if you are blocking ICMP (like our firewall scripts do) then the traditional ping will not work. In that case, you may need to use a higher level application, like Telnet, to test your connection.

Checking your Red Hat Linux networking configuration

The Red Hat Linux gateway, described in Chapter 2 uses two Ethernet interfaces to connect your private network to the Internet. We described the process of troubleshooting the Ethernet NIC configuration in the section, "Troubleshooting Linux Networking," earlier in this chapter. You should consult that discussion for information on verifying that your NICs are correctly configured and capable of communicating on their respective sub-networks.

Beyond the basic NIC configuration, additional, higher-level issues are involved when dealing with the configuration of a dual-homed gateway. Both NICs must be configured with the correct IP address for their respective networks. Make sure that one NIC is assigned to each sub-network.

Run the ubiquitous ifconfig command to check the NICs. For our gateway example the result should look as follows:

```
eth0      Link encap:Ethernet  HWaddr 00:50:BA:DE:25:35
          inet addr:192.168.1.254  Bcast:192.168.1.255  Mask:255.255.255.0
          UP BROADCAST RUNNING MULTICAST  MTU:1500  Metric:1
          RX packets:1470774 errors:0 dropped:0 overruns:0 frame:0
          TX packets:1561190 errors:0 dropped:0 overruns:0 carrier:0
          collisions:16996 txqueuelen:100
          Interrupt:12 Base address:0xe400

eth1      Link encap:Ethernet  HWaddr 00:50:DA:0F:CE:C2
          inet addr:192.168.32.254  Bcast:192.168.32.255  Mask:255.255.255.0
          UP BROADCAST RUNNING MULTICAST  MTU:1500  Metric:1
          RX packets:700502 errors:0 dropped:0 overruns:0 frame:0
          TX packets:602736 errors:0 dropped:0 overruns:0 carrier:0
          collisions:12 txqueuelen:100
          Interrupt:10 Base address:0xe000

lo        Link encap:Local Loopback
          inet addr:127.0.0.1  Mask:255.0.0.0
          UP LOOPBACK RUNNING  MTU:3924  Metric:1
          RX packets:18 errors:0 dropped:0 overruns:0 frame:0
          TX packets:18 errors:0 dropped:0 overruns:0 carrier:0
          collisions:0 txqueuelen:0
```

The first NIC, eth0, is used to communicate with the private network. The second, eth1, connects to either the DSL device directly or indirectly through the DMZ network. You should be able to ping eth0, 192.168.1.254, from any machine on your private network.

If you're using the DMZ model, you can ping the eth1 NIC, 192.168.32.254, only if you aren't running a firewall on the gateway. If you're connected to the Internet, disconnect before turning off the firewall to perform the test. You can do so by disconnecting the DSL device from the wall jack or turning off the power.

If you're using the DCWAN, turn off your Internet connection and then your firewall. Try pinging the DSL device from the gateway. You can also try using Telnet to communicate with the device. Success by either method verifies connectivity.

Checking your gateway routes and IP forwarding

After you verify both NICs' connectivity, the next step is to check your routes. The Internet gateway must connect the private network with the Internet, which means that the kernel must pass private network IP packets destined for the Internet from eth0 to eth1. You have to resolve several configuration issues for this process to work:

◆ Make sure that you have a route for both Ethernet NICs and the loopback interfaces.

◆ Make sure that the packets destined for the Internet have a default route.

◆ Turn on IP packet forwarding in the kernel.

◆ Use IP NAT.

First, the routes allow packets with destination addresses for the two networks to be routed to their respective NICs. Packets with destination addresses on the 192.168.1.0 network are sent to eth0; those destined to 1921.68.32.0 go to eth1. (Internal packets are sent to loopback interface, lo.)

The routing table for both of this book's example networks looks as follows:

```
Kernel IP routing table
Destination      Gateway          Genmask          Flags Metric Ref    Use Iface
192.168.1.0      *                255.255.255.0    U     0      0        0 eth0
192.168.32.0     *                255.255.255.0    U     0      0        0 eth1
127.0.0.0        *                255.0.0.0        U     0      0        0 lo
default          cisco.paunchy.n  0.0.0.0          UG    0      0        0 eth1
```

With the loopback and individual sub-network routes in place, you also need to make sure that the default route is configured correctly. (The default route is the catchall for all packets whose destination addresses don't match any explicit route.)

Both network models used in this book designate the default route on the Internet gateway to send packets to the Internet. The default route points to the DSL device. Packets arriving from the private network that are destined for the Internet are sent to the second NIC. From there, the DSL device picks them up and sends them to the ISP and their final destination.

TIP Setting up the default route correctly can be a little confusing at first. One common mistake is to set the default route so that it points to a local inter-face rather than the next router downstream. For instance, if you set the route on the gateway as **route –net default gw 192.168.32.254**, packets remain on the gateway and never find their way to the DSL device and the Internet. The correct command **command route –net default gw 192.168.32.1** points to the DSL device and the packets find their way out. The same is true for any computer or network device — the default route must point to the device that's responsible for sending the packets to the next router downstream.

In order for a packet to transverse from one NIC to the other on the gateway, you must turn IP packet forwarding on. If IP packet forwarding is set to off, the kernel won't allow packets to be sent from one interface to another, and the gateway won't function correctly.

You can check the status of IP forwarding by examining the /proc/sys/net/ipv4/ip_forward file. Forwarding is turned on if the value is set to 1; it's off when the value is set to 0. Running the command sysctl –a |grep ip_forward also displays the status. You can turn IP forwarding on by changing the value of /proc/sys/net/ipv4/ip_forward to 1. You can also change the net.ipv4.ip_forward value to 1 in the /etc/sysctl.conf file and then run the sysctl –p command; changing the value in /etc/sysctl.conf file assures that for-warding is turned on whenever you boot the gateway.

Our network models use NAT, also called masquerading, so that we can route packets originating from our private network on the Internet. The IP specifies that addresses from the private networking address spaces, such as 192.168.1.0, aren't to be routed on the Internet. NAT maps those non-routable addresses to the valid one our ISP provides. Packets from our private network appear as though they origi-nated from the IP our ISP designated for our DSL WAN connection.

Our IP filters handle the NAT function, which we describe in the section "Checking your firewall scripts," later in this chapter.

Checking your firewall scripts

The IP filtering firewall scripts, described in Chapter 4, are responsible for protect-ing your network and permitting your packets to be routed on the Internet. The scripts achieve the protection function by denying most external packets access to your gateway and private network. NAT is used to masquerade packets originating from the private network so that they appear to come from your ISP.

If the filter rules are set up in such a way as to deny packets that you want to allow in or out of your private network, then you're not going to have the access that you want. This problem is common because of the ever-present conflict between security and access. Expect that your firewall rules will always be in flux.

Sometimes, minimizing the IP filtering rules is helpful when debugging the firewall. Use extreme caution when doing so if you're connected to the Internet because your protection is minimal at best.

The following commands are used to set the basic filtering policies of your firewall. First, flush the IP filters and reset the default policies to allow packets in and out.

```
iptables -F
iptables -P input ACCEPT
iptables -P output ACCEPT
iptables -P output ACCEPT
```

Next, turn masquerading on.

```
iptables -m ....
```

Your firewall is now set to minimal state. All packets will be allowed out to the Internet and properly masqueraded as your ISP address. Packets won't be routed into your private network, but your gateway/firewall server is still vulnerable because packets can conceivably reach their DMZ NIC if they can get through your DSL device. (Getting through the DSL device depends on what kind of device you have and how it's configured).

You can test your firewall now. If you can connect out to the Internet, then start working back towards a full-fledged firewall, adding rules from the script described in Chapter 4 until you find the problem. If you can't communicate, then the firewall probably isn't your problem.

Checking your kernel modules and flags

One common problem with misbehaving firewalls is related to kernel modules. Several applications require specific kernel modules to operate. For instance, to use RealAudio, you must have the *ip_masq_raudio.o* module. Unfortunately, the new 2.4 Linux kernel doesn't have all modules for iptables that ipchains does.

Until iptables catch up with ipchains, you may have to use the latter. Though not as sophisticated as iptables, ipchains is adequate to protect a network.

Using network sniffing tools

You can use a number of tools to look at network traffic to determine what is or isn't passing through a firewall. Programs such as tcpdump, nmap, and netstat — which we describe in the following sections — provide powerful debugging tools.

TCPDUMP

This highly configurable and quite readable (with a little time) program prints information about packet headers.

Assume, for instance, that you're unable to connect to the Internet from your private network. You've concluded that Linux networking is configured correctly on

both client workstations and the gateway, and you've reduced the firewall to a minimal state, but you can't get access to the Internet. By using tcpdump, you can
examine packets coming into the gateway and see whether they make their way out.

Run the following command to examine HTTP packets (port 80) arriving on the
private network NIC eth0. You examine port 80 because it's commonly used and
filters out all the other packets; you need to reduce the noise as much as possible
while leaving enough information to serve the debugging purpose.

```
tcpdump -i eth0 port 80
```

You should see traffic similar to the following (assuming someone is browsing
the Net).

```
23:21:57.131639 < 192.168.1.10.1283 > www.amazon.com.www: . 838:838(0) ack 270 w
in 8492 (DF)
23:21:57.135099 < 192.168.1.10.1283 > www.amazon.com.www: F 838:838(0) ack 270 w
in 8492 (DF)
23:21:57.142324 < 192.168.1.10.1284 > www.amazon.com.www: S 307988737:307988737(
0) win 8192 <mss 1460,nop,nop,sackOK> (DF)
```

Without going into the details of tcpdump, you can see that communication
directed towards Amazon.com is coming into eth0, but nothing's coming back.

Now look at eth1.

```
tcpdump -i eth1 port 80
```

Nothing. Two possible causes that come to mind are routing misconfiguration and
lack of IP forwarding. Check both following our instructions in the section Checking
your Gateway Routes and IP Forwarding earlier in this chapter. In this case,
/proc/sys/net/ipv4/ip_forward is set to 0. After changing it to 1 (*echo "1" > /proc/sys/
net/ipv4/ip_forward*), check eth0 again and you see two-way communication.

```
23:28:58.079921 < 192.168.1.10.1288 > www.amazon.com.www: . 860:860(0) ack 16061
win 8760 (DF)
23:28:58.094195 > www.amazon.com.www > 192.168.1.10.1288: P 16061:17521(1460) ac
k 860 win 32120 (DF)
23:28:58.115370 > www.amazon.com.www > 192.168.1.10.1288: P 17521:18981(1460) ac
k 860 win 32120 (DF)
```

NMAP

nmap belongs to a class of programs called port mappers; port mappers send packets in various states of contortion and misconfigurations to determine what ports
are open. It modifies the packet headers in ways that the IP never intended. The
modified packets cause their target machine to respond in ways that provide information about that machine.

NETSTAT

Netstat is a Linux utility that displays information about your computer's networking interfaces, routes and TCP connections. This utility is a powerful diagnostic tool that you can use for troubleshooting. Use it to examine the state of your Linux computer's network.

Using Additional Information

One of Linux's strengths is the availability of information and help both on the Internet and in books like this one. The following list provides hints about where to find this sort of information:.

◆ **Howto documents:** One of the most common methods for distributing information about all Linux topics, howto documents come with the Red Hat Linux distribution (see the HOWTO....rpm packages). You can also find them on the Internet. As you may suspect, the Internet-based documents tend to be more up-to-date than those that come with the Linux distributions:

- `www.redhat.com/mirrors/LDP/HOWTO/Net-HOWTO/index.html`

- `www.redhat.com/support/docs/tips/Network-Config-Tips/Network-Config-Tips.html`

- `www.redhat.com/mirrors/LDP/HOWTO/Cable-Modem/index.html`

- `www.redhat.com/support/docs/howto/rhl71.html`

◆ **Your DSL provider's knowledge base:** We use Qwest Communications, for instance, and they maintain a knowledge base at `www.qwest.com/jump/dsl`. Most providers will provide information about your type of connection. Consult your provider to access their information databases.

Summary

As you can see, troubleshooting is not very mysterious. It uses simple logic and a general knowledge of where problems occur. By working from the simple to the complex, you can track down most problems.

You should note one more thing before proceeding to the fun stuff. You have the perfect platform for learning how to troubleshoot computers. Before Linux, an individual rarely had the opportunity to work on an advanced computer system without fear of destroying valuable data and hardware. However, with Red Hat Linux, you can build a powerful server on an inexpensive platform to work on with impunity.

This chapter covers the following topics:

◆ **Troubleshooting your network:** We introduced you to the concept of troubleshooting. Identify the problem and then work your way to the solution by first eliminating the simple causes and then the harder ones.

◆ **Introducing the fault tree concept:** Using a rooted tree to represent the relationship between a problem and its root cause, this concept reduces problem solving into logical, manageable steps by helping you view a problem and its solutions in a hierarchical manner,. With the fault tree, you're less likely to need to know a system intimately before you attempt to fix it.

◆ **Using the fault tree to address common Red Hat Linux networking problems:** Systematically check the subsystems that Linux uses to connect a computer to a LAN. Checking each possible problem will eventually lead you to the solution.

◆ **Looking at problems common to getting a DSL Internet connection:** Identify common problems with connecting, using, and configuring the DSL device. Also use the resources provided by the DSL provider and ISP, such as their help desk to find the solution to your problem.

◆ **Dealing with firewall problems:** We examined in detail the basic IP filtering firewall our Internet gateway uses.

Part II

Building a World Wide Web Server

Chapter 6

Configuring a Basic Apache Server

IN THIS CHAPTER

◆ Introducing the HTML and HTTP protocols

◆ Exploring the Apache Web server

◆ Creating a basic Web site

◆ Developing a virtual Web site

APACHE IS OPEN SOURCE and is packaged with Red Hat Linux. The Apache Web server is largely responsible for the creation of the World Wide Web (WWW), which defines most of the Internet today; Apache was originally designed by the National Center for Supercomputer Applications (NCSA). Today, over 50 percent of Web servers are based on Apache – more than the combined total of all other servers. In the Web's early days, Apache's availability made it possible to start and expand Web sites.

This chapter describes how Apache works and how to configure it. We'll start by exploring the protocols that run the WWW in this chapter. We'll look at the Apache Web server and its configuration, too. Finally, we'll look at how to construct a basic Web server.

Introducing the HTML and HTTP Protocols

You use HyperText Markup Language (HTML) to create Web pages. HTML controls the format of content on a Web server. You use HyperText Transport Protocol (HTTP) to choreograph the interaction between Web servers and clients. We introduce the basics of HTML and HTTP in this section.

Presenting the HTTP protocol

The HTTP is designed to facilitate the access of a wide range of information across the Internet. An application level protocol, HTTP makes use of TCP-level connections to ensure that all a connection's HTTP packets are delivered in sequence.

HTTP uses the concept of requests and responses. For instance, when an HTTP client, such as a Mozilla browser, sends a request to an HTTP server, the client specifies the server's address and the type of request. The HTTP server responds to the request by sending the appropriate information back to the server. (The TCP/IP stacks on all interacting machines takes care of the delivery process.)

The typical HTTP session follows this sequence:

1. The client requests information from the server in the form of a universal resource language (URL). For instance, the following URL wants to view the Red Hat home page:

```
www.redhat.com
```

2. The client browser sends the following HTTP request:

```
GET /index.html HTTP/1.0
```

The index.html is the name of a file on the server that contains HTML code. (We describe HTML in the following section.)

3. The interacting machines use the TCP/IP protocol to route and guarantee the delivery of the request.

4. The server responds by sending the following response:

```
HTTP/1.0 200 OK
Date: Sun, 20 Jan 2002 16:12:02 GMT
Content-Type: text/html
Content length: 1211
...Contents of requested document index.html
```

HTTP doesn't use the concept of sessions. Each chunk of information that an HTTP server sends to the client uses a separate TCP connection. The TCP/IP stack uses a three-step handshake process to set each TCP connection up. Building multiple TCP connections is inefficient and makes viewing the Web more time-consuming.

Introducing the HTML standard (HTML is not a protocol)

HTML is a scripting language used to build and display Web pages. Describing it in any detail is well beyond the scope of this book, so we'll use the sample HTML Web page that's included with the Apache RPM package. That file contains enough HTML directives and tags to provide you with a starting point. You can build useful and informative Web pages with this simple basis. Apache provides a sample Web page, shown in Figure 6-1.

This file provides examples for displaying text, graphics, and links to other Web pages. The links reference both local and remote sites. Listing 6-1 shows the contents of the /var/www/error/noindex.html file:

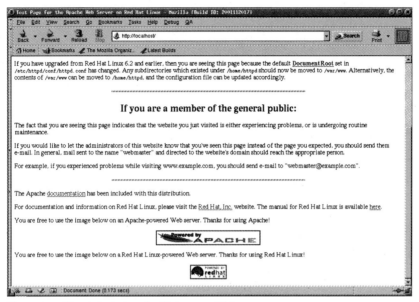

Figure 6-1: The default Apache Web server Web page

Listing 6-1: The /var/www/error/noindex.html file

```
<!DOCTYPE HTML PUBLIC "-//W3C//DTD HTML 3.2 Final//EN">
<HTML>
 <HEAD>
  <TITLE>Test Page for the Apache Web Server on Red Hat
Linux</TITLE>
 </HEAD>
<!-- Background white, links blue (unvisited), navy (visited), red
(active) -->
 <BODY BGCOLOR="#FFFFFF">

  <H1 ALIGN="CENTER">Test Page</H1>
  This page is used to test the proper operation of the Apache Web
server after it has been installed.  If you can read this page, it
means that the Apache Web server installed at this site is working
properly.

  <HR WIDTH="50%">

  <H2 ALIGN="CENTER">If you are the administrator of this
website:</H2>
```

Continued

Listing 6-1 *(Continued)*

```
    <P>
    You may now add content to this directory, and replace this page.
Note that
    until you do so, people visiting your website will see this page,
and not your
    content.
    </P>


    <P>If you have upgraded from Red Hat Linux 6.2 and earlier, then
you are
    seeing this page because the default <A

href="manual/mod/core.html#documentroot"><STRONG>DocumentRoot</STRON
G></A>
    set in <TT>/etc/httpd/conf/httpd.conf</TT> has changed.   Any
subdirectories
    which existed under <TT>/home/httpd</TT> should now be moved to
    <TT>/var/www</TT>.   Alternatively, the contents of
<TT>/var/www</TT> can be
    moved to <TT>/home/httpd</TT>, and the configuration file can be
updated
    accordingly.
    </P>


    <HR WIDTH="50%">
    <H2 ALIGN="CENTER">If you are a member of the general public:</H2>


    <P>
    The fact that you are seeing this page indicates that the website
you just
    visited is either experiencing problems, or is undergoing routine
maintenance.
    </P>


    <P>
    If you would like to let the administrators of this website know
that you've
    seen this page instead of the page you expected, you should send
them e-mail.
    In general, mail sent to the name "webmaster" and directed to the
website's
    domain should reach the appropriate person.
```

```
   </P>

   <P>
   For example, if you experienced problems while visiting
www.example.com,
   you should send e-mail to "webmaster@example.com".
   </P>

   <HR WIDTH="50%">

   <P>
   The Apache <A HREF="manual/index.html" >documentation</A> has been
included
   with this distribution.
   </P>

   <P>
   For documentation and information on Red Hat Linux, please visit the
   <a href="http://www.redhat.com/">Red Hat, Inc.</a> website. The
manual for
   Red Hat Linux is available <a
href="http://www.redhat.com/manual">here</a>.
   </P>

   <P>
   You are free to use the image below on an Apache-powered Web
   server.  Thanks for using Apache!
   </P>

   <P ALIGN="CENTER">
   <A HREF="http://www.apache.org/"><IMG SRC="/icons/apache_pb.gif"
ALT="[ Powered
by Apache ]"></A>
   </P>

   <P>
   You are free to use the image below on a Red Hat Linux-powered Web
   server. Thanks for using Red Hat Linux!
   </P>

   <P ALIGN="center">
```

Continued

Listing 6-1 *(Continued)*

```
  <A HREF="http://www.redhat.com/"><IMG SRC="poweredby.png" ALT="[
Powered
by Red Hat Linux ]"></A>
  </P>
 </BODY>
</HTML>
```

The syntax is simple: The primitives are encapsulated between less-than — < — and greater-than — > — symbols.

The following list examines the basic primitives:

◆ `<!DOCTYPE HTML PUBLIC "-//W3C//DTD HTML 3.2 Final//EN">`: Defines the HTML document type and version.

◆ `<HTML>`: Defines the beginning of the HTML document.

◆ `</HTML>`: Terminates the `<HTML>` tag.

◆ `<HEAD>`: Sets the document's heading.

◆ `</HEAD>`: Terminates the `<HEAD>` tag.

◆ `<TITLE>`: Creates the document's title. The title is displayed in the title bar of your browser when viewing the page and is also used as the label for bookmarks.

◆ `</TITLE>`: Terminates the `<TITLE>` tag.

◆ `<BODY BGCOLOR="#FFFFFF">`: Sets the body background's color. In this case, the background is white and unvisited links are blue.

◆ `<H1 ALIGN="CENTER">Test Page`: HTML provides for hierarchical headers — analogous to the section headers in this book — which are helpful for organizing Web page information. This tag creates a level 1 heading, "Test Page," that's displayed on the Web page, aligned to the center of the page.

◆ `</H1>`: Terminates a `<H1>` header.

◆ `<H2 ALIGN="CENTER">If you are the ...`: An example of a second level header. This header uses a smaller font than the H1 level header, as you can see in Figure 6-1.

◆ `</H2>`: Terminates a `<H2>` header.

◆ `<HR>`: Creates a horizontal line on the Web page and is useful for separating information.

◆ `<P> You may now add content ...`: Paragraph tags display the text that they straddle in an organized format.

◆ `</P>`: Terminates the Paragraph `<P>` tag.

◆ `<A HREF="manual/index.html" >documentation`: Though this example specifies a local URL, the `<A HREF` tag references both local and remote URLs. The URL points to a file on the local host — `manual/index.html` — that's an HTML document located in the Document Root directory. The `manual/index.html` file is part of the apache-manual package. We describe the Document Root in the section "Introducing the Apache Configuration File," later in this chapter.

◆ `<A HREF="http://www.apache.org/">`: An example of a remote URL reference, this URL is located on another machine — and in this case, on another network. (If you reference your own Web server, any queries directed at that URL will go through your local Web server, rather than going through your local file system, as in the preceding bullet point.)

◆ `<IMG SRC="/icons/apache_pb.gif"`: This tag references a graphical image.

◆ `ALT="[ Poweredby Apache ]">`: This tag directs the Apache server to display an alternative image if it can't find the primary one. In this case, the Apache server displays the text string `Poweredby Apache` if it can't locate the image `apache_pb.gif` (from the preceding bullet).

◆ `</A>`: Terminates the `<A>` tag.

You now have a basic introduction to HTML.

 We describe how to handle input and dynamic content in Chapter 7.

Exploring the Apache Web Server

The Apache Web server is the dominant Web server on the Internet. Apache is packaged with all major Linux distributions but you can also download it from www.apache.org. Apache is a light-hearted acronym that stands for A PatCHEy Web server.

Apache consists of these three primary parts:

◆ httpd daemons

◆ Configuration files for the httpd daemons

◆ Web-server content

The httpd daemons respond to HTTP requests that arrive via the host's network interfaces. The daemons process the requests, interact with the content that they control, and transmit information back to the requesting party as appropriate. The httpd configuration files determine how the httpd daemons work.

The following configuration files control Apache:

- ♦ `httpd.conf`: The main configuration file, controlling most of the Apache functions.

- ♦ `magic`: Apache handles many media types. The `mod_mime_magic` modules identify the media type by matching the *finger prints* – short binary sequences – contained in this file.

The `httpd.conf` file, which we describe in more detail in subsequent sections, contains the primary configuration for the httpd server.

Introducing the Apache configuration directives

The `httpd.conf` file contains numerous directives that control the httpd daemon's behavior. We describe the basic ones in this section by stepping through the default `httpd.conf` file. First, however, you need to understand the `httpd.conf` syntax.

Apache syntax is divided into variable assignments and block directives and also uses comments. The former consists of a variable name and its value. The latter uses a beginning and end tag that encompasses one or more variable definitions. Following is a description of both syntax types:

- ♦ **Directive:** A *directive* assigns a variable or option value. The syntax is as follows:

  ```
  <variable or option name><white space><value>
  ```

- ♦ **Container and/or blocks:** Apache uses structures called *containers* and *blocks* to combine one or more directives into a single entity. A container and block consists of a beginning and end tag to bind one or more directives together. The beginning tag defines the container. The syntax is as follows:

  ```
  <container beginning tag>
          <directive or option name><value>
          <directive or option name><value>
  <End tag>
  ```

Comments are defined by a pound – # – sign.

The next section describes the most commonly used Apache variables and directives in more detail.

Introducing the Apache configuration file

The Red Hat Linux Apache RPM package includes a default `httpd.conf` configuration file. The configuration file is over 20 pages, much of which is devoted to comments (very helpful) and boilerplate language, module, and other definitions. We're skipping most of it to concentrate on the more commonly used functions.

The configuration file is divided into these three sections:

◆ **Global environment:** Defines the behavior of the httpd processes (daemons). The daemons determine the overall operation of the Apache Web server within the Linux environment. For instance, the default configuration file starts eight httpd daemons.

◆ **Main server:** The directives and variables in this section set the Apache Web server's default behavior. For instance, this section defines the location of the `htdocs` directory, which contains the Web page documents.

◆ **Virtual hosts:** Apache can host virtual Web servers, which appear as independent sites but are actually controlled by the primary Web server. Virtual sites are most commonly used by ISPs to provide their subscribers with their own Web sites.

The following sections describe the most commonly used variables and directives of the three sections.

EXPLORING THE GLOBAL ENVIRONMENT

The global environment sets the parameters of the Apache httpd process environment. The environment describes such things as the Apache server root directory's location, how many daemons to start at boot time, how many daemons above and below that amount can be run, and so on. The following list describes the interesting variables:

◆ **ServerRoot:** The httpd configuration files are located in the ServerRoot; `httpd.conf` and other files are stored in this location. The default setting is `/etc/httpd`.

◆ **LockFile:** The `/etc/init.d/httpd` control script uses the LockFile — `/var/run/subsys/httpd` — to coordinate the start-up and shut-down process.

◆ **PidFile:** The initial httpd daemon's process identification (pid) is stored in this file. The `/etc/init.d/httpd` control script consults this file in order to control the running `httpd` daemons.

◆ **ScoreBoardFile:** Apache uses this file to store its own process state. You do not need to access or modify this file.

◆ **Timeout:** This variable sets the time, in seconds, before a connection ceases to function.

◆ **MinSpareServers:** Sets the floor on the number of spare httpd daemons the system is to use to handle transient loads. The root httpd server periodically polls the other httpd processes and determines how many, if any, are waiting to service requests. More spares are spawned if there are fewer idle processes than the value of MinSpareServers. The default MinSpareServers is five.

MinSpareServers, and the following two parameters – MaxSpareServers and StartServers defines a server pool. Apache uses the concept of a server pool to dynamically adapt to the load placed on it. The StartServers and MinSpareServers parameters set the range of httpd processes running necessary to handle a steady state load. The MaxSpareServers sets the maximum number of httpd processes that Apache can start to handle load spikes.

◆ MaxSpareServers: Sets the ceiling on the number of spare httpd daemons the system is to use to handle transient loads. The root httpd server periodically polls the other httpd processes and determines how many, if any, are waiting to service requests. The server allows excess spares to timeout and cease operation when the number of daemons exceeds the MaxSpareServers value. The default MinSpareServers is 20.

◆ StartServers: Sets the number of httpd daemons to start when the control script is run. The default is eight, which should be more than enough for a personal or small business Web site. (Broadband Internet connections at the consumer DSL level should effectively limit access to your Web site so that values in this range will be reasonable.)

◆ MaxClients: This parameter limits the number of simultaneous connections to your server pool. The server prohibits any new connections when the number of current connections exceeds the MaxClients value. The default value of 150 matches the default server pool size settings.

◆ MaxRequestsPerChild: Sets an effective lifetime on httpd processes, which prevents problems, such as memory leaks, from corrupting the system. The daemons process up to this number of requests – the default is 1000 requests – and then die.

◆ Listen: This parameter tells the server to bind to specific network interfaces and/or ports. For instance, setting the value to `Listen 192.168.1.254` binds the httpd daemons to that address; using the value `Listen 8080` configures the server to use the 8080 port and using 192.168.1.254:8080 binds explicitly to both the 192.168.1.254 IP address and port 8080. (Actually no, that statement implies more than is true. 192.168.1.254:8080 binds *only* to port 8080 on address 192.168.1.254.)

◆ BindAddress: Configures the server to any, or specific, IP addresses when using virtual hosts.

◆ LoadModule: Apache supports a wide range of functionality via the use of Dynamic Shared Objects (DSO), which are essentially libraries. The LoadModule parameter specifies which DSOs to use. The syntax is

LoadModule `some_module` modules/somemodule.so. For instance, the following LoadModule directive loads the module that permits CGI functionality:

```
LoadModule cgi_module        modules/mod_cgi.so
```

You must load the modules before you can use the function.

The following excerpt from `httpd.conf` shows several of the DSOs that are configured as part of the default Apache installation:

```
LoadModule env_module         modules/mod_env.so
LoadModule config_log_module  modules/mod_log_config.so
LoadModule agent_log_module   modules/mod_log_agent.so
LoadModule referer_log_module modules/mod_log_referer.so
#LoadModule mime_magic_module modules/mod_mime_magic.so
LoadModule mime_module        modules/mod_mime.so
LoadModule negotiation_module modules/mod_negotiation.so
LoadModule status_module      modules/mod_status.so
LoadModule info_module        modules/mod_info.so
LoadModule includes_module    modules/mod_include.so
LoadModule autoindex_module   modules/mod_autoindex.so
LoadModule dir_module         modules/mod_dir.so
LoadModule cgi_module         modules/mod_cgi.so
LoadModule asis_module        modules/mod_asis.so
LoadModule imap_module        modules/mod_imap.so
LoadModule action_module      modules/mod_actions.so
```

You can conditionally load modules by sandwiching the `LoadModule` directive between `<IfDefine>` and `</IfDefine>` tags.

◆ **AddModule:** This directive tells Apache to load a module, and is usually used in conjunction with the LoadModule directive, as shown in the following excerpt:

```
AddModule mod_env.c
AddModule mod_log_config.c
AddModule mod_log_agent.c
AddModule mod_log_referer.c
#AddModule mod_mime_magic.c
AddModule mod_mime.c
AddModule mod_negotiation.c
AddModule mod_status.c
AddModule mod_info.c
AddModule mod_include.c
```

◆ **ClearModuleList:** This directive removes modules from Apache. You can conditionally load modules by sandwiching the `LoadModule` directive between `<IfDefine >` and `</IfDefine>` tags. For instance, the following block checks to see whether PHP is available, and then conditionally adds `mod_php.c` if true (php was derived from Personal Home Page Tools and is a system that Apache can use to access databases):

```
<IfDefine HAVE_PHP>
AddModule mod_php.c
</IfDefine>
```

This section introduced the global environment variables. The following section describes the primary configuration options found in the httpd.conf file.

CONFIGURING THE MAIN SERVER

This section shows you how to configure the Apache server's behavior to HTTP requests that it doesn't handle as virtual servers. It is divided between simple and block directives. The *simple directives* define the Web server's overall behavior. *Block directives* group together directives to perform a single function. For instance, a block of directives may define who gets to access a single directory.

INTRODUCING BASIC APACHE DIRECTIVES   The following list describes simple Apache directives:

- **Listen:** Sets the port on which httpd listens. The `httdp.conf` configuration file sets the default port to 80. You can set the port to 8080, which is an alternative to port 80. (All ports greater than 1024 are unprivileged, and you can create user-land services that work with them.)

- **User/Group:** This directive sets the user and group of the httpd processes. The default is the apache user and group. The first Apache daemon starts as root and spawns additional processes that run as this user and group. Running Apache in user space ensures that any exploited vulnerability won't automatically result in a root shell or process.

- **ServerAdmin:** Defines the e-mail address to which to send server-related error messages. The default is the root user on the local machine — `root@localhost`. You may want to change this address to one from which you manage the system. For instance, change the address to `webadm@cancun.paunchy.net` if you regularly work from that workstation.

- **DocumentRoot:** Essentially the Web server's home page, this directive sets the base — root — directory from which the Web server provides documents. This directory or its subdirectories houses all HTML and other files; symbolic links may point to locations outside of the DocumentRoot tree.

- **FollowSymLinks:** Enables Apache to follow symbolic links within the DocumentRoot structure.

◆ **AllowOverride:** Allows access files such as .htaccess to override <Directory> block configurations. Options are All, None, Indexes, Includes, FollowSymLinks, ExecCGI, and MultiViews; All and None can't include any of the options. In this case, AllowOverride None prevents an access file from overriding a <Directory> block.

◆ **Order allow, deny:** Specifies the sequence that allows and prevents access to the directory block. The sequence *allow, deny* configures the sequence to first allow, but then deny access and the denial option takes precedence.

◆ **Allow from all:** Permits access from anywhere. The Allow directive can permit access from specific hosts and networks, too. For instance, setting `Allow from 192.168.1.0/24` permits access from that network.

◆ **AccessFileName:** Defines the file name that the server uses to provide auxiliary access. The previously defined access control directives directly control the Web server via the `httpd.conf` file. Files placed within the DocumentRoot can also control access. The default access file name is `.htaccess`. You can place any number of `.htaccess` files within the DocumentRoot tree to control access to the directories, and subdirectories where they reside. Control directives, such as *Allow from* and *Order*, are placed in the `.htaccess` file. The control directives perform the same functions when placed in an access file as when they are put in the `httpd.conf` file.

◆ **UserDir:** Apache permits you to serve personal Web pages from individual user accounts. The default is `public_html`. For instance, setting `UserDir public_html` forces Apache to append the string "public_html" onto a user's home directory path. The Web server at `some.webserver.com` looks to the directory `/home/lupe/public_html` when it receives a request for the URL `http://some.webserver.com/~lupe`.

◆ **ErrorLog:** Apache performs error logging. The ErrorLog directive sets the error log's name and location. The default error log file is `log/error_log`, which is located in the `/var/www/html/logs` directory.

◆ **LogLevel:** Apache provides several levels of error logging. The levels are the same as the Linux syslog system; the default is `warn`.

◆ **LogFormat:** Controls error logging's format.

◆ **CustomLog:** Apache permits the construction of custom logs. The default is logs/access_log combined, which log records connections to your server.

◆ **AddLanguage:** You can configure Apache to interpret a country domain suffix and use the appropriate language for specified files. Table 6-1 lists the available languages and their suffixes.

APACHE BLOCK DIRECTIVES, ALIASES, AND ICONS

The following list describes Apache block directives:

◆ **<Directory ...> ... </Directory>:** You can limit access, redirect to another
location, and perform other processes to each directory within the
DocumentRoot tree by using this block. Using the appropriate directives
within these tags controls access to the specified file system. The first
<Directory> container effectively sets the default behavior of all sub-
sequent <Directory> containers.

```
<Directory /var/www/html>
    Options Indexes FollowSymLinks
    AllowOverride None
    Order allow, deny
    Allow from all
</Directory>
```

The `<Directory /var/www/html>` tag specifies that the container control
starts at the top of the DocumentRoot. (Recall that DocumentRoot was
defined earlier in the httpd.conf file as `/var/www/html`. This container's
control starts at `/var/www/html`.)

◆ **Alias:** Aliases map and allow access to file systems outside the
DocumentRoot. This directive permits the Web server to provide objects
not normally accessible, such as icon images. The default is to map icons
to `/var/www/icons` as follows:

```
Alias /icons/ "/var/www/icons/"
```

Access to aliased directories, such as icons, is as follows:

```
<Directory "/var/www/icons">
    Options Indexes MultiViews
    AllowOverride None
    Order allow,deny
    Allow from all
</Directory>
```

◆ **ScriptAlias:** Access to the local file system is normally limited to directories specified by the DocumentRoot. However, the Web server must be able
to access certain files outside of that space. Aliases are one example of
such files. ScriptAlias is another. ScriptAlias maps one directory to another
and allows the server to access directories that contain executable server
scripts. The default is to map `cgi-bin` to `/var/www/cgi-bin` as follows:

```
ScriptAlias /cgi-bin/ "/var/www/cgi-bin/"

<Directory "/var/www/cgi-bin">
```

```
    AllowOverride None
    Options None
    Order allow,deny
    Allow from all
</Directory>
```

◆ **Redirect:** Redirects browsers to other locations. You can move your Web page from one domain to another, for instance, and automatically transfer your clients to the new location, so your clientele won't be left stranded if you move your ISP-based home page to your own domain.

◆ **DefaultIcon:** You use the DefaultIcon icon when no explicit icon is available. The default is the unknown.gif icon.

TABLE **6-1** LANGUAGES AND SUFFIXES FOR ADDLANGUAGE

Language	Suffix
Brazilian Portuguese	pt-br
Catalan	ca
Czech	cz
Danish	da
Dutch	nl
English	en
Estonian	ee
French	fr
German	de
Greek-modern	el
Italian	it
Japanese	ja
Korean	kr
Luxembourgeois	ltz
Norwegian	no
Polish	pl
Portuguese	pt

Continued

TABLE 6-1 LANGUAGES AND SUFFIXES FOR ADDLANGUAGE *(Continued)*

Language	Suffix
Russian	ru
Spanish	es
Swedish	sv

This list shows the languages that Apache can work with.

CONFIGURING VIRTUAL HOSTS

Normally Apache operates as a single Web server. That Web server can handle multiple simultaneous connections but all the connections access the same information. You can also configure Apache to operate as one or more virtual servers. Virtual servers provide different information and services than the actual one; they also appear as domains and host names different from the physical host. Using virtual servers permits a single platform to economically provide many different Web pages.

Virtual hosts are divided into two classes: name-based and IP-based. The former defines each virtual host via a name, while the latter uses a numeric IP address. Numeric IPs require that you define a unique IP address on the Web server host and/or the local DNS system. Name-based IPs require you to define only one unique IP.

Name-based virtual servers don't provide any clear advantage over IP-based ones if you run only a small number of virtual hosts. However, using IP-based virtual hosts can present a problem if you need to create many virtual hosts; especially when a dearth of IP addresses are available on your network.

You can configure virtual servers with the same directives that the physical Web server uses, which we described in the section "Configuring the main server," earlier in this chapter. The only difference is that you must encapsulate virtual host containers within the <VirtualHost...> and </VirtualHost> tags. Otherwise, Virtual hosts are configured in the same way as the Main server. The following directives provide the virtual server configuration:

- ◆ NameVirtualHost: Defines name-based virtual hosts. The default value is an asterisk – * – that will match any value. You can also specify a particular machine, such as your Web server host.

- ◆ <VirtualHost ...>: This tag starts the NameVirtualHost container. The default value is an asterisk. The asterisk makes the container respond to any virtual host. Setting the tag to a particular value creates a virtual host named by that value. You must provide a minimal amount of configuration for that server. You must specify a ServerName and DocumentRoot, and you should supply a ServerAdmin and logging directives. Otherwise, you can use nearly every Apache directive and container within a VirutalHost container.

The following example illustrates the basic structure of a virtual host container:

```
<VirtualHost 192.168.1.253.>
    ServerName www.virtual.com
    DocumentRoot /var/www/virtual
    ScriptAlias /var/www/virtual/cgi-bin
</VirtualHost>
```

The `VirtualHost` directive specifies the beginning of the container and also the IP address that it will listen to. This happens when you connect to the virtual Web server and   the address, 192.168.1.253. The Virtual host's HTML files are found in the `/var/www/virtual` document root directory and it's executable scripts and programs live in `/var/www/virtual/cgi-bin`.

This section introduced the Apache Web server. The basic Apache configuration file and the directives it contains were also described. The next section describes how to construct an example Web server.

Creating a Basic Web Site

Creating a Web site is straightforward. The Apache Web server packaged with Red Hat Linux is configured to run right out of the box. This section describes the process for running that server. We also describe how to make simple modifications.

The Apache server installation and configuration process consists of the following steps:

1. Installing the Apache Web server.

2. Configuring the Apache Web server (optional).

3. Controlling the Apache Web server.

4. Accessing the Apache Web server.

5. Controlling access to the Web server with .htaccess and .htpasswd.

These steps are detailed in the following sections.

The default Web server's content is stored in the `/var/www` directory. The `/var/www/html/index.html` file contains a good cross section of the HTML code. The `/var/www/icons` directory stores all of the graphics images to which the `index.html` file points.

Installing the Apache Web server

Installing Apache is generally a simple process. You simply use the rpm utility to install the base Apache package (**rpm –ivh http-2***) and optionally the Apache configuration and manual packages (**rpm –ivh http-conf*** and **rpm –ivh http-manual***). All the Apache software is packaged in RPM form with the Red Hat distribution.

However, you may not have all of the supporting Apache packages installed depending on how you've built your computer. The RPM will inform you when there are packages missing. You can determine what packages are needed, install them, and then install Apache.

Apache provides a script, `/etc/init.d/httpd`, that controls the operation of the httpd daemons; we describe the script's use in the section "Controlling the server," later in this chapter. However, the Apache RPM package does not configure itself to run at system start-up. You can configure Apache to automatically start by running the command **chkconfig httpd on**. This sets soft links in all of the run directories (`/etc/rc.d/rc1.d`, `etc/rc.d/rc3.d` and `/etc/rc.d/rc5.d`) to the Apache service script `/etc/init.d/httpd`. Apache is started every time you boot the computer.

Configuring the Apache Web server

Running the basic server doesn't require any configuration. Apache comes pre-configured with a reasonable and useful default configuration.

Tweaking parameters, should you need to, is a straightforward process. For instance, you may want to decrease the server pool size if you're running an information Web site for yourself or a small company – nine httpd processes may be more than you need. In that case, change MinSpareServers, MaxSpareServers, and StartServers to 2, 4, and 2, which should be enough for your purpose.

The following list shows the first part of the default `httpd.conf` file that's installed with the Apache RPM file. The listing shows the interesting directives and blocks with the comments removed. Most of the comments and many of the repetitive lines describing modules and languages, and the last section on virtual hosts have been removed in order to better illustrate Apache's basic configuration. Showing the boiled down configuration file really helps to understand it. Please consult the previous section for explanations of the directives.

```
### Section 1: Global Environment
ServerTokens OS
ServerRoot "/etc/httpd"
PidFile run/httpd.pid
Timeout 300
KeepAlive Off
MaxKeepAliveRequests 100
KeepAliveTimeout 15

<IfModule prefork.c>
```

```
    StartServers        8
    MinSpareServers     5
    MaxSpareServers    20
    MaxClients        150
    MaxRequestsPerChild  1000
</IfModule>

Listen 80
Include conf.d/*.conf

LoadModule access_module modules/mod_access.so
LoadModule auth_module modules/mod_auth.so
...
LoadModule rewrite_module modules/mod_rewrite.so

### Section 2: 'Main' server configuration
User apache
Group apache
ServerAdmin root@localhost
UseCanonicalName Off
DocumentRoot "/var/www/html"
<Directory />
    Options FollowSymLinks
    AllowOverride None
</Directory>

<Directory "/var/www/html">
    Options Indexes FollowSymLinks
    AllowOverride None
    Order allow,deny
    Allow from all
</Directory>

<LocationMatch "^/$>
    Options -Indexes
    ErrorDocument 403 /error/noindex.html
</LocationMatch>

<IfModule mod_userdir.c>
    UserDir disable
    #UserDir public_html
</IfModule>

DirectoryIndex index.html index.html.var
AccessFileName .htaccess
```

```
<Files ~ "^\.ht">
    Order allow,deny
    Deny from all
</Files>
TypesConfig /etc/mime.types
DefaultType text/plain
<IfModule mod_mime_magic.c>
#    MIMEMagicFile /usr/share/magic.mime
    MIMEMagicFile conf/magic
</IfModule>
HostnameLookups Off
ErrorLog logs/error_log
LogLevel warn
LogFormat "%h %l %u %t \"%r\" %>s %b \"%{Referer}i\" \"%{User-
Agent}i\"" combined
LogFormat "%h %l %u %t \"%r\" %>s %b" common
LogFormat "%{Referer}i -> %U" referer
LogFormat "%{User-agent}i" agent
CustomLog logs/access_log combined
ServerSignature On

Alias /icons/ "/var/www/icons/"
<Directory "/var/www/icons">
    Options Indexes MultiViews
    AllowOverride None
    Order allow,deny
    Allow from all
</Directory>

Alias /manual "/var/www/manual"
<Directory "/var/www/manual">
    Options Indexes FollowSymLinks MultiViews
    AllowOverride None
    Order allow,deny
    Allow from all
</Directory>

<IfModule mod_dav_fs.c>
    # Location of the WebDAV lock database.
    DAVLockDB /var/lib/dav/lockdb
</IfModule>

ScriptAlias /cgi-bin/ "/var/www/cgi-bin/"
<Directory "/var/www/cgi-bin">
    AllowOverride None
```

```
        Options None
        Order allow,deny
        Allow from all
</Directory>

IndexOptions FancyIndexing VersionSort NameWidth=*
AddIconByEncoding (CMP,/icons/compressed.gif) x-compress x-gzip

AddIconByType (TXT,/icons/text.gif) text/*
AddIconByType (IMG,/icons/image2.gif) image/*
AddIconByType (SND,/icons/sound2.gif) audio/*
AddIconByType (VID,/icons/movie.gif) video/*

AddIcon /icons/binary.gif .bin .exe
AddIcon /icons/binhex.gif .hqx
DefaultIcon /icons/unknown.gif

IndexIgnore .??* *~ *# HEADER* README* RCS CVS *,v *,t

AddEncoding x-compress Z
AddEncoding x-gzip gz tgz

Alias /error/ "/var/www/error/"

<IfModule mod_negotiation.c>
<IfModule mod_include.c>
    <Directory "/var/www/error">
        AllowOverride None
        Options IncludesNoExec
        AddOutputFilter Includes html
        AddHandler type-map var
        Order allow,deny
        Allow from all
        LanguagePriority en es de fr
        ForceLanguagePriority Prefer Fallback
    </Directory>

    ErrorDocument 400 /error/HTTP_BAD_REQUEST.html.var
    ErrorDocument 401 /error/HTTP_UNAUTHORIZED.html.var
    ErrorDocument 403 /error/HTTP_FORBIDDEN.html.var
    ErrorDocument 404 /error/HTTP_NOT_FOUND.html.var
    ErrorDocument 405 /error/HTTP_METHOD_NOT_ALLOWED.html.var
    ...
    ErrorDocument 506 /error/HTTP_VARIANT_ALSO_VARIES.html.var

</IfModule>
```

```
</IfModule>

#
# The following directives modify normal HTTP response behavior to
# handle known problems with browser implementations.
#
BrowserMatch "Mozilla/2" nokeepalive
BrowserMatch "MSIE 4\.0b2;" nokeepalive downgrade-1.0 force-
response-1.0
BrowserMatch "RealPlayer 4\.0" force-response-1.0
BrowserMatch "Java/1\.0" force-response-1.0
BrowserMatch "JDK/1\.0" force-response-1.0

BrowserMatch "Microsoft Data Access Internet Publishing Provider"
redirect-carefully
BrowserMatch "^WebDrive" redirect-carefully
```

Please note that the preceding Error alias and Error block shown are used to create a standard method of handling requests that Apache doesn't know how to handle. Using this convention, Apache processes all errors as it does a Web page. Erroneous httpd requests are passed to the /var/www/error block directive where they are sorted according to type. For instance, when a request is made for a file that the server cannot find, the error type is determined to be number 404. That server then displays the HTTP_NOT_FOUND.html.var file located in the /var/www/ error directory. This system makes it easy to handle different languages and also implement new error types.

The initial Apache Web page is no longer stored in the index.html file in the document root — /var/www/html — as in previous Apache versions. In fact, no HTML file is stored in the document root. When you browse your newly installed Apache server's home page, it looks for but does not find an index.html file in the /var/www/html directory — which is what it's programmed to look for by default. When no file is found, Apache examines the Error alias and goes to the /www/html/error directory where it finds the noindex.html file. Apache then displays the noindex.html file. This elegant convention makes it easy to provide the simple, traditional initial Web page without cluttering up the document root.

The httpd.conf file controls every aspect of Apache's performance and function. The default Apache configuration file shown in the preceding example has been stripped of comments and repetitive directives to better show its structure. The following section describes how to start and stop Apache:

Controlling the Apache Web server

The Apache package provides a control script, /etc/init.d/http, which you use to start, stop, and restart the httpd daemons. The script can also provide the server's status.

```
Start the apache Web server by running the control script
/etc/init.d/httpd start. You can stop the Web server with
this script: /etc/init.d/httpd stop. You can use httpd to
display the Web server's status like so: /etc/init.d/httpd
status. Running the script shows the following pids of the
running httpd processes:httpd (pid 9083 9082 9081 9080 9079
9073) is running....
```

Send the hangup (HUP) signal to the running httpd processes with the script /etc/init.d/httpd reload. The HUP signal forces the running processes to reload their configurations, which is faster than restarting the processes.

The default Apache configuration starts nine httpd daemons. All but one of the daemons run in user space as the Apache user and have no special privileges; the first httpd daemon starts as the root user and spawns the subsequent user space daemons.

Accessing the Apache Web server

Accessing the Apache server is a matter of pointing a browser towards it. For instance, once you install the server, start Mozilla on the same machine and enter the following URL in the Location: space: http://localhost. (Or, if you're on another machine, enter http://192.168.1.254, or whatever the server's address is.) When you connect to the default Apache Web server you see the sample home page as shown previously in Figure 6-1. The default Web page actually provides useful links to Apache.org that you can use to gain information about the system.

Apache is infinitely configurable, and describing the possibilities in detail is beyond the scope of this chapter. (Chapter 7 provides more information about how to place content on your Web site.)

Controlling access to the Web server with .htaccess and .htpasswd

Apache controls access to directories within its DocumentRoot, via <Directory> tags, within the httpd.conf file. An alternative to the httpd.conf file places directives within a file on the Linux file system. The *AccessFileName* directive controls the access file's name. The default httpd.conf has the following access directive:

```
AccessFileName.htaccess
```

The default tells Apache to look for the .htaccess file within the DocumentRoot. The .htaccess files contents will have directives similar to the following:

```
AuthUserFile    /var/www/html/secure/.htpasswd
AuthName        User

<Limit GET>
order deny,allow
allow from all
require user lupe
</Limit>

<Limit PUT POST>
deny from all
</Limit>
```

This file stipulates that a user must specify a password to access the secure directory. The htpasswd program places a hashed password in the .htpasswd file. The user lupe specifies that only the user lupe can access this directory. The user lupe must also supply the correct password.

The .htaccess file, in this case, tells the server to allow GETs from anywhere, but limits access to the user lupe. The file also prohibits any POSTs or PUTs, effectively making the directory read-only.

The following command places the password in the .htpasswd file:

```
htpasswd -c .htpasswd username
```

Using ApacheConf

Apache is highly configurable. You can do most or all configuration by modifying the httpd.conf file, and we advise that you learn to do so. Learning the Apache configuration from the ground up assures that you understand the system. However, you can use a graphical configuration system if you don't have the time or desire to understand Apache. Red Hat Linux packages its own graphical Apache configuration utility redhat-config-httpd. You can install the tool, if necessary, by logging in as root and running the following command:

```
rpm -ivh /mnt/cdrom/RedHat/RPMS/redhat-conf-httpd*.rpm
```

Using the Apache Configuration tool is self-explanatory. You can use the tool to configure numerous aspects of Apache, just as you would manually.

The `-c` option creates the password file. In this case, the file created is `.htpasswd`, but you can use your own naming convention if you wish. The username specifies for whom the password is created. For instance, the following command creates the `.htpasswd` file and places the hashed password in that file — after prompting you twice (once to verify) for the password:

```
htpasswd -c /var/www/html/secure/.htpasswd lupe
```

The contents of the file will look as follows:

```
lupe:a@#$dsf^12df
```

Developing a Virtual Web Site

Apache provides the ability to host virtual Web sites. Virtual hosting makes a single Apache Web server appear as many. ISPs use virtual hosting to provide customers with their own home pages. The customers rent the virtual site and need only to provide content. Without virtual hosting, you have to register a domain name and construct a server.

Virtual hosting is also useful to individuals and businesses who want to appear as many different sites or provide their employees with Web pages. We describe how to configure virtual hosts in this section.

Virtual hosts come in two flavors: IP-based and name-based. The former requires that you provide an IP address for each virtual host. The latter associates a name with each server and doesn't require the allocation of an IP address. The method doesn't matter very much when using non-routable, private address space, such as we use in our examples. When using registered addresses, though, you might find it better to use a name-based host because you can access the virtual server by specifying a registered name.

In this example, we're using the IP-based virtual host because the ease of configuration works well with our network example. We don't have to worry about proving that we efficiently use IP addresses, because our servers hide behind our firewall and use NAT to access the Internet.

The VirtualHost directive in the `httpd.conf` file controls virtual hosting. The following instructions describe how to configure a simple virtual host:

1. Edit the `/etc/hosts` file and add an alias for the virtual host:

   ```
   192.168.1.254atlasatlas.paunchy.net virtual1
   ```

   The alias `virtual_1` points to our physical Web server.

2. Create a directory to act as the virtual Web server's DocumentRoot. The directory's location is arbitrary. We like to consolidate our Web pages together, so we're placing the virtual's DocumentRoot in the `/var/www` directory. You may want to place your DocumentRoot in a more spacious

location such as /home; in that case, you also may want to create a user account from which to manage the virtual server:

```
mkdir /var/www/virtual1
```

Or, create a dedicated user account:

```
useradd virtual1
```

3. Create the htdoc and log directories in the DocumentRoot:

```
mkdir /var/www/virtual1/htdocs
mkdir /var/www/virtual1/logs
```

Alternatively, create the directories in the user account:

```
mkdir /home/virtual1/htdocs
mkdir /home/virtual1/logs
```

4. Create the virtual host's content. For instance, copy the /var/www/htdocs/index.html file, and modify it to create a dummy file:

```
cp /var/www/htdocs/index.html /var/www/virtual1/htdocs
```

Or, use the following command if using a dedicated virtual user account:

```
cp /var/www/htdocs/index.html /home/virtual1/htdocs
```

Modify the default index.html file to indicate that it's the virtual Web server. For instance, change the title from "Test Page" to "Virtual Test Page." The HTML code for this example is shown below.

```
<H1 ALIGN="CENTER">Virtual Test Page</H1>
```

5. Change the ownership of the new virtual server DocumentRoot to the Apache user. The Apache httpd daemons run as the Apache user and can fully access the directory and files because they own them:

```
chown -R apache /var/www/virtual1
```

Use the following command if using the dedication virtual user account;

```
chown -R virtual1 /home/virtual1
```

6. Edit the httpd.conf file and set the NameVirtualHost directive to the physical host's IP address:

```
NameVirtualHost192.168.1.254
```

7. Create a virtual host container. The following container creates a virtual host whose name is www.dummy.com:

```
<VirtualHost 192.168.1.254>
ServerName virtual1
ServerAdmin webmaster@paunchy.net
DocumentRoot /var/www/virtual1
</VirtualHost>
```

8. Create a directory block for the virtual server (optional):

```
<Directory "/var/www/virtual1/htdocs">
Options Includes (unless you give a reason that you want to
FollowSymLinks, you shouldn't.  Think about this security
problem:  "ln -s / front.jpg"
AllowOverride Limit FileInfo
Order allow,deny
Allow from all
</Directory>
```

You set up the directory block up the same as for a standalone server. (The virtual server thinks it's a standalone server.)

9. Restart the Apache server and browse the new page:

```
/etc/init.d/httpd restart
```

In this example the VirtualHost container performed the following functions:

NameVirtualHost specifies that the server found at 192.168.1.254 is used for name-based virtual hosting.

<VirtualHost 192.168.1.254> starts the virtual container.

ServerName www.dummy.com defines the virtual host server name.

ServerAdmin webmaster@paunchy.net defines who gets e-mail about the virutal domain.

DocumentRoot /var/www/virtual_1 sets the root html directory for the virtual host.

<Directory...> sets up the directory information for the virtual host.

Using SSL with Apache

With Red Hat Linux you can easily use SSL with your VirtualHosts. SSL stands for Secure Sockets Layer and basically provides two things: traffic encryption and identity authorization. The SSL layer of Apache is not inherently part of Apache, but it is included as an Apache module by Red Hat and is installable in the mod_ssl RPM package. To utilize SSL successfully with Apache, we will need to perform a few steps:

◆ Installing the mod_ssl package

◆ Negotiating the SSL handshake and the need for certificates

◆ Creating SSL certificates

◆ Configuring httpd.conf to enable SSL-based VirtualHosts

Installing mod_ssl package

The installation is very straightforward. You will need the following command:

```
rpm -ivh mod_ssl*rpm
```

Make sure that the prerequisite `openssl` package is installed first.

SSL's negotiation and certificates

SSL is essentially another layer through which the Web server has to go in order to server-out content. But even before SSL's encryption is applied to an outgoing Web server's reply, the client browser and server must negotiate the SSL connection. This involves an SSL *handshake*, which is a process where both the server and browser exchange information about their encryption strength capabilities and their identities. Encryption strength is typically either 40 bits (*weak* encryption) or 128 bits (*strong* encryption). Identity information is exchanged by way of certificate swapping. Typically, a browser won't have a certificate, but a Web server *must* have a certificate to negotiate an SSL connection successfully with the browser.

Web server certificates contain a few items of interest; a lot could be said about the format and layout of certificates, but for our purposes we will talk about the three basic pieces of information they contain:

◆ Server's public key

◆ Server's information that is its name, IP address, and contact information

◆ Signature of a CA, or Certificate Authority

The Web server's public key is used during the later stages of SSL negotiation to pass information securely from the browser to the server. This will allow encryption, but not authentication. Imagine what SSL Web browsing would be without authentication. Let's say that you visited one of the world's largest Web retailers: Amazon. In your Web browser's URL space, you enter `https://www.amazon.com`, and you see a Web page that is presumably from Amazon. Since you are employing encryption, you can safely order online and pass your credit card number and physical address information to the Web server, right? Wrong! While you *are* using encryption, and other third parties won't be able to decrypt your information, you have no guarantee that you were in fact communicating with *the* amazon.com. Maybe your local DNS server has been compromised and told you consistently to give out an incorrect IP address when queried about the `www.amazon.com` resource record. Maybe Amazon's own DNS servers have been compromised, and *they* are inadvertently misdirecting Web requests to a Web server that isn't Amazon-operated whatsoever! Not a pretty scenario. The fact that your Web browser is using encryption with *somebody* isn't nearly enough; we also want to be assured that we are communicating with a *known* organization that we can trust. Adding authentication to encryption is the key to the security that SSL provides. This is where Certificate Authorities come into play.

Certificate Authorities

A *Certificate Authority*, or *CA*, certifies that a remote organization is who they claim to be. Essentially, a CA is a trusted third party that verifies the legitimacy of other organizations. For example, popular Certificate Authorities such as Thawte (http://www.thawte.com) and Verisign (http://www.verisign.com) stake their reputations on the certifications they provide. They will verify that a business is registered locally with a specific state or provincial government; that the organization has a bank account and phone number; and that for all practical intents, the organization really exists. When a CA has done its job of verification, it will issue a certificate to be used by the organization's Web server.

Setting up Apache for HTTPS with SSL

There are several items that need to be configured for Apache to make it work with SSL. Fortunately, 95 percent of the work is already finished because Red Hat's configuration is already set up to enable serving secure Web sites. All we need are certificates . . . But wait, they already exist, too! The default certificates are simply self-signed, to be used for SSL server test purposes. Notice the IfDefine that activates the default SSL virtual host in the stock httpd.conf file:

```
<IfDefine HAVE_SSL>
<VirtualHost _default_:443>

SSLEngine on
SSLCertificateFile /etc/httpd/conf/ssl.crt/server.crt
SSLCertificateKeyFile /etc/httpd/conf/ssl.key/server.key

</VirtualHost>

</IfDefine>
```

Those three SSL keywords — SSLEngine, SSLCertificateFile, and SSLCertificate KeyFile — are the basic Apache directives that enable a working SSL Web server. The IfDefine HAVE_SSL will always evaluate to be true if we have the mod_ssl and openssl packages installed. Assuming that you have these two packages, start the Web server and try pointing the Mozilla Web browser on the Web server at https://localhost/. You should see the warning about the certificate, "The certificate was issued by a Certificate Authority that Mozilla does not recognize." Inside of every Web browser capable of SSL there is a list of trusted Certificate Authorities. Clearly, our own local machine is not on the list of trusted CAs. Click on the Continue button to allow the Web browser to accept the certificate temporarily and display the default Web page.

Making CA-signed Certificates

While the testing of SSL Web servers obviates the need for free, self-signed certificates, once we take our Web site to the outside world, we may not want Web clients to see the message, "There is a problem with the certificate that identifies localhost.localdomain. Do you want to continue?" In this case, we will need to create a certificate signing request file (CSR) that Certificate Authorities will require (along with proof of identity and their fee) when giving your organization its certificate. Fortunately, making a CSR isn't complicated:

```
[root@thunderbird certs]# cd /usr/share/ssl/certs
[root@thunderbird certs]# make server.crt
umask 77 ; \
/usr/bin/openssl genrsa -des3 1024 > server.key
Generating RSA private key, 1024 bit long modulus
............++++++
...............++++++
e is 65537 (0x10001)
Enter PEM pass phrase: hello9
Verifying password - Enter PEM pass phrase: hello9
umask 77 ; \
/usr/bin/openssl req -new -key server.key -x509 -days 365 -out
server.crt
Using configuration from /usr/share/ssl/openssl.cnf
Enter PEM pass phrase: hello9
You are about to be asked to enter information that will be
incorporated into your certificate request.  What you are about to
enter is what is called a Distinguished Name or a DN.
There are quite a few fields but you can leave some blank
For some fields there will be a default value,
```

   If you enter ".", the field will be left blank.

```
-----
Country Name (2 letter code) [GB]:US
State or Province Name (full name) [Berkshire]:North Carolina
Locality Name (eg, city) [Newbury]:Raleigh
Organization Name (eg, company) [My Company Ltd]: Not quite Red Hat
Organizational Unit Name (eg, section) []: IS/IT Dept.
Common Name (eg, your name or your server's
hostname)[]:www.example.com
Email Address []: webmaster@example.com
```

   This process just created our server.crt file and the required server.key file. They should look something like this:

```
[root@thunderbird certs]# cat server.crt
-----BEGIN CERTIFICATE-----
MIID2TCCA0KgAwIBAgIBADANBgkqhkiG9w0BAQQFADCBqjELMAkGA1UEBhMCVVMx
FzAVBgNVBAgTDk5vcnRoIENhcm9saW5hMRAwDgYDVQQHEwdSYWx1aWdoMRowGAYD
VQQKExF0b3QgcXVpdGUgUmVkIEhhdDEUMBIGA1UECxMLSVMVvSVQgRGVwdC4xGDAW
BgNVBAMTD3d3dy51eGFtcGxlLmNvbTEKMCIGCSqGSIb3DQEJARYVd2VibWFzdGVy
QGV4YW1wbGUuY29tMB4XDTAyMDgwNjAzMTEwMVoXDTAzMDgwNjAzMTEwMVowgaox
CzAJBgNVBAYTA1VTMRcwFQYDVQQIEw5Ob3J0aCBDYXJvbGluYTEQMA4GA1UEBxMH
UmFsZW1naDEaMBgGA1UEChMRTm90IHF1aXR1IFJ1ZCBIYXQxFDASBgNVBAsTC01T
L01UIER1cHQuMRgwFgYDVQQDEw93d3cuZXhhbXBsZS5jb20xJDAiBgkqhkiG9w0B
CQEWFXd1Ym1hc3R1ckBleGFtcGxlLmNvbTCBnzANBgkqhkiG9w0BAQEFAAOBjQAw
gYkCgYEAtC7R1sm1yb6Kwrq01rf+TO5q4CqnCEACM7c0Wetlv2MXh287kzMKvuzx
TgaB66Bc1GBDAtCzLXXPK+VDfp2MvD80n3i0/pHn1K4i0AsFbhKyuurWQL1T2ktI
YWxSkpUh99mTunXtf4vn77mV6zLGQz54QoL+gIeKnZxAiajTAXkCAwEAAaOCAQsw
ggEHMB0GA1UdDgQWBBRJYCbG+EeaUTq1dN/4KUWZNssBUzCB1wYDVR0jBIHPMIHM
gBRJYCbG+EeaUTq1dN/4KUWZNssBU6GBsKSBrTCBqjELMAkGA1UEBhMCVVMxFzAV
BgNVBAgTDk5vcnRoIENhcm9saW5hMRAwDgYDVQQHEwdSYWx1aWdoMRowGAYDVQQK
ExF0b3QgcXVpdGUgUmVkIEhhdDEUMBIGA1UECxMLSVMvSVQgRGVwdC4xGDAWBgNV
BAMTD3d3dy51eGFtcGxlLmNvbTEKMCIGCSqGSIb3DQEJARYVd2VibWFzdGVyQGV4
YW1wbGUuY29tggEAMAwGA1UdEwQFMAMBAf8wDQYJKoZIhvcNAQEEBQADgYEAhIeq
ddNCEhLD8yI09J1nbuFnA03C/hHB9RJ3E8sXDCABwStfKk82yVImktvo09jFqiaA
wKzXu+7J02u+vJ0e9qAHXopNAsGrovbowf1IMGBecbZb3y6fn/eLuU5ngU5386f1
pFEmvzre0z69C01XvkBqaI1BkESJavmkSdxCwjQ=
-----END CERTIFICATE-----
[root@thunderbird certs]# cat server.crt
-----BEGIN RSA PRIVATE KEY-----
Proc-Type: 4,ENCRYPTED
DEK-Info: DES-EDE3-CBC,CEE0B851D800A797

CHqU4MEcgerrXfj99oHmEN10n5ZEg4s1LIrADdDfgabpiF4GxVgBhsPGAi+itpsV
3aaBeATShmI/tcGOmCJNHoQxoTA+Qocitf89DgiyDthdOA7U35u8wC1Io8fzZKP4
kB1CAGbBW/1DpboAejoM/Tx+9jsTqKpEi6tPYNSR4cx+NCNPjq8FiLOq1FmvCYXC
eWBuyOov9YjzR5MUitZWfBDqewfQU2ZVXkaysC9YkMSYqhaJD7AEYY0PG1EY8jrV
da3Hjgo8BYZgOgbfCMv5aAE5w09Jkfdyo1q4oTTtzpTXarQqr60a0zHE6xkAH1dZ
wyTri9paFcaAwdG7i+Y2aXnKtvxx0/2IY91QxXrfP45eRcg8mjHuLKBAC0eX66kP
agAFA6V9dprpriL05Mdzu6Cvq/YQIo1EyGYs425cQ5zDhyw0k/XK5fcGCPbCOiFK
8S1ZC44UUQzyG8qz9k7H5Y3jS4+STMBzUxKetg8HH/Q24znkb+zc0papvg0TWXuH
rn8xHhJG0AViN4oCtpXr+vZRc4wHXFaOLYeiBi6gc0SsGO4PELfoTBAnkCC1FcwV
512bBYoekugXvksx9tcFtpuyEo7cFVzOy3qEmLJx9tR01ox3sp1jIC6GH+2Td00y
QGWT6j1KiqhUbSm9AmOjpAQYwiy+hUxB8/1K6A/h1anOPbjYt7xWK8SmhVABC7Km
4SIneKMVYhKFvfm0wsyQLtCnBjvA7DtZoKcRyjT2wBg+ke1B/GTUH+M89HIkDQgS
wM60ngw900kA5pDGcMoY+0TwnawbG9/bEeGKVKO8ht0TIodjy2ADmA==
-----END RSA PRIVATE KEY-----
```

Copy the server.key file to /etc/httpd/conf/ssl.key/, and guard it well. It contains the identity of your server! Next, send your server.crt file to a CA. Each CA will have a specific list of requirements, but they will all require a CSR file.

After they create and sign a certificate for you, it will be up to you to copy it to the /etc/httpd/conf/ssl.crt/ directory. If you will be using more than one IP-based SSL virtual host (indeed, you can't use name-based virtual hosts with SSL), take care to name the certificate files such that they won't overwrite each other.

Troubleshooting

You can troubleshoot the Apache server systematically. Apache is a classic client-server system so three things have to happen for it to run correctly: the server must be running and configured correctly, the Web browser client must be working correctly, and both must be able to communicate. Because running a Web browser like Mozilla is trivial, and we discuss general network troubleshooting in other chapters, we'll focus here on making sure that the server works correctly.

The following sections suggest the following areas to investigate if your Web server isn't working correctly:

◆ Inspecting the Linux system logs

◆ Connecting locally

◆ Checking your Apache configuration

◆ Using a simplified httpd.conf, if possible

◆ Adding new directives incrementally

Inspect the Linux system logs

The Linux system logs, controlled by syslogd, can show problems. For instance, syslog announces a problem if you don't configure the VirtualHost container correctly. The following /var/log/message excerpt shows a problem:

```
Jan 20 12:15:54 atlas httpd: [Sun Jan 20 12:15:54 2002] warn NameVirtualHost
192.168.1.13:80 has no VirtualHosts
```

This log indicates a configuration problem that's verified when inspecting the httpd.conf file. In this case, the virtual host container hasn't been associated with a Virtual Host, as shown here:

```
<VirtualHost *>
      ServerName    virtual_1
      ServerAdmin   webmaster@paunchy.net
      DocumentRoot  /var/www/virtual_1
</VirtualHost>
```

In this example, the VirtualHost container tag retains its default configuration. Change the tag to <VirtualHost 192.168.1.254> and you can start the Web server.

Inspect the Apache logs

Apache can log any errors that occur within its system. The following `httpd.conf` directives control error logging:

```
LoadModule config_log_module  modules/mod_log_config.so
LoadModule agent_log_module   modules/mod_log_agent.so
LoadModule referer_log_module modules/mod_log_referer.so
AddModule mod_log_config.c
AddModule mod_log_agent.c
AddModule mod_log_referer.c
ErrorLog logs/error_log
CustomLog logs/access_log combined
LogLevel warn
LogFormat "%h %l %u %t \"%r\" %>s %b \"%{Referer}i\" \"%{User-Agent}i\""
combined
LogFormat "%h %l %u %t \"%r\" %>s %b" common
LogFormat "%{Referer}i -> %U" referer
LogFormat "%{User-agent}i" agent
CustomLog logs/access_log combined
```

The first lines deal with loading and enabling the logging related modules. They're necessary to enable logging on the server. The ErrorLog and CustomLog directives set the location of the logs – they're relative to the ServerRoot, which is `/etc/httpd`. The LogLevel sets the type of error logging and uses the Linux syslog levels – debug, warning, and so on. Finally, you can configure the formatting of the log files with the LogFormat directive.

Try accessing a nonexistent document on the server. For instance, try to load `http://localhost/badfile`. No such file exists in the DocumentRoot, so the server places the following information in the `/etc/httpd/logs/error_log` file (that is a symbolic link that points to `/var/log/httpd/error_log` by default):

```
[Sun ...] [error] [client 127.0.0.1] File does not exist: /var/www/html/badfile
[Sun ...] [error] [client 127.0.0.1] File does not exist:/var/www/html/badfile
```

Connect locally

You want to eliminate as many potential networking problems as you can. If possible, run a browser on the Web server itself to eliminate any network connectivity problems that may be the root cause of your problem. If the local browser works, then your network is most likely the culprit – your firewall may be preventing connections, for example. Consult Chapter 5 for solutions. If you can't run a browser locally, try running one on the same sub-network as the Web server.

Check your Apache configuration

You can make the `httpd.conf` configuration file simple or complex. The default configuration should run automatically. Save a copy of the original configuration — for instance, `cp httpd.conf httpd.conf.orig` — and reinstall the backup copy if you have problems. Work toward your desired configuration after reinstalling the original configuration. (You should definitely mention "httpd –t" here, for syntax and document root checking, which is a wonderful way of finding hidden typos.)

Use a simplified httpd.conf, if possible

Problems often arise from using an unintended configuration. The `httpd.conf` comes pre-configured with many comments and options, but you likely won't use the majority of them. Removing the unused options and comments — clutter, really — makes the configuration file simpler and easier to read, which means that problems are easier to identify.

Add new directives incrementally

Common sense dictates that taking single, logical steps is best when creating new systems, including Web servers. The learning curve is steepest at the beginning, so don't try to create a new system in one big step. Create the simplest system as possible. For instance, create the simple virtual Web server described in the preceding section. Start with the default `index.html` file, and then verify that you can serve the default index file before moving onto more substantial ones.

Summary

This chapter introduces the Apache Web server. Apache is the most widely used Internet Web server, and probably the most used service bar none. The Internet owes much of its popularity to Apache. Apache is highly configurable, open source software that you can use to serve up Web pages from the curious individual to the biggest conglomerate.

This chapter starts by describing the underlying protocols on which Apache is based. The HTML and HTTP protocols form the basis for creating Web pages and delivering the information across networks and the Internet. HTML defines the structure and format of Web pages using the concept of tags and attributes. HTTP is an application layer Internet Protocol that handles the interaction between Web clients (browsers) and Web servers. Together, HTML (it should be noted that there are other Web-based languages, such as SGML, that can substitute for HTML) and HTTP form the underpinnings of the World Wide Web.

Next, the most widely used Apache configuration file was introduced. The configuration file — httpd.conf — controls how the Apache server interacts with its environment and provides its Web services. The httpd.conf file contains directives and blocks that control everything from the number of Apache daemons — httpd — run at any time, to the directory that a Web page is stored in.

The protocol configuration files were followed by some simple configuration examples. An Apache Web page is easy to configure. Apache comes pre-configured to work immediately upon installation. The default Web page is simple but provides a good starting point to construct more useful configurations.

The chapter ends by providing troubleshooting hints. Troubleshooting is a complex task. However, you can fix most Apache Web server problems by following the basic principle of breaking a problem into simple parts. Once you break a problem into its components, you can more easily identify the cause.

Chapter 7

Connecting a Database to the Web Server

IN THIS CHAPTER

- ◆ Introducing Structured Query Language
- ◆ Creating a simple MySQL database server
- ◆ Accessing the MySQL database by using the interactive MySQL client
- ◆ Connecting to the MySQL database by using Perl scripts
- ◆ Securing your MySQL database

THE APACHE WEB SERVER comes ready to run out-of-the box, making it very simple to configure. The /var/www/html/index.html file is the default HTML Web provided by the Apache RPM package. This Web page is a good example of a static Web page.

Static Web pages are capable of providing very useful information. However, many functions require the ability to provide dynamic content to your Web page. You can provide dynamic content in a number of ways, but attaching your Web page to a database is one of the most common and useful methods.

This chapter introduces the concept of Structured Query Language (SQL) databases, a varied and complex field. We'd really need an entire book to cover SQL in any depth, so we're relying heavily on specific examples to introduce the concept of dynamic Web content. The examples in this chapter provide enough information to get a simple, dynamic Web page running. You can then develop and expand on the examples to gain more sophistication.

Introducing SQL

SQL is a system that provides an interface between you and your database, as well as a language that you can use to manipulate and extract information from SQL databases. An SQL system consists of databases, tables, rows, fields, and elements. An entire set of data is called a *database*; each of your system users can have a separate and independent database. Databases contain tables consisting of columns of data types and rows of data. Table 7-1 shows an example database table.

TABLE 7-1 SAMPLE SQL TABLE: MACHINES

Alias	IP	FQDN	ID
atlas	192.168.1.254	atlas.paunchy.net	1
chivas	192.168.1.250	chivas.paunchy.net	2
veracruz	192.168.1.10	veracruz.paunchy.net	3
pachuca	192.168.1.11	pachuca.paunchy.net	4

SQL is based on a *relational database model*, meaning that you can interconnect, or relate, multiple databases and tables. Relational databases allow you to search and correlate data very easily. SQL databases provide the following capabilities, which allow you to provide dynamic Web content to your Web page:

◆ Adding data

◆ Removing data

◆ Modifying data

◆ Searching for data

Many SQL servers are available for Red Hat Linux. Oracle, Postgres, and MySQL are the most popular ones. We choose to use MySQL (pronounced My-S-Q-L) for the following reasons:

◆ **MySQL is free, except for certain commercial uses:** You can't sell MySQL to another party or bundled with another product, nor can you install and maintain it at a client site. Please consult the MySQL Web site at `www.mysql.com/` for more information.

◆ **MySQL supports many programming interfaces:** These interfaces include C, C++, Java, Perl, Python, and PHP.

◆ **MySQL is very fast when relating tables:** MySQL uses the method `one-sweep multijoin` that is very efficient at simultaneously combining the information from multiple tables.

◆ **MySQL enjoys a large user base, which provides troubleshooting and other help:** A large base of pre-compiled programs based on MySQL is also publicly available.

In the following sections, we describe how to configure and use MySQL by creating and manipulating an example MySQL database. We use two different methods to manipulate the database: manual access via MySQL client application, using Perl scripts and integrating PHP directly into the Apache server.

Installing and Configuring MySQL

Red Hat Linux bundles MySQL with its distribution. The process of installing and configuring MySQL, which this section describes, is straightforward.

Red Hat Linux distributions include these four MySQL RPM packages:

♦ Base system

♦ Server

♦ Client

♦ Development

You need to install the base, server, and client packages. Install the packages as follows:

1. Log in as root to your database server and download the mysql packages from Red Hat's anonymous FTP site: ftp.redhat.com:

```
mount /mnt/cdrom
```

2. Install the MySQL database packages as follows:

```
rpm -i /mnt/cdrom/db/mysql*
```

3. Start the MySQL database server like so:

```
/etc/rc.d/init.d/mysqld start
```

The mysql_install_db script initializes the MySQL system the first time that you start it up. This script creates two databases — mysql and test. The script creates six tables (user, db, host, tables_priv, columns_priv, and func) in the MySQL database. These databases and tables are useful for learning about the MySQL database system.

4. You can verify the database's correct installation via several methods. For instance, you can test the database by running the following command:

```
mysqladmin version
```

MySQL should return the following information:

```
mysqladmin  Ver 8.23 Distrib 3.23.52,for pc-linux-gnu on i686
Copyright (C) 2000 MySQL AB & MySQL Finland AB & TCX
DataKonsult AB
This software comes with ABSOLUTELY NO WARRANTY. This is free
software,
```

and you are welcome to modify and redistribute it under the
GPL license

```
Server version         3.23.52
Protocol version       10
Connection             Localhost via UNIX socket
UNIX socket            /var/lib/mysql/mysql.sock
Uptime:                3 sec
```

```
Threads: 1  Questions: 1  Slow queries: 0  Opens: 6  Flush
tables: 1  Open tables: 0 Queries per second avg: 0.333
```

5. You can also test whether the database is running by using the
   mysqladmin ping command, which returns the following message,
   if you are successful:.

   ```
   mysqld is alive
   ```

6. Use the following command to see which databases are available:

   ```
   mysqlshow
   ```

   This command returns a list of the two databases created by the
   `mysql_install_db` script:

   ```
   +-----------+
   | Databases |
   +-----------+
   | mysql     |
   | test      |
   +-----------+
   ```

7. Show the tables in the MySQL database by entering the following
   command:

   ```
   mysqlshow mysql
   ```

   This variation of the `mysqlshow` command displays the following.

   ```
   Database: mysql
   +--------------+
   |    Tables    |
   +--------------+
   | columns_priv |
   | db           |
   | func         |
   | host         |
   | tables_priv  |
   | user         |
   +--------------+
   ```

TIP Installing the `mysql-server` RPM package creates the directory */var/lib/ mysql/mysql* where the database and tables are stored. The package also creates the `mysql` user account.

Accessing the SQL Server

Once the database server is running you can use the MySQL client to execute SQL commands, create databases and tables, manipulate data within the databases, and access and search for data. Start the MySQL client program by entering the following command:

```
mysql
```

The MySQL client starts and you are presented with the MySQL prompt as shown below.

```
Welcome to the MySQL monitor.  Commands end with ; or \g.

Your MySQL connection id is 9 to server version: 3.23.52


Type 'help;' or '\h' for help. Type '\c' to clear the buffer.

mysql>
```

You're now ready to start laying your database's framework. Be sure to use a password with the database. For simplicity's sake, we're not dealing with passwords for the time being, but we show you how to use the MySQL client to access specific users, with passwords, later in this chapter in the section, "Securing Your MySQL Database."

Creating a database

We're going to create a sample database called `inventory`, which we'll use to store information about the machines that comprise our network. Follow these steps to do so:

1. Create the new database called `inventory` like so:

   ```
   create database inventory;
   ```

   The SQL command returns the following information, which verifies that the command has been executed:

   ```
   Query OK, 1 row affected (0.02 sec)
   ```

2. Display the databases to which the server can connect as shown here:

```
show databases;
```

If this database is the first you've created, the following text appears:

```
+-----------+
| Database  |
+------------------+
| mysql     |
| inventory |
| test  |
+-----------+
3 rows in set (0.00 sec)
```

3. Now you can create the tables used to store data about your machines. Start by telling the MySQL server to use the inventory database as shown here:

```
use inventory
```

4. Next, create the table like so:

```
create table machines (
   alias char(12) NOT NULL,
   ip  char(20),
   fqdn char(20),
   owner char(40),
   misc char(80),
   ostype int,
   id int auto_increment primary key);
```

5. Exit the MySQL client application by typing the following:

```
quit
```

You've created a table within the inventory database. The following list describes each of the elements that you just created in more detail:

- ◆ create table machines tells the SQL server you're trying to create a table called machines. You must include each element within the table between an open and close parenthesis (and). Therefore the first SQL command (create) must contain an open parenthesis.

- ◆ alias CHAR(12) NOT NULL, creates a column named alias that can contain up to 12 ASCII characters. This column defines each machine's alias, or nickname (chivas, for instance). We choose to force you to always fill this field with a value so that we can use it as a reference. The NOT NULL parameter specifies that this column can never be blank.

◆ `ip CHAR(16),` creates a column called `ip`. This column defines each machine's IP address.

◆ `fqdn CHAR(20),` creates a column called `fqdn`. FQDN is the machine's Fully Qualified Name; it contains the alias and domain name. The FQDN of `chivas` in the `paunchy.net` domain is `chivas.paunchy.net`.

◆ `own CHAR(40),` defines machine owner's name, which is 40 characters long. The value of 40 is arbitrary and is chosen because it will allow long names to be specified.

◆ `misc CHAR(80),` creates a column for general information about the machine. You can include information like a short description of the machine's purpose, location, or anything you want.

◆ `ostype INT,` describes the machine's platform type. For instance, 1 is Red Hat Linux, 2 is Solaris, and 666 is Windows. This simple integer is the first non-alphanumeric column included in our database.

◆ `id INT AUTO_INCREMENT PRIMARY KEY);` uses an integer field used to identify each record in the table. The primary key parameter specifies that the contents of this column determine the data's order. Lower numbers occur before higher ones.

You can enter and manipulate data now that you've created the database. Continuing to use the MySQL client, the following section describes how to enter data manually into the `inventory` MySQL database.

Using the MySQL database

We continue to use the `mysql` client to access and manually manipulate the inventory database we created in the preceding section. We use SQL commands to add data to the `machines` table. The following instructions show how to start the MySQL database, load the table and then enter the data.

1. Re-enter the MySQL client as follows:

   `mysql`

2. Connect to the inventory database like so:

   `use inventory;`

3. Examine the contents of the machines table as follows:

   `describe machines;`

The contents of the machines table should display as shown here:

```
+---------+----------+------+-----+---------+----------------
+
| Field   | Type     | Null | Key | Default | Extra
|
+---------+----------+------+-----+---------+----------------
+
| alias   | char(12) |      |     |         |
|
| ip      | char(16) | YES  |     | NULL    |
|
| fqdn    | char(20) | YES  |     | NULL    |
|
| owner   | char(40) | YES  |     | NULL    |
|
| misc    | char(80) | YES  |     | NULL    |
|
| ostype  | int(11)  |      |     | NULL    |
|
| id      | int(11)  |      | PRI | NULL    | auto_increment
|
+---------+----------+------+-----+---------+----------------
+
7 rows in set (0.02 sec)
```

4. Insert a row of data into the database. The following example enters one of the machines we have used throughout this book:

```
insert into machines (alias, ip, fqdn, owner, misc, ostype,
id)  values ("chivas", "192.168.1.250",
"chivas.paunchy.net","Dell 410 dual processor w/ 1GB RAM", 1,
12);
```

Note that character fields must be in quotes.

5. Show the data by running the following command:

```
select * from machines
```

6. Enter the exit command when you finish using the MySQL client.

```
exit
```

The MySQL client, or any other SQL database client, is useful for learning the SQL language and for performing quick tasks. However, SQL's real power appears when you automate the process of modifying and accessing databases. The following section introduces the concept of using a programming language (Perl, in this case) to access and modify a SQL database.

Interacting with the SQL Server by Using Scripts

The Data Base Interface (DBI) module separates the SQL database from the language that accesses it. DBI works in the abstraction layer; the abstraction layer is also referred to as *middleware*. Figure 7-1 shows how DBI deals directly with the database engine. The user-defined program passes all of its SQL requests to the DBI module. By placing an abstraction layer between the database and accessing programs, the programmer doesn't have to deal with the database's details, increasing his or her ability to write transportable programs and decreasing the difficulty of migrating to a different database.

 DBI is bundled with Red Hat Linux. You can obtain more information and also download DBI, written by Dan Bunce, from `http://cpan.perl.org/`.

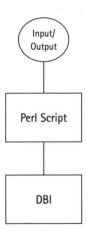

Figure 7-1:
The DBI module
abstraction layer

Displaying MySQL database data

We modified the following Perl scripts, which were written by Mohammed Kabir. They access and modify the MySQL `inventory` database that we introduced in the previous section. The following instructions tell you how to install the DBI modules and use the scripts:

1. Log in as `root` on the database server and download the packages from Red Hat's anonymous FTP site, `ftp.redhat.com`:

```
mount /mnt/cdrom
```

2. Install the DBI packages like so:

```
rpm -ivh /mnt/cdrom/db/perl-DBD*
rpm -ivh /mnt/cdrom/db/perl-DBI*
```

3. Run the script `list_ip.pl` to show the data that you entered into the machine's table in the inventory database as follows:

```
/mnt/cdrom/db/list_ip.pl
```

We described an example for entering data in the previous section. You can find the script, shown in Listing 7-1, on the companion CD-ROM.

Listing 7–1: The list_ip.pl script

```perl
#!/usr/bin/perl
# Command line script to list ips from SQL database

use DBI;

# Definitions - You will need to change these
my $db = "inventory";
my $table = "machines";
my $user = "root";
my $password = "iamnotanumber";

# End of definitions

# Tell the script that we will be using
# a MySQL database
my $drh = DBI->install_driver( 'mysql' );

# Establish a connection with the database
my $dbh = $drh->connect($db, $user);

# A simple check to see if we connected
die "Cannot connect: $DBI::errstr\n" unless $dbh;

# Get input from user
print "IP address: ";
my $ip= <STDIN>;
chomp($ip);
```

```
print "\n";

# Build and execute the SQL statement
my $SQLstatement = "select alias, ip, fqdn, ostype from $table where
ip=\"$ip\"";
my $sth = $dbh->prepare($SQLstatement);
my $howmany = $sth->execute;

die "Couldn't match $name in database\n" if $howmany eq "0E0";

print "$howmany matches found in database\n\n";
printf ("%18.12s %20.15s %24.20s    %s \n",
         "ALIAS", "IP", "FQDN", "OSTYPE");

# loop through all the matches and print them
for (my $i = 0; $i < $howmany; $i++) {
    my ($SQLalias, $SQLip, $SQLfqdn, $SQLostype) =
        $sth->fetchrow_array;
    printf ("%17.14s %20.16s %30.20s    %2d \n",
            $SQLalias, $SQLip, $SQLfqdn, $SQLostype);

}

my $dbh = $dbh->disconnect();
```

> This program prompts you to enter an IP address. After you enter the IP, the program searches the machine table in the `inventory` database by using the following SQL statement:
>
> ```
> select alias, ip, fqdn, ostype from $table where ip =
> \"$ip\"";.
> ```
>
> Note that the matching criteria `where ip =` requires an exact match to occur.

4. The `$ip` variable holds the name you enter at the command prompt. For example, running the script in Step 3 should produce the following result (assuming that you entered the data described in the previous section):

   ```
   IP: 192.168.1.250
   ```

   Running the script shows the following output:

   ```
   1 matches found in database

   ALIAS       IP             FQDN                OSTYPE
   Atlas       192.168.1.254  atlas.paunchy.net   1
   ```

The script modifies the list_ip.pl script to match partial IP addresses instead of exact ones. The script is modified to use an SQL statement that makes use of the like options instead of the is search criteria. The important line in the script is:

```
$SQLstatement = "select alias, ip, fqdn, ostype from $table where ip
like \"%$ip%\"";
```

Listing 7-2 shows the list_fqdn.pl script.

Listing 7-2: The list_ip_partial.pl file

```perl
#!/usr/bin/perl

# ---> list_ip_partial.pl <---
# Command line script to select from SQL database
# Revised to match substrings

use DBI;

# Definitions - You need to change these if you use a different db
$db = "inventory";
$table = "machines";
$user = "root";
$password = "iamnotanumber";

# End of definitions

# Tell the script that we will be using
# a MySQL database
$drh = DBI->install_driver( 'mysql' );

# Establish a connection with the database
$dbh = $drh->connect($db, $user);

# A simple check to see if we connected
die "Cannot connect: $DBI::errstr\n" unless $dbh;

# Get input from user
print "IP: ";
$ip= <STDIN>;
chomp($ip);
print "\n";

# Build and execute the SQL statement
```

```
$SQLstatement = "select alias, ip, fqdn, ostype from $table where ip
like \"%$ip%\"";
$sth = $dbh->prepare($SQLstatement);
$howmany = $sth->execute;

die "Couldn't match $name in database\n" if $howmany eq "0E0";

print "$howmany matches found in database\n\n";
printf ("%17.14s %20.16s %30.20s    %s \n",
        "ALIAS", "IP", "FQDN", "OSTYPE");

# loop through all the matches and print them
for ($i = 0; $i < $howmany; $i++) {
    ($SQLalias, $SQLip, $SQLfqdn, $SQLostype) =
        $sth->fetchrow_array;
    printf ("%17.14s %20.16s %30.20s    %2d \n",
            $SQLalias, $SQLip, $SQLfqdn, $SQLostype);


    }
```

At this point, you're prompted to enter an IP address just like before. However, entering a partial address, such as the following, results in success:

```
IP: 192.168.1

4 matches found in database
ALIAS     IP               FQDN                  OSTYPE
atlas     192.168.1.254    atlas.paunchy.net     1
chivas    192.168.1.250    chivas.paunchy.net    1
veracruz  192.168.1.10     veracruz.paunchy.net  1
pumas     192.168.1.11     tigres.paunchy.net    1
```

One feature of the new script is that if you enter a null value, then every record in the database is displayed.

Inserting data into a MySQL database

The new SQL command that takes care of inserting data is shown here:

```
insert into $table (alias,ip, fqdn, owner, misc, ostype) values
(\"$alias\", \"$ip\", \"$fqdn\", \"$owner\", \"$misc\", \"$ostype\")
```

The script shown in Listing 7-3 is designed to enter data into the database.

Listing 7-3: The insert_ip.pl script

```perl
#!/usr/bin/perl

# ---> insert_machine.pl <---
# Command line script to insert records into the SQL database

use DBI;

# Definitions - You need to change these if you use different db
$db = "inventory";
$table = "machines";
$user = "root";
$password = "iamnotanumber";

# End of definitions

# Tell the script that we will be using
# a MySQL database
$drh = DBI->install_driver( 'mysql' );

# Establish a connection with the database
$dbh = $drh->connect($db, $user);

# A simple check to see if we connected
die "Cannot connect: $DBI::errstr\n" unless $dbh;

# Get input from user
print "Alias: ";
$alias = <STDIN>;
chomp($alias);
print "\n";

print "IP: ";
$ip= <STDIN>;
chomp($ip);
print "\n";

print "FQDN: ";
$fqdn= <STDIN>;
chomp($fqdn);
print "\n";

print "Owner: ";
$owner= <STDIN>;
chomp($owner);
```

```
print "\n";

print "Misc: ";
$misc= <STDIN>;
chomp($misc);
print "\n";

print "OS type: ";
$ostype= <STDIN>;
chomp($ostype);
print "\n";

# Build and do the SQL statement
$SQLstatement = "insert into $table (id, alias, ip, fqdn, owner,
          misc, ostype)
   values (\"0\", \"$alias\", \"$ip\", \"$fqdn\", \"$owner\",
            \"$misc\", \"$ostype\" )";
$sth = $dbh->do($SQLstatement);
```

The following instructions describe how to use the insert_ip.pl script.

1. Run the script as follows:

   ```
   /mnt/cdrom/db/insert_ip.pl
   ```

2. You're prompted to enter data, as shown in the next example; this
   sequence inserts a record into the machine's table:

   ```
   Alias: cementeros

   IP: 192.168.1.100

   FQDN: cementeros.paunchy.net

   Owner: Me

   Misc:  Windows box

   OS Type: 2
   ```

The insert_ip.pl script makes entering records into a database a simple process.
The following section shows how to devise a script to modify existing records.

Modifying MySQL database data

Use the following script to modify data that already exists in a database. The SQL
command that performs the modification is shown here:

```
$updatestatement = "update $table set alias = \"$SQLalias\",
                        ip = \"$SQLip\",
                        fqdn =\"$SQLfqdn\",
                        owner = \"$SQLowner\",
                        misc = \"$SQLmisc\",
                        ostype = \"$SQLostype\"
                where id = $SQLid";
```

This script prompts for a modification of the record's alias. You enter the alias,
and the script finds all the rows that match. You are then prompted to enter the new
information that will replace the old. The script is shown in listing 7-4 below.

Listing 7-4: The modify_machine.pl file

```perl
#!/usr/bin/perl

# ---> modify_machine.pl <---
# Command line script to modify the SQL database

use DBI;

#Definitions - You need to change these if you use a diff db
$db = "inventory";
$table = "machines";
$user = "root";
$password = "iamnotanumber";

# End of definitions

# Tell the script that we will be using
# a MySQL database
$drh = DBI->install_driver( 'mysql' );

# Establish a connection with the database
$dbh = $drh->connect($db, $user);

# A simple check to see if we connected
die "Cannot connect: $DBI::errstr\n" unless $dbh;

# Get input from user
print "Alias: ";
$alias = <STDIN>;
chomp($alias);
print "\n";

# Build and execute the SQL statement
```

```
$SQLstatement = "select id, alias, ip, fqdn, owner, misc, ostype
   from $table where alias like \"$alias\"";
$sth = $dbh->prepare($SQLstatement);
$howmany = $sth->execute;

die "Couldn't match $alias in database\n" if $howmany eq "OEO";
print "$howmany matches found in database\n\n";

#Define local variables
($i, $input, $SQLalias, $SQLip, $SQLfqdn, $SQLowner,
        $SQLmisc, $SQLostype);

# loop through all the matching rows,
# ask user for new data, then update
#  the row to reflect the changes made
for ($i = 0; $i < $howmany; $i++ ) {

  ($SQLid, $SQLalias, $SQLip, $SQLfqdn, $SQLowner, $SQLmisc,
        $SQLostype)= $sth->fetchrow_array;

  printf("%17.15s %20.15s %12.10 %20.20 %12.10 %4.1 \n",
        "ALIAS", "IP address", "FQDN", "OWNER", "MISC", "OStype");

  printf("%17.15s %20.15s %12.10 %20.20 %12.10 %4.1 \n",
        $SQLalias, $SQLip, $SQLfqdn, $SQLowner, $SQLmisc,
        $SQLostype);

  printf "Alias [$SQLalias]: ";
  $input = <STDIN>;
  chomp($input);
  $SQLalias = $input || $SQLalias;

  printf "IP [$SQLip]: ";
  $input = <STDIN>;
  chomp($input);
  $SQLip = $input || $SQLip;

  printf "FQDN name [$SQLfqdn]: ";
  $input = <STDIN>;
  chomp($input);
  $SQLfqdn = $input || $SQLfqdn;

  printf "Owner [$SQLowner]: ";
  $input = <STDIN>;
```

Continued

Listing 7-4 *(Continued)*

```
    chomp($input);
    $SQLowner = $input || $SQLowner;

    printf "Misc [$SQLmisc]: ";
    $input = <STDIN>;
    chomp($input);
    $SQLmisc = $input || $SQLmisc;

    printf "ostype [$SQLostype]: ";
    $input = <STDIN>;
    chomp($input);
    $SQLostype = $input || $SQLostype;

    $updatestatement = "update $table set alias = \"$SQLalias\",
                                ip = \"$SQLip\",
                                fqdn =\"$SQLfqdn\",
                                owner = \"$SQLowner\",
                                misc = \"$SQLmisc\",
                                ostype = \"$SQLostype\"
                                where id = $SQLid";

    $dbh->do($updatestatement);
}
```

The following instructions describe how to use the modify_machine.pl script.

1. Run the script as follows:

   /mnt/cdrom/db/modify_machine.pl

2. Enter the alias as shown here:

   Name: atlas

3. The script returns any matches like so:

   ```
   1 matches found in database
       ALIAS       IP              FQDN                OSTYPE
       atlas       192.168.1.254   atlas.paunchy.net 1
   ```

4. Enter the new information and the script replaces the existing record.

The modify_machine.pl script simplifies the task of modifying database records. Using a script is vastly easier than entering SQL commands. The next section describes how to make life even easier by accessing scripts through a browser.

Using a CGI script to access a SQL database via a Web browser

The previous Perl scripts demonstrate SQL's power. The next advance requires that you adapt these scripts to work with your Apache Web server. This section shows you how to modify the Perl scripts to work as a CGI script.

Listing 7-5 shows a CGI script that provides the same functionality of the previous scripts. Install the script in Apache's `cgi-bin` directory, and you can access the database from your browser. The script presents an HTML form that allows you to search for machines based on any field. Note that we use the Common Gateway Interface (CGI) module (`CGI.pm`) to interact with the Apache server. The CGI modules provide some of the common functions necessary for working with the Web server.

TIP You can find information about CGI.pm, which is written by Lincoln Stein, at `http://cpan.perl.org/`.

Listing 7-5: list_ip.cgi

```perl
#!/usr/bin/perl

# ---> select.cgi <---
# CGI to select data from a SQL database
use CGI;
use DBI;
$q = new CGI;

# Definitions - You need to change these if you use a different name
$db = "inventory";
$table = "machines";
$user = "root";
$password = "iamnotanumber";
# End of definitions

# This is the main branch.  The first time through
# display the form to the user, when the user submits
# the form then we process the input
if ($q->param('field') eq "") {&printform()} else {&results()}

sub printform {

  print $q->header;
```

Continued

Listing 7-5 *(Continued)*

```
    print $q->start_html(-title=>'Network Machines Database',
                         -BGCOLOR=>'black',
                         -TEXT=>'white');
    print "<CENTER><H1>Network Machines Database</H1></CENTER><HR>";
    print $q->startform;
    print "Find all machines whose ";
    print $q->popup_menu(-name    => field,
                         -values  => [("alias", "ip",
                                          "fqdn", "ostype")],
                         -default => "alias");
    print $q->popup_menu(-name    => searchtype,
                         -values  => [("is", "contains")],
                         -default => "is");
    print $q->textfield(-name => text,
                        -size => 16), "<BR>";
    print $q->submit;
    print $q->endform;
    print $q->end_html;
}

sub results {

    $field = $q->param('field');
    $searchtype = $q->param('searchtype');
    $text = $q->param('text');
    @table=();
    print $q->header;
    print $q->start_html(-title=>'Database Results',
    -BGCOLOR=>'black',
    -TEXT=>'white');

    # Tell the script that we will be using
    # a MySQL database
     $drh = DBI->install_driver( 'mysql' );

    # Establish a connection with the database
    $dbh = $drh->connect($db, $user);

    # A simple check to see if we connected
    if (!$dbh) {
       print "Cannot connect: $DBI::errstr<BR>";
       print $q->end_html;
       die;
```

```
   }

   # Build and execute the SQL statement
   ($SQLstatement);
   if ($searchtype eq "contains") {
      $SQLstatement = "select alias, ip, fqdn, ostype from $table
                       where $field like \"%$text%\"";
   } else {
      $SQLstatement = "select alias, ip, fqdn, ostype from $table
                       where $field = \"$text\"";
   }
   my $sth = $dbh->prepare($SQLstatement);
   my $howmany = $sth->execute;

   # Display an error message if we can't find
   # any matches
   if ($howmany eq "0E0") {
      print$q->h3("<font color=red>Couldn't match $text in
         "."database</font>");
      die;
   }

   print "$howmany matches found in database<br><br>";
   push (@table,$q->th(["Alias", "IP", "FQDN", "OStype"]));

   # loop through all the matches and store
   # them in @table
   for (my $i = 0; $i < $howmany; $i++) {
       my ($SQLalias, $SQLip, $SQLfqdn, $SQLostype) =
          $sth->fetchrow_array;
      push (@table,$q->td([$SQLalias, $SQLip,
                          $SQLfqdn, $SQLostype]));

   }

   # print the table of data we got from the
   # SQL database
   print $q->table({-border => 1, -align => center},$q->Tr(\@table));
   print $q->end_html;
}
```

Figure 7-2 shows the HTML form in a Web browser.

Enter the search criteria into the HTML form. The CGI script retrieves the data from the MySQL database and formats before displaying on your browser. Figure 7-3 shows an example of the resulting output page.

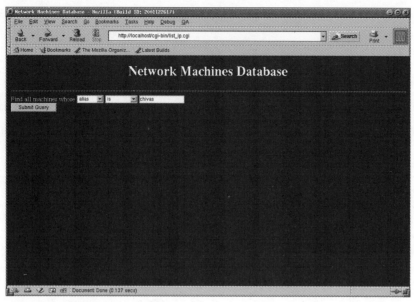

Figure 7-2: The HTML form screen

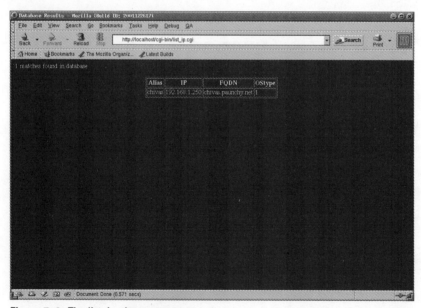

Figure 7-3: The list_ip.pl output screen

CGI scripts can perform the same functions we described in the previous section, such as inserting, updating, and deleting records from the database. Listing 7-6 shows the cmdline.insert.pl script modified to work as a cgi-bin script.

Listing 7-6: The insert.cgi file

```perl
#!/usr/bin/perl

# ---> insert.cgi <---
# CGI to insert data into the SQL database
use CGI;
use DBI;
$q = new CGI;

# Definitions - You need to change these if you use a different db
$db = "inventory";
$table = "machines";
$user = "root";
$password = "iamnotanumber";
# End of definitions

# This is the main branch.  The first time through
# display the form to the user, when the user submits
# the form then we process the input
#if ($q->param('field') eq "") {&printform()} else {&results()}
&printform();

sub printform {

  print $q->header;
  print $q->start_html(-title=>'Network Machines Database',
                       -BGCOLOR=>'black',
                       -TEXT=>'white');
  print "<CENTER><H1>Network Machines Database</H1></CENTER><HR>";
  print $q->startform;
  print "Alias: ", $q->textfield(-name => alias,
                                 -size => 16), "<BR>";
  print "IP address : ", $q->textfield(-name => ip
                                 -size => 16), "<BR>";
  print "FQDN name: ", $q->textfield(-name => fqdn,
                                 -size => 16), "<BR>";
  print "Owner: ", $q->textfield(-name => owner,
                                 -size => 16), "<BR>";
  print "Misc: ", $q->textfield(-name => misc,
                                 -size => 16), "<BR>";
  print "OS type: ", $q->textfield(-name => ostype,
                                 -size => 16), "<BR>";
  print $q->submit;
  print $q->endform;
```

Continued

Listing 7-6 *(Continued)*

```
  print $q->end_html;
}

sub results {

  ($alias, $ip, $fqdn, $owner, $misc, $ostype);

  $alias = $q->param('alias');
  $ip = $q->param('ip');
  $fqdn = $q->param('fqdn');
  $owner = $q->param('owner');
  $misc = $q->param('misc');
  $ostype = $q->param('ostype');

  print $q->header;
  print $q->start_html(-title=>'Database Results',
  -BGCOLOR=>'black',
  -TEXT=>'white');

  # Tell the script that we will be using
  # a MySQL database
  ($drh, $dbh);
  $drh = DBI->install_driver( 'mysql' );

  # Establish a connection with the database
  #   $dbh = $drh->connect($db, $user);

  # A simple check to see if we connected
  if (!$dbh) {
     print "Cannot connect: $DBI::errstr<BR>";
     print $q->end_html;
     die;
  }

  # Build and execute the SQL statement
  $SQLstatement = "insert into $table
(alias,ip,fqdn,owner,misc,ostype)
                       values (\"$alias\",\"$ip\",\"$fqdn\",\"$owner\"
                               \"$misc\",\"$ostype\"";
  dbh->do($SQLstatement);

#   print "$name added to database<br><br>";
#   print $q->end_html;
}
```

We started this chapter by demonstrating how to interface directly with the MySQL database by using SQL commands. We then devised several Perl scripts to ease the task of working with MySQL. Finally, we showed how to use a Web browser to interface with MySQL by using CGI and the Perl scripts. Using CGI and Perl insulates the user from the underlying system.

These Perl scripts provide an improvement over using the manual MySQL client. However, as a general-purpose language, Perl is necessarily more complex than is absolutely necessary. Other languages are designed specifically to work with SQL databases. The next section describes one such language.

Securing Your MySQL Database

We deliberately neglected to secure the example MySQL databases with passwords after the installation in order to simplify the process. Now we'll describe the process of assigning passwords to the database server:

1. Log in as `root`.

2. Configure the database access privileges like so:

   ```
   mysql -u root mysql
   ```

3. Set the root password from the `mysql>` prompt as shown here, replacing the string `iamnotanumber` with your own password:

   ```
   mysql> SET PASSWD FOR root=PASSWORD('iamnotanumber');
   ```

4. The MySQL RPM package manager creates the MySQL user account during the installation process. Create a password for the MySQL user in addition to the root user as follows:

   ```
   mysql> SET PASSWD FOR mysql=PASSWORD('iamanumber');
   ```

5. Locate the following line in each script:

   ```
   $dbh = $drh->connect($db, $user);
   ```

   Change that line to following so that a password is used:

   ```
   $dbh = $drh->connect($db, $user, $password);
   ```

6. You'll need to enter the MySQL user password whenever you try to access the database server. Use the following command to tell the server which user you are and what server you want to access:

   ```
   mysql -u mysql -h localhost
   ```

7. You're prompted to enter the password.

8. By default, the password for the server's administrative account (root) isn't set, so use the following command to set the password:

```
mysqladmin _u root password iamnotanumber
```

You have now added a password to the database. Anyone who wants to access the database as root must authenticate. Authentication greatly improves the security of your database.

Summary

This chapter introduced SQL, a powerful database language that becomes much more effective and useful when used in conjunction with Perl and CGI scripts. In this chapter, we also described how to install and configure the powerful MySQL, a very popular SQL server for Linux. You learned to create simple databases containing simple tables. Finally, you learned to access the data in the databases by using various methods, such as the command line or via CGI scripts.

Chapter 8

Building a Simple Audio Streaming Server

THE TRADITIONAL LINUX SERVER PROVIDES functions such as Web pages, e-mail, DNS, and file sharing services. However, there is a world beyond those bread-and-butter services. One of the most popular and important new services is streaming multimedia. Needless to say, you can use your Red Hat Linux server to create your own Internet radio, video, or information station.

Multimedia data transmission, or *streams*, is one of the truly interesting and useful technologies to become widely used on the Internet. This technology provides the Internet-transmission medium for audio, video, and other types of data. You can listen and/or view both live and prerecorded information via streaming-data technology.

As an introduction to this technology, this chapter describes how to install, configure, and run Icecast, which is an Open Source audio stream server. Icecast works with both the Open Source Ogg-Vorbis and closed MP3 formats (although you must use different versions of Icecast for each format). After completing the installation and configuration, you should be able to serve basic media streams.

Introducing Streaming Technology

Most people are familiar with multimedia streaming technology from a user's perspective. Starting a client such as XMMS and connecting to an MP3 stream is familiar to many. Several components are necessary to create a streaming client-server system that makes it possible to connect to such a stream. The following components compose a streaming client-server system:

◆ **Multimedia client:** XMMS is an example of a client that connects to a streaming server. For example, when you connect to an Icecast server with XMMS, it plays the audio stream for you.

◆ **Multimedia-streaming server such as Icecast:** Icecast is an application that acts as an interface between a media source (also called an encoder or streamer) and clients accessing the source. Icecast receives a stream from a source. Icecast then accepts network connections from clients and sends those clients a stream that comes from the source.

◆ **Source:** Sources get their content from either fixed or dynamic sources. Fixed sources typically come from prerecorded audio or video files. Dynamic sources come from sources such as microphones. Ices is one application that reads information from a source such as an Ogg Vorbis or MP3 encoded music file. It then feeds that information to Icecast. The stream source acts as a front end to the streaming server.

This chapter describes how to install and configure an audio streaming Icecast server and Ices source. The audio client XMMS is used to listen to the Icecast server.

Introducing the Xiph.org Foundation

The Xiph.org Foundation — www.xiph.org — is a nonprofit corporation devoted to developing open source systems. Xiph.org is currently developing several projects. Two of the projects — Icecast and Ogg — are oriented toward streaming multimedia and signal processing. The Ogg project — www.xiph.org/ogg/index.html — is Xiph.org's primary project and itself comprises three subprojects: Ogg Vorbis, Ogg Theora (a video encoding project), and Ogg Tarkin; Ogg Vorbis is the subproject we're interested in and is devoted to developing an audio compression format and encoding technique. Icecast is devoted to developing an audio broadcast system.

 Xiph is short for Xiphophorus helleri, a small Swordtail fish popular to small aquariums. Ogg Vorbis is a science-fiction character. (Icecast is a variation on the name Shoutcast.) There's no particular connection between the fish or sci-fi character and the xiph.org foundation, other than the developers like them.

Ogg Vorbis consists of two complimentary systems. Ogg is the audio compression format, and Vorbis is the encoding system. Ogg is equivalent to MP3 but has the advantage of being developed more recently and, thus, taking advantage of newer and better techniques. Ogg produces smaller audio files than MP3 does. Both Ogg and MP3 strip information from the audio content, but Ogg claims to produce higher-fidelity files — equivalent to MP4.

The most popular streaming technology used today is proprietary and closed source. For instance, RealNetworks, Inc.'s RealAudio and Microsoft's formats provide most of the streaming content currently available on the Internet. MP3 is another widely used proprietary protocol.

Regardless of fidelity issues, Ogg Vorbis was written from scratch in order to completely exclude any patented or proprietary techniques or software and is licensed under the GNU General Public License (GPL). Ogg Vorbis is Open Source, thus a completely open protocol. Even though MP3 currently owns more market share, Ogg Vorbis's higher fidelity and open nature will prove to be attractive to many artists and organizations.

Popular Open Source media players such as XMMS are Ogg compatible. Windows-based players such as WinAmp, FreeAmp, and Sonique, as well as the MacOS Unsanity Echo, also play Ogg. Ogg is compatible with enough client applications to make it a viable alternative to other formats.

Icecast — www.icecast.org — is an Open Source audio streaming server. It is designed to broadcast Mpeg (for instance, MP3) and Ogg Vorbis streams.

Xiph.org's other two projects are Paranoia IV and MGM. Paranoia IV consists of the familiar cdparanoia, an audio ripping program; Red Hat Linux bundles cdparanoia with its distribution. MGM consists of several utilitarian applications that are not applicable to this chapter.

Serving MP3 Streams with Icecast Version 1

Icecast streams protocols such as Mpeg Layer III (MP3) and Ogg Vorbis over a network. Icecast is designed to provide an Open Source alternative to Nullsoft's — www.nullsoft.com — commercial Shoutcast system. Icecast is generally Shoutcast compatible.

Three of the most popular applications used to provide audio content to Icecast are: Ices, Shout, and Liveice. Shout is usable but outdated. Liveice is the most flexible of the three but more difficult to use. Ices is easy to use and is currently being developed on an ongoing basis.

Red Hat doesn't bundle Icecast in their distribution. However, a copy is provided at http://www.wiley.com/compbooks/sery (and also www.xiph.org) where you can download Icecast, Ices, Shout, and Liveice. You also must compile and install the packages once you obtain the source code.

Introducing MP3 MIME Types

The following table outlines the MP3-oriented MIME types.

MIME Type	File Suffix	Description
audio/x-scpls	pls	shoutcast.com MP3 streams
audio/mpegurl	3u	icecast.org MP3 streams
audio/x-mpegurl	m3u	mp3.com for their MP3 streams
audio/mpeg	mp3	Generic
audio/x-mpeg	mp3	Generic
audio/mp3	mp3	Generic
audio/x-mp3	mp3	Generic

Installing and configuring Icecast

As of this writing, Icecast does not come prepackaged in RPM form. You need to perform the following tasks to get Icecast up and running:

- Unpack the Icecast tarball.
- Configure the Makefile.
- Compile and install the binaries.
- Slightly modify the Icecast configuration file.
- Manually start the server (you'll configure the system to run as a daemon later on).

The following instructions outline how to compile and install Icecast.

1. Create a directory to work from. For instance, many people install software in the /usr/local directory.

   ```
   mkdir /usr/local/icecast
   cd /usr/local/icecast
   ```

2. Unpack the source code from the copy of Icecast that we provide on our Web site.

   ```
   tar xzf /mnt/cdrom/xiph/icecast*
   ```

   You can download the most recent Icecast version from www.icecast.org/download.html.

3. Go into the newly created directory and configure the Makefile.

```
cd icecast-1.3.12
./configure
```

4. Run make.

```
make
```

5. Install the newly compiled programs.

```
make install
```

6. Rename the following files in the `/usr/local/icecast/conf` directory.

```
mv mounts.aut.dist mounts.aut
mv users.aut.dist users.aut
mv groups.aut.dist groups.aut
mv icecast.conf.dist icecast.conf
```

7. Modify the following parameters in the `icecast.conf` file.

```
Server  atlas.paunchy.net
```

Use the name of your server in place of the preceding example.

8. Start your Icecast server.

```
/usr/local/icecast/bin/icecast
```

You should see the following output.

```
OneIcecast Version 1.3.12 Initializing...
Icecast comes with NO WARRANTY, to the extent permitted by
law.
You may redistribute copies of Icecast under the terms of the
GNU General Public License.
For more information about these matters, see the file named
COPYING.
Starting thread engine...
[07/Sep/2002:16:44:01] Icecast Version 1.3.12 Starting..
[07/Sep/2002:16:44:01] Starting Admin Console Thread...
-> [07/Sep/2002:16:44:01] Starting main connection handler...
-> [07/Sep/2002:16:44:01] Listening on port 8000...
-> [07/Sep/2002:16:44:01] Listening on port 8001...
-> [07/Sep/2002:16:44:01] Using 'atlas.paunchy.net' as
servername...
-> [07/Sep/2002:16:44:01] Server limits: 900 clients, 900
clients per source, 10 sources, 5 admins
-> [07/Sep/2002:16:44:01] WWW Admin interface accessible at
http://atlas.paunchy.net:8000/admin
-> [07/Sep/2002:16:44:01] Starting Calender Thread...
```

```
-> [07/Sep/2002:16:44:01] Starting UDP handler thread...
-> [07/Sep/2002:16:44:01] Starting relay connector thread...
-> -> [07/Sep/2002:16:44:01] [Bandwidth: 0.000000MB/s]
[Sources: 0] [Clients: 0] [Admins: 1] [Uptime: 0 seconds]
->
```

9. Stop the Icecast server for now. Enter the command **shutdown** at the -> prompt.

The listing shows that the Icecast server has started. It's listening on TCP ports 8000 and 8001 on the server chivas.paunchy.net. The Icecast server can handle up to 900 client streams and can be accessed via a Web server listening on port 8000. No streams are being served out, so no bandwidth is being used.

Installing and configuring Ices

The next step is to feed Icecast some content to serve out. Icecast is designed to serve MP3 streams by default. Shout/Ices, Iceplay, and Liveice are three programs capable of streaming information to Icecast. Their functions are as follows:

◆ Shout is an executable program that streams — encodes — MP3 files to Icecast. Ices is a completely rewritten version of Shout. You run both from the command line. Shout is no longer supported.

◆ Iceplay is an older Per script that streams MP3 files to Icecast. Iceplay was the first Linux-based streamer but is no longer supported.

◆ Liveice is a streamer that supports variable bit rates between the MP3 source and Icecast. Liveice achieves the variability by first decoding the MP3 stream and then reencoding at the desired rate. Liveice also permits you to mix multiple MP3 streams with a live input. For instance, you can mix the output from a microphone with music from an MP3 stream to create your own radio station.

Liveice is the most powerful and sophisticated of the three systems. However, Ices provides the most straightforward method for getting your streaming server started. The following instructions describe how to feed an MP3 stream to Icecast with Ices.

1. Create a working directory.

```
mkdir /usr/local/ices
cd /usr/local/ices
```

2. Unpack the source code from the copy of Icecast stored on the companion CD-ROM.

```
tar xzf /mnt/cdrom/xiph/ices*
```

You can download Ices from the Icecast Web page, `www.icecast.org/download.html`.

3. Configure Ices.

   `./configure`

4. Compile Ices.

   `gmake`

5. Install Ices.

   `gmake install`

   Make copies of the Shout binary to the `/usr/local/icecast/bin` directory; it also creates the `/usr/local/icecast/etc` directory and copies the Shout configuration file there.

6. Rename the Ices configuration file in the `/usr/local/icecast/etc` directory.

   `mv ices.conf.dist ices.conf`

7. Rename the Ices modules in the `/usr/local/icecast/etc/modules` directory.

   `mv ices.pm.dist ices.pm`
   `my ices.py.dist ices.py`

8. Modify the password in the `ices.conf` file to match the one found in icecast.conf. The default icecast password is "hackme." Locate the following parameter:

   `password letmein`

9. Change the password to the following:

   `password hackme`

Now that you've created the MP3 encoder, you'll want to test it. But it is beyond the scope of this book to describe how to create your own content. Therefore, you might consider using preexisting material.

Serving up MP3 streams

One simple way to test your Icecast system is to use an existing MP3 file. It is, of course, illegal to broadcast copyrighted material to the public. However, you can legally listen to copyrighted material that you own. This section describes how to use your Web server to broadcast content over the loopback interface on your Linux computer. You'll essentially create a glorified MP3 player.

1. Locate an MP3 file. For instance, you might go to www.mp3.com and download a sample MP3 track (you're going to play it to yourself, not to the Internet).

2. Create a Playlist file that Shout will use to feed the MP3 stream to Icecast. Let's assume that you download a sample MP3 file called, for example, `listentome.mp3` into the `/tmp` directory. Create the `/usr/local/icecast/etc/ices.playlist` that follows.

```
#EXTM3U
#EXTINF:251,Future Famous - listentosomething
/tmp/listentosomething.mp3
```

3. Start your Icecast server again.

```
/usr/local/icecast/bin/icecast &
```

4. Start streaming the MP3 file to the `icecast` process with the `ices` encoder.

```
/usr/local/icecast/bin/ices
```

   Shout will start streaming the content of the MP3 file. By default, it will continuously loop through the file, showing a string of dots as a simple progress meter. Entering Control-C will stop the stream. Control-Z will pause the process and place it in the background.

5. Start XMMS.

6. Open the Icecast stream with XMMS. Press `Ctrl-L` or right click on the XMMS window and select `Play Location`.

7. Enter the Icecast URL in the Enter Location to play: window. Icecast listens to port 8000 on the loopback interface by default, so enter the URL `http://localhost:8000` and click OK.

You've just broadcast an MP3 stream on your internal loopback interface. Only you can listen to the stream on your computer. However, you can readily expand the broadcast to your LAN and the Internet.

TIP   The Web page yp.icecast.org contains a database of Icecast and Shoutcast servers. You can use this information to find MP3 and Ogg Vorbis streams that you can listen to with players such as XMMS and MPG123.

You'll have to find content that you can legally broadcast, of course. Once you do, change the Icecast and Ices configuration files to use your server's Ethernet NIC. (Don't forget to change the passwords from their default values!)

Introducing the Icecast URL (Link) format

You need to supply your audio player application, such as XMMS, with a proper URL when connecting to an Icecast server. The audio player parses the URL and uses the information to both connect to the Icecast server and select the stream to play. The general format of the URL is as follows:

protocol://address:port/MountPoint

Components displayed within square brackets — [ ] — are optional. The URL is divided into the following components:

An example URL is shown next:

http://someserver.somenetwork.com:8000/Example1.ogg

This URL format works for both Icecast version 1 and 2. The following list describes the function of each URL element:

- ◆ **Protocol:** Icecast uses HTTP packets to encapsulate audio streams. HTTP is convenient because many, if not most, firewalls allow that protocol to pass through.

- ◆ **Address:** The Icecast server IP address. The address can either be a domain name or in numeric form.

- ◆ **Port:** The port number that Icecast uses to listen for TCP connection requests. Icecast uses port 8000 by default; the port can easily be changed by modifying the Icecast configuration file.

- ◆ **MountPoint:** This component specifies the Icecast stream to connect to. Icecast is currently capable of playing two streams.

Serving Ogg Vorbis Streams with Icecast Version 2

You can use the Ogg Vorbis format to encode audio files. Unlike other formats such as MP3, there are no patents that encumber Ogg Vorbis. Therefore, you can encode your own content with Ogg Vorbis and not ever worry about paying royalties to the format developers; you, of course, need to pay royalties when encoding material that you do not own.

Ogg Vorbis provides the foundation for formatting your audio content into small, high-quality files; it is roughly equivalent to MP4. However, you still need to find a way of streaming the audio files. Icecast2 and Ices2 provide a reasonable system for streaming Ogg Vorbis files to a network.

Ogg Vorbis is the most mature technology that Xiph.org produces. Icecast version 2 –, which will be referred to as Icecast2 – is used to stream Ogg Vorbis. Icecast2 is still in the beta-development phase, however, and is available only via xiph.org's Concurrent Versions System (CVS) repository. CVS is a system that facilitates code development by allowing many programmers to work on the same software without interfering with each other.

Streaming Ogg Vorbis locally

You'll need to have access to an example audio file to create a streaming Ogg Vorbis server. One simple method is to copy music off a CD that you own and store it to an Ogg Vorbis file. You can then feed the Ogg Vorbis file to the Icecast2 server and connect to that server with XMMS. This will all happen on the loopback interface of your computer and will be perfectly legal and you'll be creating a complicated stereo system.

1. Insert an audio CD in your computer.

2. You can use the cdparanoia application to copy the tracks from the CD to files on your computer. The files are stored in Wave – wav – format by default.

   ```
   cdparanoia -B
   ```

3. Convert the Wave files to Ogg Vorbis using the Ogg encoding application oggenc. Red Hat bundles and installs the Vorbis-tools package that contains utilities such as oggenc.

   ```
   oggenc *wav
   ```

4. You can listen to the Ogg files using the ogg123 program.

   ```
   ogg123 xyz.wav
   ```

You now should have several Ogg Vorbis formatted audio files. Those files will be used to provide Icecast2 with streaming content. You'll use the X MultiMedia System – XMMS – to connect to those streams.

OBTAINING ICECAST2 AND ICES2

Icecast2 is in beta and is still being updated. Therefore, it's best to download the most recent code rather than use an older version that we provide at http://www.wiley.com/compbooks/sery. The following instructions describe how to download and install both Icecast2 and Ices2 from xiph.org's CVS repository (that is the term used to describe the directory tree where CVS software is stored).

1. Select a location to work from. For instance, the /usr/local/src is a good place to start.

```
cd /usr/local/src
mkdir icecast2
cd icecast2
```

2. Download the software from xiph.org's CVS repository. Start by logging into the CVS server.

```
cvs -d :pserver:anoncvs@xiph.org:/usr/local/cvsroot login
```

3. Use the string anoncvs as your password.

4. Download Icecast2.

```
cvs -d :pserver:anoncvs@xiph.org:/usr/local/cvsroot -z 9 co
icecast
```

The download process creates a directory called icecast in the current working directory. The Icecast2 software is downloaded from the CVS repository and stored in the icecast directory.

5. Next, download Ices2 and its library libshout.

```
cvs -d :pserver:anoncvs@xiph.org:/usr/local/cvsroot -z 9
co ices
cvs -d :pserver:anoncvs@xiph.org:/usr/local/cvsroot -z 9
co libshout
```

The download process creates two directories — ices and libshout — in your current working directory. The software from each repository is stored in its respective directory.

In case you have trouble downloading Icecast2 and Ices2, plus the shout libraries — CVS can be tricky to use sometimes — the source code is provided at http://www.wiley.com/compbooks/sery. All three systems are stored in the file icecast2.tar in the /mnt/cdrom/xiph directory.

COMPILING ICECAST2 AND ICES2

You need to compile and install the Icecast2 and Ices2 packages. The following instructions describe how to use the configuration scripts included with those systems.

1. Go to the newly created icecast directory, and run the autogen.sh script.

```
cd /usr/local/src/icecast2/icecast
./autogen.sh
```

2. Clean out any existing object files (just to be safe).

```
make clean
```

3. Compile the code.

```
make
```

4. Install the newly compiled code.

```
make install
```

The executable `icecast` file is moved to the `/usr/local/bin` directory.

5. Repeat steps 1 through 4 in the `libshout` and `ices` directories, respectively; `ices` depends on `libshout`, so you need to compile `libshout` first. Note that the `libshout` libraries are copied to `/usr/local/lib` and that the executable `ices` file is copied to `/usr/local/bin`.

CONFIGURING ICECAST2 AND ICES2

The next process requires you to configure Ices2 and Icecast2 to work together. Ices2 feeds Ogg Vorbis audio streams to Icecast2; Ices2 obtains its audio information from static sources such as Ogg Vorbis formatted music files. Icecast2 serves out the Ogg Vorbis audio streams that it gets from Ices2, to clients over an IP based network.

Both systems are configured by default to communicate over the loopback (127.0.0.1) interface. Using the loopback interface provides a simple method for testing your configuration. Icecast uses port 8000 to communicate with its stream source and port 8001 for administration.

Configure Icecast2 first.

1. Copy the sample Icecast2 configuration file to the `/usr/local/etc` directory.

```
cp /usr/local/src/icecast2/icecast/conf/*xml /usr/local/etc
```

2. Most of the default Icecast2 configuration file — `icecast.xml` — settings will work for the simple system being built here. However, two changes need to be made. The first is to uncomment the parameters that make Icecast2 communicate through the loopback interface (127.0.0.1) on ports 8000 and 8001. (XML comments take the form of <-- and --->.)

```
<hostname>i.cantcode.com</hostname>
<port>8000</port>
<bind-address>127.0.0.1</bind-address>

<master-server>127.0.0.1</master-server>
<master-server-port>8001</master-server-port>
```

3. The second change is to configure Icecast2 to run as the user and group nobody. The default `icecast.xml` configuration file contains the hooks for running the icecast daemon as the user nobody and group nogroup. Uncomment the parameters changowner section as follows. Keep the user nobody but change the group nogroup to nobody.

```
<security>
    <chroot>0</chroot>
  <changeowner>
```

```
           <user>nobody</user>
           <group>nobody</group>
        </changeowner>  -->
   </security>
```

4. Save the changes, and start the Icecast2 server.

```
icecast -c /usr/local/etc/icecast.xml &
```

Your Icecast2 server starts but is like a radio station transmitter without a feed. You need to configure Ices2 in order to provide content for Icecast2 broadcast. Next, configure Ices2:

1. Copy the Ices2 configuration files to the /usr/local/etc directory.

```
cp /usr/local/src/icecast2/ices/conf/*xml /usr/local/etc
```

 Ices2 is capable of relaying both live and static streams to Icecast2. The ices-live.xml configuration file deals with live streams while the ices-playlist.xml configures static streams. This book only deals with static streams.

2. When streaming static content, Ices uses a configuration file called a playlist to determine the content to stream to Icecast2. Playlists describe one or more audio files that Ices2 streams to Icecast2. Create a file called playlist.txt and add one or more of the example Ogg Vorbis files to it.

```
echo "somemusicfile.ogg" > /usr/local/etc/playlist.txt
```

You can place multiple files in the playlist.txt file — **echo *ogg > /usr/local/etc/playlist.txt**.

3. Modify the ices-playlist.xml file to include the name and location of your playlist file. For instance, modify the <param name="file"> option, in the <input> section, as follows, if you place the playlist.txt file in the /usr/local/etc directory.

```
<input>
   <module>playlist</module>
   <param name="type">basic</param>
   <param name="file">/usr/local/etc/playlist.txt</param>
   <param name="random">0</param>
   <param name="once">0</param>
</input>
```

4. Save the changes and start Ices2.

```
ices /usr/local/etc/ices-playlist.xml &
```

Ices2 starts, reads its playlist, and opens the designated Ogg Vorbis file or files. Ices2 reads the audio information from the playlist files and feeds it to Icecast2 on port 8000. You can use an audio player like XMMS to connect to Icecast2 and listen to the audio stream. The next section describes how to connect to an Icecast2 stream.

CONNECTING TO YOUR ICECAST2 SERVER

Connecting to an Icecast2 server is straightforward. However, you must use an Ogg Vorbis enabled audio player. Ogg Vorbis modules are included with XMMS, as of Red Hat Linux 8.0. You can obtain Ogg Vorbis modules from www.xmms.org when using earlier XMMS versions.

1. Start XMMS.

2. Select the Open Location option by right clicking anywhere on the XMMS window or pressing the Control-L keys.

3. Enter the URL of your Icecast2 server. For instance, in this example, it is http://127.0.0.1:8000/example1.ogg.

   XMMS will connect to the Icecast2 server and start playing the stream.

Streaming Ogg Vorbis on the Internet

The previous instructions describe how to configure a simple Icecast2 server to stream static Ogg Vorbis files on the loopback interface. The Icecast2 server provides access only to audio clients on the same machine on which it is running. This section describes how to reconfigure Icecast2 to broadcast streams over a network; that network can be the Internet.

You perform most of the configuration work in the previous section. You have only to change the icecast.xml and ices-playlist.xml files so that they work on an external network interface.

1. Change the Icecast2 configuration file — /usr/local/etc/icecast.xml — to work on the 192.168.1.0 network used throughout this book. This example uses the server Chivas that is used as an example server throughout this book; the arbitrary IP address 192.168.1.200 is also selected as an example.

   ```
   <hostname>chivas</hostname>
   <port>8000</port>
   <bind-address>192.168.1.200</bind-address>
   <master-server>192.168.1.200</master-server>
   ```

   Here, the hostname and IP address are changed to the name and address of the machine that the Icecast2 server runs on. The port remains unchanged.

2. Change the passwords from their default values.

```
<source-password>givememusic</source-password>
<relay-password>givememusic</relay-password>
```

3. Optionally, change the location and e-mail information.

```
<location>Hi-Fi Paunchy</location>
<admin>paul@paunchy.net</admin>
```

4. Change the Ices2 configuration file—/usr/local/etc/ices-playlist.xml — to contact the Icecast2 server on Chivas.

```
<hostname>chivas</hostname>
<port>8000</port>
<password>givememusic</password>
<mount>/mystream.ogg</mount>
```

5. Restart both the icecast and ices daemons.

```
killall -HUP icecast
killall -HUP ices
```

6. Connect to the Icecast2 stream with XMMS.

```
xmms http://192.168.1.200:8000/example1.ogg
```

Alternatively, you can specify the DNS name in place of the numeric IP address (assuming Chivas resolves to 192.168.1.200). For instance, you can enter the following URL.

```
xmms http://chivas:8000/example1.ogg
```

Icecast2 streams the Ogg Vorbis formatted bit stream to port 8000 at IP address 192.168.1.200. You can listen to the stream from any networked computer that can access that address. That includes listening from the Internet if you provide access through your firewall.

Summarizing the Icecast2 and Ices2 configuration files

This section describes the Icecast2 and Ices2 configuration files in more detail. XML tags delimit all configuration parameters. The beginning tag takes the form of ⟨ ... ⟩ and the end tag as ⟨/ ...⟩.

INTRODUCING ICECAST2 CONFIGURATION PARAMETERS

The configuration parameters for both versions of Icecast are similar. The following list describes the Icecast2 parameters. Please refer to the HTML formatted file /usr/share/doc/icecast-1.3.12/manual.html for information about Icecast1 configuration parameters.

◆ **Location:** Provides information about where your server is located. This information is useful to listeners but not essential; it's useful to know where your stream is coming from.

◆ **Admin:** Indicates the e-mail address of the Icecast server administrator.

◆ **Limits:** Uses the following parameters to set boundaries on your Icecast server:

■ **Clients:** Sets the limit on the number of clients that can connect to the server.

■ **Sources:** Sets the limit on the number of sources that can feed the server.

■ **Client timeout:** Indicates how long the server will wait before closing an inactive client connection.

■ **Source Timeout:** Indicates how long the server will wait before closing an inactive source connection.

◆ **Source password:** Sets the password that a source or relay must send in order to connect to the server.

◆ **Relay-password :** Sets the password that the server and relay must use to set up relaying.

◆ **Hostname:** Indicates the DNS name of the Icecast server (for instance, sets the name to `chivas.paunchy.net` or just `chivas`).

◆ **Port:** Indicates the port on which clients connect to the server.

◆ **Bind-address:** Indicates the numeric IP address of the server.

◆ **Master-server:** Denotes the IP address that the Icecast server uses for administrative connections.

◆ **Master-server-port:** Indicates the port that the Icecast server uses for administrative connections.

◆ **Logging:** Icecast logs two types of information: connections and problems. The following parameters tell Icecast the logging level, the name of the log files, and where to save those files.

■ **logdir:** Denotes the directory where Icecast writes its log.

■ **loglevel:** Icecast provides four log levels: 4 Debug, 3 Info, 2 Warn, 1 Error.

Debug provides the most information and is used for troubleshooting. Info provides less information than Debug. Warning and Error provide information when problems occur.

- ■ **accesslog:** Sets the name of the file used to log connections to the Icecast server.

- ■ **errorlog:** Sets the name of the file used to log errors.

- ◆ **Security:** Icecast provides two security-oriented options. The `chroot` option is not yet implemented, but the change owner is.

   - ■ **chroot Future:** Icecast versions will support the chroot function. You can force Icecast to operate from a subtree of the server's file system. When you use chroot on a process, that process cannot access any directories above the root node of the subtree.

   - ■ **changeowner:** Allows you to change the owner of the Icecast process. You increase the security of your server by not running processes such as Icecast as root. Running a network-based process like Icecast opens your computer to vulnerabilities such as stack overflows. If a hacker breaks into your computer via a process running as root, he or she will have root access.

INTRODUCING ICES2 CONFIGURATION PARAMETERS

This section describes the Ices2 configuration file — `ices-playlist.xml` — in more detail. This chapter focuses on static playlists and uses only the ices-playlist.xml configuration file. (It is beyond the scope of this book to describe dynamic playlists.) The Ices2 configuration file is written in XML format. Each function section is referred to as a module.

- ◆ **XML version:** Defines the version of XML in which the file is written.

- ◆ **background:** Ices runs in the foreground when set as a 0, but a 1 forces it to run as a background process. This option is not implemented yet.

- ◆ **logpath:** Sets the location to store Ices log files.

- ◆ **logfile:** Sets the name of the log file.

- ◆ **loglevel:** Sets the level of details of the logs.

- ◆ **consolelog:** Setting this option to 1 forces the log to be written to the system console. The default is 0, which writes the log to the location set by `logfile` and `logpath`.

- ◆ **stream:** Encapsulates all the parameters — for example, the metadata, input, and instance parameters — that define each stream. Currently, Ices2 can handle up to two streams, so you can define one or two streams in the `ices-playlist.xml` configuration file.

- ◆ **metadata:** Defines the information about the stream to be broadcast with the stream. The metadata components are described as follows. (The metadata information is not broadcast with the Ices stream. This feature will be implemented in the future.)

- **Name:** Indicates the text string that you want associated with the stream.

- **Genre:** Denotes the type of music that represents the stream.

- **Description:** Indicates a short message that you want to associate with the stream.

◆ **input:** Informs Ices2 where to get the data to stream to the Icecast2 server. The following parameters define the data stream.

- **module:** Sets the type of data input. In this case, the input takes the form of a playlist.

- **Type:** Sets the type of module to be used as the data input source. In this case, it is a basic playlist. (The only module type currently defined is basic.)

- **Name:** Defines the name of the module. In this case, it sets the name to `playlist.txt`. Ices obtains the names of the files from the playlist.txt file and then streams the data from those files to the Icecast server.

- **Random:** Ices randomly opens the files listed in the playlist.txt file when the option is set to 0. Otherwise, when the option is set to 1, Ices opens the files sequentially.

- **Once:** Ices continuously opens the files in the playlist.txt file and streams them to the Icecast2 server when the option is set to 0. Otherwise, when the option is set to 1, Ices only opens each file once.

◆ **instance:** Ices can stream simultaneously its input data to one or more servers; it can also simultaneously send multiple streams to different mount points on the same server. The instance module defines where each stream will be directed.

- **hostname:** Defines the host name of the Icecast2 server.

- **port:** Defines the port that Ices2 will use to connect to the server.

- **password:** Sets the password that Ices2 will use to connect to the server.

- **mount:** Defines the mount point that the clients will use to connect to the data stream.

- **reconnectdelay:** Sets the frequency that Ices will try to reconnect to the Icecast2 server when an existing connection fails.

- **reconnectattempts:** Sets the number of times that Ices2 will try to reconnect with the Icecast2 server when a current connect fails.

- **maxquelength:** Defines the amount of data that Ices2 will buffer from a source.

◆ **encode:** Ices2 supports both live and static encoding. This module defines the parameters for either option. However, this book covers only static encoding.

■ **nominal-bitrate:** Defines the bits per seconds (bps) that Ices will stream data to the server.

■ **samplerate:** Sets the bps that Ices reads data from its source. The default rate for static Ogg Vorbis files is 441000 bps.

■ **channels:** Sets the number of channels that Ices2 can send streams on.

Listing 8-1 shows the Icecast2 configuration file. These listings are based on the configurations built from the previous examples. They are provided to summarize the examples and assist you when configuring your own system.

Listing 8-1: An example Icecast2 configuration file

```
<icecast>
    <location>Paunchy Heavy Industries</location>
    <admin>paul@paunchy.net</admin>

    <limits>
        <clients>100</clients>
        <sources>2</sources>
            <threadpool>5</threadpool>
            <client-timeout>30</client-timeout>
            <header-timeout>15</header-timeout>
            <source-timeout>10</source-timeout>
    </limits>

    <source-password>abetterpassword</source-password>
    <relay-password>abetterpassword</relay-password>

    <directory>
        <touch-freq>5</touch-freq>
        <server>
            <host>chivas</host>
            <touch-freq>15</touch-freq>
            </server>
    </directory>

    <hostname>chivas</hostname>
    <port>8000</port>
    <bind-address>192.168.1.254</bind-address>
```

Continued

Listing 8-1 *(Continued)*

```
<master-server>192.168.1.254</master-server>
<master-server-port>8001</master-server-port>
<!--<master-update-interval>120</master-update-interval>-->
<!--<master-password>hackme</master-password>-->

<fileserve>1</fileserve>

<paths>
    <basedir>/usr/local/icecast</basedir>
    <logdir>/tmp</logdir>
    <webroot>/usr/local/icecast/web</webroot>
</paths>

<logging>
    <accesslog>access.log</accesslog>
    <errorlog>error.log</errorlog>
    <loglevel>4</loglevel> <!-- 4 Debug, 3 Info, 2 Warn, 1 Error
-->
</logging>

<security>
    <chroot>0</chroot>
    <changeowner>
        <user>nobody</user>
        <group>nobody</group>
    </changeowner>
</security>
</icecast>
```

 You'll need to change parameters such as the IP address to match your own server. You should also change the passwords. You may want to change parameters such as the location of the log files.

Listing 8-2 shows the Ices2 configuration file.

Listing 8-2: An example Ices2 configuration file

```
<?xml version="1.0"?>
<ices>
        <background>0</background>
```

```
        <logpath>/tmp</logpath>
        <logfile>ices.log</logfile>
        <loglevel>4</loglevel>
        <consolelog>0</consolelog>
        <stream>
                <!-- metadata used for stream listing (not currently used) -->
                <metadata>
                        <name>Example stream name</name>
                        <genre>Example genre</genre>
                        <description>A short description of your
stream</description>
                </metadata>
    <input>
<module>playlist</module>
<param name="type">basic</param>
<param name="file">
<param name="random">0</param>
<param name="once">0</param>
</input>
<instance>
<hostname>atlas</hostname>
<port>8000</port>
<password>abetterpassword</password>
<mount>/example1.ogg</mount>
<reconnectdelay>2</reconnectdelay>
<reconnectattempts>5</reconnectattempts>
<maxqueuelength>80</maxqueuelength>
<encode>
<nominal-bitrate>64000</nominal-bitrate>
<samplerate>44100</samplerate>
<channels>2</channels>
</encode>
</instance>
        </stream>
</ices>
```

Introducing the Icecast2 XML-based configuration files

Both Icecast2 and Ices2 use eXtensible Markup Language (XML) for their
configuration files. XML is similar to HTML in look and feel.

The Fraunhofer Institute, a German think tank, and the French Thomson Multimedia Company own the MP3 patent. Fraunhofer and Thomson charge royalties for every commercial MP3 player sold. However, as of this printing, they do not charge for noncommercial MP3 players such as the X MultiMedia System — XMMS. There is currently some doubt as to the status of MP3 players bundled with Red Hat Linux distributions. Even though you can download Red Hat's Linux distribution for free, you have to purchase their box CD set. That implies that XMMS is a commercial product. Unfortunately, it's up to the lawyers to decide the status of Red Hat bundled MP3 players. Red Hat, Inc. no longer includes any MP3 capability in any of its software, such as XMMS, because of these uncertainties.

Introducing RealServer

RealNetworks, Inc. produces RealSystems, a suite of software that includes RealProducer, Pro/RealProducer Plus, RealServer, and RealPlayer, which are multimedia-streaming encoders, servers, and client software. RealSystem serves up the familiar RealAudio streams used to provide many commercial multimedia streams such as radio stations.

RealServer interacts with streaming media clients and encoders. The *clients* are the content consumers, and the *encoders* are the content producers, supplying the *server* with content. For instance, the encoder may supply the server with a short, prerecorded audio clip, a live radio broadcast, or maybe even a movie. The server then accepts the data stream from the encoder and transmits it to the client.

As you can see, the server has to deal with a large range of data. The server may simply store an audio clip on a local disk after receiving it from the encoder, but a live feed has to be supplied to the server continuously. The server may store a movie, with its large amount of data, locally as a file, or a studio may stream the content to the encoder and then the server.

You can use RealServer to deliver multimedia content via three methods:

◆ **On-demand:** This method stores the content to be transmitted. The transmission starts when it's requested. You can transmit the information nonsequentially, meaning you can rewind, pause, and stop the transmission without losing data.

◆ **Live:** This method broadcasts an event, such as a radio transmission, as it occurs. The transmission must proceed in a sequential manner; you don't have the ability to start, pause, or stop the transmission without losing data.

◆ **Simulated live:** Similar to a tape-delayed television broadcast, with this method the prerecorded event appears to be live but isn't.

This section introduces the methods that RealServer uses to transmit media streams. The next section describes the networking protocols that RealServer uses to deliver those streams.

Introducing the RealServer protocols

By default, RealServer uses Transmission Control Protocol (TCP) to control media streams and User Datagram Protocol (UDP) to transfer information. (We describe the TCP and UDP protocols in Chapter 2.) TCP uses full-duplex (two-way) communication and guarantees delivery of all packets. TCP is an expensive protocol because providing those two functions requires extra overhead. Therefore, by default, RealServer uses TCP to control the connection, but not to deliver the data stream.

UDP provides one-way communication and doesn't guarantee delivery of packets. UDP is less expensive than TCP because it doesn't require the overhead necessary to check that all packets arrive. At first, UDP seems to be a curious choice for delivering a data stream. However, in most cases, a few packets in a data stream can be lost without ill effect. Analogous to radio or television static, each lost packet in an audio or video stream produces a small, and in many cases unnoticed, hiccup or glitch in the presentations.

Today's Internet works surprisingly well for streaming content, but it's not perfect. All packets are effectively treated the same, and you can't prioritize their transmission. Until you can, you're better off using UDP and assuming that you're going to lose some percentage of packets. Otherwise, if you use TCP for data transmission, you run the risk of losing an entire transmission because the extra overhead can cause the connection to bog down.

That said, sometimes you have to use TCP for data transmission. If you use a firewall that doesn't permit RealServer to establish a UDP connection back into your network, your only solution may be to use HTTP, a TCP-based protocol. Because HTTP is typically allowed out through firewalls — the firewall in Chapter 3 is such a firewall — you often have to piggyback streams on that protocol.

Introducing RealServer MIME types

RealServer uses the Apache Web server to support configurable MIME types. Apache must define the Multipurpose Internet Mail Extensions (MIME) types of which RealServer makes use so that it knows how to handle RealServer media streams. To function properly, RealServer only requires the .ram and .rpm MIME types. The following list shows the MIME types, their functions, and their extensions:

Continued

Introducing RealServer *(Continued)*

◆ **audio/x-pn-realaudio:** Identifies the source as an audio source belonging to the RealAudio protocol. This MIME type is built into RealServer, so RealServer functions as its own Web server in this case. *Extensions:* `.ra`, `.rm`, or `.ram`.

◆ **audio/x-pn-realaudio-plugin:** Identifies the source as an audio belonging to the RealAudio protocol, but it requires a plug in for access. *Extension:* `.rpm`.

◆ **application/x-pn-realmedia:** Identifies the source as a multimedia belonging to the RealMedia protocol. *Extension:* `.rp`.

◆ **application/smil:** Identifies the source as a programmable multimedia. *Extension:* `.smi` or `.smil`.

◆ **application/sdp:** *Extension:* `.sdp`. Identifies the Session Description Protocol (sdp).

◆ **image/gif:** Identifies the source as a static graphical belonging to the Graphic Interchange Format (GIF) protocol. This MIME type is built into RealServer, so RealServer functions as its own Web server in this case. *Extension:* `.gif`.

◆ **image/jpg:** Identifies the source as a static graphical using the Joint Photographic expert Group (JPG) protocol. This MIME type is built into RealServer, so RealServer functions as its own Web server in this case. *Extensions:* `.jpg` or `.jpeg`.

◆ **text/html:** Identifies the source as a text belonging to the HTML protocol. This MIME type is built into RealServer, so RealServer functions as its own Web server in this case. *Extensions:* `.html` or `.htm`.

This section describes the MIME types important to RealServer. The following section describes how RealServer parses a URL. The URL is used to tell RealServer what protocol to use as well as where to find the media stream.

Introducing the RealServer URL (Link) format

RealServer URLs, or *links*, use the following general format:

```
protocol://address:port/MountPoint/[path]/file
```

Components displayed within square brackets — [ ] — are optional. The URL is divided into the following components:

◆ **Protocol:** This component refers to the three streaming protocols that RealServer uses: RTSP, PNM, and HTTP. We describe each component in more detail in the following section.

◆ **Address:** The RealServer IP address. The address can either be a domain name or in numeric form.

◆ **Port:** The port number that RealServer uses to listen for TCP connection requests. We describe the ports in the next section.

◆ **MountPoint:** This component specifies the RealServer base path, which locates the streaming content, on the local file system.

◆ **Path:** The path is a continuation of the base path and is optional. RealServer uses the path when it needs to access content stored in the MountPoint's subdirectories.

◆ **File:** This is the name of the file containing the content.

Introducing RealServer software components

RealServer has several components. Each part performs a task necessary to the system's overall function. The following list describes each subsystem:

◆ **rmserver:** The daemon that acts as the interface between the client and encoder, rmserver runs on the Linux server. You can place it on the DMZ network to provide streams to the Internet. It serves your Intranet if placed on your private network.

◆ **rmserver.cfg:** As the rmserver configuration file, rmserver.cfg contains the information that determines how rmserver functions.

◆ **Plug-ins:** The server uses *plug-ins* (applications that provide specific functions) to provide specific functionality — beyond that which is built into rmserver itself — to the clients. Third parties can design plug-ins because RealSystems uses an open architecture.

◆ **License files:** Files that enable you to use RealServer.

◆ **RealSystem Administrator:** Web-based system for controlling and monitoring RealServer.

◆ **Tools:** RealNetworks provides utilities to manage its systems.

RealServer handles the following media formats:

◆ **Audio:** WAV, AU, MPEG-1, MPEG-2, MP3. (Optional plug-ins from Digital Bitcasting support MPEG-1, MPEG-2, and MP3. For more information, go to www.bitcasting.com.)

◆ **Video:** AVI, QuickTime.

◆ **Other:** GIF, JPEG, SMIL, Real G2 with Flash.

Continued

Introducing RealServer *(Continued)*

You can use a technique called *Splitting* to direct your server to serve up content streamed from another RealServer.

For information about creating content with RealNetworks' RealProducer, look in the section "Creating an On-Demand Source with RealProducer Plus" in the documentation that's bundled in the RealServer RPM package. If you're running a Web server on the same computer on which you installed RealServer, you can find the document at `file://realserver/RealAdministrator/Docs/Manual/realsrvr.htm`.

RealServer uses the following protocols to transmit information over networks (LANs as well as the Internet).

◆ **Real Time Streaming Protocol (RTSP):** Designed for multimedia streams, RTSP is an open protocol, so anyone can use and develop applications for it. RTSP gives clients the ability to control the transmission — starting, stopping, and pausing, for example — of data streams. SureStream (tm) provides multiple bandwidth encoding and automatically optimizes the use of available bandwidth, and RTSP is the only protocol it can use. SureStream is a RealNetworks product that is part of their RealProducer Plus product.

RTSP works under both TCP and UDP. RTSP/TCP is used to control media streams and uses TCP port 554 by default; RTSP/UDP is used for data transmission and uses UDP port 554 and the alternate port 8554 (TCP/UDP). Although RTSP connections typically use both TCP and UDP ports, you can use RTSP over TCP-only connections.

RTSP URLs use the following format:

`rtsp://someaddress.com:554/contentdir/someclip.rm`

◆ **Progressive Networks Audio (PNA):** PNA is a proprietary protocol designed by RealNetworks. RealServer understands PNA in order to provide backward compatibility to RealSystems version 5.0 and earlier clients. PNA connections typically use both TCP and UDP ports, but you can use PNA over TCP-only connections.

PNA URLs use the following format:

`pna://someaddress.com:7070/contentdir/someclip.rm`

◆ **Hypertext Transport Protocol (HTTP):** HTTP is the ubiquitous protocol used to transport Web content. RealServer uses HTTP for the initial access to streaming contents. Accessing content typically involves connecting to a Web page with a browser and opening a URL. The browser uses HTTP to download a metafile. The metafile (identified by the .ra and .ram file suffix) points to the actual media content, and an application, such as XMMS, uses it to initiate the multimedia data stream.

HTTP is often the only protocol allowed through firewalls to transmit the stream. RealServer can encapsulate data streams within HTTP in order to pass through firewalls. HTTP only uses TCP. HTTP URLs have the following format:

`http://someaddress.com:8080/contentdir/someclip.rm`

The client controls the media stream that the server provides using this URL format.

MODIFYING YOUR FIREWALL TO PROVIDE ACCESS TO YOUR ICECAST SERVER

You do not need to modify the Internet firewall if you wish to provide streaming services to the Internet. Since Icecast communicates over port 8000, you only need only to add one rule to your firewall. Add the following rule to permit port 8000 through your firewall.

```
iptables -A INPUT -I $EXT -p tcp --dport 8000 -m state NEW,
ESTABLISHED -j ACCEPT
```

Add this new rule to the Iptables script in /usr/local/etc. Run the script, and save the new rules for later use by running the following script:

```
iptables-save > /etc/sysconfig/iptables
```

This script saves the current iptables rule sets to the /etc/sysconfig/iptables file. The run-level script /etc/init.d/iptables uses this file to start and stop the firewall at boot and shutdown time.

Troubleshooting

If you encounter problems getting your MP3 or Ogg Vorbis Icecast server to work, you should consider the following possible problems (not necessarily in the following order):

◆ Verify that your Ogg Vorbis or MP3 Icecast server is running. Run the command **ps –ef | grep icecast**. Start the server if necessary.

◆ Verify that your Ogg Vorbis or MP3 streamer – ices – is working. Run the command **ps –ef | grep ices**. Start the server if necessary.

◆ Make sure that you're accessing the correct audio format. Icecast version 1.X and Ices version 1.X can stream MP3 streams but not Ogg Vorbis. The reverse is true for Icecast version 2.X and Ices version 2.X (referred to as Icecast2 and Ices2 in this book).

◆ Verify that your Ogg or MP3 player is capable of playing the desired formatted audio stream. Start by verifying that the player can play audio to your speakers. The easiest way is to insert an audio CD and try playing a track. If you can't hear the audio you may need to configure your computer's audio system.

You can check what audio libraries you have by right clicking the XMMS window and selecting Options→Preferences. The Preferences window opens and displays XMMS's audio libraries. For instance, you may not have the Ogg Vorbis library if you're using a version of XMMS distributed with Red Hat Linux 7.3 or earlier (Red Hat added the Ogg Vorbis module in version 8.0). You can download additional libraries from www.xmms.org.

TIP There is doubt about the legality of bundling Open Source MP3 capable players such as XMMS with commercial Linux distributions. As of this writing, Red Hat has removed MP3 capability from it bundled version of XMMS and has altogether removed MPG123. If that remains the case, you'll not be able to listen to MP3 streams with XMMS. You can, however, download XMMS from www.xmms.org to use with MP3. Since xmms.org does not sell their player, it — for the time being — does not have to pay royalties to Fraunhofer Thomson.

◆ Verify that your Icecast configuration file is set up properly. Check the example configurations provided throughout this book. Pay close attention to the following items:

■ **Passwords:** make sure that the source password matches the Ices password.

■ **Hostname:** ensure that the hostname matches the actual hostname of your Icecast server. Use the command **uname −n** to obtain the host name.

■ **Port:** verify that you're using port 8000. You can use another port if necessary but make sure that its value matches the one that Ices connects to.

- **Bind address:** verify that the address matches the IP address of the NIC that you want to stream onto. For instance, if you're using the loopback address — 127.0.0.1 — no other computer on your network will be able to connect to the stream.

- **Comments:** make sure that your critical parameters such as the Password, Bind address, and so on are not commented out. For instance, the Bind address in the default Icecast2 configuration file (`/usr/local/icecast2/icecast/conf/icecast.xml`) is commented out.

◆ Verify network connectivity. Make sure that the computer you're using as the Icecast server is properly connected to your network. Consult Chapter 5 for basic network troubleshooting tips.

Also verify that the computer you're running the audio player application from is properly connected to the network. The audio player will obviously not connect to the Icecast server without a network connection.

◆ Check the log files. Both Icecast and Ices write to log files. The log files are stored in the `/tmp` directory by default. Icecast writes to two log files: `access.log` and `error.log`; the former shows who and what connects to the Icecast stream, and the latter shows problems that occur. Ices writes to `ices.log` and shows information such as when it connects to the Icecast server.

You can find many problems by looking at these three log files. For instance, the following Icecast `error.log` entry shows that the Ices password (the giveaway is that the entry, `/example1.ogg`, is set in the `ices-playlist.xml` file) is not set correctly.

```
error.log:[2002-09-14  13:40:25] INFO
connection/_handle_source_request Source (/example1.ogg)
attempted to login with invalid or missing password
```

Summary

This chapter introduces Icecast and Ices that you can use to provide audio MP3 and Ogg Vorbis audio streams. Ogg Vorbis is an Open Source audio format that you can use to store and stream audio information. Icecast provides audio streams to a network (including the Internet). Ices provides dynamic and static audio streams to Icecast. Using these systems, you can broadcast audio (and in the future, video) streams to the Internet. You can create your own radio station and broadcast to the Internet or just your own home!

Part III

Providing Basic Internet Services

Chapter 9

Building a Domain Name Server

IN THIS CHAPTER

- ◆ Introducing Domain Name Service (DNS)
- ◆ Understanding resource records
- ◆ Configuring a basic DNS server
- ◆ Adding security measures
- ◆ Creating multiple zone files
- ◆ Configuring a split-domain DNS server

THE DOMAIN NAME SERVICE (DNS) is the system used to convert human-readable Internet addresses into machine-readable form. For instance, people generally find it much easier to remember the Red Hat Web site as www.redhat.com, rather than 216.148.218.195 (and much, much easier than 11011000...) Computers, however, must use the numeric address in order to traverse the Internet. DNS maps names to numbers.

Human-readable addresses take the form of a text string, such as www.redhat.com. The string separates the address into a host and domain name. For instance, the address www.redhat.com consists of the host name – www – and the network, or domain name – redhat.com. When you browse the Red Hat Web server, the domain name identifies the network where the Web server is located and the host name identifies the machine that serves the Web page.

This chapter first describes how the DNS protocol works. It then shows you how to configure a DNS server for the example networks introduced in Chapter 1.

Introducing Domain Name Service (DNS)

The Internet is designed around the concept of distributing work across many interconnected networks and machines, which work together because they speak the same language (or *protocols*). That language is, of course, the Internet Protocol (IP), which we introduced in Chapter 2.

Because of the Internet's distributed nature, you need to devise systems to provide common services—such as name resolution—that cooperate across networks that have no knowledge of each other. DNS works by using a distributed database system to store the information necessary to map names to addresses. The distributed database is organized in a hierarchical manner. Top level DNS servers, called *root* servers, provide direction to the Internet about where to find information about specific domains. DNS servers located in or near individual domains provide information about specific machines and networks.

Domains

DNS organizes information about itself by using the concept of domains and domain names. The data that maps host names to IP addresses is organized into a tree structure where the branches and leaves represent domains and subdomains. The concept of domains allows many different hosts and networks to distinguish themselves from each other.

Internet domains are organized in a hierarchical manner where the top level domain (TLD) is the root of all domains and is designated by a dot (.). The next domain levels are the ubiquitous `.com`, `.org`, `.edu`, and so on. These domains roughly divide the function of their subdomains into business, non-commercial organizations, educational, and so on. Individual organization's domains occupy the next hierarchical level; we're using our own terminology and referring to them as major domains. Red Hat, for instance, is a commercial enterprise and uses the domain space `redhat.com`. IDs can optionally have subdomains of their own. Red Hat, for instance, maintains subdomains such as `beta.redhat.com`. Individual machines—computers, routers, and other network devices—live within the owner's domain or subdomains.

When you diagram the domain organization we just described, it looks like an inverted tree. The root domain mimics the tree's root. The trunk corresponds to the major domain. Individual domains make up the branches, and subdomains, if they exist, are secondary branches. Finally, individual hosts are the leaves.

You must register your domain when constructing a network that you want to have an Internet identity. The domain name and its network address is stored at the top of the DNS hierarchy in what is called a root server. The root servers store the location of the domain's authoritative name server. Authoritative name servers store the host name to IP address maps for the domain. The addresses of the numerous root servers can be displayed by running the dig command without any parameters.

Zones

Domains are divided into *zones*. Domains map into one or more zones. Zones can divide a name space into one or more parts or sub-zones.

Take for example, the domain `paunchy.net`. Internally, `paunchy.net` is divided into two subdomains, `dmz.paunchy.net` and `priv.paunchy.net`. If you maintain two separate name servers, each of which is authoritative to one subdomain, then you have two zones. Otherwise, if you have only one authoritative name server, then you have one zone. Figure 9-1 shows the configuration.

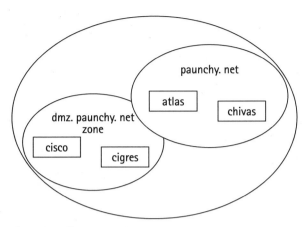

Figure 9-1: Two `paunchy.net` zones

Authoritative name servers

Zones are served by one or more authoritative name servers. Authoritative name servers maintain the detailed information specific to each zone. They maintain, as the name suggests, authority over their zones. Authoritative name servers contain the majority of information in the distributed DNS database.

For instance, assume that you register the domain `mydomain.com`. As part of the registration, you create an authoritative name server. That name server contains the information about the machines on your private network `mydomain.com`.

This section discusses the following types of name servers:

◆ Primary master servers

◆ Secondary name servers

◆ Stealth name servers

◆ Caching name servers

PRIMARY MASTER SERVERS
The Primary Master server is the authoritative name server that maintains the master copy of one or more zone databases. The Primary Master obtains the mapping data for the zones it controls. The data is stored in zone files (also called master files). The zone files contain simple text that describes the name to IP address maps for the zone.=Secondary name servers.

Secondary name servers (often called slave name servers) provide backup authoritative name resolution to the primary master. You can configure one or more secondary name servers for each zone that you control. The secondary name server obtains name mapping information via a process called *zone transfer*. The master and the secondary negotiate zone transfers; the secondary ends up with copies of the master's zone files.

Bind introduces the ability to authenticate zone transfers by using key transfers. The master and secondary share encrypted keys, which they exchange before a zone transfer takes place. The zone transfer takes place when the primary server authenticates the secondary. Using authentication ensures that unauthorized people can't obtain your zone maps.

STEALTH SERVERS

The zone's NS records (see the discussion of NS records in the section "Caching name servers") define the authoritative name servers. However, you can create a name server for a zone without explicitly defining it — such name servers are called Stealth Name Servers, Stealth Servers for short. Stealth Servers are authoritative for a zone.

Stealth Servers are used as backups for the primary servers. Stealth servers also speed up name server queries by obviating the need to perform zone transfers.

CACHING NAME SERVERS

You can create a name server that does not require any explicit zone information. Caching name servers accept domain name queries and redirect them to other name servers. When caching server receives the answer and relays it to the client. The caching name server also saves the answer in memory and builds a data base of such answer. Since the caching server retains all name query answers, it can very quickly answer subsequent duplicate requests.

Understanding client name resolution

When a client requests the resolution of a domain name, a process is started that requires several steps to occur. Following these processes will help you better understand how DNS works overall. This section describes the steps that must occur for a client name request to be answered.

Following a sample name service request

Several processes must occur to answer a name service request. There are three separate systems used to satisfy a name request: a local mechanism that tells networked devices where to get names resolved, a server mechanism that stores names and their addresses for specific domains, and an umbrella system (root domain name servers) that points name requests to the appropriate domain server. Figure 9-2 shows how the systems interact.

The three functions work together in a hierarchical, tree-structured fashion as follows:

1. A client application, such as a Web browser, requests access to a Web page. For instance, you enter the address www.redhat.com into the address box in Mozilla or Netscape.

2. The application makes a call to the host computer's — for example, the host computer cuernavaca — resolver library. In the case of a Linux or UNIX system, the library consults its `/etc/resolv.conf` file. The `resolv.conf` file contains the names (or numeric addresses) of DNS servers. A sample `/etc/resolv.conf` file is shown below:

```
domain paunchy.net
nameserver 192.168.1.250
```

3. The client computer consults its local name cache. If the cache doesn't contain an answer, then the computer sends a name request to the first server.

4. The DNS server `192.168.1.250` — `chivas.paunchy.net` — in this case, processes the request. The DNS server is responsible — authoritative in DNS terminology — for the `paunchy.net` domain only. Because you're requesting address information for another domain, chivas decides that it needs to find the information externally. (Of course, the local name server answers the request directly if the name request is for the local domain.)

5. Chivas needs to find the DNS server that is authoritative for the `redhat.com` domain. The nameserver on chivas consults the `/var/named/named.ca` that contains the locations of the Internet's root servers. One of the root servers sends back the address of redhat.com's name server.

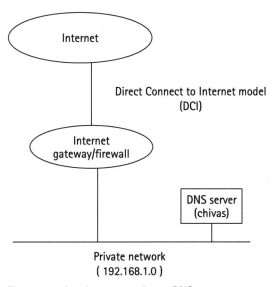

Figure 9-2: Local, server, and root DNS

The root servers are an example of one of the few consolidated—non-distributed—Internet services. These machines provide information about the authoritative name servers for every registered Internet domain. When you register a domain name, such as `redhat.com` or `paunchy.net`, with the InterNIC, that information is stored on these root servers.

6. Chivas gets the address of `ns.redhat.com` and sends a name request to it.

7. `ns.redhat.com` returns the addresses (Red Hat maintains two Web servers for load balancing purposes) of `www.redhat.com` back to chivas.

8. Chivas returns the address of `www.redhat.com` to the cuernavaca.

9. Cuernavaca processes the requests by using Netscape and exchanges information with `www.redhat.com`.

Figure 9-3 shows the relationship between the three parties involved in making DNS work.

You can use the dig command to demonstrate this process. (You can use dig interactively or in a batch mode to display information about hosts and domains.) Run the following command:

```
dig www.redhat.com T_ANY
```

You should see the information displayed in Listing 9-1.

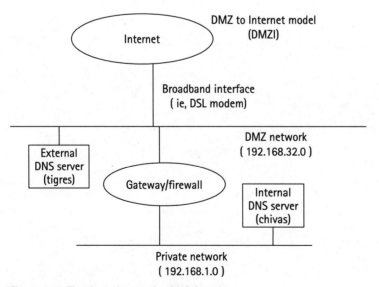

Figure 9-3: The three, interactive DNS functions

Listing 9-1: Dig displays the domain information about the Red Hat's Web server

```
; <<>> DiG 9.2.1 <<>> www.redhat.com
;; global options:  printcmd
;; Got answer:
;; ->>HEADER<<- opcode: QUERY, status: NOERROR, id: 15284
;; flags: qr rd ra; QUERY: 1, ANSWER: 2, AUTHORITY: 3, ADDITIONAL: 3

;; QUESTION SECTION:
;www.redhat.com.                        IN      A

;; ANSWER SECTION:
www.redhat.com.         600     IN      A       216.148.218.197
www.redhat.com.         600     IN      A       216.148.218.195

;; AUTHORITY SECTION:
redhat.com.             600     IN      NS      ns1.redhat.com.
redhat.com.             600     IN      NS      ns2.redhat.com.
redhat.com.             600     IN      NS      ns3.redhat.com.

;; ADDITIONAL SECTION:
ns1.redhat.com.         157562  IN      A       66.187.233.210
ns2.redhat.com.         157562  IN      A       66.77.185.41
ns3.redhat.com.         157562  IN      A       63.240.14.66

;; Query time: 103 msec
;; SERVER: 192.168.1.254#53(192.168.1.254)
;; WHEN: Tue Sep 10 21:02:46 2002
;; MSG SIZE  rcvd: 166
```

Look towards the end of Listing 9-1, in the AUTHORITY SECTION, and you see that dig consulted the "A" root server A.ROOT-SERVERS.NET. The root-level name server contained the address of redhat.com's name server. That information allowed the dig query to recursively traverse its way from the root server to the authoritative name server for redhat.com and eventually find the addresses for www.redhat.com.

Understanding Resource Records

Resource Records (RR) provide the foundation for authoritative name servers. RR defines the basic information about a zone, such as the name and mail servers. RR also defines the IN, A, and PTR maps. You find RR in the named.conf file and the zone files.

Using Start Of Authority (SOA) resource records

The following snippet from a zone file shows the general parameters that define the DNS server's behavior; in this case, the zone is for the fictitious mydomain.com domain.

```
@       IN      SOA     mydomain.com. root.mydomain.com.  (
                                2002091002 ; Serial
                                10800      ; Refresh
                                3600       ; Retry
                                3600000    ; Expire
                                86400 )    ; Minimum
        IN      NS      ns.mydomain.com.
        IN      MX      10  mail.mydomain.com.
```

This section in the mydomain.com zone file specifies the Start Of Authority (SOA) for mydomain.com. The following list describes each resource record's function:

◆ @: This symbol means that the SOA is the same as the domain.

◆ IN: IN is a name server class that provides IP addresses. When used in conjunction with A, PTR, or CNAME records, it maps names to IP addresses, and vice-versa.

◆ SOA: Start Of Authority indicates that the subsequent names define the primary name server, as well as the point-of-contact's e-mail address, for a domain.

◆ mydomain.com: This is the SOA's domain name. Note that the dot — . — is a delimiter that specifies an absolute domain name. If the trailing dot is left out, then the specified name is relative to the previously defined domain name. For instance, mydomain.com. means that mydomain.com is the full domain name. If you specify a name like ns, then the name server prepends the ns to mydomain.com and the result is ns.mydomain.com, which is the fully qualified domain name. Another way to look at it is that the dot ends the interpretation of the name.

◆ root.mydomain.com: This is the point of contact for mydomain.com. In this example, the point of contact (POC) is the root user on the machine.

◆ Named operational parameters: Within the parentheses are five parameters that define the operational aspects of the named daemon. They are as follows:

■ Serial number: An arbitrary value that assists the DNS server's administrator in keeping track of changes. The serial number is incremented every time the zone file is changed. The convention is to use the current date with an appended integer. For instance, if today is December 1, 2001, then the serial number is 2001120100. The next time the zone file is changed, the number is incremented to 2001120101. By comparing the numbers, master and secondary name servers can synchronize themselves.

- **Refresh time:** Defines the time, in seconds, that a secondary name server waits – if necessary – before copying a new zone file.

- **Retry:** Specifies the frequency, in seconds, that a secondary server retries to transfer a zone file, but only if the refresh fails.

- **Expire:** Defines the time, in seconds, that a secondary server will wait to cease answering name queries after it can't transfer a zone file.

- **Time to live:** Sets the time, in seconds, that caches are valid.

◆ **NS:** The Name Server specifies the name, or IP address, of the zone's DNS server.

◆ **Mail eXchanger (MX):** The MX record defines what machine(s) to route e-mail to for the domain and/or individual hosts. Defining an MX record for a domain tells everyone sending e-mail to people and machines in that domain with whom to communicate.

For instance, when an e-mail message is sent the redhat.com domain, the local mail server will look up the MX record of redhat.com. The answer is mx1.redhat.com and mx2.redhat.com; the secondary server is used as a backup to the primary. When the local server receives the answer it tries to send the message to one of the two servers. One of the remote servers receives the message and delivers it to the recipient within the redhat.com domain (this may involve relaying the message to another machine or to the person directly).

TIP

The following list defines the number of seconds in an hour, day, and week.

- 1 hour = 3600 seconds

- 1 day = 86400 seconds

- 1 week = 604800 seconds

- You can substitute the macro 1H for 3600 seconds, 1D for 86400 seconds and 1W for 604800 seconds. You can also use multiples of the macros such as 3H or 2W.

Defining a zone resource records

You use the following parameters to map host names to IP addresses, to map IP addresses to host names, and specify how to route e-mail:

- ◆ **Address (A) records:** Map host names to their IP addresses.

- ◆ **PoinTeR (PTR) records:** Map IP addresses to host names. PTR records perform the reverse function of A records.

- ◆ **Cononical name (CNAME) records:** Define the cononical name for a host. In DNS terminology, cononical really means alias. For instance, assume you map a name to an address with an A record. You can then specify one or more CNAMES to the A name.

- ◆ **Host Information (HINFO):** Allows you to set information about a host in a zone file. HINFO records are a convenient method for transmitting vital information about your domain. Be careful, however: Any information that you include in your DNS server may be used against you by hackers.

- ◆ **TXT:** Specifies text information about the devices within the zone.

These are the items that you can define for a zone. By using the resource records you can create a domain name system. The following section describes how to configure the named daemon.

Introducing bind configuration statements and parameters

You configure bind via the `named.conf` file. (We use bind version 9 – bind9 – for the examples in this book.) The `named.conf` file provides both general and zone specific control. Control is provided through the use of statements and parameters; comments are allowed in order to provide information to the administrator. The `named.conf` syntax uses the following convention:

```
statement {
      parameter;
      [parameter;]
      };
// comments
```

The statement name defines the beginning and end of a configuration section. Parameters are defined within the statement section. For instance, parameters defined by a zone statement tell named where to find the zone's database. The statement section itself is delimited by a beginning and end squiggly bracket – { and } respectively. The end of the parameter and statement section is designated by a semicolon – ;.

The following statements provide the most important control features for named:

- ◆ **options:** You define general purpose parameters within this section. This parameter defines such things as where zone files are stored. For instance, the following configuration tells named that the default configuration file location, including zone databases, reside within the /var/named directory:

```
options {
directory "/var/named";
}
```

◆ **acl:** You can define access control lists (ACLs) that limit who can access information from your DNS server. Access control lists help improve security and also minimize administration costs. The following acl limits access to machines on our private network:

```
acl private { 192.168.1.0/24; };
```

Here, we define the label – or variable – `private`, which corresponds to our private network. (Note that the `/24` is shorthand for a netmask of `255.255.255.0`. Class A and B networks use the shorthand of `/8` and `/16`, respectively.) Once defined, you can use the label anywhere else in the configuration file to limit access to its defined value; in this case the private network.

◆ **zone name:** This statement defines zone definitions. The zone statement defines the type – master or secondary (slave) – the domain name and the zone database file name. Option parameters set options, such as who is allowed zone transfers. The following example defines the `paunchy.net` zone:

```
zone "paunchy.net" {
type master;
file paunchy.zone;
allow-query { any; };
allow-transfer { 192.168.1.0/24 };
}
```

The zone is a master in this case. All mapping information is contained within the `paunchy.zone` file; `paunchy.zone` is found in the `/var/named` directory, as defined by the directory parameter in the options statement. We allow queries from anyone, although the firewall prevents any Internet user from making one. Transfers are allowed to any machine on our private network, allowing us to set up secondary name servers.

Note that we could substitute an acl variable for the explicit network address if we define one in the configuration file. For instance, by defining the acl – `acl private { 192.168.1.0/24; };` – we can change the transfer parameter to permit transfers.

TIP The name of the zone map file `paunchy.zone` is arbitrary and can be anything. Traditionally, zone files have used the `.db` suffix — for instance, `paunchy.db` — to describe them as databases. The word `zone` has been used more frequently as either a prefix or suffix. We use `.zone` to stay current.

The following options are used to set up various name server security-based features:

- ◆ **key:** Sets up the encryption key for the name server.

- ◆ **trusted keys:** Provide a list of keys from other machines that the name server trusts.

- ◆ **logging:** Sets up logging on the name server. Logs are important to see what machines are accessing the name server and have performed zone transfers. Logs are important because they provide an audit trail of zone transfers and a way of verifying that your keys and access lists are working as designed.

Some of the major parameters are as follows:

- ◆ **allow-query:** Defines which machines can query the local name server.

- ◆ **allow-recursion:** Defines which name servers can recursively query the local name server.

- ◆ **allow-transfer:** Defines which name servers can perform zone transfers with the local name server.

- ◆ **forwarders:** Lists which machines that the local name server can forward queries to

- ◆ **masters:** List of servers that are authoritative for a domain.

- ◆ **slave:** List of secondary servers for a domain.

- ◆ **Comments:** Comments are defined by two sequential slashes — //. Comments are used to document the named configuration file.

The options described here are used to determine which machines a name server will cooperate with. Specifying which machines can and can't interact with each limits the opportunities that hackers can have. Using these options can significantly enhance the security of a name server.

Introducing the /var/named/ configuration files

The zone files' location is arbitrarily defined in the /etc/named.conf file. The default directory is defined in the options statement section with the directory parameter. The /var/named directory is the de facto default location for named's zone and other configuration files. Our examples use that standard.

The bind RPM package doesn't install any configuration files by default. We're constructing our initial files from the examples that the bind package gives. Those files are as follows:

◆ `named.ca`: Contains the addresses and other information about the InterNIC's *root name servers*. Root name servers store name service information for all the top level domains – `.com`, `.org`, `.net`, and so on – and are used to start name searches.

◆ `localhost.zone`: Defines the name of the configuration file that allows name queries to be sent to the local caching name server.

◆ `some_domain.zone`: Defines the name to IP address mapping information for an arbitrary zone.

◆ `reverse_domain.zone`: Defines the IP address to name mapping information for an arbitrary zone.

The `named.conf` file defines several configuration files. Those files were introduced in this section. The next section describes how to configure an actual DNS server.

Configuring a Basic DNS Server

Recall from Chapter 1 that we designed two network examples to use in this book. The first one is called Direct Connect to Internet – DCI – and is a simple network that connects to the Internet via a firewall/gateway router server. The second is called DMZ to Internet and consists of two networks separated by a Linux firewall; DMZ stands for DeMilitarized Zone and is used to refer to a network that's exposed to the outside world. The internal network is private and generally inaccessible from the Internet (only Secure Shell connections are allowed in), while the external DMZ network provides services to the outside world.

We'll start by designing a DNS server for the DCI model in this section. It will handle the name resolution for our private network but won't provide information to the outside world – internal clients will be provided with external DNS information, of course. The DCI network model is suitable for anyone who wants to build a private network that isn't going to provide services to the outside world. By design, our DCI model off-loads certain services, such as a Web site and e-mail, to an ISP.

The DNS server for the DCI network resides on the private network. In our example, we use the server chivas with the IP address of `192.168.1.250`. The firewall blocks incoming DNS queries (port 53), allowing us to use the default bind9 configuration; we don't need to define acls to limit access.

Configuring a primary name server

The server chivas functions as our primary name server. It uses the non-routable network address of `192.168.1.250`. This server will use the forward option to resolve external DNS queries. All external requests will be forwarded to our local ISP's DNS server.

We must install the bind RPM package, which you can get from Red Hat at `ftp.redhat.com`.

We use the following named configuration files (mostly stock named configuration files because we're building a simple server):

◆ `/etc/named.conf`

◆ `/var/named/named.ca`

◆ `/var/named/localhost.zone`

◆ `/var/named/paunchy.zone`

◆ `/var/named/1.168.192.zone`

The bind RPM package doesn't provide the general-purpose files `named.conf` and `named.ca`. Therefore, we create basic configurations that will work for a basic DNS server. The basic server will be adequate for a simple network, such as our DCI model.

The following sections examine each of sample DNS server's files in more detail.

CREATING THE NAMED CONFIGURATION FILE — NAMED.CONF

This file controls the overall operation of a DNS server. The following named.conf file provides an example of a simple, authoritative name server for the `paunchy.net` domain.

```
options {
        directory "/var/named/";

};

zone  "." {
        type hint;
        file  "named.ca";
};

zone  "localhost" {
        type master;
        file  "localhost.zone";
};

zone  "paunchy.net" {
        type master;
        file  "paunchy.zone";
};

zone "1.168.192.addr" {
        type master;
        file "1.168.192.zone";
};
```

This file defines both general and specific parameters. The options statement defines all the general parameters. In this example the default directory is set to the standard /var/named; without this statement, we'd have to explicitly define each statement's directory. We also set the optional allow-query parameter to our private sub-network. Limiting queries is good practice, even though a firewall protects the private network.

Every subsequent statement defines a new zone. The root and localhost zones are standard configurations.

CREATING A HINTS FILE — NAMED.CA

This file contains a list of addresses for root servers. Recall that the root servers contain maps of the *top level domains* (TLD). A name server consults the TLD root servers when it doesn't know how to resolve a request. The TLDs point to the name server of the domain that should contain information about the host in question. The following hints file has been edited for brevity's sake.

```
;       This file holds the information on root name servers needed
to
;       initialize cache of Internet domain name servers
;       (e.g. reference this file in the "cache  .  <file>"
;       configuration file of BIND domain name servers).
;
;       This file is made available by InterNIC registration
services
;       under anonymous FTP as
;           file                /domain/named.root
;           on server           FTP.RS.INTERNIC.NET
;       -OR- under Gopher at    RS.INTERNIC.NET
;           under menu          InterNIC Registration Services (NSI)
;               submenu         InterNIC Registration Archives
;           file                named.root
;
;       last update:    Aug 22, 1997
;       related version of root zone:   1997082200
;
;
; formerly NS.INTERNIC.NET
;
.                       3600000   IN  NS   A.ROOT-SERVERS.NET.
A.ROOT-SERVERS.NET.     3600000       A    198.41.0.4
;
; formerly NS1.ISI.EDU
;
.                       3600000       NS   B.ROOT-SERVERS.NET.
B.ROOT-SERVERS.NET.     3600000       A    128.9.0.107
```

```
;
; formerly C.PSI.NET
;
.                          3600000    NS    C.ROOT-SERVERS.NET.
C.ROOT-SERVERS.NET.        3600000    A     192.33.4.12
;
; formerly TERP.UMD.EDU
;
.                          3600000    NS    D.ROOT-SERVERS.NET.
D.ROOT-SERVERS.NET.        3600000    A     128.8.10.90
;
; formerly NS.NASA.GOV
;
.                          3600000    NS    E.ROOT-SERVERS.NET.
E.ROOT-SERVERS.NET.        3600000    A     192.203.230.10


{...Lines delete for brevity ...}


;
; housed in Japan, operated by WIDE
;
.                          3600000    NS    M.ROOT-SERVERS.NET.
M.ROOT-SERVERS.NET.        3600000    A     202.12.27.33
; End of File
```

This zone file should rarely if ever change. However, you may want to periodically update it by downloading and installing a new bind RPM package from Red Hat's Web page (or one of its mirrors). Run the command **rpm –Uvh bind*** to perform the upgrade. Updating bind is a good idea whether or not the named.ca file should be changed. Updating bind will implement any security fixes that have occurred, which is a good thing.

CREATING A LOCALHOST ZONE FILE – LOCALHOST.ZONE

The localhost interface exists entirely within the Linux kernel. This logical interface is used for internal communications. The DNS requires that you define a localhost zone to satisfy name service requests by applications using the localhost interface. The following /var/named/localhost.zone file defines the localhost zone:

```
$TTL 86400
@      IN      SOA     @ root.localhost (
                2002091002 ; serial
                10800 ; refresh
                3600 ; retry
                604800 ; expire
                86400 ; ttl
```

```
                )

@       IN      NS      localhost.


@       IN      A       127.0.0.1
```

This configuration begins just like all other zone files. Parameters, such as the serial number and TTL, are defined in the header. The NS resource record is defined as the localhost. An A record that maps the standard 127.0.0.1 IP address (the localhost interface) is also defined.

CREATING A ZONE FILE – PAUNCHY.ZONE

The following file contains the map for our example DCI network. The domain paunchy.net maps to a single zone in this case.

```
@               IN      SOA     ns.paunchy.net. root.paunchy.net. (
                2001120100
10800
3600
3600000
86400 )
                IN      NS      ns.paunchy.net.
                IN      MX      10 mail.paunchy.net.
                IN      A       192.168.1.250
$ORIGIN paunchy.net.
; servers
fw              IN      A       192.168.1.254
atlas           CNAME   fw


www             IN      A       192.168.1.251
tigres          CNAME   www


ns              IN      A       192.168.1.250
chivas          CNAME   ns


gw              IN      A       192.168.32.1
toluca          CNAME   gw


; printers
lp              IN      A       192.168.1.240
lp2             IN      A       192.168.1.241
hplj            CNAME   lp
Epson           CNAME   lp2


; linux workstations
```

```
puma            IN     A     192.168.1.101 ; Sony Vaio
cementeros      IN     A     192.168.1.102 ; Toshiba Satellite
cancun          IN     A     192.168.1.103 ; Toshiba Satellite

; windows workstations
pachuca         IN     A     192.168.1.11  ; laptop
veracruz        IN     A     192.168.1.12  ; workstation
cuernavaca      IN     A     192.168.1.13  ; workstation
```

This zone file is straightforward and easy to configure. The file provides the name sever with the ability to map numeric IP addresses to names. The next section shows an example reverse name lookup zone file.

EXAMINING REVERSE DNS MAPS STORED IN THE 1.168.192.ZONE FILE

The PTR resource record maps numeric IP addresses to names. The reverse mapping for our example paunchy.net domain is shown here:

```
$TTL 86400
@       IN      SOA     paunchy.net.  root.paunchy.net(
                        1 ; serial
                        28800 ; refresh
                        7200 ; retry
                        604800 ; expire
                        86400 ; ttk
                        )


@       IN      NS      paunchy.net.


;       servers
254.1.168.192  IN     PTR    atlas.paunchy.net.
250.1.168.192  IN     PTR    chivas.paunchy.net.


;       workstations
101.1.168.192  IN     PTR    puma.paunchy.net.
103.1.168.192  IN     PTR    cancun.paunchy.net.
```

Start the named daemon by running the following command:

```
/etc/rc.d/init.d/named restart
```

Using the restart parameter forces any running named daemons to stop before being started again. The named daemon responds to any queries about the paunchy.net domain by returning the IP and/or name of associated hosts.

Configuring a secondary name server

Secondary name servers backup primary name servers. Rather than explicitly maintaining their own zone databases, they download zone information from their primaries. Configuring a secondary name server is quite straightforward. The secondary requests a zone transfer, and the primary transfers copies of its zone file. The following /etc/named.conf file defines two new secondary zones. (We prepend a tag of "2nd" to each secondary zone file. This arbitrary naming convention distinguishes the primary and secondary zone files.) We use the machine pachuca — 192.168.1.251 — as our secondary name server; recall from the chivas's named.conf file in the previous section that we configured the primary to allow zone transfers to pachuca.

```
options {
        directory "/var/named/";
};

zone    "." {
        type hint;
        file  "named.ca";
};

zone    "localhost" {
        type master;
        file  "localhost.zone";
};

zone    "paunchy.net" {
        type slave;
        masters { 192.168.1.250; };
        file  "2nd.paunchy.zone";
};

zone "1.168.192.addr" {
        type slave;
        file "2nd.1.168.192.zone";
};
```

This named.conf file is similar to the primary name server's. The difference is found in the type directive. Setting type to slave forces the named daemon to download its zone file from the master. Maintaining any local zone files is unnecessary.

Adding Security Measures

Bind provides three, easy-to-implement security systems:

◆ The ability to set acls that limit which machines can transfer information from primary name server.

◆ The ability to create transfer keys that verify the name servers' identity.

◆ The ability to run the service from within a chroot environment.

Using these measures greatly increases your name service system's security. The following sections describe how to use these features.

Using ACLs

If you allow zone transfers with any servers that aren't part of your domain, hackers can gain information about your domain simply by asking for it. Bind provides the following ACLs for limiting who can gain such information:

◆ **allow-query {list}**: This parameter specifies the individual hosts or networks that can ask the name server questions. You can use allow-query in the options section, to specify global acls, or in individual zones sections. For instance, adding the following line to named.conf on chivas restricts queries to machines on the local sub-network:

```
allow-query { 192.168.1.0/24; };
```

◆ **allow-recursion {list}**: This parameter specifies the individual hosts or networks that can ask the name server recursive questions. You can use allow-recursion in the options section, to specify global acls, or in individual zones sections. Using the following acl restricts recursive queries to the local subnet:

```
Allow-recursion { 192.168.1.0/24; };
```

◆ **allow-transfer {list}**: This parameter specifies the individual hosts or networks that can request and receive zone transfers from the name server. You can use allow-transfer in the options section, to specify global acls, or in individual zones sections. The following acl restricts transfers to the machine at 192.168.1.251, which could be a secondary name server for the paunchy.net domain:

```
allow-transfer { 192.168.1.251; };
```

The following acl restricts zone transfers to all non-routable networks between 192.168.0.0 to 192.168.128.0:

```
allow-transfer { 192.168.0.0/16; };
```

◆ **allow-update {list}**: The list parameter specifies the individual hosts or networks that can send dynamic updates to the name server. You can use allow-update in the options section, to specify global acls, or in individual zones sections. For instance, using the following parameter restricts dynamic updates to a list of specific machines:

```
Allow-update { 192.168.1.251; 192.168.2.250; 192.168.3.250; };
```

TIP Bind permits you to set acl statements. You can assign IP addresses to an acl statement and then use it to specify permissions, which saves having to write out all the IP addresses for each acl. For instance, if you set up the acl statement acl xyz { 192.168.1.251; 192.168.2.250; 192.168.3.250; };, then you use it in the acl statement allow-update { xyz; };. Acl statements also use the following built-in values:

- any: All addresses.

- none: No addresses.

- localhost: Maps to all addresses that exist on the local machine.

- localnets: All networks to which the local machine is connected.

ACLs help increase the security of your name server. However, hackers can still impersonate your IP addresses and potentially access your zone files. The next section describes how to use digital signatures to ensure that zone transfers are performed by authenticated hosts.

Using Transfer Signatures

You use Transfer Signatures (TSIG) to verify that remote name servers are who they claim to be. TSIGs represent a machine's fingerprint. Two machines verify who they are by transferring secret keys and running the keys through a mathematical algorithm. The result either confirms or denies that the other machine is valid. Positive results permit zone transfers and other information to proceed.

You must generate TSIGs and write them into each name server's named.conf file. The following example configures chivas and pachuca to use TSIGs:

1. Generate the key on chivas (**Note:** You start on any machine, but for this example, we're using chivas):

```
dnssec-keygen -a hmac-md5 -b 128 -n HOST xferkey
```

- The -a hmac-md5 option specifies the type of key to generate.

- The -b 128 option specifies the length in bits of the key. The longer the key, the harder it is to break. However, bigger keys require more processing time to encode/decode.

- The -n HOST xferkey option specifies the type of key to create. You have four choices HOST, ZONE, ENTITY, and USER.

- The `xferkey` option is an arbitrary file name prefix in which to store the results.

2. Extract the shared secret from the result file that ends with the suffix `.private`. The `.private` file should look something like the following:

```
Private-key-format: v1.2
Algorithm: 157 (HMAC_MD5)
Key: ByrncUulmYoA8fLXQXYTog==
```

The string `ByrncUulmYoA8fLXQXYTog==` represents the secret.

3. Place the secret in the `/etc/named.conf` file as follows:

```
key xferkey. {
algorithm hmac-md5;
secret "ByrncUulmYoA8fLXQXYTog==";
};
```

4. Copy the `named.conf` key section that contains the secret to the second machine. In this case, the second machine is pachuca:

```
key xferkey. {
algorithm hmac-md5;
secret "ByrncUulmYoA8fLXQXYTog==";
};
```

5. Add the following section to `named.conf` on chivas to force chivas's named to verify the keys before allowing transfers to pachuca:

```
server 192.168.1.251 {
keys { xferkey. ; };
};
```

6. Add the following to `named.conf` on pachuca to allow transfers from chivas:

```
server 192.168.1.250 {
keys { xferkey. ; };
};
```

7. Restart named on both machines:

```
/etc/init.d/named restart
```

No other name server can perform zone transfers after you configure TSIG on both machines. Adding the appropriate `key` and `server` sections to the `named.conf` file on other machines will allow them to get zone transfers from the master server.

Running named in a chroot environment

The chroot command creates a virtual file system. The virtual file system is rooted to some arbitrary point within an existing one. A "chroot'd" file system limits access of processes running within it to a constricted file system. The constricted environment enhances security because intruders don't have access to as many tools as they otherwise would.

A hacker gaining access to a system through named is always a danger. Designed to respond to external network queries, named is a popular target. Running named within a chroot'd environment increases its security. Anyone who finds and exploits a named vulnerability is limited to working within the chroot. We're going to create a chroot environment that contains almost nothing with which to work.

The chroot file system must contain all the applications, libraries, and miscellaneous systems. Fortunately, named requires only a few systems to operate. We're going to create an arbitrary directory /chroot to use as the root of the chroot environment. The required directories within /chroot are /chroot/etc, /chroot/var/run, and /chroot/var/named.

Move the named configuration files from /etc to /chroot/etc and from /var/named to /chroot/var/named; those files are named.conf, hints.db, localhost.zone, paunchy.zone, and 1.168.192.zone. The /chroot directory should contain the following files:

- ◆ /chroot/etc/named.conf
- ◆ /chroot/var/run
- ◆ /chroot/var/named/hints.db
- ◆ /chroot/var/named/localhost.zone
- ◆ /chroot/var/named/paunchy.zone
- ◆ /chroot/var/named/1.168.192.zone

Add the following lines to the /etc/rc.d/init.d/named script as follows:

```
OPTIONS=-t named
ROOTDIR=/chroot
```

The OPTIONS parameter forces the named daemon to run in user space; the user named is dedicated to running the named daemon. Setting the ROOTDIR variable forces named to run in the chroot environment; in this case, named runs in the chroot environment rooted within /chroot.

Starting and stopping the name server

The /etc/rc.d/init.d/named script controls the bind9 daemon and provides information about the running service. You start the daemon by running the script with the start parameter: /etc/rc.d/init.d/named start. You stop named by using the stop parameter: /etc/rc.d/init.d/named stop; you can restart it as follows: /etc/rc.d/init.d/named restart. You can force named to reread its configuration by sending the HUP signal to the named daemon as follows: `killall -HUP named`.

Alternatively, you can use the `rndc` utility that is packaged with bind. If you do not specify any options, rndc displays the named status. Depending on what options you give rndc, it will start and stop the named daemon. Rndc can also be configured to use keys to authenticate itself to named.

Creating Multiple Zone Files

This section expands the previous example to include additional subdomains. We're going to create an additional zone for each subdomain. This example expands the `paunchy.net` domain to include two new subdomains: `lab.paunchy.net` and `syseng.paunchy.net`. The new sub-networks are going to use the non-routable network addresses `192.168.2.0` and `192.168.3.0` and will be routed to `paunchy.net` — `192.168.1.0` — through a triple-homed Linux router as described in Chapter 1.

We'll manage these subdomains entirely within our official `paunchy.net` domain; we don't have to register the subdomains with the InterNIC.

We're going to create a zone for each new sub-network, and we'll also create a name server for each new zone. The new name servers will be connected to the sub-networks that they serve.

The new configuration will require the following modifications to the single domain/zone (described in the section "Configuring a Basic DNS Server"):

♦ Retain chivas as the primary name server for the `paunchy.net` domain: Chivas will be modified to act as a secondary name server for the new subdomains. Its `named.conf` file will require modification, but its zone files remain unchanged.

♦ Create primary name servers for the new subdomains `lab.paunchy.net` and `syseng.paunchy.net`: The new servers are pachuca and toluca, respectively.

Assuming that you create two Linux boxes to act as the name servers, you have to perform the following steps to modify the previous example to work with the new subdomains:

1. Add new secondary zones to chivas's `/etc/named.conf` file as shown here:

```
options {
directory "/var/named/";
};

zone  "." {
type hint;
file  "named.ca";
};

zone  "localhost" {
type master;
file  "localhost.zone";
};

zone  "paunchy.net" {
type master;
file  "paunchy.zone";
};
# zone for the dmz subdomain dmz.paunchy.net
zone  "lab.paunchy.net" {
type slave;
masters { 192.168.2.250; };
file  "dmz.paunchy.zone";
};

# zone for the private network priv.paunchy.net
zone  "priv.paunchy.net" {
type slave;
masters { 192.168.3.250; };
file  "priv.paunchy.zone";
};

# end new zones
```

2. Create the authoritative dmz name server on the `192.168.2.250` Linux box. Create the following `named.conf` file:

```
options {
directory "/var/named/";
};

zone  "." {
type hint;
file  "named.ca";
};

zone  "localhost" {
```

```
type master;
file  "localhost.zone";
};

zone  "paunchy.net" {
type slave;
file  "paunchy.zone";
};
# zone for the lab subdomain lab.paunchy.net
zone  "lab.paunchy.net" {
type slave;
masters { 192.168.2.250; };
file  "lab.paunchy.zone";
};
# zone for the private network priv.paunchy.net
zone  "syseng.paunchy.net" {
type slave;
masters { 192.168.3.250; };
file  "syseng.paunchy.zone";
};

# end zones
```

3. Create the lab zone file on the `192.168.2.250` name server. For instance, the following zone file defines the lab subdomain's gateway, file server, and so on:

```
$TTL 86400
$ORIGIN lab.paunchy.net
@ IN SOA paunchy.net. root.paunchy.net(
1 ; serial
28800 ; refresh
7200 ; retry
604800 ; expire
86400 ; ttk
)


@ IN NS paunchy.net.

gw IN A 192.168.2.254
fileserver IN A 192.168.2.251
ns IN A 192.168.2.250
```

4. Repeat Steps 2 and 3 for the syseng subdomain name server `192.168.3.250`. (Make the appropriate changes for the syseng subdomain, of course.)

Configuring a Split-Domain DNS Server

Increasing security is important once you provide DNS to the Internet. Your domain's zone information provides a map of your internal network, which hackers can use to attack you. With the configuration we use, no one needs to know the private network's internal layout. Recall from Chapter 2 that we allow internal access to our private network via an OpenSSH proxy — e-mail is routed to an IMAP server from the Internet as well. We also use non-routable IP network address space (192.168.0.0), so without configuring a post-routing NAT on our firewall, packets originating on the Internet can't find their way into our private network.

We use a system called a Split-Domain system to satisfy our two demands. A *Split-Domain system* maintains two different zone maps for internal and external use. Each map must be run on its own server. One server runs on the private network, the other works off of the DMZ.

The internal zone map contains information about both the private network and the DMZ network. The external map contains information about only the DMZ network, which makes sense when you recall that the DMZ network provides external services such as a Web server, sendmail relay, and so on. The internal name server provides the following information to the private network:

◆ Host names for all zones that you maintain.

◆ Name resolution for Internet domains (by accessing external name servers via the forwarding and root server systems).

The external name server provides the following functions to the DMZ network, and to any machine on the Internet:

◆ Name resolution for the DMZ zone.

◆ MX records to the Internet (which allows our e-mail relay system to function).

The Split-Domain system requires at least two DNS servers. Each functions as a primary name server. You can use additional secondary name servers. For simplicity, we're going to build two primary name servers. The first server will function on the private network and the second on the DMZ.

The key to running a Split-Domain system is to configure the acls correctly. The private (internal) network name server must provide the following access:

◆ All our private network machines (the 192.168.1.0 sub-network in this example).

◆ The DMZ network.

The DMZ (external) name servers require the following access lists:

◆ The private network machines.

◆ The DMZ name server Ips.

Configuring the Split-Domain private name server

The private network name server is similar to the one we configured in the section "Configuring a Basic DNS Server" early in this chapter. The difference is that we're adding access lists and a zone for the DMZ network.

The private named is configured similarly to our basic primary name server. We use the following /etc/named.conf file for our Split-Domain name server on our private network:

```
options {
        directory "/var/named/";
        allow-query { 192.168.1.0/24; };
        allow-transfer { 192.168.1.251; };
};

zone "." {
        type hint;
        file  "named.ca";
};

zone "localhost" {
        type master;
        file  "localhost.zone";
};

zone "paunchy.net" {
        type master;
        file  "paunchy.zone";
};

zone "1.168.192.addr" {
        type master;
        file "1.168.192.zone";
};
```

We use /var/named/paunchy.zone as the private name server zone file. The zone file is exactly the same as the basic name server's — we include the zone file contents here for your convenience:

```
$TTL 86400
@             IN SOA  ns.paunchy.net. root.paunchy.net. (
```

```
2001120100
                          10800
                          3600
                          3600000
                          86400 )
                  IN      NS      ns.paunchy.net.
                  IN      MX      10 mail.paunchy.net.
                  IN      A       192.168.1.250

; servers
fw                IN      A       192.168.1.254
atlas             CNAME   fw

www               IN      A       192.168.1.251
tigres            CNAME   www

ns                IN      A       192.168.1.250
chivas            CNAME   ns

gw                IN      A       192.168.32.1
toluca            CNAME   gw

; printers
lp                IN      SA      192.168.1.240
hplj              CNAME   lp
lp2               IN      A       192.168.1.241
Epson             CNAME   lp2

; linux workstations
puma              IN      A       192.168.1.101 ; Sony Vaio
cementeros        IN      A       192.168.1.102 ; Toshiba Satellite
cancun            IN      A       192.168.1.103 ; Toshiba Satellite (new)

; windows workstations
pachuca           IN      A       192.168.1.11  ; Sony laptop
veracruz          IN      A       192.168.1.12  ; Toshiba laptop
cuernavaca        IN      A       192.168.1.13  ; HP workstation
```

Configuring the Split-Domain DMZ name server

The DMZ name server is stripped of most of the zone information you find on the primary one. The private server, however, requires more restrictive acls. Following is the /etc/named.conf file:

```
options {
        directory "/var/named/";
        allow-query { 192.168.1.0/24; };
        allow-query { 192.168.32.0/24; };
};

zone   "." {
        type hint;
        file  "named.ca";
};

zone   "localhost" {
        type master;
        file  "localhost.zone";
};

zone   "paunchy.net" {
        type master;
        file  "dmz.zone";
};
```

Note that we're using the same domain — paunchy.net — but a different zone. The dmz.zone is limited to the DMZ network.

The following zone file — /chroot/var/named/dmz.zone — configures the DMZ name server:

```
$TTL 86400
@           IN      SOA   ns.paunchy.net. root.paunchy.net. (
                          2002091002
                          10800
                          3600
                          3600000
                          86400 )
                    IN    NS    ns.paunchy.net.
                    IN    MX    10 mail.paunchy.net.
                    IN    A     192.168.32.250

; servers
fw                  IN    A     192.168.32.254
atlas               CNAME fw


www                 IN    A     192.168.32.240
tigres              CNAME www


ns                  IN    A     192.168.32.250
```

```
chivas CNAME ns

gw              IN    A     192.168.32.1
dslmodem        CNAME gw
```

Troubleshooting

Troubleshooting the name server consists primarily of verifying that your named configuration files are configured correctly and queries can be processed. Verifying the named configuration requires testing the various named configuration files. You can check whether queries are processed correctly by sending test queries to your server. The applications discussed in the following sections serve as useful troubleshooting tools.

named-checkzone

This application checks your zone files by examining the syntax for correctness and displaying any discrepancies. Configuration errors are easily corrected once identified. For instance, run the following command to check your zone file:

```
named-checkzone /var/named/paunchy.zone
```

The utility returns a simple "OK" if the zone file is constructed correctly. If the zone file contains mistakes then the named-checkzone program will be displayed. For instance, if one of the A records has an incorrect IP address, named-checkzone returns the following message:

```
dns_rdata_fromtext: /chroot/var/named/paunchy.zone:13: near eol: bad dotted quad
dns_zone_load: zone /chroot/var/named/paunchy.zone/IN: loading master file
/chroot/var/named/paunchy.zone: bad dotted quad
```

This response tells you that the zone file has a bad IP address. Indeed, looking at the file reveals the following malformed address:

```
atlas IN A 192.168.322.254
```

named-checkconf

This application checks the named configuration files by examining the `named.conf` syntax for correctness and displaying any discrepancies. Configuration errors are easily corrected once identified. Running named-checkconf against a valid `named.conf` results in no errors being displayed. Named-checkconf shows errors when `named.conf` has problems. The following display indicates a problem:

```
/etc/named.conf:6 parse error near 'ooptions'
```

In this case, a misspelled options parameter — ooptions { — is the culprit.

dig

This application sends named queries to either the default — as specified by
/etc/resolv.conf — or an arbitrary name server. You can use dig to query single
or multiple hosts.

host

This application looks up a host's name or address. Specify the -v option to display
detailed information about the results. For instance, running the command host **–v**
www.redhat.com displays the following information:

```
Trying "www.redhat.com"
;;  >>HEADER<<- opcode: QUERY, status: NOERROR, id: 49497
;; flags: qr rd ra; QUERY: 1, ANSWER: 2, AUTHORITY: 3, ADDITIONAL: 3

;; QUESTION SECTION:
;www.redhat.com.                   IN    A

;; ANSWER SECTION:
www.redhat.com.           592  IN    A     216.148.218.197
www.redhat.com.           592  IN    A     216.148.218.195

;; AUTHORITY SECTION:
redhat.com.       70599 IN    NS    NS1.redhat.com.
redhat.com.       70599 IN    NS    NS2.redhat.com.
redhat.com.       70599 IN    NS    NS3.redhat.com.

;; ADDITIONAL SECTION:
NS1.redhat.com.           48731 IN    A     66.187.233.210
NS2.redhat.com.           48731 IN    A     216.148.218.250
NS3.redhat.com.           48731 IN    A     63.240.14.66

Received 166 bytes from 68.35.172.5#53 in 18 ms
```

The returned information provides you with the following information:

- ◆ The first three lines give information about what was queried. For
  instance, we are looking for the address of www.redhat.com, no errors
  occurred, and so on.

- ◆ The Question section reiterates the fully qualified domain name we're
  looking for.

◆ The answer section provides the numeric IP address of every machine that answers to www.redhat.com. In this case, Red Hat maintains two Web servers; multiple servers are used to increase reliability and speed.

◆ The authority section provides the names of every DNS server that is authoritative for the redhat.com domain.

◆ Finally, the additional section provides the IP addresses for each of the DNS server.

The host utility provides a quick and easy way of finding IP addresses. The host command also can give you information about what DNS servers are authoritative for a domain.

tcpdump

This application causes name queries to travel as UDP packets through IP networks. Queries must reach their destination to return information to their host — which means that your network must be working correctly. Introduced in Chapter 5 as a general purpose troubleshooting tool, tcpdump is also quite useful for debugging named problems. Use tcpdump to verify that name queries are traversing your network.

Summary

This chapter describes the basics of the DNS protocols. You use DNS to map names to numeric IP addresses, and vice versa. DNS is designed as a distributed database where the detailed information about registered Internet domains are stored locally, while the information about how to find those maps is spread across the Internet.

Building a DNS server is straightforward when you only have to serve a single zone for a single domain. The process becomes more involved as your domain becomes more complex. We began this chapter by describing how to build a simple, single-zone DNS server. We branched out from there to describe more complex configurations ending with a Split-Domain DNS server. The Split-Domain server increases security by preventing external access to your detailed zone maps.

Chapter 10

Creating an SMTP E-mail Server

IN THIS CHAPTER

- ◆ Understanding mail queues
- ◆ Understanding configuration parameters
- ◆ Handling unsolicited commercial e-mail
- ◆ Setting up important files
- ◆ Using commands to process datafiles
- ◆ Examining important parameters in main.cf
- ◆ Understanding e-mail server terminology
- ◆ Sample configurations

A NUMBER OF MAIL SYSTEMS are available for Linux. The best known and most widely used on servers is probably Sendmail. But although Sendmail is a truly powerful mail system, it is highly complex. It is not at all uncommon for a new system administrator to look at a Sendmail configuration file and immediately feel overwhelmed. The number and complexity of rules in a typical Sendmail installation can seem daunting to someone who has not received explicit training in the subject. And a thorough Sendmail manual can be as large as an urban telephone book.

It is no wonder, then, that there are several alternatives to Sendmail in the Linux world. Many, such as Qmail and Postfix, have sought to deliver much of the power of Sendmail without the associated complexity. In this chapter, we will focus on Wietse Venema's popular Postfix package.

A Little Mailer Theory

When considering the security issues surrounding a mailer, it is useful to know something about the program's operational structure. Knowing the operational structure of the program helps determine the program's vulnerabilities to attack, as well as its possible performance issues.

A monolithic approach to mail processing, for example, can create a single efficient program to handle the task. But a single program increases the danger that the entire mail process can be compromised if a cracker exploits one portion of the program. Such a program also has to be designed well enough to handle many concurrent tasks, so that a slowdown in one activity does not create delays in all forms of mail processing.

Postfix takes a different approach, however. Instead of employing a monolithic design, Postfix uses a coordinated multiple-process strategy. A master process creates daemons to handle certain tasks as needed. These daemons stay resident in memory for as long as needed, plus a wait time specified by the system administrator. When there has been no work to do in the specified amount of time, a given daemon kills itself.

This design has a number of advantages. First, it means that individual services provided by Postfix can be turned on and off at will. If certain features are not needed, the related processes can be shut down. This is a win in at least two ways: it reduces the ability of malicious crackers to try to exploit the program, and it increases performance by eliminating unneeded code in the system.

Mail systems are a frequent subject of attack by crackers. Why? Because even a well-run server needs to provide mail services to its owner. So even when most other services are disabled to prevent malicious mischief, the mail port is almost always open. Security in a mail server is an absolutely critical matter. Since Postfix allows you to turn off particular mail services you don't need, there is less for crackers to probe and exploit. This reduces your risk while providing you with the services you require.

The ability to remove unneeded processes also helps with performance. When a process no longer exists, it needs no CPU time and takes up no space in memory. That leaves you with more resources to get work done on the server and reduces unnecessary overhead.

Compatibility

Because Postfix was created after Sendmail, Postfix was fully established as the predominant mail system on Unix-like systems and was designed to coexist peacefully with Sendmail servers. This means that it not only tries to faithfully implement the same mail protocols as Sendmail, but that it tries to preserve the key elements of the user interaction, mainly through the files (such as .forward) that many Sendmail users already employ.

Performance

Postfix's design has shown that it is capable of handling substantial volumes of mail. It runs very quickly, reportedly faster than many other mail transports, yet it is capable of handling tens of thousands of messages per hour on a properly tuned server.

Making use of it all

Now that we have covered some of the things that Postfix can accomplish, we can start to explore how Postfix goes about doing its work. In particular, the queues and configuration files drive the process. By understanding the queues and the configuration parameters, one can learn how to control Postfix.

Understanding Mail Queues

Postfix utilizes a number of queues to control its actions. Each queue facilitates a different part of the mail system.

◆ **Incoming queue:** This queue contains new mail messages that have been received from the network for delivery, as well as new messages from the local host.

◆ **Activequeue:** This queue contains the small number of messages that Postfix has opened for delivery.

◆ **Deferred queue:** This queue contains mail messages that could not be successfully delivered. Delivery is retried at periodic intervals after the initial unsuccessful attempt.

◆ **Corrupt queue:** This queue contains damaged e-mail messages that require administrator inspection.

Understanding Configuration Parameters

The configuration of Postfix is accomplished through manipulation of certain files. The main configuration file is called main.cf, and it normally resides in the /etc/postfix directory. A few smaller files also usually reside at that location. We will spend some time examining them in detail.

The main configuration file is capable of holding dozens of parameters that can control the behavior of the program. Thankfully, Postfix is quite functional as installed on most systems. A standard set up successfully delivers mail on the local machine and sends mail to reachable hosts. It normally takes only a few modifications to permit Postfix to act as the mail server for an entire domain or to allow it to send mail through a mail router on a firewall.

Parameter information and syntax

Configuration information is broken down into a series of parameters. These parameters supply the information Postfix needs to do its work. Parameters may be specified as values, files, databases, or tables.

Values

Values are simple substitutions for the parameter. Values are text, numbers, or lists of text and/or numbers.

Syntax for setting values looks like this:

```
someparameter = itsvalue
someparameter = onevalue, anothervalue, yetanothervalue
```

Files

Files are references to external text files that normally contain a group of values. Files are generally used when there are too many values to list inline in the configuration.

Syntax for setting values via a file looks like this:

```
someparameter = /file/name/here
```

If the file contains regular expressions, the syntax becomes this:

```
someparameter = regexp:/file/name
```

If it is a special UNIX file, like the password file, the syntax becomes as follows:

```
someparameter = unix:/etc/passwd
```

Databases and tables

Databases are similar to files, except that they are processed into a binary format of some type. There are many possible types of databases.

A general database file looks like this:

```
someparameter = dbm:/etc/mail/aliases
someparameter = db:/file/db
```

A hash table looks like this:

```
someparameter = hash:/etc/postfix/aliases
```

A hash table is another name for a simple Unix-style database.
A Postfix PCRE (Perl Compatible Regular Expression) table:

```
someparameter = pcre:/etc/postfix/filename
```

Handling Unsolicited Commercial E-mail

Any modern mail administrator needs to be sensitive to Unsolicited Commercial E-mail (UCE). The amount of UCE or spam that crosses a mailserver these days can be horrific. It is necessary, then, to enable settings that help limit the amount of UCE that is successfully delivered to your domain. The trick, of course, is to succeed at that task without blocking the delivery of legitimate mail that might be mistaken as spam.

Many of the parameters in the `main.cf` file can be helpful in handling UCE. The particular settings you choose need to reflect the realities of the mail traffic you receive. As we discuss the parameters, we will make some suggestions for handling UCE.

Examining Important Parameters in main.cf

There are many parameters and values that can be set in the `main.cf` configuration file. This chapter is not meant to provide an exhaustive list. Rather, it is meant to highlight many of the most useful parameters available to you.

Again, remember that these parameters are generally installed with sensible defaults. Adjustments to the parameters are best left to changing behaviors not currently configured on your Postfix system.

queue_directory

The `queue_directory` parameter points to the directory that holds the various Postfix queue files. On most systems, it is sensible to leave the default value alone, as shown in the following example.

```
queue_directory = /var/spool/postfix
```

command_directory

The `command_directory` parameter indicates the directory containing all the Postfix-related programs that start with the letters *post*. As changing this parameter means that you need to move executables around to match the new value, and as this defeats the intentions of the RPM package to give you version control over your software, it is best to leave this with its installed value.

```
command_directory = /usr/sbin
```

daemon_directory

This is the directory containing the various Postfix daemons found in the master.cf file. For the reasons given in the preceding discussion of the command_directory, this parameter is best left unchanged.

```
daemon_directory = /usr/lib/postfix
```

mail_owner

This is the name of the owner of the Postfix queue and daemons. For the sake of security, this should be set to a unique user on the system. The user should not own any other files or programs, nor should it share a group with any other users on the system. This owner should not have root privileges under any circumstances. Most installations create and utilize a dedicated user named postfix to handle this situation.

This greatly reduces exposure in the case where an exploit is discovered in the Postfix system. If the owner of the processes can only touch the Postfix system, it cannot be compromised and used to corrupt other software or files on the computer. This is a case where an ounce of prevention is worth a pound of cure. By following these guidelines, you limit the impact of the worst-case scenario, should a cracker find a way to issue system commands through the Postfix program.

```
mail_owner = postfix
```

default_privs

This parameter sets the privileges that the Postfix programs will have when interacting with external programs. For security sake, this should not have the same value as mail_owner; the value should not give system privileges (such as root).

On most Linux boxes, the user nobody works well. This user is frequently used where a daemon requires basic nonprivileged access to run on the system.

```
default_privs = nobody
```

myhostname

This specifies the fully-qualified domain name that will be used by Postfix whenever the $myhostname variable is specified. The $myhostname variable allows you to refer to the hostname again and again in the configuration, all controlled by the value of this single entry. If the hostname needs to be changed, it can be accomplished throughout the entire Postfix system by simply altering this value.

If this value is not specified, Postfix will use the system-default hostname value returned by the gethostname() system service call.

```
myhostname = host.domain.name
```

If Postfix is to operate on a virtual server, you can specify the virtual domain instead:

```
myhostname = virtualhost.domain.name
```

mydomain

The mydomain parameter is similar to myhostname, except that that host portion of the full-qualified name is not used. If the name of your machine is frogs. mypetanimals.com, the value of mydomain should be set to mypetanimals.com Like the myhostname parameter, if this value is omitted, it will be derived from the default system value.

```
mydomain = domain.name
```

myorigin

The myorigin parameter is used for sending mail. It provides the apparent origin of the e-mail to the receiver. If this value is not set, the default is $myhostname However, if you are configuring Postfix to act as the mail server for an entire domain, you should change this value to $mydomain You may also want to set up an alias database so that the origin will contain the name of the node within the domain employed by that user.

```
myorigin = $myhostname
```

inet_interfaces

The inet_interfaces parameter configures mail delivery. It controls the IP addresses for which Postfix will accept incoming mail. If not specified, all incoming mail will be accepted.

```
inet_interfaces = all
inet_interfaces = $myhostname, localhost
```

mydestination

When mail is received, the Postfix program needs to know if it is responsible for the local delivery for the message. The mydestination parameter will tell Postfix what local mail it is responsible for delivering. If not explicitly set, it will assume a value of `$myhostname` + `localhost.$mydomain` If your Postfix installation will be responsible for delivering mail to your entire domain, this parameter should be set as follows:

```
mydestination = $myhostname, localhost.$mydomain $mydomain
```

Addresses already specified by the `inet_interfaces` parameter will already be served by Postfix. Note that virtual addresses should not be listed here. The appropriate place to set up virtual addresses is through the use of the `virtual` file.

local_recipient_maps

The `local_recipient_maps` parameter allows you to configure Postfix to reject any incoming mail that does not belong to the list of users you supply. If you supply this parameter, Postfix will compare the address of all incoming messages to the list you provide. If the address is not in the list or table you supply, the message will be rejected. This is useful when you need to control the list of acceptable users on the system or in the domain. This can also set up the criteria for accepting mail for users on other machines in the domain.

```
local_recipient_maps = $alias_maps unix:passwd.byname
```

masquerade_domains

The `masquerade_domains` is an optional parameter that lists domains that need to have the subdomain structure removed before sending messages.

```
masquerade_domains = $mydomain
```

masquerade_exceptions

The `masquerade_exceptions` provides a list of user names to be exempted from the masquerading activity. By default, there are no exceptions to the masquerade logic.

```
masquerade_exceptions = root,mailer-daemon
```

local_transport

The `local_transport` parameter specifies the transport to use for delivering local mail. By default, Postfix uses the transport called `local`, which is defined in the master.cf configuration file.

```
local_transport = lmtp:unix:/file/name
local_transport = local
```

alias_maps

The `alias_map` parameter tells Postfix which database tables to employ for user aliasing. Postfix will search the alias tables for a match against the names on incoming mail. Aliases provide a way to redirect incoming mail to different accounts on the local machine or domain.

By default, Postfix will search the local alias database and then the NIS alias database (if the Postfix machine is using NIS).

```
alias_maps = hash:/etc/postfix/aliases
```

alias_database

The `alias_database` parameter is similar to the `alias_maps` parameter, except that `alias_database` is restricted to tables built by Postfix that were compiled using the `newaliases` command. This is in contrast to the `alias_maps` command, which can refer to tables that reside outside of Postfix itself.

```
alias_database = dbm:/etc/mail/aliases
```

home_mailbox

The `home_mailbox` parameter allows you to change the directory that receives incoming mail. The value is a directory specification given in relation to the user's home directory. So a value of `Maildir/` places mail in that subdirectory in the user's home directory, much in the same way Qmail does. By default, incoming mail is usually directed to `/var/spool/mail`.

```
home_mailbox = Maildir/
```

mail_spool_directory

The `mail_spool_directory` parameter is a pointer to the directory that contains the traditional Unix-style mailbox files. On most Linux systems, the default value is /var/spool/mail.

```
mail_spool_directory = /var/spool/mail
```

mailbox_command

The `mailbox_command` parameter allows you to specify a program to be executed in lieu of normal local mail delivery. The program is run with the identity and privileges of the receiving user. This allows the use of the `procmail` command, a local delivery program often used in Sendmail installations.

This parameter is somewhat unique in that it does not substitute Postfix variables, which begin with the dollar sign ($). This allows you to specify shell environment variables, which begin with the dollar sign instead. In particular, this command sets environment values for the following:

- SHELL
- HOME
- USER
- EXTENSION
- LOGNAME
- LOCAL
- DOMAIN

```
mailbox_command = /usr/bin/procmail -a $DOMAIN -d $LOGNAME
```

mailbox_transport

If you have specified an optional mail transport mechanism in master.cf, this parameter will cause it to be invoked after .forward files and aliases have been processed. This parameter takes precedence over other related parameters such as mailbox_command.

```
mailbox_transport = newtransport
```

fallback_transport

The fallback_transport parameter is similar to the mailbox_transport parameter, except that it is invoked only for users not listed in the password file.

```
fallback_transport =
```

luser_relay

The luser_relay parameter is very useful for delivering mail to users who do not have accounts on the machine. If an incoming message is addressed to someone unknown on the current machine, a bounce message is usually returned to the sender. With luser_relay set, mail to unknown users is sent to a different user, even on a different machine.

Certain special variables are available for use in this parameter:

- $recipient is the full address name.
- $shell is the recipient's shell.

- ◆ $user is the recipient's username.

- ◆ $local is the recipient's local information.

- ◆ $domain is the recipient's domain information.

Also, a Boolean syntax is available to substitute values conditionally. Specifying `${variable?value}` causes the value of `variable` to be used if it exists or causes `value` to be used if $variable does not exist.

```
luser_relay = $user@other.host
```

smtpd_recipient_limit

The `smtpd_recipient_limit` sets the maximum number of recipients that can be addressed in a single message.

```
smtpd_recipient_limit = 1000
```

smtpd_timeout

The `smtpd_timeout` parameter sets the amount of time allowed between SMTP responses before a timeout is declared. The number is followed by s for seconds, m for minutes, or h for hours.

```
smtpd_timeout = 300s
```

mynetworks_style

The `mynetworks_style` is used to establish which machines are to be trusted by this machine. Trust can be set for an entire network class (A, B, or C), a particular subnet, or the local host alone. Once the machine is determined to be trusted or untrusted that fact can be used to determine activities and restrictions by Postfix.

```
mynetworks_style = class
mynetworks_style = subnet
mynetworks_style = host
```

mynetworks

If you do not use the `mynetworks_style` parameter to declare trusted networks, you can use the `mynetworks` parameter to explicitly declare the networks and nodes to be trusted by Postfix.

```
mynetworks = 166.100.19.0/28, 127.0.0.0/8
```

allow_untrusted_routing

The `allow_untrusted_routing` parameter can prevent sender-specified routing of messages from untrusted clients to domains listed in the relay_domains parameter. Spammers sometimes ask backup MX hosts to forward mail to the primary MX host. The primary MX host, having received the messages from the trustedMX backup, is then tricked into relaying the spam to the world. This parameter can prevent this scenario from happening.

```
allow_untrusted_routing = no
```

maps_rbl_domains

The `maps_rbl_domains` parameter allows you to specify domains that host blacklists of known spammers. This allows Postfix to reject messages that come from commonly known spamming domains. By default, no such check is made.

```
maps_rbl_domains = blackholes.mail-abuse.org
```

smtpd_client_restrictions

The `smtpd_client_restrictions` parameter gives you power to reject clients for a number of reasons. For example, you can check the header information of the incoming mail and look it up against a table of regular expressions and reject the message if it satisfies a rule calling for a rejection. The `reject_unauth_pipelining` value can be used to reject mail from mass mailing programs that try to speed up delivery by pipelining commands (sending them ahead of time). The `reject_unknown_client` value rejects mail supposedly sent from invalid domain names. The `reject_maps_rbl` parameter rejects mail from any domain listed in the `$maps_rbl_domains` variable, which contains a list of known spamming domains. The `permit_mynetwork` allows access to trusted hosts.

```
smtpd_client_restrictions =
    check_client_access hash:/etc/postfix/client_access,
    reject_unknown_client,
    reject_unauth_pipelining,
    reject_maps_rbl
```

smtpd_sender_restrictions

The `check_sender_access` value allows the sender's domain name to be checked against regular expressions. The `reject_unknown_sender_domain` value causes the connection to be rejected if the DNS server does not know the hostname. The `reject_non_fqdn_sender` causes rejection if the sender name is not a fully qualified domain name.

```
smtpd_sender_restrictions =
    check_sender_access hash:/etc/postfix/sender_access,
    reject_unknown_sender_domain,
    reject_non_fqdn_sender
```

smtpd_recipient_restrictions

The `smtpd_recipient_restrictions` parameter directs Postfix to reject messages if the recipient name does not pass muster. The `check_recipient_access` value allows the recipient name to be filtered via regular expressions. The `reject_unknown_recipient_domain` value causes the connection to be rejected if the recipient's host is not known to the DNS server. The `reject_non_fqdn_recipient` causes rejection if the recipient name does not contain a fully qualified domain name. The `check_relay_domains` value allows the message to go through if the client or recipient hostname is covered by an entry in the `$relay_domains variable`.

```
smtpd_recipient_restrictions =
    check_recipient_access hash:/etc/postfix/recipient_access,
    reject_unknown_recipient_domain,
    reject_non_fqdn_recipient,
    check_relay_domains
```

smtpd_helo_required

The `smtpd_helo_required` parameter forces the mail-sending program to use the `HELO` command when initiating contact to the mail server. The `HELO` command requires that the sender specify the name of the host sending the mail. This allows Postfix to investigate the domain name and take action according to the restrictions specified in the `smtpd_helo_restrictions` parameter that follows:

```
smtpd_helo_required = yes
```

smtpd_helo_restrictions

The `smtpd_helo_restrictions` parameter specifies the conditions under which Postfix rejects connections once a `HELO` message is received. The `check_helo_access` value allows the domain name included in the `HELO` command to be checked against regular expressions. The `reject_unknown_hostname` and `reject_invalid_hostname` values cause the connection to be rejected if the hostname is not known to the DNS server or if the hostname syntax is incorrect, respectively. The `reject_non_fqdn_hostname` causes rejection if the domain name is not fully qualified. The `permit_mynetworks` parameter allows access to trusted nodes.

```
smtpd_helo_restrictions =
    check_helo_access regexp:/etc/postfix/helo_access,
    reject_unknown_hostname,
```

```
reject_invalid_hostname,
reject_non_fqdn_hostname
```

smtpd_delay_reject

Much UCE is sent by spammers who specify an invalid return address. By default, Postfix rejects the e-mail after receiving the intended receiver. By specifying no here, Postfix rejects the e-mail as soon as it is apparent that the e-mail is unacceptable.

```
smtpd_delay_reject = no
```

strict_rfc821_envelopes

The strict_rfc821_envelopes parameter can enable Postfix to reject any addresses that do not meet the RFC 821 standards. Although this may block some messages generated by spammers, it also may block messages from badly written mail clients.

```
strict_rfc821_envelopes = yes
```

header_checks

The header_checks parameter helps fight spam. Use it to point to files containing regular expressions that will reject e-mails that fail the header checks. The regular expressions should be in the general form of: /^header-name: things that indicate this is spam/ REJECT

```
header_checks = regexp:/etc/postfix/hdr-chks-filename
```

body_checks

The body_checks parameter is similar to the header_checks parameter, except that the regular expressions act on the body of the message.

```
body_checks = regexp:/etc/postfix/bdy-chks-filename
```

message_size_limit

The message_size_limit parameter controls the maximum size allowed for an incoming message. By default, Postfix limits the maximum size to 10 megabytes. To reduce possible ill effects from spammers, many people lower the maximum limit to around 2 megabytes. Obviously, this parameter needs to reflect the legitimate traffic you expect to receive on your server.

```
message_size_limit = 2048000
```

relay_domains

The `relay_domains` parameter allows you to place restrictions on the relaying of mail through the SMTP server. By supplying a file, database, or list of domains and/or hosts, you can specify which systems Postfix will relay mail to and from. If not specified, the value of this parameter is set to $mydestination.

Note that systems already specified by the `inet_interfaces`, `mydestination`, and `virtual_maps` parameters will be handled by Postfix in those contexts, so those hosts and domains do not need to be added to this list.

```
erelay_domains = $mydestination
```

mynetworks

The `mynetworks` parameter tells Postfix what networks are local to this machine. This is critical for preventing use of the mail relay by unknown hosts — a favorite trick of many spammers. You can specify the network using the `your.IP.number.here`/mask either directly or in a file.

```
mynetworks = $config_directory/mynetworks
```

smtpd_banner

For security reasons, most system administrators do not want to reveal the versions of software they are using. However, some people prefer to display the software name or version upon connection to the SMTP server. The information is transmitted as part of the 220 status code. If this is not specified, none of the software information is returned in the 220 status code.

By Internet convention, the first parameter must be $myhostname.

```
smtpd_banner = $myhostname ESMTP $mail_name ($mail_version) (Red Hat)
```

A proposed US law would make it illegal to send unsolicited commercial mail to any mail server that includes the string NO UCE in the banner.

```
smtpd_banner = $myhostname NO UCE ESMTP
```

local_destination_concurrency_limit

The `local_destination_concurrency_limit` controls the number of concurrent mail deliveries that can be made to the local client. Since deliveries to an individual mailbox must be done in serial, it makes sense to keep this number very low if there are only a few valid mailboxes on the local node.

```
local_destination_concurrency_limit = 2
```

default_destination_concurrency_limit

Similar to `local_destination_concurrency_limit`, this parameter controls the number of transfers that can take place at one time. Every message transport (like UUCP or SMTP) has its own limit for the number of concurrent transfers. If the value is not specifically described for a particular transport, the default parameter is used.

```
default_destination_concurrency_limit = 10
uucp_destination_concurrency_limit = 100
smtpd_destination_concurrency_limit = 1000
```

debug_peer_list

The `debug_peer_list` parameter is a list of hosts or domains that will produce debugging messages in the log file upon connection.

```
debug_peer_list = 127.0.0.1
```

debug_peer_level

The `debug_peer_level` parameter sets the level for debugging messages logged when connecting to a node covered by the `debug_peer_list` parameter.

```
debug_peer_level = 2
```

debugger_command

The `debugger_command` parameter specifies the shell command to be executed when the `-d` debug argument is passed on invocation of Postfix. The inclusion of a `sleep` command in the syntax gives the debugger a few seconds to connect before the process continues.

```
debugger_command =
     PATH=/usr/bin:/usr/X11R6/bin
     xxgdb $daemon_directory/$process_name $process_id & sleep 5
```

disable_vrfy_command

The `disable_vrfy_command` can be turned on so that spammers cannot easily extract e-mail addresses.

```
disable_vrfy_command = yes
```

Now that we have seen many of the parameters used in constructing the main configuration file, we will briefly examine how to approach some of the other configuration files found in a typical Postfix installation.

Setting Up Important Files

As we have seen, the main.cf configuration file contains critical information regarding Postfix's activity. However, there are other configuration files which provide important information as well. While these files will not require as much attention as the main configuration, it will be useful to understand how to set them up according to need.

Setting up master.cf

This table lists the services available within Postfix. It also specifies some of the characteristics of each service, including whether the service is run as root and what command is executed to provide the service.

Unless you will be customizing your services, you probably will not need to add to this file.

Setting up the aliases file

The format and function of the Postfix aliases file is identical to that of Sendmail. The concept of the file is simple: redirect mail from one address to another. This is very helpful for redirection of mail that might be addressed to generic accounts such as admin or root to the appropriate individuals. It can also redirect mail addressed to synthetic accounts (such as info or help) to real people.

The basic format is:

```
user:    targetaccount
```

To redirect mail addressed to admin, the entry might look like:

```
admin:    therealadmin@domain.name
```

Setting up the virtual file

The virtual file sets up redirections that Postfix uses. The redirections can be either local or nonlocal. Redirections affect delivery, but they do not affect message headers. The administrator must also be aware that the rules are recursive.

Typical entries might include:

```
virtual.domain
```

This instructs Postfix to accept mail addressed to virtual.domain.

```
someuser@virtual.domain receiver@local.domain
```

This redirects e-mail addressed to a particular user in the virtual domain to the specified user in the local domain.

Consult the man page for virtual if you anticipate setting up an extensive virtual file. Certain entries take precedence over others, but we will not deal with that here.

Setting up the canonical file

The canonical file is used to clean up addresses. Typical uses might include translating node-based usernames to a corporate standard `First.Last@company.com`. Another use is to fix up the e-mail addresses that older legacy systems have generated. The format of the file is simply:

```
pattern result
```

When an e-mail address matches the pattern, it is replaced with the corresponding result.

Setting p the access file

The access file directs the Postfix SMTP server to accept or reject mail based on the host or recipient's address information. The format of each line is straightforward:

```
pattern result
```

The `pattern` portion is basically almost any part of an e-mail address. It can be a full e-mail address such as `user@domain.com`, a domain or network name such as `domain.com`, or a user specification such as `user@`.

The `result` portion is usually either the word *REJECT* or *OK*. If the `result` contains a number and some text, it will cause a rejection returning the specified error number and the accompanying text. If the result contains any other value, it is treated as OK.

Once these files have been configured properly, a basic few commands will be helpful to manipulate your Postfix installation.

Using Commands to Process Datafiles

The `postmap` command takes Postfix text files and makes a table out of them.

```
postmap helo_access
```

Use this command to find out the version of Postfix:

```
postconf mail_version
```

Display Postfix default settings:

```
postconf -d
```

Display Postfix nondefault settings:

```
postconf -n
```

Delete a message from a Postfix queue:

```
postsuper -d queuename
```

Delete all messages from all queues:

```
postsuper -d ALL
```

Flush the mail queue:

```
postfix flush
```

Based on the summary of possible configuration parameters for postfix the second half of the chapter discusses common scenarios and situations for postfix parameters.

Understanding E-mail Server Terminology

When discussing e-mail, a lot of specialized terminology is used. The terms MUA, MTA, message store, envelope headers, and message headers will be explained here.

The standards that define how e-mail is transmitted from one server to another are ancient by the standards of Internet time. They were written at a time when Internet-wide e-mail was still just beginning, and though the Internet has grown beyond anyone's expectations, the standards for mail haven't changed a whole lot. The original standard, the venerable RFC 821, is dated 1982, and still moves all e-mail that is transported across the Internet. It has recently been updated in rfc 2821, which makes the protocol clearer for implementers but does not change the core concepts of Internet e-mail.

Mail User Agents

When you read your e-mail, you do so with a program that is technically referred to as a *Mail User Agent* (MUA), sometimes referred to as *UA*.

Some examples of MUAs are Microsoft Outlook, Netscape Mail, Eudora, mutt, or pine. The primary job of the MUA is to read e-mail in a message store (usually on a disk) or from a server (that is, using a POP3 or IMAP server) and to present that e-mail to a user in a readable fashion. The MUA also submits messages to the MTA in a format that lets the MTA route the message to its intended recipient. This can be accomplished using a command line client or, as is more common now, an SMTP server.

Message stores

A *message store* is an abstract term for usually one or more files on a server. The term message store is used when discussing where e-mail that has been delivered goes, because the standards don't define how you have to store your e-mail. This may seem strange, but consider how much computers have changed since 1982. If how messages were stored on disk were codified in the standard, the standard would have ceased to be relevant a long time ago.

Mail Transport Agents

Most people are aware that their mail arrives on a server. Mail server systems are correctly referred to as Mail Transport Agents (MTAs). Sendmail, qmail, and postfix are examples of MTAs. An MTA serves two purposes. The first is to accept e-mail messages from a mail client and transmit it across a network to another server. The second is to accept e-mail from another server and deliver it to a mail store to be picked up by an MUA, where it can be read by the user to whom it has been sent.

Message headers

When you view an e-mail message, you see information regarding the person it came from, whom it was sent to, the message's subject, and probably other, less important information. Each piece of information occupies one line. These lines are called message headers. These are lines of information that MUAs insert into messages for their own reasons. For instance, some MUAs insert information about what MUA and what version was used to send the e-mail, what the name of the user is set to, and so on. These headers can all be set by the MUA and won't necessarily bear any relationship to reality if the message's sender doesn't want it to.

Envelopes

The information in message headers is separate and distinct from the message's *envelope*. The envelope information is what servers use to determine how the message really gets delivered. The term *envelope* references traditional snail-mail. A postal mail will always have the name of the person it's intended for, the person's address, and other information needed to send the mail. The post office will always stamp mail with a mark that indicates the post office that the mail was first delivered to, and the mail will usually have a return address (which may or may not be useful). E-mail is similar.

For instance, have you ever had a friend send a message to 10 people, and when you get it, you see that the message is apparently addressed to a nonexistent user? This is because the message header has been filled with useless and possibly misleading information. However, when you use Postfix it saves the envelope information in special headers that you can use to glean some useful information. When you use Postfix, it saves the envelope information in special headers. The important information that gets saved is the IP address and name of the server that has sent the e-mail, the IP address and the name of the server that has received the e-mail, the supposed name of the sender, and the intended recipient of the message. The IP addresses of the servers are preserved in headers that begin with Received. The senders claimed e-mail address is in the line beginning with Return-Path:. The final recipient e-mail address is stored in the line beginning with Delivered-To:. If e-mail has gone through more than one server, which happens a lot, at each stage a Received: header will be inserted, and there will be a single Delivered-To: header. For a mailing list, where the message has been delivered, there may be an additional Delivered-To: header. However, the only headers which you can be sure are accurate portions of the envelope are the last Received: and the Delivered-To:. The last envelope headers inserted are usually at the top of the message headers.

It's important to have this information in mind when examining e-mail for correct mail routing and possible configuration issues and when detecting and preventing spam. Now that some of the language has been defined, let's look at some examples where it can be used.

Sample Configurations

Now we present scenarios that can take place in real life and show how to solve them using Postfix based on a standard Redhat Postfix package.

All of the following examples assume that you're setting up a server called mail.example.com and that it is the main mail server for example.com*. mail.example.com will have one ethernet interface. This interface will be used to deliver e-mail and for users to check e-mail. This interface will be at 192.168.0.2, and the network it is on has the IP addresses 192.168.0.0-192.168.0.254, which will be considered trusted for the sake of sending e-mail in our examples.

Please note that example.com can't be used and is reserved and set up in such a way so that no mail will ever go to or from it.

Example 1: Sending mail

The most basic task for a new mail server is to allow users to send e-mail to each other. The Postfix rpm comes with most of the necessary configuration already done for you in main.cf. If you've ever tried to setup Sendmail, you'll be pleased to find that all of the options are well documented in the configuration file as it ships and that they can appear in almost any order.

Postfix has a command called postconf, which can be used to edit the configuration file automatically. We're going to use postconf for the configuration examples to be more concise and to focus on the relevant settings.

```
# postconf -e 'myhostname = mail.example.com'
# postconf -e 'mydomain = example.com'
# postconf -e 'inet_interfaces = all'
# postconf -e 'mydestination = $myhostname, $mydomain,
localhost.$mydomain'
```

After changing these variables in main.cf, run

```
# postfix reload
```

as root; the server will now accept mail for example.com and mail.example.com. Any user on the system will now receive e-mail as user@example.com.

Example 2: Accepting e-mail for multiple domains

Let's suppose that your company has a new product and has registered another domain to help sell and support it. The new product is called the wowwidget, so your company wants to receive e-mail sent to them at wowwidget.com as well as example.com. For now, though, everyone's e-mail address will be the same. So the employee who currently receives e-mail as john@example.com will also receive e-mail as john@wowwidget.com. Postfix administrators sometimes refer to this as *Sendmail style virtual domains*.

This change is very simple. As long as DNS is setup correctly (we'll look at this shortly), the only change that needs to be made is to add names to the `mydestination` variable:

```
# postconf -e 'mydestination = $myhostname, $mydomain,
localhost.$mydomain, wowwidget.com'
```

If you expect your company to be adding a lot of new domains, you can see how quickly appending names to this line can become cumbersome. Even though Postfix's configuration syntax allows you to continue lines by beginning the next line with a whitespace, Postfix has a way of making the management of long lists of hosts (or other data) much easier. Postfix allows you to put lists of data into files outside of main.cf. If your company starts to increase the number of domains you have to receive e-mail for, to 10, 20, or more domains that you need, you can make managing your configuration much easier by doing this:

```
# postconf -e 'mydestination = $myhostname, $mydomain,
localhost.$mydomain, /etc/postfix/mydestination'
```

This tells Postfix that there will be a file called /etc/postfix/mydestination that will have a list of domains that should be associated with the mydestinationparameter.

If your company wants to receive e-mail for `newwowwidget.com` and `thebest-wowwidget.com`, the file `/etc/postfix/mydestination` will look like this:

```
wowwidget.com
newwowwidget.com
thebestwowwidget.com
```

After this file is altered, `Postfix reload` must be run for the changes to take effect.

Example 3: Postfix-Style virtual domains

Let's say that your company has decided that the wowwidget product line should be developed into its own unit. The first step is to have e-mail sent to info@wowwidget.com to go to a different address than e-mail sent to info@example.com. The person now in charge of answering e-mail sent to info@example.com is john@example.com. The person who responds to info@wowwidget.com is fred@example.com.

> Even though to other systems on the Internet, example.com and wow widget.com are treated the same — they have users, they accept e-mail, and e-mail will come from addresses at both domains — there is an important difference in how Postfix treats the two domains. When you set up a Sendmail-style virtual domain, as in example 2, mail is delivered to what is considered a local user. This means that e-mail addressed to a user at example.com or wowwidget.com is delivered to a message store on the example.com server. When you set up a Postfix-style virtual domain, mail is never delivered locally; it is always forwarded to another address where mail can be delivered locally. The other address can be on the same server or on a remote server — it makes no difference.

Forwarding from virtual address to virtual address

You should know that you can forward to an e-mail from a virtual address to another virtual address, and under most circumstances you won't encounter any problems. One case of this is that if two virtual e-mail addresses forward to each other, they will create a forwarding loop that will, in principle, never end. In fact, MTAs are usually smarter than that, and when a certain number of Delivered-To: or Received: headers have been reached, the mail will be bounced to the sender as undeliverable. Some MTAs will also bounce a looping message if they see themselves in the `Delivered-To:` headers too many times. If you get unexplained bounces involving a virtual user (or any kind of alias), it's worth examining the `Delivered-To:` headers with this in mind when you're determining the cause of the bounce.

To start enabling virtual domains in Postfix, do the following:

```
# postconf -e 'virtual_maps = hash:/etc/postfix/virtuals'
```

The preceding line looks similar to what is done in the example for extending the mydestination parameter in example 2. The notable difference is that before the path to a file is the word, *hash*. In the context of the configuration file, it means that Postfix should reference a file that is compiled from a plain text file into a specialized file-type on disk that makes accessing large amounts of data easy and fast. One other advantage of using this file format is that when changes are made to the file, Postfix does not need to be restarted to have those changes affect the way the system works.

The contents of /etc/postfix/virtuals should contain the following:

```
wowwidget.com virtual
info@wowwidget.com fred@example.com
```

The first line is present to indicate that the domain wowwidget.com is virtual. However, the word *virtual* isn't important. You can put any word in, but the word *virtual* is an appropriate choice.

After doing this, you should run the postmap command:

```
# postmap /etc/postfix/virtuals
```

This creates the hash file from the text file. After running postmap, you should have a new file in /etc/postfix called virtuals.db.

Last, we should alter our configuration to reflect that wowwidget.com is now a Postfix-style virtual domain instead of a Sendmail-style virtual domain by removing wowwidget.com from /etc/postfix/mydestination. After all this is done, reload Postfix, and wowwidget.com will be treated as a virtual domain.

The first problem that will arise after this is that mail that used to go to users@wowwidget.com will no longer work. Once this solution has been put in place, all e-mail addresses that will receive e-mail must be entered into the virtuals file. As the number of virtual domains grows, it is handy to break the lists of virtual domains into their own files. So if thebestwowwidget.com is also growing and you want to manage both of these in files that are mnemonically named, you can do the following (all on one line):

```
# postconf -e 'virtual_maps = hash:/etc/postfix/wowwidget.com,
    hash:/etc/postfix/thebestwowwidget.com'
```

If you rename what was the virtuals file to a file called wowwidget.com and create a similar file called thebestwowwidget.com that has the same format as the wowwidget.com file, you can more easily manage virtual domains.

It is important to note that even though the files listed in virtual_maps resemble the format of the aliases file, the features that Sendmail administrators expect in their aliases files can't be used for Postfix-style virtual servers. If you need to run commands on an alias, the aliases file is still the place to put them. However, a convenient twist is that in a similar fashion to how Postfix allows you to define multiple files for your virtual_maps, Postfix will let you define multiple alias files. To do this, define additional files in the alias_maps setting.

There is one other form of virtual domains that will not be covered in this section. It can be called "pure virtual domains." This means that the domains are all separate from one another, and all of them are virtual — that is, none of the users have any local accounts, and no one checks e-mail using system passwords. Postfix has support for delivering e-mail in this style. Some IMAP and POP3 servers such as Courier-IMAP (which supports IMAP and POP3) will work with pure virtual domains. If you want to find out more about how Postfix works in this context, you can read the file /etc/postfix/virtual. You shouldn't bother reading this until you've already become familiar with how Postfix works.

Example 4: Verifying DNS settings for e-mail

The Domain Name Service (DNS) is one of the essential protocols that make the Internet as useable as it is (although some people may argue that it's not as useable as they would like, the Internet's rampant success proves that it's good enough so far). The underlying idea for DNS is that computers should be addressable by their names, not by their IP addresses, which are unfriendly sequences of numbers, such as 127.0.0.1 or 192.168.3.1. DNS is how, after you register a domain name or decide on a name for a system that your company uses, that name gets propagated and can be used by other people on the Internet or within your company's network.

DNS under Internet Protocol Version 4 have multiple record types. These record types have short names that are usually a mnemonic contraction — names like an "A record" for "Address record," "TXT record" for "Text Record," and so on. There are three records important for tracking down e-mail issues. These are the Name Server record, the Mail eXchanger record, and the Address record. The odd capitalization exists because the abbreviations for the records are "NS," "MX," and "A" records, respectively.

IPv4 is used Internet-wide right now. You may hear things about IPv6, but don't worry about it — it won't be something you have to worry about for a couple of years.

If you've never dealt with DNS before, A records are going to be the most familiar. An A record translates a name such as slashdot.org into an IP address. Most DNS tools will, by default, look up A records. For example, we'll get the following output if we use the `host` command (included in the `bind-utils` package on Redhat systems):

```
# host slashdot.org
slashdot.org has address 64.28.67.150
```

 This may change sometime in the future, but at the time of this writing, what you see is the actual output of the host command.

The first rule of investigating DNS issues is not to use nslookup. nslookup has many behaviors that can encourage an incorrect diagnosis of problems, so the examples presented here won't use it. Instead, we'll be using two similar programs that are better behaved. They're the `host` command and the `dig` command. You've just seen the host command being used. The same information that precedes this section can be obtained by doing the following:

```
# dig -t a slashdot.org
; <<>> DiG 9.2.1 <<>> -t a slashdot.org
;; global options:  printcmd
;; Got answer:
;; ->>HEADER<<- opcode: QUERY, status: NOERROR, id: 13438
;; flags: qr rd ra; QUERY: 1, ANSWER: 1, AUTHORITY: 0, ADDITIONAL:
0
;; QUESTION SECTION:
;slashdot.org                    IN    A

;; ANSWER SECTION:
slashdot.org          51868      IN    A    64.28.67.150

;; Query time: 27 msec
;; SERVER: 10.0.0.1#53(10.0.0.1)
;; WHEN: Tue Aug 27 02:12:47 2002
;; MSG SIZE  rcvd: 46
```

The `-t` in the preceding command is telling dig what record type to query. By default, dig and host will look for an A record, but if we are looking for other record types, `-t` is necessary for both commands. From now on, we'll use `-t` whenever we issue a query.

As you can see, dig gives you a lot more information by default than host does. You can get more information from host by adding the -d flag, that is:

```
# host -d -t a slashdot.org
Trying "slashdot.org"
;; ->>HEADER<<- opcode: QUERY, status: NOERROR, id: 48363
;; flags: qr rd ra; QUERY: 1, ANSWER: 1, AUTHORITY: 0, ADDITIONAL:
0

;; QUESTION SECTION:
;slashdot.org                    IN    A

;; ANSWER SECTION:
slashdot.org          51533   IN    A    64.28.67.150

Received 46 bytes from 10.0.0.1#53 in 33 ms
```

The output is a little different between the two tools, but all of the important information is the same. The information to focus on is the answer section.

```
;; ANSWER SECTION:
slashdot.org          51533   IN    A    64.28.67.150
```

The answer tells us that slashdot.org has an A record in the IN class that points to 64.28.67.150 with a time to live in the cache of 51,533 seconds. This means the cache we're querying will wait that many seconds before it will reconfirm that A record. That number will go down one for every second. If you run the same query a few times over a few minutes, you'll see that number go down.

It's highly unlikely that you'll ever see a class other than "IN" (short for "INternet"). Other classes were in use when DNS was first developed, but all others have fallen out of common usage.

To find out about MX records, you need to tell host or dig that you want them, like so:

```
# host -t mx slashdot.org
slashdot.org mail is handled by 10 mail.egl.net.
```

This response makes sense at first, except that unlike the answer to the query for an A record, this response has the number 10 floating in the middle. This is called the MX preference. The MX preference allows multiple servers to be defined as valid receiving systems for e-mail. This allows mail service for an organization to be more tolerant of failure of a particular system or network. The MX preference for a hostname can be anywhere from zero to 32,767. Any MX records with a value of zero are tried first. If the mail delivery succeeds, no other mail servers are tried. If there are issues with all of the servers with a preference of zero, any other servers with a higher number preference will be tried in order, from next lowest to the highest available.

There can be multiple servers with the same MX preference, but it's usually a good idea to specify a lowest-preference server and subsequently specify higher-preference servers unless you have specific reasons for doing otherwise.

Also, if you are sending e-mail to a domain name that has no explicit MX record but that does have an A record, that A record acts like an explicit MX record with a value of zero.

The last important record that needs to be talked about is NS. In the same way that mail servers handle e-mail, name servers handle DNS names. To find out what name server is handling names for a particular domain, you can run the query:

```
# host -t ns slashdot.org
slashdot.org name server ns1.osdn.com.
slashdot.org name server ns2.osdn.com.
slashdot.org name server ns3.osdn.com.
```

As you can see, slashdot.org has multiple name servers. Unlike MX records, NS records do not have associated preference values. When a name is looked up, all name servers are contacted, and the first response is used. Even though the servers are named sequentially (for example, ns1, ns2, ns3), those numbers don't indicate any kind of special order to networked computers.

DNS works by querying servers in a top-down fashion. That is, there are a few top-level servers. These are called the root servers. They're the ones that all the others branch out from. These servers have their own domain, root-servers.net. The names of the root servers are a.root-servers.net through m.root-servers.net. You can check the addresses of the active root servers by running, for instance:

```
# host c.root-servers.net
c.root-servers.net has address 192.33.4.12
```

It's important to know about these servers because they let you trace names right from the top when you have problems. You need this power because all IP protocol-using computers rely on a caching name server to look up names. If these servers are broken, or sometimes when they're working properly, they can cause problems.

The name servers that a Linux system is using can be discovered by looking in the file /etc/resolv.conf. Each line beginning with the word nameserver and followed by a numeric IP address is one of the caching name servers you are using. For the sake of the examples, we'll use a name server at 10.0.0.1, which is a private IP address. A real system should probably have a different name server listed, as well as more than one server that it can use in case there are issues with one. More than four aren't usually any use.

```
# cat /etc/resolv.conf
nameserver 10.0.0.1
```

Until now, we've been implicitly asking our caching name server to answer for us. But if there are problems, the mail administrator will have to start near the top and simulate what should happen if his or her caching name server(s) were working properly. Let's imagine that mail sent to a friend at slashdot.org isn't reaching him or her. First it should be confirmed that the e-mail actually hasn't made it off of our system and over to the remote MTA. You determine this by running the `mailq` command and seeing that your message is still in the local queue on mail.example.com. The next thing to do is check the maillog in `/var/log/maillog`. It could reveal that Postfix has deferred delivery of this message because of a name service error. That could look like the following (though it would appear on a single line in the logs):

```
Aug 22 12:29:43 mail postfix/smtp[960]: CED42BF48:
to=<friend@slashdot.org>, relay=none, delay=44641, status=deferred
(Name service error for slashdot.org: Host not found, try again)
```

There are other possible errors besides `host not found`. But let's investigate this error. Let's see if we can find slashdot.org on our own. First, ask a root name server for information about slashdot.org's name servers:

```
# host -t ns slashdot.org a.root-servers.net
Using domain server:
Name: a.root-servers.net
Address: 198.41.0.4#53
Aliases:
```

That's entirely useless. So, use the -d switch to see if the information we need is hidden somewhere in there.

```
# host -d -t ns slashdot.org a.root-servers.net
Trying "slashdot.org"
Using domain server:
Name: a.root-servers.net
Address: 198.41.0.4#53
Aliases:

;; ->>HEADER<<- opcode: QUERY, status: NOERROR, id: 17155
;; flags: qr rd; QUERY: 1, ANSWER: 0, AUTHORITY: 13, ADDITIONAL:
13

;; QUESTION SECTION:
;slashdot.org                          IN    NS

;; AUTHORITY SECTION:
```

```
org                172800   IN   NS   A.GTLD-SERVERS.NET.
[ A through M, in no particular order ]
org                172800   IN   NS   M.GTLD-SERVERS.NET.

;; ADDITIONAL SECTION:
A.GTLD-SERVERS.NET.   172800   IN   A   192.5.6.30
[ A through M, in no particular order ]
M.GTLD-SERVERS.NET.   172800   IN   A   192.55.83.30
```

This hidden information is telling us that the root servers don't have the information we've asked for, but that if we want it (and we do) we should next ask one of the name servers for the .org domain, which are all in the GTLD-SERVERS.NET zone. It may not make sense for the root servers to forward to a set of gtld servers. The reason for this is that there are many top-level domains. There are country-specific domains like .us, .it, .uk, and so on, as well as the Generic Top-Level Domains (that's what gtld stands for), which have to be accommodated. So the root servers have their hands full just telling caching name servers what other name servers should be queried next. The authority section of the response tells us which servers we should treat as authoritative for a particular domain, and the additional section passes on the information, including the IP address of the server we should be asking.

The next time, we'll query one of the gtld-servers given to us in the authority section. So let's make another query, this time:

```
#  host -t ns slashdot.org a.gtld-servers.net
Using domain server:
Name: a.gtld-servers.net
Address: 192.5.6.30#53
Aliases:

slashdot.org name server NS1.OSDN.COM.
slashdot.org name server NS2.OSDN.COM.
slashdot.org name server NS3.OSDN.COM.
```

Now we're getting to some answers. You don't have to look at debugging information. Instead of returning a referral to another server (the contents of the authority section in the last example), we're seeing that the gtld-servers do have NS records that are directly related to the domain we're looking for. This indicates that we're progressing without any problems. Very often, the next step is where real problems occur. However, sometimes if a domain is in transition or has been newly registered, or the name server hasn't been properly setup for this domain, you won't get results for the prior query. The response you get might be:

```
#  host -t ns wowwidget.com a.gtld-servers.net
Using domain server:
Name: a.gtld-servers.net
Address: 192.5.6.30#53
```

```
Aliases:

Host wowwidget.com not found: 3(NXDOMAIN)
```

If you get this answer when you're trying to send e-mail to someone else's system, you can stop looking for the problem – you've found it. When a mail server gets an NXDOMAIN as a response to a query for the domain an e-mail is addressed to, it will bounce the e-mail. An NXDOMAIN is classified as a *hard* error, one that is not caused by a failure that will pass. This is distinguished from a *soft* error, one that may pass if some time is given and tried again. Soft errors can be caused by problems such as all name servers being unavailable when the mail is being delivered, or by all of the receiving MTA's being unavailable or refusing connections. If a name server is unreachable, the error will look like the following (very contrived) example:

```
# host -t ns wowwidget.com 10.0.0.2
;; connection timed out; no servers could be reached
```

This will not trigger a bounce – it will tell the mail server to try repeatedly for five days at intervals that increase to prevent the server from spending all of its time on mail that is less likely to be delivered. When there's a problem, it's generally better to give the people in charge of the system time to sort it out.

Now that the name servers for slashdot.org have been identified, let's see if they have the information Postfix needs to deliver e-mail.

```
# host -t mx slashdot.org ns1.odsn.com
Using domain server:
Name: ns1.osdn.com
Address: 64.28.67.51#53
Aliases:

slashdot.org mail is handled by 10 mail.egl.net.
```

In a properly working configuration, all of the name servers for a domain will have records that indicate that the same hostname (in this case, mail.egl.net) and each name server will respond with the same preference value for the name (in this case the preference value is 10). Any variations could indicate an error in the data on the server(s) that do not agree with the others and could indicate an issue that could prevent mail from being delivered properly.

The last test for confirming that DNS is configured properly for mail is to confirm the A record of the mail exchanger. To do this, we'll ask the root servers who the mail servers are for egl.net and then ask those name servers for the A record of mail.egl.net:

```
# host -t ns egl.net
egl.net name server NS2.egl.net.
```

```
egl.net name server NS3.CW.net.
egl.net name server NS.egl.net.
# host -t a mail.egl.net ns.egl.net
Using domain server:
Name: ns.egl.net
Address: 208.159.114.2#53
Aliases:

mail.egl.net has address 208.159.114.4
```

In your investigations of mail servers, you may have an easier time than this. Many domains do not have MX records, only A records, which cuts out some of the steps that have been detailed here. Remember that if the host just has an A record, Postifix will try to deliver to that host. Be aware, however, that if the DNS admin means for mail to go to another system by using an MX record, mail will bounce after five days. This is because Postfix will attempt to deliver to the host specified in the A record, not the host that should have been specified by the erroneously non-existent MX record. As a mail administrator, if you see such a situation, you have to make a judgment call as to what is supposed to happen. If you are confused, you should contact the postmaster at the domain in question and see if he or she can help resolve the confusion.

When any situation preventing e-mail from being delivered is corrected (in the case of a misconfiguration, the configuration being fixed, or in the case of a system or network outage, the system or network coming back up), you can try to hurry the process along by running the postfix command with the flush option:

```
# postfix flush
```

This tells Postfix to try to deliver all mail that is currently backlogged. You can also specify an e-mail in the queue. Let's suppose that after running the mailq command, a mail with the queue id of 4BCA31F5F3 is found. Let's say that the recipient of that e-mail is jouser@slashdot.org. We've done the investigation, and whatever problems we had before sending e-mail to slashdot.org are now resolved. So let's move that e-mail on its way:

```
# postfix flush 4BCA31F5F3
```

Now, if the slashdot.org MX systems are accepting e-mail, that mail will go out, and pretty soon the entry 4BCA31F5F3 will be delivered, no longer residing in the mail queue.

There is one thing to look out for. New DNS admins who are trying to host multiple domain names on a single IP address sometimes think that they should use a special record called a CNAME. If, at any stage in this, you encounter a CNAME in your lookups where we've demonstrated an MX, an A, or an NS record, the DNS administrator has made a mistake. Unlike A, NS, and MX records, which can all be associated with the same name, CNAME records cannot have other record types associated with them. This means that when we query slashdot.org, it has an A record. It can have more than one A record, and that would be fine. Slashdot.org can also have an MX record associated with it, and everything still works. However, if slashdot.org is a CNAME, it cannot have an A record or an MX record, and mail cannot be delivered to any users @slashdot.org. In other words, expecting a CNAME to work with mail is asking for failure.

A variety of other DNS failures are more subtle than those we've discussed here. Lame servers and lame delegations exist, where servers that are listed as authoritative (listed in the authoritative part of the response) aren't responding as authoritative servers should. This happens when a name server that is acting as a cache is listed as a primary server for a domain. This problem can be ignored as long as there are other servers that can be queried. However, if other name servers go offline, the still functioning, misconfigured name server will first be returning nonauthoritative answers. This will cause funny behavior and later will lose the entry for the mail server from its cache, making the domain unavailable. Both of these are usually soft errors, but even though the mail won't bounce back, it will not be delivered.

Example 5: Directing all mail through a central mail hub

In many companies, it's desirable to have a single host through which all e-mail is processed. This allows the company to reduce the number of systems that need to access the Internet and the number of potential points of confusion when delivering e-mail. In Sendmail, a server put to this purpose was called a smarthost, because it would be the system on the network that had the proper mail-routing information. The term mail hub is in more common use these days, probably because it is often security, antivirus, and network policy that dictates that e-mail go through a single system, not the complexity of maintaining the configuration of a mail server that must work between multiple legacy mail protocols. Also, because the term smarthost isn't evocative of much of anything we won't use it.

If you are setting up a Linux desktop that will handle e-mail for its user, that system's MTA should be sending e-mail through the mail hub rather than trying to send e-mail end-to-end by itself.

To forward all mail from a desktop system through a mail hub, Postfix has a configuration variable called relayhost, which would be set as follows to use the mail hub:

```
# postconf -e 'relayhost = mail.example.com'
```

Then postfix reload should be run. After this, Postfix will route all e-mail through a properly configured mail hub (see the next example), which will then deliver the e-mail properly, whether its destination is another user on the same server or across the Internet.

Example 6: Acting as a mail hub

The most basic requirement for a mail hub is that it relay e-mail for a certain set of local IP addresses, which it considers trusted. By default, Postfix will notice which network interfaces and addresses are active when it starts up, and it will automatically configure itself to relay for clients that are directly attached to these networks. The setting to explicitly enable this behavior is:

```
# postconf -e 'mynetworks_style = subnet'
```

However, suppose that there is an office in another building that is connected to the example.com main office via a WAN link. Suppose it is on the network 192.168.1.0, with a netmask of 255.255.255.0. By the preceding setting, the Postfix server won't allow that second office to send e-mail through it, so mail.example.com won't be a capable mail hub.

The way to fix this is to explicitly set the mynetworks variable to the networks that mail.example.com will be hosting, like so:

```
# postconf -e 'mynetworks = 192.168.0.0/24, 192.168.1.0/24'
```

This says that 192.168.0.0/24, the network that mail.example.com is on, is to be trusted, as is the network in the other building. That /24 at the end is another way of notating a netmask of 255.255.255.0. Now this server will work as a mail hub for example.com and for its satellite office.

Example 7: Reducing unwanted e-mail

This section isn't, strictly speaking, an example. This section is going to discuss unwanted e-mail and a few approaches to tackling the issue. The reason that this section is not going to be strong on examples is that there is no single way of eliminating undesired e-mail, and some methods that may work acceptably well for one user (for example, a sysadmin or a programmer) may not work for less technical users (for example, a manager or CEO). Such nontechnical users may become irate when e-mail they expect does not arrive, which will happen on occasion with almost any automated mail-filtering software.

First, what kinds of e-mail might be easily categorized as unwanted? The first thing that comes to mind is Unsolicited Commercial E-mail (UCE). The other name for this is spam. This is e-mail sent to you commonly trying to sell you a product, trying to sell you pornography, or trying to bilk you by trying to sell you a scam. This e-mail is often sent with false headers and often through systems that are misconfigured to allow others to relay through them (that is, all systems on the Internet are considered trusted).

The second variety of unwanted e-mail is virus-laden. There have been many incidences of MUAs being tricked into executing the content of a message attachment. Sometimes, even valid content such as .doc word-processing documents may have what are known as macro viruses capable of infecting the system the MUA is on. The trickiest part of these e-mail viruses is that they are not generated by a malicious user. They are often e-mailed from infected friends or business contacts who don't realize that their computer is being used to launch an attack on you.

Common sense dictates that, as much as possible, both kinds of e-mail should be dealt with and made safe. Doing this requires consistent work on the part of the people who are responsible for this job. There really is no single solution, but some strategies will be presented here.

The first thing we'll approach is UCE. UCE is usually mailed in large quantities from specific systems, and the message is usually from a fake address. The last thing the sender of UCE wants is for an irate recipient to be able to track the e-mail back to him or her. This often requires the sender to find vulnerable servers and abuse them in a hit-and-run fashion. The sender then uses the server until that server is either taken off line or until relay-prevention is implemented properly. This advantageous use of misconfigured sites has led to the growth of blackhole lists. These are lists that are propagated using DNS. If a DNS query is made to one of these lists and it succeeds in returning a record, the MTA making the request is expected to deny mail from that server on the basis that it is statistically far more likely to be UCE than it is to be valid e-mail. To configure this, the configuration parameter `maps_rbl_domains` must be set to one or more servers that maintain a so-called real-time blackhole list of domains that are offenders. The default setting for Postfix is as follows:

```
# postconf -e 'maps_rbl_domains = blackholes.mail-abuse.org'
# postconf -e 'smtpd_recipient_restrictions =   permit_mynetworks, \
        check_relay_domains, \
        warn_if_reject, reject_maps_rbl'
```

The backslashes tell the shell to make sure all of the variables get passed to postconf on one line — postconf will not accept multiple lines for configuration variables without this. Make sure not to put spaces or other characters after that backslash.

The first configuration option tells Postfix what blackhole list to reference. The second line tells Postfix to keep two items from the default configuration. `permit_mynetworks` and `check_relay_domains` enforce behavior that we've documented earlier — namely allowing local networks to relay through Postfix and to allow trusted domains that we've defined to relay through the server. The last two options enable our new behavior. The option `warn_if_reject` changes the meaning of the following restriction — if the next restriction matches, instead of outright rejecting the e-mail, Postfix will log a warning. This is a way of testing that a particular method you're considering putting into production won't eliminate valid e-mail and will match e-mail that you don't want. You should check your mail logs after reloading Postfix with these options and see if the phrase `reject_warning` appears in your logs. If it does, you can begin verifying whether or not the e-mail that would have been rejected is UCE or legitimate and extend this over time into whether the blackhole list you are using is appropriate for your needs.

To begin experimenting with how effective this method of blocking is for you, you should find a good search engine (google is my favorite) and use the search terms open relay dns list to find lists of relays you can use. For each list you try out, you should run postconf to set the given list to be the one you want to use:

```
# postconf -e 'maps_rbl_domains = some-blackhole.server'
```

If you find one or more blackhole lists that satisfy your needs, after you are done testing you should run the following command:

```
# postconf -e 'smtpd_recipient_restrictions =    permit_mynetworks, \
        check_relay_domains, \
        reject_maps_rbl'
```

to let postfix begin enforcing the restriction by rejecting e-mail from blackholed domains.

The only difference between this and the prior configuration command is that now there is no warn_if_reject clause, which would let potentially unwanted e-mail through. As usual, a Postfix reload should be run after any changes are made using postconf when you are ready to test the changes.

The second variety of unwanted e-mail, viruses, and other attacks, are usually approached on the desktop with antivirus software. There are packages that will work with postfix to perform virus checking and disinfection on the mail server. The project "AmaViS – A Mail Virus Scanner" at http://www.amavis.org – will provide you with a postfix-compatible package you can use to eliminate messages with particular headers, particular subject lines, or specific attachment types. AMaViS works with a package called avacl (which I think means antivirus access control list), which extends this capability. Also, AMaViS allows you to incorporate a commercial virus scanner, some of which allow free use for noncommercial or personal Linux systems. Links are available from the AMaViS home page, as well as specific installation instructions if this is something you or your organization needs.

Spamassassin basics

Another form of self-defense are programs which will let users implement their own protection policies. One way is allowing users to implement what are known as personal *whitelists* and *blacklists*. Systems like TMDA (Tagged Message Delivery Agent) allow users to specify who they will allow e-mail from. For particularly beleaguered users, there is the option of requesting that anyone who is sending them e-mail for the first time send them a special second e-mail confirming that they're a real person to whom responses can be sent, and with whom a conversation can be held. Almost no spam can be replied to, and there are rarely people at the other end.

TMDA mainly works on a per-user basis. Spamassassin, on the other hand, can be made to easily work system-wide. Spamassassin is a program that scans messages for signs of spam keywords in the subject or message, certain patterns (repetition of a phrase over and over is a common one for spam), and what server the e-mail was received by. However, spamassassin does more then just reject a message. It includes a score – the higher the score, the more likely the message is unasked for and unwanted.

Using a score, each user can judge for themselves how to treat the message, and he or she can also see the reasons for the score so the user can judge for themselves how much to rely on spamassassin. For instance, if a message has 8 or more points, it's highly unlikely that it is anything but spam. Most MUAs can filter messages with specific headers, and so a user can throw mail with high scores into a spam folder that they don't have to look at.

In addition, spamassassin lets you tap into a collaborative effort called "Vipul's Razor" (commonly just called "razor" and the new version is called "razorv2") where users can send in e-mails which they believe are spam, and complex heuristics will be generated from this e-mail and can be downloaded by spamassassin users to provide you with always current spam identifiers. TMDA, spamassassin, and Vipul's Razor can all be easily found by doing a search on the Web.

Summary

This chapter introduced the basic terminology of e-mail servers, including the definition of MTA, MUA, message store, headers, and the envelope. The relevant standards documents were referenced in case you want to gain a more thorough knowledge of e-mail. These terms described how to use Postfix in a number of sample configurations that are commonly asked for in an organization. The most basic example was how to configure a default Postfix installation to the bare minimum of sending e-mail for your domain. Then two forms of virtual hosting – Sendmail style virtual hosts and Postfix style virtual hosts – were described along with how to implement each style along with some things to consider when choosing which style to implement for your own purposes.

You were then introduced to DNS, the Domain Name service, and the subset of the DNS protocol that is relevant to delivering e-mail. This contributed to a discussion of a method of troubleshooting DNS settings along with particular words of wisdom (don't use nslookup to troubleshoot DNS problems). After this, we spoke about the roles that a mail sever usually plays in an organization, either that of a mail client or a mail hub. The client would be a desktop or similar system that would deliver to a mail hub, but shouldn't try to deliver to anything except its mail hub. A mail hub is a system that is configured with more information than a mail client, and is setup to receive e-mail from clients in the organization and to deliver e-mail to other organizations. Mail hubs are commonly implemented to limit the amount of work needed to keep e-mail flowing, since its much easier to manage one or two systems instead of trying to manage and configure every system on every users desktop individually.

Lastly, we covered the forms of unwanted e-mail — Unsolicited Commercial E-mail (UCE) a.k.a. spam, and virus-laden e-mail. You were introduced to a few approaches and some free software to help you reduce the amount of spam and viruses that your organization receives.

Chapter 11

Configuring FTP

IN THIS CHAPTER

- ◆ Introducing the FTP protocol
- ◆ Introducing WU-FTP
- ◆ Configuring a Real Mode FTP Server
- ◆ Configuring Guest Accounts
- ◆ Configuring Anonymous Accounts
- ◆ Troubleshooting the WU-FTP Server

THE FILE TRANSFER PROTOCOL (FTP) is one of the most commonly used methods for transferring files across the Internet and across Intranets. Designed in the period when the Internet was young and idealistic, FTP is an insecure protocol. You can still use it without unduly exposing its host server to the dangers of the Internet if you're careful, and a significant portion of this chapter deals with doing so. You can use FTP to transfer files from password protected private accounts or anonymously from public ones. This chapter shows you how to configure FTP to perform both functions.

Introducing the FTP Protocol

Most protocols use a single port to conduct their business, but the FTP protocol (yes, it's redundant) is different because it uses two ports by default. You use port 21 — the designated control port — to connect to an FTP server, but you transfer data on port 20. The FTP client establishes one port while the FTP server establishes the second. When you connect to a server, the FTP client initiates the connection to the server on port 21. The client-server negotiates the authentication and establishes the TCP connection on port 21. However, when the client asks for data (whether in the form of a directory listing or file transfer) the server opens a new TCP connection back to the client on port 20 in order to transfer the data.

The use of two ports is usually transparent to the FTP user. Although it doesn't affect the FTP server configuration, it does impact firewall configuration, so you have to take care when constructing IP filters to allow FTP access. Doing so isn't difficult once you understand the protocol, but you do have to factor that information into the firewall design process. Fortunately, iptables accommodates the use of multiple ports via the RELATED state option. The RELATED option is described in the section "Introducing stateful IP packet filters (Netfilter/iptables)" in Chapter 4.

FTP allows three service modes:

♦ **Real:** The FTP client connects to the server and provides a Linux user name and password. The FTP server negotiates the login process just like any other login. Once authenticated, the FTP client gains access to the user account home directory. This form of FTP access is the most dangerous. FTP nominally provides access to the user's home directory. However, Linux doesn't take any specific precautions to tighten security on the FTP server process. If the FTP client finds and exploits a vulnerability, then the entire Linux file system can potentially be compromised. As you'll soon see, methods are available for locking the FTP client in a reduced Linux file system. (You can create a reduced file system by configuring the Linux kernel to change the root file system for a process. The chroot utility is used to change the root of a process's file system.)

♦ **Guest:** The FTP client connects to the server and provides a Linux user name and password. After the login process is complete, however, the system uses `chroot` to limit access to the overall file system. This process takes place within the Linux kernel, and although not foolproof, it definitely helps increase security.

♦ **Anonymous:** The user supplies an e-mail address as the password, and the FTP client connects to the server anonymously. Obviously, supplying a fake e-mail address is quite easy, but the FTP server doesn't use the so-called password for authentication. In fact, no authentication takes place at all. Authentication is unnecessary because the FTP server gives the FTP client access to a public directory intended to serve anyone without restriction. The public login directory is generally configured as read-only, but mechanisms are available to allow limited, public write access. The FTP server uses `chroot` to further limit access to the overall system.

Be aware that you need to transmit your Linux login password in clear-text across the public Internet to access both Real and Guest FTP modes. We urge you to use Secure Shell (SSH) if you need to transfer files from user accounts across the Internet.

You can tailor the security level to your FTP server by judiciously using these access methods. Real FTP access may be perfectly adequate within a small, private network, but in general, you should use only Guest and/or Anonymous FTP access on an Internet server.

Introducing Washington University FTP (WU-FTP)

Red Hat Linux provides the *Washington University FTP* (WU-FTP) server on its distributions. You can download the RPM package from Red Hat's anonymous FTP site, `ftp.redhat.com`, if necessary. WU-FTP is a popular and flexible version of an FTP. WU-FTP also has the advantage of automatically using `chroot` for all guest and anonymous logins. `chroot` increases security by creating a virtual file system for a process. The virtual file system limits access to an arbitrary subset of the directory tree; the subset is usually in the process's home directory. With WU-FTP, `chroot` limits logins to either the public directory, in the case of anonymous logins, or the guest account home directory, in the case of guest logins.

WU-FTP has six configuration files:

- ◆ `/etc/xinetd.d/wu-ftpd`: This file controls the xinetd deamon, which launches the wu-ftpd daemon — the FTP server — whenever necessary. This configuration file controls several aspects of the wu-ftpd daemon, such as whether it is enabled.

- ◆ `/etc/ftpaccess`: Controls what user accounts can be logged in by the FTP server. Any account name that is included in this file will be denied access. For instance, the root user is included in this configuration file by default and therefore you can't log in directly to the FTP server.

- ◆ `/etc/ftpconversions`: Instructs the FTP server to pass files through various filters when being downloaded. You can specify file compression filters such as gzip to compress a file or files during transfers.

- ◆ `/etc/ftphosts`: This file configures the FTP server to allow or deny login access from specified hosts.

- ◆ `/etc/ftpusers`: This file contains a list of users who are not permitted to login to the FTP server.

The most recent version of WU-FTP has deprecated the last two files. Originally meant to deny certain hosts and users from accessing the WU-FTP server, those functions have been folded into the `ftpaccess` file. We describe the configuration files in detail later in this chapter.

Installing WU-FTP

Follow this simple process to install WU-FTP :

1. Download the wu-ftp package from `ftp.redhat.com`.

   ```
   mount /mnt/cdrom
   ```

2. Run the following command to install the WU-FTP RPM package, which you just downloaded from Red Hat (or obtained from one of their CD-ROMs):

```
rpm -ivh /mnt/cdrom/ftp/wu-ftpd*
```

3. If you want to allow anonymous FTP, then install the anonftp package. (The decision to use anonymous FTP depends on what information you want to distribute and to whom. Anonymous FTP is ideally suited for distributing information that you want to give to everyone. For instance, Red Hat Linux wants to allow everyone to download their Linux distribution and provides aand nonymous server at ftp.redhat.com.):

```
rpm -ivh /mnt/cdrom/ftp/anonftp*
```

The anonftp package installs the files that chroot needs to change the root directory for anonymous FTP connections. chroot requires that a miniature, but self-sufficient, file system be created at the point where the change root is going to occur. The anonftp package contains libraries and binaries that are going to be stored in the /var/ftp directory, the point where the change root will occur for anonymous logins.

4. Edit the /etc/xinetd.d/wu-ftpd configuration file and change the disable option to no as shown below:

```
disable = no
```

5. Restart the xinetd daemon to make the change take effect:

```
/etc/rc.d/init.d/xinetd restart
```

6. Test WU-FTP by connecting to it:

```
ftp localhost
```

7. The WU-FTP login prompt displays:

```
Connected to chivas.paunchy.net.
220 chivas.paunchy.net FTP server (Version wu-2.6.1-16)
ready.
Name (chivas:paul):
```

You can now log in to your user account and use FTP to transfer, delete, and perform other tasks to your home directory files. Please be aware that the default WU-FTP configuration is fairly insecure at this point. Don't allow Real mode logins if your WU-FTP server is accessible from the Internet.

WU-FTP provides chroot capability to Guest and Anonymous mode connections, so we recommend discarding Real mode connections in favor of the other two. You can make "real" users into "guests" by using the getuser * option in the ftpaccess file, a process we describe later.

Introducing the WU-FTP/xinetd configuration file

Red Hat Linux 7.0 introduced the *Extended Internet Services* (xinetd) daemon, which replaces the traditional inetd daemon (also known as the Super Daemon). xinetd provides more control of each service that it launches than inetd did. It also integrates access control that previously required the separate tcp_wrappers system.

The xinetd daemon controls wu-ftpd. wu-ftpd has a control file located in the */etc/xinetd.d* directory. The /etc/xinetd.d/wu-ftpd configuration file controls all aspects of the server's operation. The default configuration file is as follows:

```
# default: on
# description: The wu-ftpd FTP server serves FTP connections. It uses \
# normal, unencrypted usernames and passwords for authentication.
service ftp
{
        socket_type             = stream
        wait                    = no
        user                    = root
        server                  = /usr/sbin/in.ftpd
        server_args             = -l -a
        log_on_success          += DURATION USERID
        log_on_failure          += USERID
        nice                    = 10
        disable                 = yes
}
```

The first two options are set by the type of service that WU-FTP is, and you never need to change them. Following is a quick explanation of the remaining options:

- ◆ **user:** The server process's user id (UID). This option is set to root by default; therefore, the WU-FTP process runs as root. You may not want the server process to run as root for security reasons. If a hacker discovers and exploits a vulnerability in WU-FTP, she may gain root access because the program was running as root. If the server is running with a non-privileged UID and an exploit occurs, the hacker achieves non-root access.

- ◆ **server:** The server program's name and location. In this case, the program /usr/sbin/in.ftpd is a hard link to /usr/sbin/wu-ftpd.

- ◆ **server_args:** The *arguments* (options) to give the server when you start it. In this case, -l causes the FTP server to log all FTP sessions, and -a enables use of the ftpaccess configuration file.

- ◆ **log_on_success:** Determines what information is logged after a successful log in. This configuration records the time from log in to log out (DURATION) and the user ID (USERID).

◆ **log_on_failure:** This option tells the FTP server to log unsuccessful connection attempts. The user ID is set in this case.

◆ **nice:** Sets the server process priority. The Linux kernel controls how many processor cycles per second each process gets by its priority. Higher numbers mean fewer cycles and lower numbers mean more. nice is a way of modifying a process priority relative to the default priority.

◆ **disable:** Enables or disables the service. Services are set to be disabled (disable = yes) by default. You must set this value to disable = no in order to use a service.

This section described wu-ftp works with xinetd. The xinetd acts as a gatekeeper to the FTP server providing additional security and control. The next section describes how to control access directly from the wu-ftp server daemon.

Introducing the ftpaccess configuration file

Most of the important WU-FTP configuration information is defined in the ftpaccess file. This file is responsible for controlling the general behavior of the FTP server.

Each line uses the following format:

```
keyword   one or more options
```

Red Hat supplies a default /etc/ftpaccess file, which is shown in Listing 11-1.

Listing 11-1: The default /etc/ftpaccess file

```
# This file controls the behavior of the wu-ftpd
# ftp server.
#
# If you're looking for a graphical frontend to
# editing it, try kwuftpd from the kdeadmin
# package.
# Don't allow system accounts to log in over ftp
deny-uid %-99 %65534-
deny-gid %-99 %65534-
allow-uid ftp
allow-gid ftp
# Chroot all users to their home directory by default
# (comment this out if you don't want to chroot most of your users)
guestuser *
# If you wish to allow user1 and user2 to access other
# directories, use the line below:
# realuser user1,user2
```

```
# realuser user1,user2
# The ftpchroot group doesn't exist by default, this
# entry is just supplied as an example.
# To chroot a user, modify the line below or create
# the ftpchroot group and add the user to it.
#
# You will need to setup the required applications
# and libraries in the root directory (set using
# guest-root).
#
# Look at the anonftp package for the files you'll need.
guestgroup ftpchroot

# User classes...
class    all    real,guest,anonymous    *

# Set this to your email address
email root@localhost

# Allow 5 mistyped passwords
loginfails 5

# Notify the users of README files at login and when
# changing to a different directory
readme   README*    login
readme   README*    cwd=*

# Messages displayed to the user
message /welcome.msg          login
message .message              cwd=*

# Allow on-the-fly compression and tarring
compress      yes          all
tar           yes          all
```

The more commonly used `ftpaccess` options are described below:

- ◆ **Archiving and compression options (`compress` and `tar`):** Using these options allows the WU-FTP server to implement the *compression* and *tar* file when necessary.

- ◆ `banner <file>`: Similar to the greeting option, the text contained within the banner (the file) displays before you enter the username and password.

◆ class (`<class> <typelist> <addrglob> [<addrglob>]`): Creates a group or type of user called a class. You can conveniently assign options and functions to a class rather than individual users, addresses, etc. The type of user and source address (or addresses) from which the connection is coming defines the class. The default WU-FTP configuration defines a class in which all types of connections (the Real, Guest, and Anonymous modes) can login from any address:

```
class all real, guest, anonymous*
```

Following are examples of different classes:

- `class private guest 192.168.1.*`: Creates a class called private that allows only guest logins from a private network address space of `192.168.1.0`.

- `classall anonymous *`: Allows only anonymous logins, but the logins can come from anywhere.

- `class all guest, anonymous *`: Creates a class called `all` that accepts Guest and Anonymous mode logins from any address.

- `class all guest, anonymous ! 192.168.1.*`: Modifies the preceding example to allow Guest and Anonymous logins from any address except the `192.168.1.0` subnet.

- `classrealprivatereal192.168.1.*`: Creates a class called `realprivate` that allows Real mode logins from the local subnet.

◆ **Command execution options:** You can allow or disallow the users you specify in the typelists to perform these functions. The typelist options include Real, Guest, Anonymous, and classes. You can specify classes to be used in the typelist. The functions are shown below.

```
chmod <yes|no> <typelist>
delete <yes|no> <typelist>
overwrite <yes|no> <typelist>
rename <yes|no> <typelist>
umask <yes|no> <typelist>
```

◆ deny `<addrglob>`: Denies access to the hosts whose source addresses match the `addrglob` parameter. Following are some examples of this option:

- deny `badguy.wiseupsucker.com`: This example denies access to the single host `badguy.wiseupsucker.com`.

- deny `wiseupsucker.com`: This example denies access to any hosts originating from the `wiseupsucker.com` subnet.

- deny `! goodguys.com`: This example denies access to all addresses except the `goodguys.com` subnet.

- deny !192.168.32.*: Alternatively, you can use numeric IP addresses in place of domain names.

◆ deny-uid <uid-range> [<uid-range> ...] or deny-gid <gid-range> [<gid-range> ...]: Deny access based on user and guest IDs. You can specify names, individual numbers, or number ranges. The percent sign (%) operator indicates a number or range of numbers. Individual numbers follow the operator immediately. You specify a numeric range by the sequence of the percent sign operator, followed by a plus (+) or minus (-) sign, and then the number. For instance, the string %-99 means all numbers below and including 99; %+65000 means 65000 and above.

◆ email <address>: The address to which you want to send system messages.

◆ greeting full|brief|terse: This option tells the FTP server how much information to display at the start of a connection (after the username and password have been successfully entered).

◆ greeting text <message>: The text to display at the start of a connection (after the username and password have been successfully entered).

◆ guestgroup <groupname> [<groupname> ...]: When a Real mode user is a member of a guestgroup, then that user is logged in as an Anonymous mode user. As a result, a chroot is executed for the login. The user must have a home directory set up properly for the chroot to occur. The guestgroup groupname must also exist in the /etc/group file.

For example, the user *myacct* belongs to the guestgroup. If the myacct has a home directory */home/ftp/myacct*, then the user will be logged into that directory. If the */home/ftp* directory is set up correctly for chroot, then the user myacct will be chroot'd to the */home/ftp/myacct*.

- guestgroup myacct: This example treats the user *myacct* as belonging to the Guest mode.

- guestgroup *: This example forces all non-anonymous users to be treated as belonging to the Guest mode.

◆ guest-root directory: This option sets a common home directory root for all guest logins, which makes constructing a chroot directory easier, because you only have to create the support directories once. For example, using guest-root /home/ftp sets a single location (/home/ftp) for all Guest mode logins.

◆ guestuser <username> [<username> ...]: Usernames associated with guestuser work in the same manner as guestgroup, except that their sessions inherit username IDs instead of the groupname IDs.

◆ `log commands [<typelist>]`: This option enables the system to log the individual commands that users enter. If you don't specify a `typelist`, then the system logs all commands. Otherwise, the `typelist` specifies which commands are logged for the three login modes: Real, Guest, and Anonymous. The following command, for instance, logs commands for guest users:

`log commands guest`

◆ `noretrieve [absolute|relative] ([class=<class_name>]| [user=<user_name>]) ... [-] <filename> <filename>`: This directive denies the downloading (get) of all the specified files. Following are some examples:

   ■ `noretrive core`: This configuration denies the retrieval of core files, wherever they are.

   ■ `noretrieve /etc/passwd /etc/group`: In this example the noretrieve option prevents the password and group files from being downloaded from the /etc directory. (You can bypass this restriction if either or both of the passwd and group files are stored in directories other than /etc.) The use of chroot negates this option, but you can still use it beneficially. It is possible that the server will be misconfigured. If you permit Real mode sessions (from your private network only, for instance), then chroot isn't used, and this command becomes essential.

◆ `realuser` or `realroup`: These options work in the opposite fashion of guestuser and guestgroup; login sessions that would normally be treated with Guest mode gain Real mode access.

◆ `timeout {various options}`: This option sets timeout intervals based on various options:

   ■ `accept`: How long to wait for an incoming connection.

   ■ `connect`: How long to wait for an outgoing connection.

   ■ `data`: How long to wait for data to appear on the connection.

   ■ `idle`: How long to wait before disconnecting an idle connection.

◆ `upload [absolute|relative] ([class=<class_name>]| [user=<user_ name>])... [-] <root-dir> <dirglob> <yes|no> <owner> <group> <mode> ["dirs"|"nodirs"] [<d_mode>] [<dirowner> <dirgroup>]`: This directive — essential for making anonymous file transfers safe — determines which classes and users are allowed to upload files and how and where the transfers can occur. You can get more information on this directive from the WU-FTP man (**man ftpd**) page, but here are a couple examples of this option in action:

- upload /var/ftp /incoming yes ftpxfer ftpxfer 0440 nodir: In this example, uploads are allowed into the *incoming* directory (the root directory is /var/ftp and the dirglob is /incoming). Transferred files are given the user and group ID of ftpxfer. The uploaded files are given user and group read-only permissions. The nodir clause prevents the anonymous user from creating subdirectories.

- upload /incoming * no: This configuration denies any files from being uploaded into the Anonymous FTP directory.

This section describes what the ftpaccess configuration file does. Each option is described along with several examples. The next section describes the ftpconversion file that controls how the FTP server handles downloads.

Introducing the ftpconversions file

This file stores instructions telling WU-FTP how to handle certain type of file transfers. The file contains file name suffixes and prefixes, along with conversion commands. When WU-FTP is used to transfer a file, it checks the ftpconversion file. If the file name suffix or prefix matches a pattern found here, WU-FTP executes the corresponding command and converts the file into another form.

The default /etc/ftpconversion file is shown here:

```
 :.Z:   :  :/usr/bin/compress -d -c
%s:T_REG|T_ASCII:O_UNCOMPRESS:UNCOMPRESS
  :    :  :.Z:/usr/bin/compress -c %s:T_REG:O_COMPRESS:COMPRESS
 :.gz:  :  :/bin/gzip -cd %s:T_REG|T_ASCII:O_UNCOMPRESS:GUNZIP
  :    :  :.gz:/bin/gzip -9 -c %s:T_REG:O_COMPRESS:GZIP
  :    :  :.tar:/bin/tar -c -f - %s:T_REG|T_DIR:O_TAR:TAR
  :    :  :.tar.Z:/bin/tar -c -Z -f -
%s:T_REG|T_DIR:O_COMPRESS|O_TAR:TAR+COMPRESS
  :    :  :.tar.gz:/bin/tar -c -z -f -
%s:T_REG|T_DIR:O_COMPRESS|O_TAR:TAR+GZIP
```

For instance, if myfile.Z is the file being transferred, then WU-FTP executes the command /usr/bin/compress -d -c myfile.Z. The -c option tells compress to pipe its output to stdout. Therefore, the file myfile.Z is uncompressed (the -d option) and sent to the stdout. WU-FTP takes the uncompressed data and does its transfer.

The ftpusers and ftpgroup files were previously used to deny access to all usernames listed within it. However, that function has been given to the deny-uid and deny-gid directive contained in /etc/ftpaccess file and the use of both files has been deprecated.

Configuring a Real Mode FTP Server

If you're creating an FTP server that will exclusively serve your private network, then you don't need to engage in any more configurations. Simply installing the WU-FTP package as described in the beginning of this chapter creates a Real mode FTP server. However, we recommend that you consider using other methods such as OpenSSH to allow users to transfer files. When users connect to the FTP server in Real mode, they send their passwords in clear-text. Once they login to their accounts they have no way to chroot their directories. You can eliminate these two problems by requiring users to use Secure Copy (scp) and Secure FTP (sftp), if available, to transfer files. Both scp and sftp are part of the OpenSSH package included with the Red Hat Linux distribution and provide file transfer capability over an encrypted channel.

You may want to configure a Real mode FTP server connected to the Internet. Don't! That type of configuration is fraught with security risks. Use Secure Shell or virtual private networks to transfer files across the Internet. Alternatively, configure WU-FTP to treat your user accounts as Guest accounts. See the next section for instructions on that process.

Configuring Guest Accounts

Using Guest mode logins increases your FTP server security. Like Real mode users, guest users authenticate their sessions with a password. However, to prevent the guest session from seeing any of the files, chroot is used to separate their home directories from the rest of the file system. The following instructions describe how to set up a Guest account.

1. Log in on the WU-FTP server as root. We use chivas for this example.

2. Create the guest user account just as you would any Linux account:

   ```
   useradd guest
   ```

3. Set the guest account password just as you would for any Linux account:

   ```
   passwd guest
   ```

4. Modify the new account in /etc/passwd to use the correct chroot syntax:

   ```
   usermod -d /home/guest/./guestftp guest
   ```

   The first part of the home directory path, before the lone dot (/./), specifies the chroot root directory. When guest logs in, his current directory is /home/guest/guestftp.

5. Copy the ftponly script to the /bin directory:

   ```
   cp /usr/share/doc/wu-ftpd-2.6.1/examples/ftponly /bin
   ```

6. Modify the user account to use the `ftponly` shell:

```
usermod -s /bin/ftponly guest
```

7. Add the `ftponly` entry to the `/etc/shells` configuration file:

```
echo "/bin/ftponly" >> /etc/shells
```

8. Copy the `chroot` support directories into the guest home directory:

```
cd /var/ftp
cp -r /var/ftp/* /home/guest
```

Note that we're using the directories set up for anonymous FTP logins by the `anonftp` RPM package. That package contains all of the directories and files that `chroot` requires.

9. Add the necessary definitions to /etc/ftpaccess. You need to define the user guest as a guest login. Add this line (or change it, if it already exists) to /etc/ftpaccess:

```
guestuser guest
```

10. Change the directory owner and permissions and make the following the directory `/home/guest/guestftp`:

```
mkdir /home/guest/guestftp
chown -R guest.guest /home/guest/guestftp
chmod 755 /home/guest/guestftp
```

11. Now try logging in as a guest. The process is the same as logging in as a Real mode user. Enter the username guest and that user's password (set in Step 3):

```
ftp localhost
```

12. If you enter the `pwd` command, you see that your home directory is as shown below:

```
257 "/guestftp" is current directory
```

Your FTP session believes that the host computer's file system is rooted at guest home directory /homeguest. `chroot` has successfully changed the root directory of the FTP process to its home directory. All of the server's files and directories are protected from any maliciousness that the FTP user may have in mind because the user can only browse the directory structure below /home/guest.

You can now use this guest account just as you would a Real mode account. You can put, get, and remove files, do directory listings, and so on. The only difference is that your FTP session is rooted at the guest account home directory.

Configuring Anonymous Accounts

Anonymous FTP servers share information with the public. The most common configuration is as a public repository of downloadable files, which can contain software, information, and almost anything else imaginable. Anonymous FTP can also function as a mechanism for people to communicate by allowing file uploads and downloads. This section describes how to construct both types of facilities.

Configuring for Anonymous logins

Constructing an Anonymous FTP server requires that you construct a special directory to serve as the common login home directory. WU-FTP automatically uses the chroot facility, so you also have to create the support structure we described in the previous section. The following simple steps describe the process:

1. Log in on the server as root. We use the example server chivas here.

2. Insert the Red Hat CD-ROM.

3. Install the anonftp RPM package. (We're assuming that you've already installed the WU-FTP package.)

   ```
   rpm -ivh /mnt/cdrom/RedHat/RPMS/anonftp*
   ```

4. Create an arbitrary sample file in the /var/ftp/incoming directory:

   ```
   echo "123456" > /var/ftp/incoming/test
   ```

5. Try logging into the server:

   ```
   ftp localhost
   ```

6. Enter the word **anonymous** or its synonym **ftp** at the prompt:

   ```
   Name (localhost:paul):ftp
   ```

7. Anonymous logins use your e-mail address as the password. As long as the e-mail address matches the proper syntax (username@somedomain.biz) then it's accepted as a password.

8. After you're logged in, enter the dir command and the following display appears:

   ```
   227 Entering Passive Mode (127,0,0,1,180,23)
   150 Opening ASCII mode data connection for directory listing.
   total 32
   d--x--x--x   2 root      root       4096 Apr 22  2001 bin
   d--x--x--x   2 root      root       4096 Apr 22  2001 etc
   drwxr-xr-x   2 root      root       4096 Apr 22  2001 lib
   drwxr-xr-x   3 root      ftp        4096 Jul 22 05:15 pub
   226 Transfer complete.
   ```

The `anonftp` packages creates and configures this `/var/ftp` directory. `chroot` uses the files in the `bin`, `etc`, and `lib` directories to set up the virtual root file system.

9. Change to the public (pub) directory:

    cd pub

10. List the directory contents by entering the `dir` command (`ls` works, too). The test file listed appears.

11. Download the file:

    get test

12. Exit from FTP:

    quit

13. You can examine the contents of the simple file that you just downloaded, store the files you wish to make public in the `/var/ftp/pub` directory, and, of course, create a more complex directory structure in that directory.

WU-FTP makes setting up an anonymous FTP server very easy. WU-FTP also implements an essential security feature by default. It limits file system access given to anonymous users by using the `chroot` facility. The two features make WU-FTP a very useful server.

Configuring for anonymous uploads

You can configure anonymous FTP servers to allow people to upload files. Doing so requires some additional security considerations, but a properly configured server is reasonably safe. The following list describes how to configure your FTP server to provide anonymous file transfers.

1. Log in on the server as root.

2. If you haven't yet installed the anonymous FTP RPM package, then do so now.

    rpm -ivh /mnt/cdrom/RedHat/RPMS/anonftp*

3. Create a new user to manage the anonymous FTP files:

    useradd ftpadm

    This user will own the anonymous FTP directory and files. Importantly, make sure that neither the anonymous FTP user nor root owns those files. Because the anonymous user is, well, anonymous, you can't tell whether that person's intentions are good or bad. And, we don't want to allow scripts or executables to operate as root. Changing to user and group ownership of a regular user prevents any FTP server related operations from running as root.

4. Create a subdirectory in /incoming to be used for uploads. The common naming convention calls this subdirectory incoming.

```
mkdir /var/ftp/incoming
```

5. Change the directory ownership to a regular user. Change the permissions on the new download directory to allow downloads.

```
chown -R ftpadm.ftpadm /var/ftp/incoming
chmod 3773 /var/ftp/incoming
```

The chmod command changes the incoming directory permissions such that root will have read, write, and execute (7) permissions, and the group and the world will have write and execute (3) permissions. chmod also sets the *sticky bit* for the directory and all its files, protecting the files from being deleted by regular users. Normally when a directory has write and execute permissions set for everyone, any user of that system can delete a file in that directory. The sticky bit stops that by allowing only the file's creator to delete the file. Because the FTP server writes the file with root as the owner, nothing but root is allowed to delete the uploaded files.

6. Add the following line in your /etc/ftpaccess file:

```
class anonftp anonymous *
```

You're going to use this new class to configure WU-FTP permit uploading.

 When multiple "class" commands are defined that can apply to a single FTP session, then only the first one will be used. For instance, let's assume that you define the follow configuration:

```
class all real,guest,anonymous *
class anonftp anonymous *
```

The first class instance will take precedence. Unfortunately, in this case, the first statement causes the FTP server to deny access because the anonymous login is not allowed in that configuration. Eliminate the "class all" statement to allow access.

7. Modify the ftpaccess files again to allow the uploading of files:

```
upload class=anonftp /var/ftp /incoming yes ftpadm ftpadm
0440 nodir
```

Here, the root directory is /var/ftp and the directory of interest is incoming, so the upload directory is /var/ftp/incoming. Uploaded files inherit the ftpadm user and group ID, and they're given user and group read-only (0440) permissions. The nodir clause prevents the anonymous user from creating directories.

If you want to give anonymous users permission to create subdirectories, remove the `nodirs` option in the preceding line. Doing so may be useful if you're creating an anonymous FTP site for use only within your private network. A private network implies more trust of the anonymous users and, thus, more flexibility.

8. The following lines prevent transferring files from the upload directory to your FTP client (downloading):

```
noretrieve /var/ftp
allow-retrieve /var/ftp/pub
```

Limit anonymous users' ability to download files to the `/var/ftp/pub` directory, and don't give them the ability to download from the upload directory. Automated systems are constantly searching the Internet for anonymous FTP sites that allow integrated uploads and downloads from the same directory. Those systems then use the directory as repositories for their own, always undesirable data. Limiting downloads to a directory different than the upload directory solves this problem. Save the changes to `/etc/ftpaccess`.

9. Create an arbitrary test file:

```
echo "abcdef" > test
```

10. Log in anonymously.

11. Change to the incoming directory:

```
cd incoming
```

12. Upload the test file:

```
put test
```

13. Try listing the newly transferred file:

```
dir
```

No directory information displays because the file permissions are configured so as not to allow display of the incoming directory. This configuration enhances security because you want to display as little information about your server as possible. People should be allowed to transfer files to your server but not retrieve them.

After you take these steps, FTP to the server as an anonymous user and make sure that you can upload files only in the specified directory. You don't have read access to the `/var/ftp/incoming` directory, so you shouldn't be able to see the files you upload by using the `ls` command. However, you'll still be able to download the uploaded files, if you supply the proper filenames.

Troubleshooting the WU-FTP Server

Troubleshooting WU-FTP is relatively straightforward. When an FTP server is misbehaving, you need to make a few basic checks. Those checks are divided into general-purpose ones and specific ones related to guest and anonymous logins. Always make sure that WU-FTP is installed and that you can start it by xinetd, and also check for basic network connectivity. Beyond checking the WU-FTP systems, you need to check the ftpaccess configuration parameters that control the guest and anonymous login modes.

The following sections outline the systems you need to check if you're having problems using WU-FTP.

Conducting general purpose checks

This section outlines the general systems — both WU-FTP specific and general networking — that may cause problems with your FTP server. Always start by checking the WU-FTP related systems, before turning to the network as the culprit. We recommend that you check the items in the order these sections appear.

MAKE SURE THAT WU-FTP IS INSTALLED

This check may seem simplistic, but sometimes it actually works. Experience has taught us to check the simple things first. Run the following command to verify that WU-FTP is installed:

```
rpm -qa | grep wu-ftp
```

CHECK THAT THE /ETC/XINETD.D/WU-FTPD (LOWER CASE PLEASE) FILE IS CONFIGURED CORRECTLY

WU-FTP depends on the xinetd daemon by default. When xinetd detects a request to connect to the FTP service, it fires up the wu-ftpd daemon. The daemon then handles the FTP client commands. Check the following xinetd subsystems to make sure that they're running correctly:

◆ **Verify that the** xinetd **daemon is running:** Start this simple process by running the following command:

```
ps -ef | grep xinetd
```

The daemon should display:

```
2704 ?        00:00:00 xinetd -stayalive -reuse -pidfil
```

If the daemon isn't running, start it as follows:

```
/etc/rc.d/init.d/xinetd restart
```

♦ Check that disable option is set to no in the `wu-ftpd` file:

```
disable = no
```

This misconfiguration is one of the easiest to have because the option is set to yes by default. If you need to change the option to `disable = no`, then you'll have to restart the xinetd daemon. See the preceding bullet for instructions on restarting the daemon.

♦ **Make sure that the /usr/sbin/wu-ftpd file is linked to /usr/sbin/in.ftpd:** The default `/etc/xinetd.d/wu-ftpd` configuration states that the `/usr/sbin/in.ftpd` daemon is to be started when someone calls for the FTP service. However, the `/usr/sbin/wu.ftpd` file is actually a soft link to `/usr/sbin/in.ftpd`, so you need to make sure that this link exists:

```
ls -l /usr/sbin/wu.ftpd
```

♦ **Verify that /etc/ftpaccess doesn't have any major misconfigurations:** If the system is to work correctly, you must be able to find the following items, which are the default settings, in the `ftpaccess` file. (Please note that you may change some of the options for the Guest and Anonymous modes. We provide the appropriate settings in the following sections.)

♦ The following deny-uid and deny-gid configuration prevents system users like root, whose uid and gids are less than 100, from logging on. All other users (regular or non-privileged) are allowed on:

```
deny-uid %-99 %65534-
deny-gid %-99 %65534-
```

♦ Verify that the `class all` accepts the three login modes (Real, Guest, and Anonymous), from any address:

```
class    all    real,guest,anonymous    *
```

VERIFY THAT YOUR NETWORK IS OPERATING CORRECTLY

If you still can't login after you're satisfied that WU-FTP and `xinetd` are configured correctly, then turn your attention to the network. Obviously, your FTP client machine and the WU-FTP server must be able to communicate. Try the following suggestions first; if they don't produce positive results, then consult the chapters in Part I, "Building a Linux Network," for more information about configuring and testing your network:

♦ **Try using an FTP client on the same machine as the server:** The following commands access the WU-FTP server from the localhost (127.0.0.1) and the local NIC (192.168.1.250), respectively. (We're using the server chivas, 192.168.1.250, in this example.)

```
ftp localhost
ftp 192.168.1.250
```

The physical networking doesn't have to be working for these tests to succeed.

◆ **Try using an FTP on a machine within the same sub-network as the server:** This eliminates any routing issues.

◆ **Make sure that your firewall — if you're running one on the WU-FTP server — is allowing your FTP client host's packets to pass in and out:** Examine the IP filtering rules for obvious mistakes. You can also use `tcp-dump` to see whether packets on ports 21 and 20 are passing through. Following is a sample `tcpdump` command:

```
tcpdump port 20 and port 21
```

`tcpdump` should display packets from the host coming through. If none are shown, then the packet filter is most likely dropping them.

If these checks fail to work, then you may want to reinstall the WU-FTP and `anonftp` packages. The process is simple and the reconfiguration painless. The following steps outline reinstallation:

1. Log in as `root`.

2. Remove the `anonftp` package. Doing so removes the files and directories from `/var/ftp`. You have to delete the `anonftp` before deleting WU-FTP because RPM will complain about dependencies. (You can override the complaints by using the `-nodep` option.)

   ```
   rpm -e anonftp
   ```

3. Remove the WU-FTP package:

   ```
   rpm -e wu-ftpd
   ```

4. Install the WU-FTP package:

   ```
   rpm -ivh /mnt/cdrom/RedHat/RPMS/wu-ftpd
   ```

5. Install the `anonftp` package:

   ```
   rpm -ivh /mnt/cdrom/RedHat/RPMS/anonftp
   ```

6. Repeat the steps described in earlier sections of this chapter according to the service modes you want to use Real, Guest, and/or Anonymous.

Often a useful method when you're first learning the system, reinstalling both packages provides a clean slate to reconfigure your server. The process is painless enough that you should feel confident that you can always start fresh if your first installations don't work correctly.

Troubleshooting Guest FTP logins

Fixing Guest FTP problems is an extension of general troubleshooting. If you're having problems with this mode, first follow the suggestions in the previous section. After exhausting those steps, then the following ones may provide the answer.

VERIFY THAT ANONFTP PACKAGE IS INSTALLED

This oversight is easy to make, but also easy to correct. Check the installation as follows:

```
rpm -qa | grep anonftp
```

Install the package if necessary from the second CD-ROM.

```
rpm -ivh /mnt/cdrom/RedHat/RPMS/anonftp*
```

CHECK THE STATUS OF THE LOGIN ACCOUNT USED FOR THE GUEST ACCOUNT

Guest mode sessions require the use of Linux user accounts. For instance, the earlier example uses the user called guest. Make sure that the account exists:

```
grep guest /etc/passwd
```

Create the account if necessary.

CHECK THE GUEST USER ACCOUNT HOME DIRECTORY

The guest user account home directory must be coordinated with the one set up in the /etc/passwd file. We set up the guest account to be used together with chroot, which creates a limited, virtual file system for the guest account to operate within. That, in turn, requires that a miniature version of the Linux operating system be copied into the guest account directory tree.

Check the guest user account home directory by viewing the output of the grep command from the preceding section. It should contain a string similar to the following:

```
/home/guest/./guestftp
```

This string specifies the guest home directory by using chroot syntax. /home/guest specifies the directory from which chroot creates a virtual root directory. /guestftp becomes the virtual current directory into which the guest account FTP user is logged. Once chroot creates the virtual root from /home/guest, /guestftp appears to the user as a directory in the root file system. The single dot (/./) separates the root from the current directories.

MAKE SURE THAT THE /BIN/FTPONLY FILE EXISTS

You substitute `ftponly` for a normal shell, such as bash. It prevents anyone from logging directly in to the guest account. If `ftponly` hasn't been created, then copy the one installed with the WU-FTP package:

```
cp /usr/share/doc/wu-ftpd-2.6.1/examples/ftponly /bin
```

VERIFY THAT FTPONLY IS LISTED IN /ETC/SHELLS

If not, then edit the `/etc/shells` file to include it. The file will look like the one below:

```
/bin/sh
/bin/bash/
/sbin/nologin
...
/bin/ftponly
```

CHECK CHROOT FOR THE CORRECT OPERATING SYSTEM FILES

WU-FTP uses `chroot` to enhance security. `chroot` requires that several operating system files exist within the guest account directory root. You should see directories such as `/bin`, `/lib`, and `/etc`. If you don't, then copy them from the `anonftp` directory:

```
cd /var/ftp
cp -r /var/ftp/* /home/guest
```

VERIFY THAT THE DIRECTORY OWNER AND PERMISSIONS ARE SET CORRECTLY

The owner and group must be guest. The permissions for the owner must be read, write, and execute; the group and everyone else get read and execute:

```
chown -R guest.guest /home/guest/guestftp
chmod 755 /home/guest/guestftp
```

VERIFY THAT YOU'RE NOT TRYING TO LOGIN WITH A SYSTEM ACCOUNT

The default `ftpaccess` file denies system account logins. The following directives deny accounts with UIDs below 99. Make sure that you are not trying to login with a system account, such as `root`, `adm`, and so on:

```
deny-uid %-99 %65534-
deny-gid %-99 %65534-
```

If none of these suggestions work, then consult the documentation in `/usr/share/doc/wu-ftpd*`. You may have to reinstall the entire system.

Troubleshooting Anonymous FTP logins

Just as with Guest, troubleshooting Anonymous FTP requires that WU-FTP be working properly. Seek solutions in the general-purpose section first. After exhausting those ideas, try the suggestions in the following sections.

VERIFY THAT ANONFTP PACKAGE IS INSTALLED

This oversight is easy to make, but also easy to correct. Check the installation as follows:

```
rpm -qa | grep anonftp
```

Install the package if necessary:

```
rpm -ivh /mnt/cdrom/ftp/anonftp*
```

VERIFY THAT THE /ETC/FTPACCESS FILE IS CONFIGURED CORRECTLY

The `/etc/ftpaccess` file must include one or more directives that permit Anonymous sessions. The default class configuration (`all`) does indeed configure that. You may want to create a specific class to more tightly control anonymous logins. In that case, make sure that the class includes the anonymous option. For instance, `class anonftp anonymous *` allows anonymous logins from anywhere.

If you want to permit uploading files, then `ftpaccess` should have directives like the following:

```
upload /var/ftp                    * no
upload /var/ftp /incoming yes ftpadm ftpadm 0440 nodirs
noretrieve /var/ftp/incoming
```

The first directive starts your anonymous FTP security by denying all uploads. The second one backs off the deny-all policy and allows uploads to a single directory. Finally, the third directive denies anonymous downloads of any of the uploaded files.

Summary

This chapter showed you how to configure an Internet-ready WU-FTP server and how to set up Real, Guest, and Anonymous mode sessions.

WU-FTP provides Real mode logins out of the box. It uses regular Linux user accounts for its login and is generally too dangerous to allow connections from the Internet. WU-FTP can be readily configured to accept Guest mode sessions. Guest mode is considerably safer than Real mode because its sessions use `chroot` to create a virtual directory with no access to the general file system. Finally, WU-FTP also permits Anonymous FTP sessions, which permit public access to files that you specify. Anonymous sessions also make use of `chroot` and are reasonably safe when configured correctly.

Chapter 12

Configuring Samba

IN THIS CHAPTER

♦ Introducing Samba

♦ Learning Samba by example

♦ Introducing SWAT

♦ Troubleshooting Samba

THIS CHAPTER FOCUSES ON configuring Samba on a Red Hat Linux server, which can replace your Windows NT/2000 file server. Samba is a suite of programs that duplicates (in other words, speaks the same language as) the Microsoft Windows 2000/NT/XP file and printer sharing function. Running a Samba server allows Microsoft and Linux clients to access a Linux server's file and printer resources across a local subnet.

You should only access Samba from within a private network. Unless you have a very good reason, don't make Samba shares available over the Internet; use a virtual private network (VPN) if you do need to share file systems across the Internet. Other system like Secure Shell, FTP, and Apache provide good alternatives for giving access to your file systems. Samba is strictly an intranet — private network — service. The term *services* is the Samba terminology for the directories and printers to be shared or exported with the network clients. We include a discussion here because it's such a useful intranet service.

Introducing Samba

Samba consists of several programs that understand and use the Microsoft Session Message Block (SMB) protocol; SMB is also referred to as NetBIOS. Windows 9x, ME, and NT/2000/XP use the SMB protocol to share files and printers across a network. You can find more information about Samba at www.samba.org.

The heart of the Samba suite consists of two daemons — smbd, which processes file and print sharing across the network, and nmbd, which provides share browsing. A single configuration file, smb.conf, controls the behavior of the system. Several other Samba programs — smbstatus, testparm, testprns, and smbclient — provide additional services.

The smbd daemon monitors the network for share requests. When it detects a share request, smbd goes through Linux to get the resource that the share represents — that is, a directory or a printer – and makes this resource available to the Samba client that requested it. The resource – a file, for example – stays on the Linux server, but the Samba client can make use of it just as if it were located on the client's disk.

The name server – nmbd – controls browsing that Windows clients do (such as when they open the Network Neighborhood), and responds to the Windows clients' requests to locate Samba servers. (A name server converts an IP name into its numeric IP address. Thus, as an arbitrary example, nmbd converts the domain name toluca.paunchy.com into its IP address of 192.168.1.1.) Both daemons read the smb.conf file when they start up to discover exactly which services to *export*. (The term *export* means to make available a service or share to one or more clients over the network.)

When you're working from a Windows workstation and want to access a directory, a file, or a printer, the operating system sends an SMB request to the appropriate server. For instance, suppose you access a file visible on a server in the Network Neighborhood. When the request makes its way to the Samba server, the smbd daemon creates a copy of itself.

Try opening the root share from the Network Neighborhood on your computer by double-clicking the computer icon; you should see a window open with the /root directory's contents – if any. If you don't see anything, try copying a file into the /root directory. Next, login to your Linux server as root and enter the following command:

```
ps -ef | grep smbd
```

You should see two smbd daemons (unless you've already started to experiment and have mounted other shares) as shown below. The process numbers you see will differ from those in the listing. Note that the grep command you entered is also shown, because it runs at the same time as the ps command. The question marks after the process IDs (PIDs) indicate that these processes aren't associated with any IO device, which makes sense because they're daemons.

```
183    ?    S    0:00 smbd -D
3664   ?    S    0:00 smbd -D
3693   p0   S    0:00 grep smbd
```

 TIP You can find complete descriptions of smbd and nmbd in their respective man pages. To view these man pages, login to your Linux box and enter the following commands: **man smbd** or **man nmbd**.

You configure the Samba daemons via the smb.conf file, which is located in the /etc/samba directory. The smb.conf file has a straightforward syntax and structure. The default smb.conf file includes numerous – and in some cases, interdependent – parameters. These parameters are included to provide general-purpose examples of various Samba functions, and we use several of the examples because they provide a good starting point. However, you can eliminate most, or all, of these superfluous parameters when you configure Samba for your own network.

Examining the smb.conf syntax

The `smb.conf` file has a simple structure, which is similar to Microsoft's WIN.INI file. The file is divided into sections. Each section contains parameters that define the shares (services) Samba is to export and their operational details. A global section defines the parameters that control the general Samba characteristics. Other than the global section, each section defines a specific service. Each section begins with a name enclosed within square brackets — for example, [home] — and continues until either the next section appears or the end of the `smb.conf` file occurs.

You specify a parameter with the following syntax:

```
name = value
```

The name can be one or more words, separated by spaces. The value can be Boolean (true or false; yes or no; 1 or 0), numeric, or a character string. Section and parameter names aren't case-sensitive. For example, the parameter `browseable = yes` works the same as `browseable = YeS`.

Comments are preceded by a semicolon (;) and can appear either as a separate line or after a name-value pair. Finally, you may continue lines from one to another by placing a backward slash (\) as the last character on the line to be continued.

Examining the smb.conf parameters

The `smbd` and `nmbd` daemons read the `smb.conf` configuration file when you start them (usually at boot time). The configuration file tells these daemons which shares to export and where and how to export them. Because security is always a top priority, you must be specific about which computers can access a share. The `smb.conf` file offers good flexibility for specifying precisely who has access to each service. As your Linux network grows, this control becomes increasingly important.

 You may already be familiar with Novell or NFS networks. They both share, or export, directory and print services to clients on the network. In this way, their function is the same as Samba's.

Examining the smb.conf structure

The `smb.conf` file has three main parts:

- ◆ Global parameters

◆ Directory shares section – including the standard [homes] section

◆ Printer shares section

The global parameters, as you may guess, set the rules for the entire system. The [homes] and [printer] sections are special instances of services. The services define who should be able to access them and how. Listing 12-1 shows a summary of the default Red Hat smb.conf file (the comments have been removed to highlight the actual parameters).

Listing 12-1: The default Red Hat smb.conf file

```
[global]
    workgroup = MYGROUP
    server string = Samba Server
    printcap name = /etc/printcap
    load printers = yes
    printing = lprng
    log file = /var/log/samba/%m.log
    max log size = 0
    security = user
    encrypt passwords = yes
    smb passwd file = /etc/samba/smbpasswd
    unix password sync = Yes
    passwd program = /usr/bin/passwd %u
    passwd chat = *New*password* %n\n *Retype*new*password* %n\n
*passwd:*all*authentication*tokens*updated*successfully*
    pam password change = yes
    obey pam restrictions = yes
    socket options = TCP_NODELAY SO_RCVBUF=8192 SO_SNDBUF=8192
    dns proxy = no

[homes]
    comment = Home Directories
    browseable = no
    writable = yes
    valid users = %S
    create mode = 0664
    directory mode = 0775

[printers]
    comment = All Printers
    path = /var/spool/samba
    browseable = no
    guest ok = no
    writable = no
    printable = yes
```

The [global] section also defines the type of security used, where the log and lock directories are located and other general parameters. Security is based either on locally stored or network-based passwords. The log files are useful for troubleshooting problems and for tuning your system. The lock files prevent multiple users from overwriting the same files.

The [homes] section defines the generic parameters for how an individual user's directories are exported. If your Microsoft Windows user name matches a Linux user name and you supply the correct password, you can double-click this icon in the Network Neighborhood and gain access to your home directory.

The [printers] section describes how printers are configured, of course.

The /etc/printcap file contains the configuration information for the Linux printers. In Red Hat Linux, the lpd daemon reads the printcap file for its configuration information. Then it monitors the system for print requests and manages the printing process.

You can expand on these special sections to create more specific services. They are useful in and of themselves, but you can also view them as templates.

The man page offers a complete description of smb.conf. To view it, enter the following command:

```
man smb.conf
```

Learning Samba by Example

One of the primary reasons for using Samba is to create a file and print server for Microsoft Windows clients. Linux clients can also use the Samba server. We assume that you have Windows machines connected to your private network, and we provide several examples for connecting Windows clients to a Red Hat Linux Samba server.

Configuring Samba to use encrypted passwords

Microsoft configures its operating systems — except for early Windows 95 and Windows 98 (pre OSR/2) versions — to encrypt passwords when accessing SMB shares. However, Samba's default configuration accepts unencrypted passwords.

To make Samba understand encrypted passwords, you must modify the smb.conf file as follows and create an smbpasswd file:

1. Edit the /etc/smb.conf file, and make sure that the security setting reads security = user.

2. Uncomment the following two lines:

```
encrypt passwords = yes
smb passwd file = /etc/smbpasswd
```

3. Create a Samba password for each user whom you want to provide with Samba access. Run the `smbpasswd` command as follows, where *iamauser* is the name of the user whose password you want to set:

```
smbpasswd -a iamauser
```

The `smbpasswd` program prompts you to enter the password twice. The *iamauser* entry in the `/etc/smbpasswd` should now look something like the following:

```
iamauser:500:834A03B3blahblahblahD80EBE5326::/home/iamauser:/
bin/bash
```

The `Xs` have been replaced with the encrypted characters to protect the innocent password.

4. Repeat this process for each user.

5. Restart the Samba daemons:

```
/etc/init.d/smb restart
```

6. Log in to your Windows client and enter a user name and password that correspond to a user you've entered in the Samba password file. That user's home directory should appear in the Windows Network Neighborhood folder.

TIP If you configure Samba to accept encrypted passwords, it will still accept plain text ones as well. When using encryption, Samba first tries to authenticate a share request against the encrypted version of the associated password. If that fails, Samba attempts to authenticate against the plain text password.

For further information on configuring Samba for encrypted passwords, read the `ENCRYPTION.txt`, `Passwords.txt`, `Win95.txt`, and `WinNT.txt` files in the `/usr/share/doc/samba-2.2.2/docs/textdocs` directory.

ADDING USERS TO THE LINUX SYSTEM

The following Samba examples require the addition of user and printer shares. Adding user and printer shares requires that Linux explicitly know users and printers. Therefore, you need to know about some basic Linux administration tasks, which we address in this section. To make use of the standard `[home]` Samba shares, you must add one or more users to your Linux box. Users are defined in the `/etc/passwd` and `/etc/group` files.

Red Hat reasonably suggests that you use Red Hat's User Configuration utility `redhat-config-users`, or command line programs `useradd` and `userdel`, to add, delete, and modify users. All are good methods that you should plan to use in general. However, it is useful to manually create a user — at least once — in order to understand what goes on under the hood. So for now, I'll explain the password file, and give instructions for modifying the /etc/passwd and /etc/group files in order to add users.

All Linux distributions have the same /etc/passwd file format, with fields separated by colons (:) in the order shown in Table 12-1. (The top item in this table corresponds to the left-most item and the bottom item to the right-most item.)

TABLE 12-1 THE /ETC/PASSWD FILE FORMAT

Field	Description
Login name	The name with which the user logs into the system.
Encrypted password	If the user has no password, this field is blank. An asterisk identifies a non-login account. Otherwise, this field shows an apparently random jumble of characters representing the encrypted password. (If you use shadow passwords, the encrypted password is moved to the file /etc/shadow, which isn't readable by anyone except root, and thus, is more secure.)
User ID	The user identification number. The number corresponds to the login name after it's set in the passwd file. You can show the numeric user ID by using the -n and -l options with the ls command (that is, ls -n -l, or, ls -nl).
Group ID	The default group identification number. The number identifies the default group to which the user belongs; users can belong to multiple groups, however. Red Hat uses the individual group convention in which each user belongs to a unique and exclusive group. (In the past, a user belonged to one or more general-purpose groups, which created problems.) The groups are defined in the /etc/group file.
Name and/or comment	This optional field contains the user's full name and other pertinent information such as office location, phone number, and pager number (especially important for systems administrators). Commas separate these pieces of information.
Home directory	The user's default directory. You go here when you log in.
Shell	Your default login shell. All Linux distributions, including Red Hat, use bash, which is the most commonly used shell in the Linux world. You can change the shell to ksh, csh, sh, or whatever you want.

Configuring Samba to authenticate from an NT server

Samba can also use an NT domain controller to authenticate requested shares. (The discussion of NT domain controllers is beyond the scope of this book.) In this case, you need to modify the /etc/samba/smb.conf file to point to the NT controller:

1. Change the security parameter to specify the use of an NT domain controller as follows:

```
security = server
```

2. Uncomment the following line:

```
password server = <NT-Server-Name>
```

3. Edit this line to include the name of the NT server, which in this case is called *my_pdc*:

```
password server = my_pdc
```

The name of your domain controller should convert into the IP address of your NT primary domain controller via DNS. **Note:** You can specify the IP address if you desire. For instance, if your controller address is 192.168.1.100, then you can enter the following line:

```
password server = 192.168.1.100
```

You must, of course, have an account on the primary domain controller.

The following listing shows the beginning of the default /etc/passwd file that Red Hat provides. Most Linux distributions use the same login names, user IDs, and group IDs through the first ten or so users (but vary in some of the directories). From there, the distributions vary according to their own needs. Don't worry, the details may vary, but they're for the system to use and don't affect your setup.

```
root:x:0:0:root:/root:/bin/bash
bin:x:1:1:bin:/bin:
daemon:x:2:2:daemon:/sbin:
adm:x:3:4:adm:/var/adm:
lp:x:4:7:lp:/var/spool/lpd:
sync:x:5:0:sync:/sbin:/bin/sync
```

The next steps show you how to add a user. (Note: We use arbitrary names , such as lidia, for creating Linux user names and Samba shares in this example. Substitute your own names as appropriate.)

1. Log in to the Windows computer `toluca` as the user `lidia`. If `lidia` is a new user, then you're prompted to enter a password. Enter the same password for `lidia` in the Windows machine as for `lidia` on the Linux computer.

2. Log in to the Linux server chivas as `root`.

3. Add the username:

   `useradd lidia`

4. Create a password by entering the following command:

   `passwd lidia`

   The passwd program prompts you for a new password.

5. Enter a password and then the confirmation of that password.

You have just created the Linux user account. The next section describes how to configure Samba to access that account's home directory.

Creating Samba shares

The following sections give you some examples of how to modify Samba shares. The first examples require only minimal modifications to the `smb.conf` file. Subsequent ones require further modifications, such as adding a printer, to your Linux system.

Any services that you had open won't be active because they were tied to the daemon you just terminated. However, they return as soon as you access them again. For example, if the computer icon `chivas` is opened from our Network Neighborhood, the same share becomes active again. If the window is still open, simply choose View → Refresh, and that same share becomes active again; the `smbd` daemon is a brand new process and has a new PIC.

Accessing an individual user's home directory

This section describes how to create a service out of the new user account, `lidia` (whose creation we showed in the preceding section). After you create a new user account on the Linux-Samba server, you can automatically access its home directory from Samba. The default `smb.conf` file is pre-configured to export the home directory of Windows clients whose usernames/passwords match the Linux username/password. The following instructions describe how to start and use Samba to access a Linux account.

1. Log in to the Windows computer `toluca` as the user `lidia`.

2. Log in to the Linux server chivas as `root`.

3. Restore your original `smb.conf` file from the backup copy:

```
cp /etc/samba/smb.conf.orig /etc/samba/smb.conf
```

4. Restart the Samba daemons:

```
/etc/init.d/smb restart
```

5. Double-click on the `chivas` icon in your Network Neighborhood, and then double-click the `lidia` icon and you see the contents of the directory.

   The contents of the `/home/lidia` directory appear.

6. Run the `smbstatus` command to see what Samba knows about your connection:

```
Samba version 2.2.5
Service uid     gid     pid    machine
-------------------------------------------------
IPC$    lidia  lidia  13057  toluca (192.168.1.1) Sep ... 2002
IPC$    nobody nobody 13057  toluca (192.168.1.1) Sep ... 2002
paul    lidia  lidia  13057  toluca (192.168.1.1) Sep ... 2002
No locked files
```

   In this case, Samba sees the user — and group — `lidia` connecting from the machine `toluca`. The service `lidia` points to the `/home/lidia` directory, which isn't shown in the `smbstatus` output. The `[homes]` services works as advertised!

7. You can read and write to this share and use it just like a local disk.

This section showed how to take advantage of Samba's default configuration. By default, Samba allows you to access all Linux home directories using the `[home]` share. The next section describes how Linux permissions supersede Samba permissions.

Introducing Linux and Samba permissions

Linux file permissions play a controlling role in how Samba shares behave. Linux permissions supersede Samba permissions. Therefore, even if Samba says that you can do something, you can't if Linux doesn't permit it.

As you know, every Linux file has file permissions for the user to whom it belongs, the group to which it belongs, and everyone else. If you do a long format listing of a directory or a file, you get a listing that includes the file's permissions — among other information — in the order just listed. For example, you may enter this command:

```
ls -l /etc/init.d/smb
```

Here's the information that this command displays:

```
-rwxr-xr-x   1 root     root          1177 Jul 20 11:12 /etc/init.d/smb
```

The characters rwx identify the permissions; as you've probably guessed, they stand for read, write, and execute – the hyphen (-) character means no permission. The order of their placement doesn't vary, so the hyphen in this example means no write permission.

These characters are grouped first as owner permission, then group, and finally other permissions. The owner is root in this case, as is the group. The other group means any user who isn't an owner or a member of the group – that is, other users.

UNDERSTANDING LINUX PERMISSIONS

Linux file permissions are important for Samba management because no matter what permission you set in the Samba configuration, it doesn't override the Linux file system permissions. For instance, if you set a share to be public but the directory that the share points to doesn't have the correct permissions set, that share won't be accessible to the public. The following example demonstrates this convention:

1. Log in to the Windows computer toluca as the user lidia.

2. Log in to the Linux server chivas as root.

3. Create a trivial file without any permissions in the /tmp directory. This file will be used to show how Linux permissions map to Samba.

   ```
   touch /tmp/test
   chmod 000 /tmp/test
   ```

4. Restore your original smb.conf file from the backup copy. (If you haven't already done so – as we advised earlier in this chapter – reverse the process and make a backup copy.)

   ```
   cp /etc/samba/smb.conf.orig /etc/samba/smb.conf
   ```

5. The [tmp] share in the smb.conf file is commented out. Remove the comments (anything following a semicolon – ; – is considered to be a comment) so the [tmp] share looks like the following code:

   ```
   [tmp]
       comment = Temporary file space
       path = /tmp
       read only = no
       public = yes
   ```

6. Save the changes, exit back to your shell prompt, and restart the Samba daemons with the following command:

   ```
   /etc/init.d/smb restart
   ```

7. Back on `toluca`, open the chivas share displayed in your Network Neighborhood. Double-click the `tmp` icon and you should see the contents of the `/tmp` directory.

8. Run the `smbstatus` command to see what Samba knows about your connection:

```
Samba version 2.2.5
Service uid      gid      pid    machine
-----------------------------------------------
IPC$    nobody   nobody   1317   toluca (192.168.1.1) Fri Sep
...
tmp     lidia    lidia    1317   toluca (192.168.1.1) Fri Sep
...
IPC$    lidia    lidia    1317   toluca (192.168.1.1) Fri Sep
...


No locked files
```

In this case, Samba once again sees the user — and group — lidia connecting from the machine `toluca` to the `tmp` service. The `tmp` service points to the `/tmp` directory. The IPC$ service is a generic share that Samba creates to send commands to the server.

9. You should be able to see the `test` file owned by `root`. If you do a long listing on the `test` file — **ls -l /tmp/test** — you'll see that only `root` has the write privilege:

```
---------- 1   root    root       7710 Sep 15 11:36 test
```

10. Try opening `test` by double-clicking on its icon.

11. You get a dialog box telling you that you don't have the permission to open the file. Change the file's permissions to allow non-owners to read but not write to the file:

```
chmod o+r /tmp/install.log
```

12. Open the share from your Windows box by double-clicking on its icon. Depending on what version of Windows you are using you might be asked what application program you want to use to open it. You can select an editor such as Microsoft WordPad and then look at the contents of the file.

13. Try modifying and then saving the file. Once again, you are told that you do not have permission. Even though you have marked the public Samba share pointing to `/tmp` as writeable, you do not have the permission from Linux to do so.

14. Add write permissions to the test file:

```
chmod o+w /tmp/test
```

You can modify the file through Samba once you provide sufficient Linux permissions. Linux permissions always supersede Samba's.

UNDERSTANDING SAMBA PERMISSIONS

In this next example, you once again export the /tmp directory. This time, however, you give world write permission on the install.log file so that you can modify it:

1. Log in to the Windows computer toluca as the user lidia.

2. Log in to your Linux-Samba server as root.

3. Change the permissions on the /tmp/install.log file as follows:

   ```
   chmod 777 /tmp/test
   ```

   This gives world read, write, and execute permission to test.

4. Restore your original smb.conf file from the backup copy (if you haven't already done so — as we advised earlier in this chapter — reverse the process and make a backup copy):

   ```
   cp /etc/samba/smb.conf.orig /etc/samba/smb.conf
   ```

5. Edit the smb.conf file, remove the comments (;) from the second [tmp] section, and change the read only parameter to yes:

   ```
   [tmp]
       comment = Temporary file space
       path = /tmp
       read only = yes
       public = yes
   ```

6. Save the changes, exit back to your shell prompt, and restart the Samba daemons:

   ```
   /etc/init.d/smb restart
   ```

7. Back on toluca, double-click on the chivas icon in your Network Neighborhood. Double-click the tmp icon and you should see the /tmp directory.

8. Run the smbstatus command to see what Samba knows about your connection:

   ```
   Samba version 2.2.5
   Service uid     gid     pid   machine
   ------------------------------------------------
   IPC$    nobody  nobody  1317  toluca (192.168.1.1) Fri Sep ...
   tmp     lidia   lidia   1317  toluca (192.168.1.1) Fri Sep ...

   No locked files
   ```

9. In this case, Samba sees the user — and group — `lidia` connecting from the machine `toluca`.

10. Do a long listing on the `test` file — ls -l test — you'll see that the world has read, write, and execute privileges:

    ```
    -rwxrwxrwx   1 root       root      0 Sep 13 20:19 test
    ```

11. Open up the `test` file from your Windows box by double-clicking the `test` file icon.

12. Modify the file in any way that you want. For instance, enter the widely used string `asdfasdf`.

13. Try saving the changes but you find that you're not allowed to do so. Even though Linux allows read, write, and execute permission to the `test` file, Samba does not allow you to do so.

14. If you wish to experiment, modify the `smb.conf` and change the `read only` to `no`. Restart Samba and this time you will be able to save any changes that you make. Be careful, however, and make only a trivial change. Once you have convinced yourself that it is possible, remove the changes.

This example shows how Samba can manipulate share privileges when the underlying Linux privileges exist.

EXPORTING THE CD-ROM

The next example involves exporting a CD-ROM, a quite useful service to your network. For example, one very productive service is sharing software — such as your Linux distribution — or other material to your network. Exporting the CD-ROM cuts down on the number of CD-ROM drives you need (although CD-ROM drives are becoming ubiquitous, some of your older machines may not have them). Plus, exporting the CD-ROM saves transporting a CD-ROM disc from machine to machine.

Once again making use of the default `smb.conf` file, the following instructions show you how to export the `/mnt/cdrom` directory:

1. Log in to the Windows computer `toluca` as the user `lidia`.

2. Log in to the Linux server chivas as `root`.

3. Restore your original `smb.conf` file from the backup copy (if you haven't already done so — as we advised earlier in this chapter — reverse the process and make a backup copy):

   ```
   cp /etc/samba/smb.conf.orig /etc/samba/smb.conf
   ```

4. Edit the `smb.conf` file and find the `[tmp]` share section. Remove the comments, and then change the `[tmp]` share name to `[cdrom]` and the `path = /tmp` to `path = /mnt/cdrom`:

```
[cdrom]
   comment = share CD-ROM
   path = /mnt/cdrom
   read only = no
   public = yes
```

5. Save the changes, exit back to your shell prompt, and restart the Samba daemons:

```
/etc/init.d/smb restart
```

6. Mount any CD-ROM disk:

```
mount -r -t iso9660 /dev/cdrom /mnt/cdrom
```

7. Double-click on the `chivas` icon in your Network Neighborhood. Double-click the `cdrom` icon and you should see the contents of the `/mnt/cdrom` directory.

8. Run the `smbstatus` command to see what Samba knows about your connection:

```
Samba version 2.2.5
Service  uid     gid     pid   machine
------------------------------------------------
IPC$      nobody nobody  3812  toluca (192.168.1.1) Sun Sep 15
23:06:40 2002
cdrom     lidia  lidia   3812  toluca (192.168.1.1) Sun Sep 15
23:07:09 2002

No locked files
```

9. In this case, Samba sees the user – and group – `lidia` connecting from the machine `toluca`. The `cdrom` service points to the `/mnt/cdrom` directory.

This section described how to configure Samba to export a specific resource. The CD-ROM drive was selected as the resource in this example in order to provide you with a useful configuration example plus a useful resource.

Exporting a service to two or more users

This section shows you how to use some of the user parameters, which we introduced in the preceding example. You can use this variable to allow any number of users access to a particular service. Though not the same as group access, the following access works in a similar fashion:

1. Log in to the Windows computer `toluca` as the user `paul`.

2. Log in to the Linux server chivas as `root`.

3. Restore your original `smb.conf` file from the backup copy:

```
cp /etc/samba/smb.conf.orig /etc/samba/smb.conf
```

4. Edit the `smb.conf` file and find the `[myshare]` share section. Remove the comments, and then change the `[myshare]` share name to `[lidia]` and the `path = /usr/somewhere/shared` to `path = /home/lidia` and `valid users = mary fred` to `valid users = lidia paul`.

```
[Lidia]
comment = Lidia and Paul's stuff
path = /home/lidia
valid users = lidia paul
public = no
writable = yes
printable = no
create mask = 0765
```

5. Save the changes, exit back to your shell prompt, and restart the Samba daemons:

```
/etc/init.d/smb restart
```

6. If you need to add the new user `paul`, follow the instructions in the section, "Adding users to Linux," earlier in this chapter, or enter the following command:

```
useradd paul
```

7. Set the password for `paul` by entering the following command:

```
passwd paul
```

8. Add `paul` to the lidia group in `/etc/group`:

```
lidia:x:500:paul
```

9. Change the permissions on `/home/lidia` to allow group access:

```
chmod g+rwx /home/lidia
```

10. Add paul's password to the `/etc/smbpasswd` file:

```
smbpasswd paul
```

11. On `toluca`, double-click your Linux-Samba computer icon — `chivas` — in your Network Neighborhood. Double-click the `lidia` icon and you should see the `/home/lidia` directory.

12. Run the `smbstatus` command to see what Samba knows about your connection:

```
Samba version 2.2.5
Service   uid    gid    pid    machine
---------------------------------------------
```

```
lidia    paul    paul    3844    toluca(192.168.1.1) Sun Sep 15
23:12:31 2002
IPC$     nobody nobody   3844    toluca(192.168.1.1) Sun Sep 15
23:12:31 2002

No locked files
```

13. In this case, Samba sees the user — and group — paul connecting from the machine toluca to the lidia share. The lidia share points to the /home/lidia directory (not shown in the smbstatus output). The fact that the user ID is paul is important because the service points to lidia's directory, which is fully owned by the user lidia. Thus, Samba has indeed allowed multiple users to access a single share.

    Unlike the earlier examples in this chapter, you can read and write to this share, using it just like a local disk!

Using Samba's macro capability

Samba can substitute macros for service parameters. Upon connection, it dynamically allocates its resources according to which machine or user is asking for each resource.

You designate a macro by adding a percent (%) symbol as the first character of any of several predefined names. Table 12-2 shows the macros.

TABLE 12-2 SAMBA MACROS

Macro	Description
%a	Remote servers architecture
%d	PID of the current server process
%g	Primary group name of %u
%h	Samba server's host name
%m	Client computer's NetBIOS name
%u	Username of the current service or share (if any exists)
%v	Samba version number
%G	Primary group name of %U
%H	The user's home directory, given by %u
%I	Client computer's IP address

Continued

TABLE 12-2 SAMBA MACROS *(Continued)*

Macro	Description
%L	Samba server's NetBIOS name
%M	Client computer's Internet name
%P	Root directory of the current service or share (if any exists)
%S	Current service or share, if it exists (if any exists)
%T	Current date and time
%U	Session username the client requested, but not necessarily the one received

The following example experiments with the %u macro. (The names used in this example, such as lidia, are optional. Feel free to use any names that you want to use.)

1. Log in to the Windows computer toluca as the user lidia.

2. Log in to the Linux server chivas as root.

3. Restore your original smb.conf file from the backup copy:

   ```
   cp /etc/samba/smb.conf.orig /etc/samba/smb.conf
   ```

4. Edit the smb.conf file and find the [pchome] share section. Remove the comments and then change the path = /usr/pc/%m to path = /home/%u, as shown below. Notice that smb.conf uses the %u macro, which expands into the Windows user's username — lidia in this case — connecting to it.

   ```
   ; The %m gets replaced with the machine name that is
   connecting.
   [pchome]
     comment = PC Directories
     path = /home/%u
     public = no
     writeable = yes
   ```

5. Save the changes, exit back to your shell prompt, and restart the Samba daemons:

   ```
   /etc/init.d/smb restart
   ```

6. On your Windows computer, double-click your Linux-Samba computer icon in your Network Neighborhood. Double-click the pchome icon, and you should see the contents of the /home/lidia directory.

7. Run the `smbstatus` command to see what Samba knows about your connection:

```
Samba version 2.2.5
Service  uid   gid   pid   machine
------------------------------------------------
pchome   lidia lidia 1346 toluca(192.168.1.1) Fri Sep ...

No locked files
```

8. In this case, Samba sees the user — and group — `lidia` connected from the machine `toluca`. The `[pchome]` service, which points to the `/home/lidia` directory (not shown in the `smbstatus` output), is active.

This Samba macro-based service attempts to connect every Windows client that comes down the pike. If a valid Linux username exists, this service automatically connects a matching Windows client to it. Using macros really simplifies the `smb.conf` file setup, because you can adapt one service section to numerous situations. If you have numerous shares to distribute (or are just plain lazy like your authors), this option is for you.

Adding network printers by using Linux and Samba

Samba provides an excellent mechanism for sharing printers across a network. In this section, we configure an Epson 777 ink jet printer that's attached to a Red Hat Linux server.

CONFIGURING A LOCAL PRINTER

Before configuring a Samba print share we connect a printer to a Red Hat Linux computer. We use chivas as the server in this example. The following steps describe how to set up Chivas as a printer server.

1. Log in to the Linux server chivas as `root`.

2. Attach a printer to your Linux computer's parallel (printer) or USB port.

3. Start the Red Hat Print Configuration utility. Click the GNOME Menu button and select System Settings→Printing.

4. Click on the Printer icon (the third icon from the top).

5. If you haven't already configured a printer, then you'll get a blank screen. To add a printer, click on the New button and the Add a New PrintQueue window opens.

6. The Local Printer radio button should already be set. Choose OK and the printer port that's detected appears.

7. Click OK, and you see the Edit Local Printer Entry window.

   The default values for the printer name, spool directory, and file limit fields should all be acceptable. (You can choose any name for the printer that you want, but by convention, the default name is lp. You can assign multiple names to a single printer.) If your printer port is detected, it should show up in the Printer Device field; if it doesn't, then choose the port yourself. Click the Input Filter Select button and you'll get the window.

8. Highlight and select the printer type that you're using and click OK, and control is sent back to the Edit Local Printer Entry window.

9. Click OK and you return to the Red Hat Print Configuration window where the new printer is displayed.

10. Test your new printer by first restarting the print daemon and then using the Tests→Print Postscript test page. Enter the command: **lpr /etc/printcap.**

11. Click on the Tests→Print Postscript test page from the Red Hat Print System Manager window (you can also choose to print a plain text file). The Red Hat Printer Configuration utility prints PostScript. You can try a more complex job by using an application like Mozilla, which is included with Red Hat's distribution.

USING SAMBA TO SHARE A PRINTER

Samba makes sharing printers across a network easy. For instance, you can use Samba to share a printer that's already connected to your Linux box. All you have to do is configure Samba to use the Red Hat Linux printer setup. The Linux setup is simple, unless you have an unusual printer or some other irregularity.

The following instructions show you how to configure a typical Linux-Samba server to work as your network's printer server:

1. Connect a printer to any Red Hat Linux computer on your network.

2. Login as root.

3. Restore your original smb.conf file from the backup copy:

   ```
   cp /etc/samba/smb.conf.orig /etc/samba/smb.conf
   ```

   Don't restart the Samba daemons just yet, however.

4. Edit the smb.conf file and find the [global] share section:

   ```
   [global]
       ...
       printing = lprng
   ```

   This section gives Samba the following information:

- The printing entry specifies which printer daemon Linux uses. (BSD is the default, but Linux also uses `sysv`, `hpux`, `aix`, `qnx`, and `plp`. Linux works well with BSD; we mention the others for the sake of being complete.) It also tells Samba the default values for the `lpr` and `lpq` commands that Linux uses to perform the actual printing.

- The `printcap name` parameter defines where the Linux printer configuration file printcap is located.

- The load printers parameter indicates whether to load all the printers defined in the printcap for browsing.

5. Next, create an explicit printer share for the Epson 777:

```
[epson777]
        comment = lp for Epson 777
        path = /var/spool/samba
        read only = No
        guest ok = Yes
        browesable = no
        writeable = no
        public = no
        printable = Yes
        printer name = epson777
        oplocks = No
```

This section gives Samba the following information:

- A comment describing what it's set up for.

- If browseable is `yes`, you can browse all the printers defined in the /etc/printcap file from a Windows client.

- If `printable` is `yes`, it allows nonprinting access to the spool directories associated with the print service. If `printable` is set to `no`, you're not prevented from printing, you're simply denied direct access to the printer spool directories — /var/spool/lpd/lp, for instance.

- If `public` is set to `no`, those Windows clients that a Linux username doesn't authenticate (the guest account, for example) can't use the Samba print services.

- If `writeable` is set to `no`, you can't write directly to the printer spool directory, but you can still print.

6. Exit from the `smb.conf` file and edit the /etc/printcap file. It contains the Linux printer configuration information, and Samba reads this information when it starts. We have a Hewlett Packard LaserJet 5L attached to our Linux computer. The following shows our printcap file:

```
#
# /etc/printcap
#
# DO NOT EDIT! MANUAL CHANGES WILL BE LOST!
# This file is autogenerated by printconf-backend during lpd
init.
#
# Hand edited changes can be put in /etc/printcap.local, and
will be included.

lp|epson777:\
        :sh:\
        :ml=0:\
        :mx=0:\
        :sd=/var/spool/lpd/lp:\
        :af=/var/spool/lpd/lp/lp.acct:\
        :lp=/dev/lp0:\
        :lpd_bounce=true:\
        :if=/usr/share/printconf/util/mf_wrapper:
```

Here's an explanation of the file's contents:

- Anything after a pound sign (#) is treated as a comment.

- Colons (:) bound variables and their parameters.

- A backslash (\) specifies that the parameter continues on the next line.

- The first line after the comments defines the printer name and any aliases by which Linux knows the printer (it can have zero or more aliases). The printer name lp (line printer) is standard.

- The sd=/var/spool/lpd/lp line identifies the printer spool directory's location. Recall that the lpd daemon spools a print file to a temporary directory. The effect is to buffer the print file so that the processor doesn't have to wait for the much slower printer.

- The mx variable specifies the largest file that you can print. Setting mx to a pound-zero (#0) removes any file limitation.

- The sh variable is a flag that prevents the printing of a burst page (header page) before each print job. This feature is only useful if you have many users printing to a single printer.

- The lp=/dev/lp0 line defines the device file (in this case, lp0 points to the first parallel port, which would be lpt0 in MS-DOS parlance).

- The :if=/usr/share/printconf/util/mf_wrapper: specifies the input filter. You use it to translate various file formats to a printer. It translates everything from PostScript into a form that the printer understands.

7. Save the changes, exit back to your shell prompt, and restart the Samba daemons:

   ```
   /etc/init.d/smb restart
   ```

   The preceding changes to your smb.conf file make all your printers available over your network, which, in this case, means that you can print to the LaserJet from any of the Windows clients. You can explicitly set parameters (such as where the spool directories are located), but we prefer to keep that information in the printcap file as much as possible.

One very useful thing that Printer Configuration does is set up printer filters for you. A printer filter can enable you to do things, such as print PostScript files to a non-PostScript printer, by translating from one protocol to another.

8. Windows may not recognize the new printer when you try to mount it. If you haven't configured the printer on your Windows PC, you have to do so. A dialog box appears asking whether you want to configure a printer. If you click the Yes button, the Windows Wizard guides you through the process with minimal confusion. You'll most likely need your Windows or printer CD-ROM to get the print driver.

9. After you have Windows configured for your Samba printer, open the Network Neighborhood icon. You should see a Samba share 1p, along with any other shares that you've configured.

10. Double-click the 1p icon and you get the Windows printer queue dialog box.

11. To test your Samba print service, click the Printer menu. Next, click the Properties menu item and you get the Windows Epson 777 Properties dialog box.

12. Click the Print Test Page button and a test page prints for you. In fact, if you keep an eye on the Epson 777 queue dialog box, you can watch the job's progress.

13. Windows processes the print job and copies it by using Samba to the print server. The Linux print server then processes the file.

   The test page is finally printed on your printer. It's a marvelous system.

TIP

You can print directly with Linux by redirecting output to a printer's device driver. For example, if you have a printer connected to your parallel port — the common PC method — you can print the content of a file as follows:

```
cat /etc/share/smb.conf > /dev/lp0
```

This method is occasionally useful — usually for troubleshooting purposes — but unadvisable in general. Linux uses a spooling system to print. The user program lp works with the daemon process, lpd to send a print job to a spool directory and then to the printer. This method efficiently and safely shares a resource among many users and processes. The /etc/printcap file contains the configuration information for each attached printer (both physically and via a network).

Introducing SWAT

The Samba team has introduced the *Samba Web Administration Tool* (SWAT) in the Samba 2.0 distribution. SWAT is a Web-based tool that enables you to configure Samba by using your Web browser. SWAT uses a specialized version of the httpd daemon to act as the interface to your Web browser. When you open SWAT with your browser, the inetd daemon kicks off the swat daemon. Introduced during the writing of this book, the tool appears to be a good one and should only get better with time.

You use the xinetd daemon to kick off other daemons on a per-use basis. The xinetd.conf configuration file controls the overall action of xinetd. Individual configuration files control each daemon. You need to modify the /etc/xinetd.d/swat file as follows before SWAT will work:

1. Change the disable parameter from yes to no:

   ```
   Disable = no
   ```

2. Restart the xinetd daemon:

   ```
   /etc/init.d/xinetd restart
   ```

3. Start up your Web browser and enter the http://localhost:901/ URL in the Location window. You're prompted to enter a username and password. Enter **root** as the user name and enter the **root** password. The SWAT interface window then appears.

SWAT is in a relatively early phase of development. It currently enables you to do all the things that you can do by manually modifying the smb.conf file. It allows you to modify the global parameters; add, modify, and create shares (printer shares, too), and view the status of open shares. For instance, to modify the Samba workgroup, click GLOBALS, change the name from WORKGROUP to MYGROUP, and then click the Commit Changes button. Look at the `/etc/samba/smb.conf` file and you see that SWAT has not only changed the workgroup parameter, but it has also completely rewritten the file.

SWAT replaces the original `smb.conf` file with one that doesn't include all the comments. Any changes that you make with SWAT are written into this new file.

One of SWAT's best features is that you can return any parameter back to its default value by clicking the Set Default button to the right of the field. It also prevents you from specifying incompatible parameters. You can display help on a subject by clicking the Help button to the left of the field.

Troubleshooting

If you have difficulty getting Samba to work, please review the steps we describe in this chapter. Pay special attention to the Samba utilities, such as `smbstatus`. Remember that if you're using Windows 98, ME, NT/2000, or newer versions of Windows 95, then you need to configure Samba to accept encrypted passwords. You can find a good troubleshooting guide in `/usr/share/doc/samba-2.2.2`.

Summary

This chapter provides an overview of the Samba file and printer sharing system. The Samba configuration file is described and then several examples show how to modify the configuration. The examples show many of the basic configurations that you'll use to set up a simple business or home network. For instance, you can take the steps for allowing two users access to one service and easily expand to a dozen users by including their names in the valid users variable.

This chapter covers these topics:

- **Expanding the client-server network by working first on the Samba configuration:** This approach offers the most efficient method for obtaining a working system because modifying a simple text file is all that's necessary.

- **Reviewing the roles of the two Samba daemons:** `smbd` and `nmbd`: Together they form the heart of Samba.

- **Restarting the Samba daemons:** A new `smbd` process starts with every new share that you export. Even so, restarting these daemons is advisable when configuring Samba to make sure that everything works the way you intend it to.

- **Describing the `smb.conf` file** — the global section, directory, and printer shares.

◆ **Giving examples of services that don't require any Linux modifications:** Shares that are public or guest types are very easy to make and serve as good starting points. Some are useful in the real world.

◆ **Demonstrating a working Samba share:** The first example shows how to make the entire Linux disk visible (but not writable).

◆ **Using the `/etc/init.d/smb` script:** The second example shows you how to start and stop the Samba daemons with the `/etc/init.d/smb` script. This method is easier and safer than doing the same thing manually.

◆ **Examining Linux and Samba permissions:** The third example illustrates how Linux permissions take precedence over Samba permissions. Even if you have Samba's permission to do something, you can't do it if Linux doesn't let you. Another example shows you how Samba permissions work alongside Linux permissions. If you have the proper Linux permissions, then you can use Samba to further tune your user's access.

◆ **Exporting your CD-ROM:** We provide an example that shows how to export your CD-ROM. Because the CD-ROM is a read-only device, you can make it publicly available, and it can provide a valuable network service.

◆ **Adding a user to Linux manually:** This process entails adding a line to the `/etc/passwd` and `/etc/group` files and creating a home directory for each new user.

◆ **Allowing multiple users to access a single share:** In the example we give, the `allow users` parameter provides that function.

◆ **Using Samba's macro capability to automate many services:** Samba provides a set of macros that expand to match things, such as the Windows machine name.

◆ **Configuring a Linux printer:** We use the Red Hat Printer Configurator to set up a printer. We then use Samba to provide network access to that printer.

◆ **Configuring Samba by using the graphical SWAT user interface:** This interface allows you to modify Samba shares without touching the `smb.conf` file.

Part IV

Managing Your Linux Servers

Chapter 13

Automating Network Backups

IN THIS CHAPTER

- ◆ Introducing automated, network-based backups
- ◆ Introducing the AMANDA backup system
- ◆ Configuring AMANDA
- ◆ Using AMANDA
- ◆ Troubleshooting backup problems

ONE OF THE MOST ESSENTIAL but underrated network services is the ability to make systematic, reliable backups of multiple clients. Backups provide both security and reliability for your network. Security comes from knowing that you can recover from break-ins and other compromises; reliability comes from the obvious ability to recover from both major and mundane disasters.

The traditional method of making backups involves connecting a tape drive to a server and using utilities such as tar and dump to manually copy data to the tape. That method is both simple to configure and use. However, manual backups quickly become labor-intensive and unreliable when you begin to manage multiple computers.

The better system is a network-based, automated client-server backup model. When using a network backup model, you attach a backup server to a storage device. The server determines when a client needs to be backed up and initiates the backup process. The server controls the client software, telling it when to start a backup and what file systems to copy. The client and server communicate over the network using specific TCP/UDP ports to transmit the backup date. The server receives the data and writes it to the backup media, which is usually a tape but can be a hard disk or other media.

The backup server also controls the data recovery process. The server keeps an index or database of the backups it has made. You tell the server what files or directories to recover and it determines the location (for instance, what tape) of the backups and then restores the data.

Introducing AMANDA

Today, AMANDA is the most widely used Open Source network backup system. AMANDA—the Advanced Maryland Automated Network Disk Archiver—was developed by James da Silva at the University of Maryland in the early 1990s. Its Web page is located at www.amanda.org.

AMANDA is a client-server system that makes use of existing Linux/UNIX backup utilities. It uses the traditional tar and dump archiving utilities on a client to back up a file system, directory, or file. The AMANDA client then copies the archive across the network to the server using its own TCP/UDP connection. The data is copied over the network to a temporary location on the server's file system, called a Holding Disk, which can be a simple directory, a file system, or an entire disk. The data is transferred from the Holding Disk to the backup media to complete the backup process.

The AMANDA server controls both the backup media and the backup schedule. The media can be any device such as tape drives, a tape library, or a hard disk.

AMANDA uses the Holding Disk to more efficiently stream data to the backup media. Tape drives typically operate most efficiently when they can constantly stream data to tape. Queuing data and then constantly writing it to a tape allows the drive to operate at a constant speed. Maintaining a constant speed prevents the time-consuming process of constantly stopping, rewinding, and restarting the write process. AMANDA optimizes its tape drive efficiency by queuing all the backup data to the Holding Disk so it won't have to wait for the data to arrive.

AMANDA does not schedule explicit full backups but instead defines the maximum time between full backups. It typically performs daily incremental backups and performs full backups when activity is at a minimum.

AMANDA maintains indexes (databases) of what client backups have been done and where they exist. The indexes allow you to perform file recoveries, and they also keep track of which tapes were used for each backup, relieving you of the burden of keeping manual data logs for each tape.

The server maintains a schedule of what to back up and when. When the server determines that a client has reached its scheduled backup time, the server daemon communicates with the client daemon to initiate the backup. The two sides manage the transfer of the data (corresponding to the file systems being backed up) across the network. The server receives the data and writes it to the storage media.

Understanding AMANDA

AMANDA uses the client-server model to conduct its backups. The server portion controls the timing of client backups and the media used to store the backups. This section describes the elements of the AMANDA client and server.

Introducing the AMANDA server and client

The AMANDA server consists of the following elements:

◆ **Server applications:** AMANDA uses several programs to control and perform the backup and restoration process. You can run the server programs manually or program `cron` to execute them.

◆ **Configuration files:** The AMANDA server configuration files are stored in the `/etc/amanda` directory by default. You create subdirectories in `/etc/amanda` for each AMANDA configuration. For instance, the `/etc/amanda/DailySet1` directory contains a sample AMANDA configuration that we use as the basis for the examples in this chapter. The configuration files are `amanda.conf`, `diskfile`, and `.amandahosts`.

◆ **xinetd system:** AMANDA uses its own protocol to transfer data and control between clients and server. The AMANDA server "wakes up" the client by connecting to the client's xinetd server and starting the AMANDA processes.

◆ **Holding Disk:** The Holding Disk is storage space where backups are stored until they can be flushed to the permanent storage media – tape or other media. By queuing dumps, the Holding Disk also helps optimize network bandwidth by allowing multiple backups to be performed at anytime rather than waiting for a tape to be free. A Holding Disk can be placed on a simple directory, a dedicated file system, or a dedicated disk.

◆ **Cron jobs:** AMANDA uses cron to automatically run backup jobs. The `cron` daemon wakes up periodically and `amdump`. `amdump` performs a backup.

The AMANDA client consists of the following elements:

◆ **Client applications:** AMANDA uses several programs to perform the client portion of a backup. The AMANDA server initiates the client programs. The client programs use the native Linux `tar` and/or `dump` utilities to obtain copies of the specified client directories. (The `diskfile` configuration file on the server and the `.amandahosts` file on the client determine what directories to back up.)

◆ **The xinetd system:** The AMANDA server controls the client via `xinetd`. When the server sends control packets to the client, the client's `xinetd` starts up the appropriate processes that start the backup process.

Here is a time-line summary of what an AMANDA backup process looks like:

1. `cron` starts the `amdump` program.

2. `amdump` runs the planner program to decide what backups to run.

3. The `amdump` program wakes up the client backup process via the `xinetd` service.

4. The client starts its own backup by using either the `tar` or `dump` utility.

5. The client process opens a network connection to the backup server.

6. The client pipes the output of the `tar` or `dump` process over the network connection to the server.

7. The server receives the data from the client and stores it to permanent storage (for instance, a tape or disk).

8. AMANDA uses several criteria to determine when to write the contents of the Holding Disk to tape. Once AMANDA decides to flush the Holding Disk, it uses the standard `mt` utility to make the write.

Introducing the network services

The AMANDA server communicates with its clients by using several network services. The server controls the client and also receives the client backup data by using several `xinetd`-based client processes. AMANDA uses four network services to perform backups:

◆ **amanda:** The `amanda` service controls the backups. This service uses both TCP- and UDP-based communication on port 10080.

◆ **kamanda:** You can configure AMANDA to use Kerberos authentication on port 10081 (TCP and UDP). It is beyond the scope of this book to discuss Kerberos-based AMANDA backups. Please consult the `KERBEROS` file in the `/usr/share/doc/amanda-server-2.4.2p2` directory for more information.

◆ **amandaidx:** When a backup is performed on a client, the index of that backup is sent to the server via the `amandaix` service. The service uses a TCP connection on port 10082.

◆ **amidxtape:** This service controls the tape.

TIP

AMANDA is designed to optimize computer and network resources. AMANDA limits the amount of a client's processor resources that it uses via its configuration. For example, you should not configure a slow client to use software compression. AMANDA conserves network bandwidth by spacing full backups as far apart as possible, and deferring backups if the load becomes too high.

The next section describes the configuration files that you need to use when creating AMANDA backups.

Introducing the configuration files

The following list describes the `amanda.conf` configuration file parameters:

◆ **org:** The string defined for this parameter is inserted into the `Subject:` line when AMANDA sends e-mail reports.

◆ **mailto:** Defines the address that AMANDA will e-mail reports to. You'll want to set this to the e-mail address of the AMANDA administrator.

◆ **define:** Provides the mechanism for constructing `dumptypes`, `tapetypes`, and `interface` definitions.

◆ **dumpuser:** Defines the user ID that AMANDA runs as. The default is the `amanda` user.

◆ **dumpcycle:** Defines the interval between full backups (dumps).

◆ **runspercycle:** Sets the number of backups – full and incremental – to run every dumpcycle.

◆ **tapecycle:** Informs AMANDA how many tapes it has access to. Note that if tapecycle is equal to 10, AMANDA will use at least 9 (10–1) tapes before rewriting a tape.

◆ **runtapes:** Defines the number of tapes that AMANDA can use during a backup.

◆ **tapedev:** Defines the no-rewind Linux device to be used for backups. The device can be a tape drive, hard disk, null device, or other media. Don't define this parameter when using a tape library (changer).

◆ **tapetype:** Associates a media type with the tapedev.

◆ **netusage:** Defines the maximum network bandwidth that AMANDA can use. AMANDA tries to reduce its use when it exceeds the threshold set by `netusage`.

◆ **labelstr:** Defines an expression to use as the basis for every tape label (AMANDA needs to create a label for every tape that it uses). If, for instance, the `labelstr` is `daily[0-9][0-9]`, AMANDA will label the first tape as `daily00`, the second as `daily01`, and so on.

◆ **infofile:** Sets the directory of the file that stores the AMANDA history database.

◆ **logdir:** Sets the directory where AMANDA stores its log files.

◆ **indexdir:** Sets the location of the optional AMANDA catalog database.

Please consult the examples provided later in this chapter for more information about the parameters.

The `disklist` file describes the clients and their directories that the server backs up. The disklist parameter format specifies the client machine name, the directory or partition to back up, and the type of backup. The following line shows the format:

```
client    partition/directory    backup type
```

The backup types are defined in the `amanda.conf` file. The default types are as follows:

- **always-full:** Specifies a full backup run at a high priority with no software compression.
- **comp-root-tar:** Uses the same configuration as `root-tar` but adds software compression.
- **comp-user-tar:** Uses the same configuration as `user-tar` but adds software compression.
- **comp-user:** This type dumps user partitions using compression and high priority.
- **comp-root:** This type dumps root partitions using compression and low priority.
- **nocomp-root:** Same as `comp-root` but without compression.
- **nocomp-user:** Same as `comp-user` but without compression.
- **high-tar:** Uses the same configuration as `root-tar` except the priority is bumped from low to high.
- **holding-disk:** This type designates that the holding-disk be flushed.
- **root-tar:** This backup type is designed for root partitions and uses GNU `tar`; it uses a low priority, no software compression, and creates an index.
- **user-tar:** This backup type uses the same configuration as `root-tar` but is designed for user partitions.

The next section describes the AMANDA utilities used to back up data, restore data, and perform administrative tasks.

Introducing AMANDA utilities

AMANDA provides a suite of programs that perform the backup and restoration functions. The suite also provides various utilities that perform secondary jobs, such as labeling tapes, controlling tape libraries, displaying logs, and so on. The following list describes each AMANDA program:

- **amadmin:** Performs AMANDA configuration file modifications; also displays information about the configuration file.

- ◆ **amcheck:** Performs configuration checks on AMANDA clients and servers.

- ◆ **amcheckdb:** Determines if the tapes listed in `tapelist` are consistent with those listed in the AMANDA database.

- ◆ **amcleanup:** Repairs AMANDA databases.

- ◆ **amdump:** Performs an AMANDA backup.

- ◆ **amflush:** Flushes backups from the Holding Disk to permanent storage (for instance, a tape).

- ◆ **amgetconf:** Checks and displays the contents of the `amanda.conf` configuration file.

- ◆ **amlabel:** Labels an AMANDA tape.

- ◆ **amoverview:** Shows the file systems that AMANDA controls.

- ◆ **amplot:** Graphically displays information gleaned from amdump files.

- ◆ **amrecover:** Interactively browses backup index files. Interactively restores selected files and directories.

- ◆ **amreport:** Computes and displays statistics about AMANDA backups.

- ◆ **amrestore:** Recovers entire backup images from permanent media to disk.

- ◆ **amrmtape:** Removes tapes from the AMANDA database.

- ◆ **amstatus:** Displays the state of an AMANDA backup.

- ◆ **amtape:** Interactively controls tape devices.

- ◆ **amtoc:** Creates and displays the table of contents of a backup.

- ◆ **amverify:** Locates tape errors if they exist.

Consult the AMANDA man page for more information about the `amanda.conf` parameters. You can find more information about this configuration file, including examples and a FAQ, in the `/usr/share/doc/amanda-server-2.4.2p` directory.

Knox Software, Inc. sells an excellent automated, network backup system called Arkeia. The system is capable of streaming multiple clients to multiple backup devices; multiple backups can also simultaneously be written to a single device. Unlike AMANDA, its backups can span multiple tapes, and recoveries are done in a single step (rather than having to step through incremental backups until the last full backup is reached). Knox Software provides a free download version of Arkeia for Linux. The free version can back up one server and two clients, and there are no other limitations than that. You can find out more information about Arkeia at `www.knoxsoftware.com`.

Tape libraries, also known as *stacks*, *autoloaders*, or *jukeboxes*, combine one or more tape drives, multiple tape slots, and a robotic arm mechanism to transfer the tapes from the slots to a drive. A simple box with a door on the front generally contains the whole system. (The biggest libraries have a slot for inserting and removing individual tapes without opening the front door). Tape libraries are generally connected to their server, but you can connect them by other methods.

Enhanced Software Technologies makes a backup system called BRU2000; you can find more information at www.estinc.com. The taper program, which comes as part of the Red Hat distribution, also provides another backup system.

Using AMANDA

AMANDA is a powerful system capable of backing up large networks. However, AMANDA's power comes at the price of complexity. Therefore, we're going to provide two examples that demonstrate AMANDA's basic operation. The first example exercises AMANDA using a null device without saving any data. The second example backs up data to a disk drive. These examples provide a reasonable method for starting on the steep AMANDA learning curve.

We construct a basic AMANDA client-server system in this section. In order to quickly build the system, we'll put both the client and server on the same computer — chivas in this example. The server will use a simple directory as its Holding Disk and the /dev/null device — also referred to as the null device — as its backup media. Using the null device provides a mechanism that everyone can access and that requires zero configuration.

After creating the simple AMANDA system using the null device, we'll move on to create a backup system that connects to an actual backup device.

Configuring AMANDA requires the following elements:

- ◆ **AMANDA server:** The computer that controls AMANDA backups and stores the data that they generate. The data does not necessarily have to be stored locally. It can be stored on an NFS mounted file system, for instance.

- ◆ **Backup device:** The device can be a single tape drive, a tape library, a disk, or other backup media.

- ◆ **One or more AMANDA clients:** AMANDA clients are controlled from the server. The server can be a client to itself. The client communicates with the server over a TCP/IP network connection.

TIP   You can find out more information about configuring and using AMANDA from the following sources: The backup guru, W. Curtis Preston, graciously provides access to the AMANDA chapter from his excellent book, *UNIX Backup and Recover*; O'Reilly, at www.backupcentral.com/amanda.html. The following Web page gives an excellent introduction to AMANDA: www.frankenlinux.com/guides/amandaintro.html.

Building a minimalist backup system

This example provides a way to learn the basics of AMANDA. We use the Linux null device as the AMANDA backup media. The null device is a virtual device that is available on all Linux systems; the null device refers to the /dev/null device. It throws away all the data sent to it, so this example will not save any data for you. However, this example is universal and can be run on all Linux computers for that reason. It is a very useful device for our purposes.

CONFIGURING THE SERVER

The following instructions describe how to configure the example server chivas as an AMANDA server. The process requires that you modify the default AMANDA configuration files on the server.

1. Log in as root on chivas.

2. Install the AMANDA packages from the companion CD-ROM if you have not already done so.

   ```
   rpm -ivh /mnt/cdrom/backups/amanda*
   ```

   Note that the AMANDA RPM packages add the user amanda and group disk to the system. All the following configurations depend on them.

3. Make a backup of the configuration files.

   ```
   cd /etc/Amanda/DailySet1
   mkdir Bak
   cp * Bak
   ```

4. Edit the default /etc/amanda/DailySet1/amanda.conf file to create a basic AMANDA server. Modify the following parameters shown. The first two create a backup system that writes to the null device (obviating the need to find or purchase backup media for the time being.) The remaining parameters define the Holding Disk — note that you may need to use a different file system depending on available space.

   ```
   tapedev "/dev/null"
   rawtapedev "/dev/null"
   ```

```
tapetype Null

define tapetype Null {
    comment "for testing purposes only"
    length 100 mbytes
    speed 100 kbytes
}

holdingdisk hd1 {
    comment "main holding disk"
    directory "/var/holdingdisk"
    use 500 Mb
}
```

5. Configure the /etc/amanda/DailySet1/disklist file to define the client
   and directory to back up. The disklist file also controls what options —
   dumptype — to use when making the client backups.

```
# server
localhost /etc always-full
```

In this particular example, we select the /home directory to back up. The
dump type of the /etc directory uses always-full, which means that a
full backup of /etc will be made whenever this client is backed up.

CONFIGURING THE CLIENT

The next step is to configure the client. In this case, the client is the server.
Combining the client and server on the same machine is simply the most straightforward example to build; making the server a client to itself removes most networking issues from the system. The following instructions describe the client
building process:

1. Log in as root on chivas.

2. Enable AMANDA by modifying the appropriate files in the
   /etc/xinetd.d directory. Change the disable parameter in the amanda,
   amidxtape. and amandaidx files to the following value:

   ```
   disable = no
   ```

3. Restart the xinetd daemon.

   ```
   /etc/init.d/xinetd restart
   ```

You've configured the simplest AMANDA system possible. Using the /dev/null
device simplifies the configuration process because it is a logical device that has no
physical significance. Everything you write to the null device goes into the Ether —
the bit stream is discarded.

TESTING THE SIMPLE BACKUP

Test the backup system now. The following instructions will exercise the simple AMANDA system you just created. Note that the client runs on the server.

1. Log in to the client machine `chivas` as the `root` user.

2. Change to the `amanda` user.

   ```
   su - amanda
   ```

   Installing the AMANDA RPM packages creates the `amanda` user. You should run all backups as the `amanda` user. Running the backups as a non-privileged user minimizes your security vulnerabilities.

3. Run the `amdump` program to start the example backup.

   ```
   /usr/sbin/amdump DailySet1
   ```

   The `DailySet1` parameter directs `amdump` to use the configuration files that you just modified in the `/etc/amanda/DailySet1` directory.

The AMANDA client runs on the server. The client runs the `tar` utility, which archives the `/etc` directory. The tar output is sent to the server on the loopback — 127.0.0.1 — interface. The server flushes the backup data to the `/dev/null` device. No data is actually saved, but this example demonstrates the basic AMANDA configuration and usage.

You can run the `amcheck` utility to display the backup status once `amdump` finishes.

```
/usr/sbin/amcheck -s DailySet1
```

You should see output similar to the following:

```
Amanda Tape Server Host Check
-----------------------------
WARNING: tapedev is /dev/null, dumps will be thrown away
Holding disk /var/tmp: 1846124 KB disk space available, that's
plenty
NOTE: skipping tape checks
Server check took 0.004 seconds
```

This shows that using `/dev/null` exercises the backup system without saving any data. It also shows the available space on the Holding Disk. This information would help you determine if you have enough storage space when using real media to make real backups. (AMANDA also e-mails the dump results to the `amanda` user.)

Building a simple backup system

As you can see from the previous section, AMANDA is not very difficult to set up. This section expands the simple "null" configuration to create a real-world backup system. We back up two clients to real backup media. We also show how to recover data from the backup.

We replace the /dev/null device with a disk drive in this section. Using the universally available disk drive ensures that every reader can configure this system. Disk drives also provide fast and reliable media. The following sections describe how to set up the server and two clients.

CONFIGURING THE SERVER

The following steps describe how to configure an AMANDA server. This server expands on the previous example "null" server by using a disk drive as its backup media.

1. Log in as root on the server chivas.

2. Restore the original AMANDA configuration files from the backup you made in the previous example.

   ```
   cd /etc/Amanda/DailySet1
   cp Bak/* .
   ```

3. Edit the default /etc/amanda/DailySet1/amanda.conf file to create an AMANDA server that flushes its backups to a hard disk. The parameters set up the device parameters so that we can use the hard disk.

   ```
   tapedev "no-device"
   rawtapedev "no-device"
   changerdev "no-device"
   ```

4. Create a new tape type that uses a hard disk as its backup medium; hard disks are cheap and you should consider using a dedicated drive as your backup medium. Set the length parameter to match the size of your disk (although you can set the values smaller than the total available space). The filemark parameter is used to define the number of bytes between reference marks on a tape. The filemark parameter is set to zero when using a disk drive because no reference is necessary.

   ```
   tapetype Disk

   define tapetype Disk {
       comment "Save to disk"
       length 100 mbytes
       filemark 0 kbytes
       speed 1000 kbytes
   }
   ```

5. Configure the Holding Disk to point to the backup disk. In the following example, an entire disk is dedicated as the backup disk. The backup disk is formatted with the ext2 file system and mounted as /backupdisk.

```
holdingdisk hd1 {
   comment "main holding disk"
   directory "/backupdisk"
   use -1 Mb }
```

The backup disk can also be a simple directory or file system. In those cases, you'd use the following respective `directory` parameters:

```
directory "/dev/hda5"
directory "/var/backup"
```

6. Set the reserve to 0.

```
reserve 0
```

7. Configure the `/etc/amanda/DailySet1/disklist` file to define the client and directory to backup. The `disklist` file also controls what options — `dumptype` — to use when making the client backups.

```
# server
toluca    /home comp-root-tar
```

This defines one Linux client `toluca`. We choose to back up an arbitrary directory — `/etc` — on the client.

This section described setting up the AMANDA server. The next section shows how to set up the client.

CONFIGURING A CLIENT

The previous examples configured a client and server on the same computer. That model provides the simplest and quickest method to construct a working system. This section expands the example to create an AMANDA client on a separate machine.

The following instructions show how to install and configure AMANDA on a client that's separate from the server:

1. Log in as root on `toluca`.

2. Install the AMANDA packages from the companion CD-ROM if you have not already done so.

```
rpm -ivh /mnt/cdrom/backups/amanda*
```

Note that the AMANDA RPM packages add the user `amanda` and group disk to the system. All the following configurations depend on them.

3. Enable AMANDA by modifying the appropriate files in the `/etc/xinetd.d` directory. Change the `disable` parameter in the `amanda`, `amidxtape`, and `amandaidx` files to the following value:

```
disable = no
```

4. Restart the xinetd daemon.

```
/etc/init.d/xinetd restart
```

5. Make a backup of the configuration files.

```
cd /etc/Amanda/DailySet1
mkdir Bak
cp * Bak
```

6. Modify .amandahosts on the AMANDA client Toluca to identify the server and user name to run the backups as follows:

```
chivas.paunchy.net amanda
```

You're now ready to start a backup from the AMANDA server. The next section describes how to run a test backup.

TESTING THE BASIC BACKUP

Test the backup system now. The following instructions will exercise the simple AMANDA system you just created. Note that the client runs on the server.

1. Log in as the root user on the server chivas.

2. Change to the amanda user.

```
su - amanda
```

Installing the AMANDA RPM packages creates the amanda user. You should run all backups as the amanda user. Running the backups as a non-privileged user minimizes your security vulnerabilities.

3. Run the amdump program to start the example backup.

```
/usr/sbin/amdump DailySet1
```

The DailySet1 parameter directs amdump to use the configuration files that you just modified in the /etc/amanda/DailySet1 directory.

The AMANDA client runs on the server. The client runs the tar utility, which archives the /etc directory. The tar output is sent to the server on the loopback — 127.0.0.1 — interface. The server flushes the backup data to the /dev/null device. No data is actually saved, but this example demonstrates the basic AMANDA configuration and usage.

You can run the amcheck utility to display the backup status once amdump finishes.

```
/usr/sbin/amcheck -s DailySet1
```

You should see output similar to the following:

```
Amanda Tape Server Host Check
-----------------------------
WARNING: tapedev is , dumps will be thrown away
Holding disk /var/tmp: 1846124 KB disk space available, that's
plenty
NOTE: skipping tape checks
Server check took 0.004 seconds
```

This shows that using a disk drive for backup media creates a system that you can use to back up your network. The system has the advantage of being fast and reliable. However, you should consider obtaining removable media at some point. One possibility is to use a writable CD-ROM. You can use utilities such as `cdrecord` or `gtoaster` to copy some or all of the backup disk contents to a CDR disc. The other alternative is to obtain a streaming tape drive or library.

The log also shows the available space on the holding disk. This information would help you determine if you have enough storage space when using real media to make real backups.

 TIP The next version of AMANDA is 2.4.3 and will provide better disk-based backup options. Version 2.4.3 is currently in beta. AMANDA source code is hosted by SourceForge (`www.sorceforge.net`) and can be found by going to `www.amanda.org/download`.

RECOVERING BACKUP DATA

You can use the `amrecover` application to selectively recover files and data when you have enabled the `dumptype` index parameter during a backup. Otherwise, you can use the `amrestore` utility to recover entire AMANDA backups whether or not a backup has any indexes.

The following instructions describe how to interactively recover data from this example backup. These instructions assume that you are recovering from a backup controlled via the `DailySet1` set up in the previous example.

1. first:Log in to the client `toluca` as `root`.

2. Add the `root` user in the `/var/lib/amanda/.amadahosts`.

   ```
   toluca.paunchy.net    amanda
   toluca.paunchy.net    root
   ```

3. Start the `amrecover` browser (specify the configuration file and AMANDA server).

   ```
   amrecover -C DailySet1 -s chivas.paunchy.net
   ```

The `amrecover` program starts and displays the prompt shown here:

```
amrecover>
```

4. Specify the dump disk to use.

```
amrecover> setdisk /home
```

5. Specify a directory to browse.

```
amrecover> add paul
```

6. Display information about the backup data.

```
amrecover> list
```

7. AMANDA displays the information about the backup.

```
TAPE /home/paul/20020930/cancun.paunchy.net._home.0 LEVEL 0
DATE 2002-09-30 /spool
```

8. Change the relocation root (optional). AMANDA will restore files and directories to that location rather than the current working directory.

```
amrecover> lcd /tmp
```

9. Set the date of the backup that you want to start browsing.

```
amrecover> setdate 2002-09-30
```

This example looks back one day.

10. Start the recovery.

```
amrecover> extract
```

If you're recovering data using tapes, you may be prompted to insert additional tapes if the backup spans multiple tapes.

11. Exit from `amrecover`.

```
amrecover> quit
```

This example shows how to interactively browse and recover files and/or directories using `amrecover`. The next example shows how to use `amrestore` to recover entire backups.

1. Log in to the client `toluca` as `root`.

2. Use the `amadmin` utility to list the backups.

```
amadmin DailySet1 find paul
```

3. You should see information about your backups.

```
Scanning /amanda...
date          host         disk           lv tape or file      file
```

```
status
2002-09-24 toluca     /home/paul     DailySet1     14 OK
2002-09-25 toluca     /home/paul     DailySet1     14 OK
2002-09-26 toluca     /home/paul     DailySet1     14 OK
```

4. Start the restore process.

```
amrestore paul
```

The entire backup image will now be restored to your disk.

This section demonstrated the process of recovering files and directories using amrecover **and** amrestore. The amrecover utility makes use of the indexes that AMANDA can optionally create; you can interactively browse AMANDA backups and select files and/or directories to restore. The amrestore utility does not make use of indexes and recovers entire backups.

Automating your backups

AMANDA is designed to run automatically via the Cron daemon. Rather than run the amdump and amcheck programs manually, as done in the two previous examples, they are started by Cron. This system is simple to configure and understand. The default AMANDA crontab is as follows:

```
0 16 * * 1-5    /usr/sbin/amcheck -m DailySet1
45 0 * * 2-6    /usr/sbin/amdump DailySet1
```

This crontab programs AMANDA to run amcheck in the afternoon (16 hours, 0 minutes) on weekdays (day 1 is Monday, 5 is Saturday) and amdump just after midnight on Tuesday through Saturday. Add the cron jobs to your system as follows:

1. Log in to the AMANDA server as the amanda user.

2. Edit the crontab.

```
crontab -e
```

On a Red Hat Linux computer, the -e option specifies that the vi editor be used to edit the user's crontab.

3. Add the two cron entries shown above. Modify the times and days as desired.

4. Exit the editor by pressing the Z key twice.

5. Verify your cron entries by entering the following command:

```
crontab -l
```

You now have programmed AMANDA to back up your network.

Troubleshooting

AMANDA is a somewhat complicated system. Several components must work together on different machines in order for backups to run and recoveries to be made. The following list outlines several AMANDA subsystems to check if you have problems. Identify the problem and do the following:

◆ Check the AMANDA log files stored by default in the /var/lib/amanda/ DailySet1 directory.

◆ Use netstat to verify that AMANDA is communicating with the xinetd daemons. You should see connections made to the AMANDA client as shown below.

```
Active Internet connections (w/o servers)
Proto Recv-Q Send-Q Local Address          Foreign
Address         State
tcp       0        0 cancun.paunch:amandaidx
cancun.paunchy.net:721  TIME_WAIT
```

If you don't see the connection, the problem might be that xinetd isn't configured correctly, the network connection isn't being made, or the server doesn't have the correct permission to start the client; in that case, verify that the .amandahost file on the client is configured correctly.

◆ Check your amanda.conf, disklist, and .amandahosts configuration files. Use amcheck to verify that the client and server configurations are valid. For instance, running the command amcheck –c DailySet1 checks the validity of the client configuration and should return a result shown below.

```
Amanda Backup Client Hosts Check
--------------------------------
Client check: 1 host checked in 0.203 seconds, 0 problems
found

(brought to you by Amanda 2.4.2p2)
```

◆ Check that the client and server can communicate over the network. Make sure that your network is configured correctly and the clients and server can communicate correctly. Consult Part I for network troubleshooting information.

Summary

This chapter introduced the AMANDA network backup system. Network-based backups are an essential component to both the reliability and security of your network.

Without backups, you can't recover from minor or major disasters; disasters can be caused by human mistakes or malice, fires, hackers, or any number of other causes. If your network consists of more than just one or two machines, you cannot rely on your backups unless they are made automatically.

It is pure drudgery to make manual backups. Human nature programs us to make mistakes in many circumstances, but especially when we are bored. Therefore, we recommend using the Open Source AMANDA system to back up the machines on your network. This chapter introduced AMANDA and outlined two example configurations that you can create on any Linux computer.

The following list describes the subjects discussed in this chapter:

◆ **AMANDA system:** We introduce AMANDA and its philosophy. It is based on the client server network model: one server can back up many clients. AMANDA is an Open Source system that was designed at the University of Maryland.

◆ **AMANDA components:** AMANDA consists of network services, utilities, and configuration files.

◆ **Network services:** The AMANDA server communicates with its clients via the `xinetd` system. Clients are controlled and backup data is transmitted via client network processes that are started by the `xinetd` daemon on the client. One process controls the client backup process while the other two transmit the backup data and index information to the server.

◆ **Configuration files:** The AMANDA server uses configuration files to describe the backup media along with the clients and client directories to be backed up. The AMANDA client configuration files identify the server and other parameters.

◆ **Very simple example:** The first example creates a minimalist backup client-server system. Both the client and server exist on the same machine. The server directs all data to the `/dev/null` device because, while no data is actually stored on the server (`/dev/null` is not connected to any physical device), the device is universally available on all Linux computers. Thus, you are not limited by hardware that you may or may not have.

◆ **Usable example:** The second example provides a simple yet usable backup system. The example uses a disk as its permanent storage media. You cannot physically change or move disk-based backup media as easily as tape. However, you can still perform backups on reliable media. Everyone has access to disk-based media, so the example is universal.

◆ **Recovering data:** The interactive `amrecover` utility and command-line `amrestore` utilities were introduced.

Chapter 14

Increasing the Reliability of a Linux Server

IN THIS CHAPTER

- ◆ Locating single points of failure
- ◆ Using the Ext3 journaling file system
- ◆ Using RAID to increase reliability
- ◆ Creating a high availability Linux cluster

YOU CAN INCREASE THE RELIABILITY of your Red Hat Linux-based Internet servers by considering several software and hardware issues. This chapter concentrates on making your hardware systems morerobust. We introduce the concept of single points of failure (SPOF) in this chapter, as well. Locating your SPOFs helps you to make intelligent choices for efficiently increasing reliability. Based on the SPOFs you find in the common PC, we address the systems that we believe will provide the most cost-effective increases in reliability.

Locating Single Points of Failure

This section outlines the typical SPOFs you find on the typical computer, and tells you what measures you can take to eliminate or ameliorate them. The following list describes the vulnerability of a computer's subsystems.

- ◆ **Central Processing Unit (CPU):** As the center of every computer, the CPU performs the tasks called for by every program – including Linux and all of the processes it manages – executed on a computer. Obviously, if the CPU fails, your computer fails. Your odds of failure actually increase if you use multiple processor computers because one of two is more likely to fail than one alone.

- ◆ **Random Access Memory (RAM):** RAM is another major computer subsystem that can cause a system failure. Although memory failure doesn't guarantee total failure, it causes significant, if not catastrophic, problems.

◆ **Mass storage:** The ubiquitous hard disk (also known as hard drive) stores the operating system, applications, and data. The mean time to failure (MTF) of modern disks is typically very long at about 300,000 hours, which is 34 years. However, being mechanical device(s) by nature they are still vulnerable to failure due to vibration, shaking, etc. Therefore, mass storage systems are major SPF. What you discover is that the probability of failure increases as you add subsystems to individual computers. (This principle is the same one that increases your odds of winning the lottery when you purchase more than one ticket.) For instance, if a single disk drive's MTF is 10 years, then the MTF for two drives is less than 10 years.

◆ **Network Interfaces:** Failing network interfaces don't necessarily cause a computer's failure; however, they do effectively destroy the availability of network-based servers and workstations.

◆ **Power supplies:** Power supplies convert alternating current (AC) into the direct current (DC) necessary to run all computer subsystems. These devices are semi-mechanical in nature because they use cooling fans. Power supplies tend to fail more than many subsystems due to their reliance on mechanical fans and transients from the power grid itself.

◆ **Miscellaneous:** Your computer can also fail due to problems with secondary systems, such as cables. Computers are also vulnerable from external systems, such as power failures, fires, and so on.

You can take various measures to minimize or eliminate SPOFs. In many cases, you can eliminate SPOFs by purchasing specialized – and expensive – equipment. For instance, you purchase redundancy if you can afford PCs with multiple CPUs, power supplies, and network interfaces. Those who can't afford the price of redundant systems can still greatly increase reliability by using several of the Linux-based utilities.

The following sections describe three of the most cost-effective Linux systems. The first two sections describe how to increase the reliability to your mass storage by adding journaling and RAID to your file systems. The final section introduces the concept of using fail-over systems to gain complete redundancy. The theme of these solutions is that they use General Public License (GPL) software to create very reliable, redundant servers from inexpensive, off-the-shelf hardware. This software is free, so Linux once again provides inexpensive and elegant solutions.

Using the Ext3 Journaling File System

The Ext3 (also called Ext3fs) journaling file system provides an important and exciting addition to the Linux world. Ext3, which stands for third Extended file system, is an important advancement because it makes your mass storage much more robust and reliable than was possible with the previous Ext2 system. Red Hat now includes Ext3 in its 7.2 release.

Ext2 has been the de facto Linux file system since its introduction over ten years ago. Ext2 is fast, reliable, and capable of handling file systems up to 4 Terabytes (TB). However, Ext2 file systems are vulnerable to corruption if you don't follow proper shutdown procedures.

Data that is to be written to an Ext2 file system is first cached in memory. Linux eventually writes the data to disk by using a process called *syncing*. However, if the power fails for some reason, then the file system will most likely be corrupted. (Corruption occurs when cached data isn't actually written to physical media.) The actual file system state won't match up with the expected state, and Linux won't allow the file system to be used until you correct the problem.

Corrupted Ext2 file systems are usually recoverable by using the fsck (file system check) utility. If the system can derive the actual state from the current state, then it can recover the file system and use it again. Anyone who has turned the power off to a Linux computer has experienced fsck recovering the file systems the next time the system is booted. Red Hat shows a simple recovery metric while the file system is being fsck'd.

Recovering a file system or systems generally presents an inconvenience for servers that use small file systems. You can recover small file systems on the order of a few gigabytes in just seconds up to a few minutes, an acceptable delay for many Internet servers. However, the recovery period can stretch into the tens of minutes and beyond when you're using large file systems, which is unacceptable for most Internet server operations.

Journaling provides the solution to the delay caused by recovering Ext2 file systems. Journaling file systems are much less vulnerable to corruption than Ext2 file systems because they keep a record of all data that is to be written to disk in a journal file — you can also think of the journal as a log. The journal permits you to know the file system's exact state at all times and in all circumstances. When you know the state, you can completely recover from a file system failure in a matter of seconds, rather than minutes or hours.

 You can find more information about jfs and the Ext3 file system at `www.redhat.com/support/wpapers/redhat/ext3/why.html`

Using the Ext3 file system is an option with Red Hat Linux starting with the 7.2 release. You have the choice of formatting or upgrading partitions with Ext3. The format option destroys any data that may already exist on the partition. The upgrade option leaves any existing Ext2 data in place and simply installs a journal file on the existing file system.

For more information on the Ext2 and Ext3 file systems consult the following Web sites: `www.europe.redhat.com/documentation/HOWTO/ Filesystems-HOWTO-6.php3#ss6.1` **and** `www.linuxdoc.org/LDP/ khg/HyperNews/get/fs/ext2intro.html`.

You can perform the Ext2 to Ext3 upgrade option manually. The process is independent of the steps involved in installing Red Hat. The following instructions describe how to convert an existing file system; we use a non-functional file system in this example. Using a test system is safer than using an existing file system, such as `/home` or `/usr`.

1. Mount the file system in the usual way:

   ```
   mount -t ext2 /dev/hda7 /mnt
   ```

   The details, such as the IDE hard disk `/dev/hda7` device file, are our own. Modern PCs use IDE devices, such as hard drives and CD-ROMs, as their standard device type. IDE devices integrate all controller electronics into the device itself. You should use your own parameters.

2. Create the journal — also known as a log — file on the file system. tune2fs –j –c 0 –m 0 /dev/hda7

3. With the `journal.dat` inode number in hand, mount the test file system again, but this time as an Ext3 system:

   ```
   mount -t ext3 /dev/hda7 /mnt
   ```

   The `journal` parameter tells the kernel that it can find the journal file at inode number `1234`. The kernel can then go directly to the data that the `journal.dat` file contains and fix any inconsistencies that may exist on the file system. The `-t ext3` parameter identifies the file system as Ext3, of course. The `noload` option prevents the kernel from using any old, invalid journal files. If this filesystem was listed in /etc/fstab, be sure to change the filesystem type from ext2 to ext3.

You can now test the new system if you like. One simple way of testing is to turn off the power to the computer. We don't recommend this method because your other file systems probably aren't journaled yet, and even if they are, doing so is just a bad practice. However, if you do power cycle your Linux server, you'll see that the test file system is mounted immediately without a `fsck` occurring. Seeing your first journal Linux file system recovery occur is a very satisfying experience.

You can use the *mke2fs –j* command to format new ext3 filesystems.

You can check the file system journal by looking for the kernel process. You should see several kernel processes when you examine the process table. Running the **ps –ef** command reveals the processes as shown here:

```
root        191     1  0 17:13 ?        00:00:00 [kjournald]
root        192     1  0 17:13 ?        00:00:00 [kjournald]
root        193     1  0 17:13 ?        00:00:00 [kjournald]
root        194     1  0 17:13 ?        00:00:00 [kjournald]
root        195     1  0 17:13 ?        00:00:00 [kjournald]
```

Using RAID to Increase Reliability

The ubiquitous hard disk is amazing in its own right because it works so well, and is constantly improving in speed and capacity. However, a hard disk still uses a rotating platter that's somewhat prone to failure. Hard disks still represents one of the most significant points of failure in the modern computer.

The Redundant Array of Independent Disks (RAID) method is a technique that greatly increases the reliability and performance of mass storage. RAID combines multiple, inexpensive hard disks in such a way that they work faster and are more reliable than if used individually. RAID improves performance by parallelizing data I/O and increases reliability by using redundancy. Depending on your needs, you can use either or both options.

Disk drives are mechanical devices that are slow relative to other electronic computer subsystems, such as memory, busses, and CPUs. The electronic subsystems must often wait for disk I/O to finish. You can minimize the disparity in speed by reading or writing to two or more disks at once by using a process called *Striping*.

You can spread data across multiple disks, increasing reliability through redundancy by using one of two methods: mirroring or parity. Mirroring simply duplicates all data, making it an effective, but expensive – you have to double all of your storage – method. Parity is a method for reconstructing data and is less expensive but sacrifices some reliability. You can recover all data stored on a parity-based system if you lose one disk. However, you may lose data if more than one disk fails.

Introducing software RAID

Until recently, no one would consider using a software-based RAID system for any important system because the cost of calculating parity in the case of RAID-5, or duplicating writes for RAID-1, plus other overhead was just too high. The Linux kernel RAID algorithms were relatively inefficient and the CPUs weren't fast enough for the task. Software-based RAID was okay for small systems but not for ones of any size.

However, the Linux kernel code has been greatly improved in the 2.4 kernel. Processing power has continued its relentless progress to the point that software RAID is adequate for most small to medium- sized systems. This advancement is exciting because implementing RAID on your servers costs almost nothing.

 Some computers use *hot-swappable disks.* Such equipment allows you to replace failed disks without powering down your server. Hot-swappable disks are another example of functionality that used to be available only from expensive, dedicated equipment, such as commercial disk arrays.

The following sections describe the major RAID modes. RAID-2 and RAID-3 are rarely, if ever, used, so we don't discuss them here.

LINEAR MODE

In linear mode, two or more disks are concatenated into a single, logical device. The second and any subsequent disks appear to be extensions of the first. The logical device's total storage capacity is the sum of the individual disks. Data fills up the first device, then continues onto the second, and so on. Any size disks can make up the Linear mode device.

This configuration provides no redundancy. Reliability is decreased, in fact, because the loss of one disk causes the loss of the whole raid system. If you lose the first disk to a catastrophic failure, for instance, then all data on the first disk is lost, as are any files that started on the first disk and continued to the second. This mode generally doesn't improve performance. You can gain de facto improvements if you do I/O simultaneously to multiple files that happen to reside on different disks. Performance will suffer when you access disks with slower I/O rates.

RAID-0 (STRIPE MODE)

RAID-0 combines two or more disks into a single, logical device as with the Linear mode; however, it divides I/O between the disks and performs I/O in parallel. Two or more devices will divide and write – or read – a chunk of data at once. I/O is speeded up because the total number of devices used effectively divides the latency of each single device, assuming that the bus speed is fast enough. For example, assume that you have two IDE disks that rotate at 5500 revolutions per minute and are attached to two 133 MHz busses – typical for today's PCs. The busses are fast enough to handle the two disks. Your RAID-0 array will be nearly twice as fast as if you use a single disk. When the computer's bus is fast enough to handle the total number of disks the formula is N*P MB/sec, where N is the number of disks and P is the speed of each disk.

RAID-0 provides no redundancy. The loss of one disk almost guarantees the loss of all data, because data streams are split between all the disks in the array. We recommend that you use disks of similar size for RAID-0. You can use different sized disks, but performance suffers when writes are sent to the high end of the RAID, because the single, large disk is accessed alone; when that occurs, all parallelism is lost.

RAID-1

RAID-1 provides complete redundancy by duplicating data to multiple disks. Data is copied to both disks in a two-disk, RAID-1 configuration. The copied data is referred to as a mirror.

Write performance is slightly degraded when using RAID-1. Data being written to the RAID must be duplicated to each disk in the array. This duplication adds overhead when using software-based RAID, such as the one we describe here, because the Linux kernel must take care of the duplication. Read performance is also affected because the kernel must access each disk in the array. You can use a spare disk to replace a failed disk. You must copy all data from the remaining functional disk to the spare. The transfer process takes time, and you should take that delay into account when deciding whether to use RAID-1.

RAID-4

RAID-4 combines striping with redundancy. Data is striped across the disks in the array to enhance performance. Calculating and saving the parity of the data being written provides redundancy. You can reconstruct data by combining the parity information with the remaining data. (The data is striped across multiple disks, so if one fails some of the original data still exists.)

RAID-4 requires a minimum of three disks — two data disks and one for parity. RAID-4 isn't widely used — Red Hat doesn't support RAID-4 — because RAID-5 is better. RAID-5, as you will see, provides the same performance without requiring a separate parity disk.

RAID-5

This system provides RAID-4's functionality — better performance and redundancy — without requiring a separate parity disk. Parity is calculated as in RAID-4 but it's saved on the data disks themselves. Data must be written to both the parity and data drives, which slows the entire system down. By writing the parity to the data disks the whole process is streamlined, and by eliminating the dedicated parity disk, the system is more economical.

RAID-5 requires three or more disks to function. You can recover data when one disk fails; however, this is not possible when two or more do. RAID-5 increases read and write performance.

Implementing Software RAID

Software RAID is available on all Red Hat Linux systems 6.1 and above. You can configure a software RAID system by using either the Red Hat Linux installation tools or the utilities provided by the raidtools RPM package. The Red Hat Linux installation process provides a simple method for configuring and formatting a software RAID device. The general process is as follows:

1. Decide how much reliability and performance you want to get out of your system. You will have less need for a RAID system if you are the only one who uses your network. However, you need to build in more reliability if you run a business network that numerous employees and customers depend on.

2. Create two or more partitions for the RAID to use.

3. Configure the /etc/raidtab configuration file. A sample configuration is shown below.

```
# sample raiddev configuration file

#
# 'persistent' RAID5 setup, with no spare disks:
#
raiddev /dev/md0
     raid-level              5
     nr-raid-disks           3
     nr-spare-disks          0
     persistent-superblock   1
     chunk-size              4

     device                  /dev/sda7
     raid-disk               0
     device                  /dev/sda8
     raid-disk               1
     device                  /dev/sda9
     raid-disk               2
```

4. Run mkraid on each partition as shown below:

   ```
   mkraid
   ```

5. Run mkfs to place a file system on the combined RAID partitions.

   ```
   mkfs /dev/md0
   ```

6. Create a mount point for the new RAID file system.

   ```
   mkdir /raid
   ```

7. Mount the RAID-based file system.

```
mount /dev/md0 /raid
```

The following instructions describe how to create a RAID-5 file system. We use individual partitions on a single disk for this example. The resulting RAID device won't be of much use because, it'll fail if the disk fails. However, this is a very good method for describing the process. You can use any disk with unused space to learn the process. You can also easily modify this example to create a useful RAID device that uses separate disks.

1. Decide how you want to configure your RAID partitions. You'll obtain the most reliability and performance by using individual hard drives for each partition. Small Computer System Interface (SCSI) disks provide more flexibility (and performance, in many cases) over IDE. You can use up to only four disks on a PC. IDE disks also suffer performance hits because the master and slave pair must share bandwidth on each bus. SCSI permits at least 6 devices, up to 14 on each bus. The busses themselves also offer more bandwidth. One side benefit is that some external SCSI chassis allow you to hot-swap (change disks without powering down).

2. Log in as `root` and download the package from Red Hat's anonymous FTP site if you have not already installed it.

```
mount /mnt/cdrom
```

3. Install the `raidtools` RPM package:

```
rpm -i /mnt/cdrom/raid/raidtools*
```

4. Format the partitions by using the `fdisk` utility. Use the `fd` option to create `Linux Raid Auto` partitions.

```
fdisk /dev/sda
```

5. Configure the */etc/raidtab* configuration file. The following example describes using partitions on the same disk.

```
#
# 'persistent' RAID5 setup, with no spare disks:
#
raiddev /dev/md0
     raid-level            5
     nr-raid-disks         3
     nr-spare-disks        0
     persistent-superblock 1
     chunk-size            4

     device                /dev/hda10
     raid-disk             0
     device                /dev/hda11
```

```
raid-disk               1
device                  /dev/hda12
raid-disk               2
```

If you're creating a "real" RAID device – using separate IDE disks, for instance – the configuration will look as follows:

```
#
# 'persistent' RAID5 setup, with no spare disks:
#
raiddev /dev/md0
    raid-level              5
    nr-raid-disks           3
    nr-spare-disks          0
    persistent-superblock   1
    chunk-size              4

    device                  /dev/hda1
    raid-disk               0
    device                  /dev/hdc2
    raid-disk               1
    device                  /dev/hdb1
    raid-disk               2
```

6. Configure the partitions into a RAID device:

   ```
   mkraid /dev/md0
   ```

7. Create a file system on the RAID partition:

   ```
   mke2fs -j -c 0 -i 0 /dev/md0
   ```

8. Start the RAID file system:

   ```
   raidstart /dev/md0
   ```

9. You can now mount and use the file system:

   ```
   mount /raid
   ```

10. You should see the kernel-based RAID processes running as follows:

    ```
    root          9     1  0 17:13 ?        00:00:00 [mdrecoveryd]
    root         15     1  0 17:13 ?        00:00:00 [raid5d]
    ```

You can test the RAID file system only if you use separate disks. (Creating the RAID file system on partitions that reside on the same disk doesn't provide any method for testing.) You can perform a simple test in the case where you have separate disks – disconnect one of the disks. The RAID will rebuild itself when you replace the disk that you disconnect. Alternatively, the RAID set can be rebuilt on a spare disk if you have one.

You can check the status of a running RAID device by examining the */proc/mdstat* file. This file contains the information about the running RAID. The following is an example of a RAID-5 running on the single-disk partitions that we just constructed:

```
Personalities : [raid5]
read_ahead 1024 sectors
md0 : active raid5 hda10[2] hda11[0] hda12[1]
        204800 blocks level 5, 64k chunk, algorithm 0
[3/3] [UUU]

unused devices: <none>
```

Creating a High Availability Linux Cluster

The previous two sections described methods for increasing the mass storage reliability on a single Linux server. Those methods provide cost-effective measures for dealing with the most important mechanical device – disk drive – that your Linux server depends on. This section advances the concept of reliability by introducing fail-over Linux clusters.

You create a cluster, or High Availability (HA), when two or more computers are tightly coupled and communicate any failures to each other. The computers appear as a single IP address to the outside world. When one computer fails, the others take over its function and the service that it provides never stops working.

HA technology has been commercially available for many years, but the cost was prohibitive for small to medium-sized organizations and almost insurmountable for the individual. In recent years, people such as Alan Robertson, Harald Milz, and many others have created a software system called Heartbeat, which provides HA to the Linux world. Heartbeat is published via the GPL and is stored at `http://www.wiley.com/compbooks/sery`. You can find more information about the Heartbeat concept and software at `http://linux-ha.org/`.

Understanding how HA works

The Heartbeat system currently makes creating a two-server cluster possible. The machines monitor each other by listening to each other's heartbeat, which is analogous to the simple communication the ICMP-based `ping` supplies. As long as machine A can detect machine B's heartbeat, and vice-versa, both machines know that their cluster is operating correctly. If machine A encounters problems and stops sending a heartbeat to B, then B knows that A is sick. The heartbeat software enables B to detect A's problems and take over its services. The cluster shares a single IP address that the outside world accesses.

You can find a good article on configuring a two-computer cluster at *System Admin* magazine: www.sysadminmag.com/articles/2001/ 0109/0109c/0109c.htm. The article discusses configuring Heartbeat on two identical Linux machines that share a common SCSI disk drive. Samba is used to share the common data.

Exploring HA fail-over modes

High Availability software uses several different modes of operations. The following list describes the fail-over modes of operations.

- ◆ **Idle Standby:** In this fail-over strategy, one machine in a cluster is the primary node and runs the services that the cluster provides to the outside world. The other machine is the backup node and is idle – on Idle Standby – until the primary fails. The backup node provides the services if and when the primary fails. You can prioritize the backup nodes so that the higher ones take over before the lower ones.

- ◆ **Rotating Standby:** Rotating Standby is similar to Idle Standby, but none of the nodes are prioritized. The node that enters the cluster first owns the service group. This strategy is useful when you don't want service interrupts caused by higher priority nodes joining a service group.

- ◆ **Simple Fallover:** This configuration uses both the primary and backup nodes to perform services. The primary node runs mission critical services, while the backup node runs non-critical ones. The backup takes over the primary's functions if the primary fails. This strategy is useful when you can't afford to maintain an Idle Standby machine.

- ◆ **Mutual Takeover:** This configuration expands the concept of an Idle Standby into a two-way Idle Standby. Each server in a two-server cluster can take over the other's function.

- ◆ **Concurrent Access:** Only the Oracle Parallel Server uses this system, so it doesn't enjoy widespread use.

Understanding fail-over modes is necessary when constructing a high availability Linux cluster. The next section describes how to create a simple two-node Linux cluster.

Creating a simple HA Linux cluster

The Heartbeat system makes the task of creating an HA Linux cluster straightforward. The process requires that you connect two Linux boxes together with a network (and optionally a serial or other communication path) and then install and configure the software. The two machines then monitor each other. One machine is configured as the master and the other as the slave. If the master fails, then the slave configures its network interface as the virtual IP address. The slave also mounts the appropriate file system and starts any necessary services. The slave continues to provide the services that the master had been running after the configuration is complete. The Heartbeat system is designed so that the master will take back its duties when it becomes operational again.

We concentrate on describing how to configure the fail-over system between two Linux servers. To that end, we skip the usual description of configuring a common mass storage system that the cluster shares. A shared mass storage system requires extra equipment, such as an external SCSI disk, an external Network File System (NFS) server, or a Storage Area Network (SAN). (If you're concerned about reliability, a SAN is the best system because more than one computer can share it and you can configure it as a RAID.)

By concentrating on the process of failing one server to another, we avoid the considerations and complications of deciding on what common storage to use and how to configure it. Our cluster provides a static Web page, so each server in the cluster uses only its own local storage. The slave uses its own file system when the master fails. This design simplifies the process of configuring a Linux Heartbeat system by removing the necessity of providing a high-availability file system. You don't have to worry about configuring a fail-over storage when configuring this system.

This process requires two Linux computers, preferably machines that are closely matched and configured. You want the machines to be similar from a hardware perspective because one machine must be able to take over from the other. Using two, identical machines reduces administrative load because you need only keep track of one configuration.

 The Heartbeat package contains extensive documentation that is stored in the /usr/share/doc/packages/heartbeat directory. The Getting Started file provides a good introduction to configuring the heartbeat on Linux machines.

Follow these steps to create the cluster:

1. Connect a null modem cable between the two computers. The cable is connected between the serial ports on each computer and provides a path on which the two machines can share a heartbeat.

2. Install a second Ethernet Network Interface Card (NIC) on each machine.

3. Connect the second Ethernet NIC to a hub or switch that is separate from your private network. The second network is used exclusively to share the

heartbeat (independent of the serial connection). We refer to this configuration as the HA network. You don't need to use a switch or a hub for the HA network. You can connect two Ethernet NICs with a Cat 5 crossover cable. We use the extra equipment because it's inexpensive and more available than crossover cables.

4. Install the Heartbeat RPM package from the companion CD-ROM onto each server:

```
rpm -ivh /mnt/cdrom/HA/heartbeat*
```

5. The Linux heartbeat relies on three configuration files that live in the `/etc/ha.d` directory: `ha.cf`, `authkeys`, and `haresources`. `ha.cf` controls the heartbeat's overall operation; authkeys authenticates the machines to each other; and haresources defines what services the cluster provides.

6. Configure `ha.cf` on each server. (Each server's `ha.cf` file is identical.)

```
        The servers, or nodes, that belong to the cluster are
set in this file. The communication interfaces (serial and
Ethernet, in this case) that heartbeat uses are also set in
this file. The parameters are shown below:
node      ha1
node      ha2
# time a system must be unreachable before considered dead
(seconds)
deadtime 10
# set up for the serial heartbeat pulse
serial    /dev/ttyS0
baud      19200
# interface to run the network heartbeat pulse
udp       eth1
# set up a log file
logfile /var/log/ha.log
```

7. Create and configure the authorization keys file – `authkeys`. This file configures the encryption keys that the machines in the cluster will use to authenticate themselves to each other. The protocol options are Cyclical Redundancy Check (CRC), Message Digest (MD5), and SHA1. We use MD5, which is the most commonly used method. The contents of an example `/etc/ha.d/authkeys` file is shown below:

```
auth 3
3 md5 ttikey
```

8. Make the `authkeys` file accessible by root only on each server:

```
chmod 0600 /etc/ha.d/authkeys
```

9. Configure the `haresources` file on each server. This file controls the services that the cluster provides by defining the scripts that the heartbeat executes when it starts. The scripts are exactly analogous to the standard Red Hat Linux scripts found in `/etc/rc.d/init.d`. The haresources script expects the scripts to be located in either the `/etc/rc.d/init.d` or `/etc/ha.d/resource.d` directories.

The `haresources` file for server ha1 is shown below:

```
ha1 10.0.0.100 httpd
```

The following `haresource` file is for ha2:

```
ha1 10.0.0.100 httpd
```

Both files configure the heartbeat on their respective systems to use the shared IP address of `10.0.0.100`. Both systems are instructed to run a Web server — `httpd`.

10. The final step requires you to populate the `/etc/hosts` file with your HA cluster information. The `/etc/hosts` file on each server must contain the addresses of the virtual server and the other node:

```
127.0.0.1      localhost.localdomain localhost
10.0.0.102     ha2
10.0.0.101     ha1
10.0.0.100     ha
```

You now have a high-availability Linux cluster. The following section describes how to test the cluster.

Testing the Heartbeat

Now you can experiment with your cluster. This section describes how to start the heartbeat on both the master and slave. You can test fail-over in a number of ways by either turning off the heartbeat on one machine or pulling the plug on the server.

Follow these steps to test the Heartbeat:

1. Create a service that doesn't require shared storage. We create a simple Web server on each machine that uses a local file system for its root directory.

2. Make sure that you can view the Web page. Remember that the master server should be the machine serving up the page.

3. Start the heartbeat by running the initialization script on both machines:

```
/etc/rc.d/init.d/heartbeat start
```

4. The script shows the heartbeat's status. If the service starts up successfully, the following line is displayed:

```
Starting High-Availability services: [  OK  ]
```

5. Test the network communication from the server to the slave — ha1 to ha2:

```
ping ha2
```

6. Repeat Step 4 on ha2.

7. Test the serial line communication from the server to the slave. Enter the following command on ha1:

```
cat < /dev/ttyS0
```

8. Enter the following command on ha2:

```
echo "iamnotanumber" > /dev/ttyS0
```

   The text string that you entered on ha2 shows up on ha1's console.

9. Repeat Steps 7 and 8 so that you test communications from ha1 to ha2.

10. Test the fail-over by stopping the heartbeat on ha1. (If you're brave, then pull out the Ethernet cable on ha1. That's an acid test!)

```
/etc/init.d/heartbeat stop
```

11. View the Web page.

You now have a high-availability Linux cluster. High-availability systems were the sole domain of expensive, proprietary hardware and software until the Linux-HA project was completed. Linux-HA is another example of the incredible functionality that Linux provides the world.

Summary

This chapter introduces the concept of identifying and minimizing single points of failure (SPOFs). Identifying SPOFs allows you to understand how your server might fail. You can take measures to minimize your failure modes once you gain that understanding.

We concentrate on three methods for minimizing SPOFs: using journal file systems, using RAID, and using High Availability fail-over servers. Journaling file systems provide the ability to quickly recover from improperly un-mounted file systems; they also provide an extra measure of protection from data loss. RAID provides an extra layer of data protection on mass storage systems. Finally, Linux High Availability (HA) provides total redundancy by allowing one Linux computer to take over from another when a failure occurs.

This chapter describes how to efficiently and economically increase the reliability of your Red Hat Linux servers. The methods used here rely on freely available software systems to increase reliability. By effectively using these systems, you can minimize the down time to which your servers are vulnerable.

Experimenting with Heartbeat on Virtual Computers

The concept of using virtual computers to create an inexpensive laboratory environment was mentioned in Chapter 1. Heartbeat is an excellent system to test with virtual computers.

VMware, Inc. creates the leading virtual computer software package available today. VMware is a commercial product not open source. However, they do provide 30-day evaluation licenses that you can use to test their system. You can download their Linux-based workstation software from their Web site: `www.vmware.com/download`. You need to fill out an information form at the same site and they will e-mail your temporary license.

Install and configure the VMware workstation on your Linux computer by following the instructions available from their Web site. Install Red Hat Linux on the first virtual machine. Create a second virtual Red Hat Linux machine by copying virtual files to a second directory. For instance, install the first virtual Red Hat machine — vm1 — in `/home/paul/vmware/linux1` (use the server installation type and install the Apache Web server). Create a second virtual machine — vm2 — by creating a directory `/home/paul/vmware/linux2` and copy the files from `/home/paul/vmware/linux1` to `linux2`. Run the VMware wizard against the new directory and you have a second virtual machine.

When you build a high availability server cluster, you need multiple paths for their heartbeat. You typically provide multiple heartbeat paths by using a second NIC and serial connection. However, you can't easily simulate a serial connection to use with Heartbeat but, fortunately, don't need to. You can use a single virtual Ethernet — eth0 — on each virtual machine to experiment with Heartbeat. The following instructions outline how to configure two virtual Linux computers to create a minimalist Heartbeat cluster.

Create the following `/etc/ha.d/ha.cf` file on both virtual machines:

```
node      vm1
node      vm2
deadtime  10

udp       eth0
```

Continued

Experimenting with Heartbeat on Virtual Computers (Continued)

Create the following /etc/ha.d/authkeys on both virtual machines (change its permissions to 0600).

```
Auth 3

3 md5 ttikey
```

Create the following /etc/ha.d/haresources file on vm1.

```
vm1 10.0.0.100 httpd
```

Create the following /etc/ha.d/haresources file on vm2. In this case, vm2 is the backup (or failover) server for vm1. The haresources file on vm2 must be configured to point to vm1 as the primary server.

```
vm1 10.0.0.100 httpd
```

Create the following /etc/hosts file on both machines.

```
127.0.0.1  localhost.localdomain localhost
10.0.0.101 vm1
10.0.0.102 vm2

10.0.0.100 vm
```

Restart the heartbeat daemon on both machines.

```
/etc/init.d/heartbeat restart
```

Test the heartbeat system as discussed in the previous sections.

Part V

Increasing Security

Chapter 15

Introducing Basic Server Security

IN THIS CHAPTER

◆ Understanding the threat to security

◆ Going beyond the patch

◆ Identifying your attackers

◆ Thinking about the attacks

◆ Considering a defense

THIS CHAPTER ON BASIC SERVER SECURITY CONCEPTS examines the nature of security vulnerabilities and shows why patching alone can't avoid compromise. It also helps you begin to understand how you can design and run your systems and networks more securely, while simultaneously making them easier to manage. Finally, we also introduce the fine art of system hardening or tightening, which we describe in greater depth in Chapter 17.

Understanding the Threat to Security

Security holes are actually bugs. They're often programming bugs, such as buffer overflows. In a buffer overflow vulnerability, an attacker supplies specially crafted Evil Input to a program's request for data; in return, the program gives him a command shell that runs with the same privilege as itself. Security vulnerabilities can also be bugs in the design, as, for example, when a program authenticates a remote user based on a spoofable parameter such as the user's IP address.

Now, for a bug to be a security hole, or *vulnerable*, two conditions have to be true:

◆ **The buggy program has to have privilege that the attacker doesn't have:** If the program being attacked runs as root, then this condition is definitely true. Then again, this program may simply be running on a remote system to which the attacker currently has no access.

◆ The bug must be (at least theoretically) exploitable in some way to get the program to do something that its designer didn't intend the program to do.

In many cases, an attacker is able to get a vulnerable program to run an interactive command shell with the original program's level of privilege. If this 'sploit doesn't work, the attacker may be able to force the program to write to a file of the attacker's choosing. For instance, the /etc/passwd file is good for getting a root account.

A security vulnerability is a threat if you're running the vulnerable program and someone can exploit that program to get more access than she's currently authorized for. The following sections of this chapter discuss handling security threats.

Going Beyond the Patch

Fortunately, as vendors or program creators discover security bugs in their programs, they often release fixes in the form of patches. You can remove a known security problem by simply applying a patch. If applying a patch was all you had to do, you wouldn't find entire chapters — or books — on system hardening. The following lifecycle of the modern security exploit demonstrates why you must do more than patch:

1. **Someone discovers a bug in a program.** The person who discovers the bug may tell one or more people about it, or he may publicly release the information to the world. Then again, he may tell no one.

2. **Someone discovers that the bug is a security hole.** This person, who may or may not be the original bug discoverer, can again tell a few people, the entire world, or no one. Bugs are frequently released publicly, but some discoverers may choose to hold the information in secret or within a small group indefinitely. In that case, a few people may know about a security vulnerability that the program vendor or creator, along with the rest of the world, never learn about or have the chance to correct.

3. **Someone creates a working security exploit.** Again, this person may be separate from the bug discoverer or the person who figured out that the bug was a security hole. Further, the exploit may be held by one person, several people, the entire attacker "underground," or even the world IT community. No matter how many people have it, the threat is now real and undeniably dangerous.

4. **Someone releases the exploit publicly.** This step may never happen, but it often does. Once the exploit is public, things become more dangerous, as every vulnerable system's odds of being attacked with this exploit increase dramatically. Then again, people often take reactive steps to fix the problem at this point.

The vendor works on creating, testing, and distributing a patch, if they haven't already. People who are running the vulnerable program may deactivate it, lower its privilege level, reduce its accessibility to the world, or at least get ready for an attack.

5. **The vendor releases a patch.** Now, it may be that the vendor was never informed of the existence of one or more problems with the program (the original bug, its security implications, or the associated exploit). Even worse, the vendor may have been informed, but chose not to commit the resources to create a patch! At this point, one of three things usually happens: the vendor responds to consumer demand (or bad press) and develops a patch; the more advanced user-base develops a patch or work-around (*if* the program in question is Open Source or otherwise manageable/accessible); the vendor ignores all warning signs and customer pleas and eventually goes bust.

The critical point in this whole explanation is actually that this step takes time. Some vendors have taken as little as a week, but the slowest have been known to take three months! The time that you spend vulnerable to a working exploit without applying a patch or other work-around is called your *window of vulnerability*. That window can be extreme, especially in the case where the hole or exploit is never publicly released or revealed to the vendor. The window can also be short, in the case where the discoverer immediately communicates with a speedy, attentive vendor who immediately begins work on an easy patch.

What do you do during this window of vulnerability? Well, during the portion of that window when you aren't aware of the vulnerability, you experience bliss — and potentially an unexplained break-in. After you do know about it, you try your own work-arounds or wait for the patch, potentially getting cracked all the while. In either case, it's not a good time for you.

The best thing you can do about these windows of vulnerability is to harden your system. Doing so involves configuring the system for lock-down, which lowers the odds that a new security hole will actually be a substantial threat to you. This means that you not only deactivate functionality that you don't need, hoping to avoid having a vulnerable subsystem activated, but that you also reduce both access to each subsystem and the level of privilege at which each subsystem operates. Although this process may sound trivial, it takes some time. On the other hand, it is extremely effective. For instance, a Red Hat 6.0 out-of-the-box Web server was vulnerable to around five security holes. If the system was hardened to serve only as a Web server, not a single one of those holes was usable to an attacker. That's pretty impressive.

The rest of this chapter discusses what you need to do to harden your systems and how you go about doing it. First, though, you need to take a look at whom you're defending your systems against, which we cover in the next section.

Identifying Your Attackers

Threats to the left of you, threats to the right of you, vulnerabilities all around you — you've got 'em right where you want 'em! No, this isn't just hopelessly sarcastic fatalism — you actually *do* want to keep your (potential) vulnerabilities where you can see them. Otherwise, only the attackers will know where your weak points are. Tiger team drills, or penetration tests, can be particularly effective because you can't properly defend something until you know everything about it, including its strengths and vulnerabilities.

Start by thinking about server security from square one. Internet servers are scarily exposed to the big bad Net and its legions of weasels. Unfortunately, they have to be that way to be useful. An unreachable Web server may be less prone to attack, but it certainly isn't going to help market or sell anything! In order to perform its function, such as providing a public presence, a server has to be accessible. Going one step further, remember that not only is your server exposed, but it also pretty much advertises this fact via the public domain name service (DNS), accessible network ports and services, and so on.

As you search for a way to protect your server from the dangers it presents to itself and the rest of the organization, the most important thing to remember is that no one solution — no silver bullet, magic wand, or pixie dust — can find and fix even a majority of your server's vulnerabilities. Whether or not you're ultimately doomed, though, really depends on the attacker in question.

Categorizing attackers

This section discusses the following types of attackers:

◆ Motivated attackers

◆ Script kiddies

◆ Problematic attackers

MOTIVATED ATTACKERS
Any sufficiently motivated attacker *will* get into one of your systems. Count on it. Fortunately, this class of attacker isn't in the majority, but the simple fact that time is on his side makes him very effective, and he frequently wins face-offs with the sysadmin and security staff.

SCRIPT KIDDIES
Not everyone who tries to get into your system is necessarily patient, crafty, and skilled. The novice attackers who just run other folks' scripts on relatively random targets are just irritating weasels who sometimes get lucky. Though we call them weasels, you've probably heard them called *script kiddies*, for their lack of skill and almost exclusive use of commonly available scripts. Their targets tend to be random, and they themselves also tend to be clumsy and "noisy" (leaving several

telltales on the affected system). Weasel attacks can certainly cause damage — they're irritating and make recovery a pain — and they pretty much fall into the non-critical category.

PROBLEMATIC ATTACKERS

The next grade of attackers goes from being a minor irritation to a major problem. They tend to have more information-gathering skills and finesse when taking over a server. The problematic attackers are usually a little more focused on their target — a specific server-type, a particular O/S-type, and so on — and they're more stealthy in getting it. They're just as likely to use the machine as a staging platform for other attacks as they are to trade its root info on IRC (Internet Relay Chat) with their buddies (though they may do that, too, when they finish with the platform). The real showstoppers, though, are the problematic attackers who can write their own exploit code, watch the intended target to gather information about it before attacking, and not get caught until the damage is done (if ever!).

Obviously, these broad classes of attackers are going to approach the problem of breaking into our system differently, use different tool sets, and have different end goals in mind. As you've probably already guessed, you're either going to have to have one, highly adaptive product that can cover all circumstances (even unexpected ones) or you're going to have to deploy multiple types of overlapping defenses that you can shore up as new attacks appear.

Thinking about the Attacks

Obviously, nothing is going to defend against every single type of attack. The people who design the attacks are smart, creative, and innovative humans. So, you're going to have to grit your teeth and construct a multi-layered security response architecture — a totally non-trivial task! You already have your motivation, now you need a model. Start by thinking of one of those multi-layered hard candy and chewy chocolate lollipops. The outer wrapper is your first, most basic line of defense; the hard candy is your second defensive shell; the chewy center is your root access and important, proprietary stuff; and, the stick is the hardware underpinning. Now, how many licks does it take to get to the center?

Well, if the attacker can't get past your border defenses (such as a firewall), then the wrapper never comes off and the lollipop center is safe. If the attacker manages to slip by the outer layer, he still has more to face before getting his prize.

Remember that an attacker has time on his side. If, in this analogy, he has unlimited time, then he'll certainly get to the center. If, on the other hand, he's continually interrupted, and maybe even set back by self-repairing security mechanisms, he may never actually reach the center (imagine putting the wrapper back on and slapping on some extra hard candy shell every night).

If the attacker manages to brute force his way in (the infamous CRUNCH! in the lollipop saga), then he wins the prize, though he'll probably also tip off the sysadmin to the compromise (and may damage what he was trying to collect).

Security through obscurity?

You're probably scratching your head and thinking, "Hey, this looks like security through obscurity. I thought most security types say that's a bad thing . . . " Well, although you're essentially hiding information about the server (if not the whole server itself), the key is that you aren't *relying* on this trick to keep the system safe.

Even if keeping your critical infrastructure confidential doesn't solve your entire security problem, it doesn't mean you should go around advertising your critical infrastructure. Remember that every additional layer and type of defense makes the bad guy's job harder. Security through obscurity is fine to use as a *component* of your security strategy, just not as your only defense.

The point of this wacky example (you can use geological strata or planetary layering models if they make the principles clearer to you) is that the key to layered defense is presenting an attacker with multiple lines and types of defense to overcome. Never depend on a *monoculture* (think "Irish Potato Famine"); rather, keep as much variety as you can reasonably manage across your systems.

We're now ready to examine some of the system security layers we've been telling you about. This list isn't exhaustive, but it provides a starting framework that you can use to evaluate your own system.

First, consider the fact that your system has a sort of split personality — things look very different depending on whether you are outside looking in or inside looking out. A system's *external face* is what you can see and extrapolate from a network standpoint. If you give away too much information about the system, then anyone who can get access to your network can scope out the best attack vector. When you put the "wrapper" on the system, the attacker suddenly gets much less information, and so is less wellprepared to give the *coup de gras*. A really opaque wrapper filters out information about the operating system flavor, the system's composition, and possibly even the system's importance to your site. A good wrapper also lowers your system's profile, possibly even taking it off an attacker's radar.

The open network ports (and related network daemons) that your system offers also affect your network profile. You can think of these things as being points of entry, small holes in the outermost wrapper. Clearly, if you punch too many holes in the wrapper, the core assets you want to protect will be far too exposed. Obviously you have to leave the services and ports associated with the server's main function open, whether that be web, or mail, or ftp. But you don't need to leave a lot of irrelevant network ports open, such as those for daytime, chargen, and echo. Unfortunately, most operating systems ship with many open by default, even though these guys don't provide any meaningful services to your system and are pretty much just a Denial of Service (DoS) attack waiting to happen. Vendors traditionally ship the O/S in this way because it leaves the system much easier to set up. Unfortunately, this practice significantly weakens the system's security stance.

What are Set-UID and Set-GID?

Set-UID or Set-GID is a special status whereby the user running the program gets enhanced, usually root, privileges for a specific task. Specifically, the program runs with its owner's user-id (UID) and group-id (GID), rather than those of the user invoking the program. For example, if user Jay runs ls, he can list directories that his UID/GID allows him to list, based on file permissions. On the other hand, if ls was Set-UID root, then it would run with root privileges no matter who ran it — Jay could list any directory on the system. A Set-UID/GID program with a security hole tends to give a user full use of the elevated privilege, which is why these programs are excellent vehicles for privilege escalation.

The system may seem fairly complex when viewed from the outside, but that's nothing compared to what's going on from an insider's perspective! Hiding what's going on from folks who have login/shell access to the machine is much harder, so you need to think about what system users can see from the inside.

Start by considering that insiders can enumerate the system's processes — something that doesn't sound so scary at first — until you think about the implications. The would-be attacker can find out what daemons are running (checking whether the process name ends with "d" is a good first cut), who owns the daemons (compromising a root-owned daemon process really hits pay dirt fast), and other interesting tidbits. See, if an attacker knows what internal and external services are running — especially if he can also find out which version — then he can really tailor his attacks to the target. Broad attacks and probes are often noisy, but highly directed ones can be very stealthy. The longer you, the admin, don't know about the attack or compromise, the longer the attacker has to get what he wants from the system.

Also remember that folks inside a system can usually locate most, if not all, of the system's Set-UI or Set-GID programs.

Because an insider can easily find Set-UID/Set-GID programs by just looking around the system, he'll know what binaries to try compromising for quick root access. Many defenders underestimate the power and significance of Set-UID/Set-GID exploits. Don't make that mistake!

If a user can find Set-UID/Set-GID binaries, then he can probably also find other dangerous permissions. World-readable files give away their contents (think about what would happen if the shadow password file were world-readable). World-readable files aren't always a bad thing — they may even be necessary (*a la* the passwd file) — but you need to know when using them is OK and when it isn't. World-writeable files also give an attacker a foothold by letting him potentially change system behavior with just a few keystrokes. Imagine what would happen if the passwd file were somehow made world-writeable, or rc.local.

At this point, an attacker starts to build a picture of your system, which she'll sketch out, and then refine as she gets more information.

A quick `netstat` command gives a good snapshot of what the system is doing with its network services:

- ◆ `netstat -rn`: Tells you what the nearest router is, along with other routing info.

- ◆ `netstat -an`: Tells you about active/listening processes and what port they are bound to and even who is connecting into that process or port remotely at the time.

- ◆ `netstat -in`: Tells you which network interfaces are configured, what those configurations are, and how they're behaving.

Whew, that's quite a bit for one little command that normally isn't restricted to privileged users!

You're providing a great deal of information, essentially for free! You may be feeling a surge of paranoia, but remember that you're here to add security layers and keep your vital information (and secrets) internal.

Considering a Defense

Enough of the attacker perspective, for now. You're ready to kick up the defense. You can reduce your profile, minimize your information leaks, and generally improve your server's security through a process called *host hardening*. Host hardening comes in two flavors. One is the install-time hardening, which we introduce in just a moment; the other is the ongoing maintenance and periodic testing, which we discuss in Chapter 16.

Before we actually show you how to do install-time hardening, we need to explain what this process is trying to achieve and why. The remainder of this chapter explores this. Chapter 17 explores the how of install-time hardening in detail.

Sensibly enough, install-time host hardening involves using many of the same surveillance techniques an attacker would. Your intentions are different, of course, but the best way to know what an attacker may find out about your server is to use the same tools and methods. Take a look at the following process listing, sorted by process identification number (pid):

```
[linux1 ~] ps -efw | sort -n -k2
UID          PID  PPID  C STIME TTY          TIME CMD
root           1     0  0 Apr03 ?        00:00:40 init
root           2     1  0 Apr03 ?        00:00:00 [keventd]
root           3     0  0 Apr03 ?        00:50:04 [ksoftirqd_CPU0]
root           4     0  0 Apr03 ?        00:47:49 [ksoftirqd_CPU1]
root           5     0  0 Apr03 ?        00:00:09 [kswapd]
root           6     0  0 Apr03 ?        00:00:00 [bdflush]
root           7     0  0 Apr03 ?        00:04:11 [kupdated]
```

```
root          8      1   0 Apr03 ?        00:00:10 [pagebuf_daemon]
root         11      1   0 Apr03 ?        00:00:00 [scsi_eh_0]
root         12      1   0 Apr03 ?        00:00:00 [scsi_eh_1]
root         13      1   0 Apr03 ?        00:00:00 [mdrecoveryd]
root         18      1   0 Apr03 ?        00:00:05 /sbin/devfsd /dev
root        434      1   0 Apr03 ?        00:00:57 syslogd -m 0
root        439      1   0 Apr03 ?        00:00:00 klogd -2
rpc         449      1   0 Apr03 ?        00:00:00 portmap
root        464      1   0 Apr03 ?        00:00:00 ypbind
rpcuser     495      1   0 Apr03 ?        00:00:00 rpc.statd
root        619      1   0 Apr03 ?        00:00:34 xinetd -stayalive -
reuse -pidfile
  /var/run/xinetd.pid
root        629      1   0 Apr03 ?        00:03:01 /usr/local/sbin/sshd
root        642      1   0 Apr03 ?        00:00:03 crond
xfs         684      1   0 Apr03 ?        00:00:00 xfs -droppriv -
daemon
daemon      694      1   0 Apr03 ?        00:00:00 /usr/sbin/atd
root        808      1   0 Apr03 tty1     00:00:00 /sbin/mingetty tty1
root        809      1   0 Apr03 tty2     00:00:00 /sbin/mingetty tty2
root        810      1   0 Apr03 tty3     00:00:00 /sbin/mingetty tty3
root        811      1   0 Apr03 tty4     00:00:00 /sbin/mingetty tty4
root        812      1   0 Apr03 tty5     00:00:00 /sbin/mingetty tty5
root        813      1   0 Apr03 tty6     00:00:00 /sbin/mingetty tty6
root        814      1   0 Apr03 ttyS0    00:00:00 /sbin/getty ttyS0
DT9600 vt100
```

This output isn't too intimidating, but just wait until you have users on the system! Even so, you do have a wealth of information here. You now know which users own key processes: root, rpc, rpcuser, xfs, and daemon. This information is important because if an attacker breaks into even the non-root accounts, she can stop, start, or alter the processes that the account owns.

You also know some of the services started at boot time, including some interesting ones: portmap, ypbind, xinetd, sshd, crond, and atd. All of these services have had fairly recent and disturbing vulnerabilities exploited with widespread success. On the other hand, all of them are considered pretty safe at the time of this writing, as long as you're using the latest version (or have applied the most recent relevant patches). RPC services (portmap and friends), for example, are notoriously short on authentication and security, but long on system access. The Secure Shell (SSH) daemons version 1.2.26 and below were subject to a buffer overflow attack — an amazing irony because SSH is the connection protocol of choice for system administrators who want to securely log into and manage their systems!

Up-to-date software is extremely important, so here are a few tips for finding out which software versions you have and which are current:

Keeping up with the kernels

To keep up with Red Hat's progress and new kernels, start at the Errata page (www.redhat.com/apps/support/errata/index.html).

You'll find three categories of Errata there: Bug Alerts, Security Alerts, and Enhancement Alerts. All Alerts provide information about the problem or issue being addressed, the solution or enhancement, and the files or other downloads needed to effect the fix.

The Red Hat Network service offers automated notifications and update delivery for a yearly fee at https://rhn.redhat.com/purchase_info.pxt and https://rhn.redhat.com/.

As for kernels, check out the canonical Linux kernel archive site (www.kernel.org/) on a regular basis.

♦ **Ask your software what version it believes itself to be:** Most software versions support a command-line option such as -v, -V, or -version. Most applications also provide some kind of notification pipeline (the author or vendor's reputation can only be hurt by keeping you in the dark about known problems). Check your application's command line arguments and info file.

♦ **Keep track of where you obtained the software:** Chances are that the author/vendor/hosting site maintains an errata and updates page.

♦ **Check for mailing lists about the software:** Unless your application is a home brew, you almost certainly won't be the only one using a given application, so neither will you be the only one who wants to keep up with current patches, additional features, and new updates. Again, the author/vendor/hosting site often offers opt-in mailing lists right on the software's information or download page.

♦ **Keep an eye on the standard sysadmin and security mailing lists and Web sites (such as the Bugtraq list and the Security Focus site):** Bugs, glitches, holes, and other nasties are usually exposed in a technical forum before they make it out to the broader audience.

Some software packages volunteer to automatically go out hunting for updates from the Web, but this nifty trick can also be dangerous. Locating the update yourself is generally the wiser choice so that you can verify the source and the patch's integrity (most sites post MD5 hashes of their updates). Accept no substitutes — make sure that you get the authentic, original, and real update!

The same goes for your kernel and other O/S bits, too: the most basic and first line of defense is a well-patched system. If you don't have that, well, the length of time an attacker needs to find the box is just a roll of the dice. One of the authors knows someone who intentionally put an old version of Linux (with a slightly outdated kernel) on a sacrifice box on his home network and then hooked up his cable modem just to see how long it would last. The box was rooted within 2½ hours! Obviously, this is not something you want to try at work with the company's production server.

Okay, so you have your current kernel, your recent patches, and your up-to-date apps, but your job has just begun, so no sneaking off for sushi or beer yet! You need to look at minimization and simplification, which should be your watchwords when you design, build, and deploy your systems. The Principle of Minimization says that if you don't need it, get rid of it. The Principle of Simplification is simplify, simplify, simplify! System administration is complicated enough without making it worse!

Here's our basic chain of reasoning:

> Minimization leads to simplification.
>
> Simplification leads to ease of maintenance.
>
> Ease of maintenance leads to better maintenance.
>
> Better maintenance leads to better security.
>
> THUS, minimization leads to better security.

Really. Think about it this way: Complex systems have very complex interactions. The more knives, balls, weasels, and flaming torches a juggler tries to keep going, the greater likelihood that someone is going to get cut, hit, bit, or set on fire. But if you can get down to just one ball . . . well, most folks can manage to juggle that just fine.

A corollary to the Principle of Minimization is Dedication of Resources. A *dedicated server* is one that runs the bare minimum set of processes necessary to support a single designated service or purpose. Fewer competing processes means less contention for resources across multiple tasks and that the system will naturally function better.

Dedicated servers also imply a distributed service architecture. If a server only offers a single service, then you need multiple servers to take care of all your site's needs. A medium-sized site may have separate log, file, Web, login, and ftp servers. When each server only provides a narrow service, it fulfills many of the following security goals:

◆ **Lower network profile:** When you minimize the network services you offer, you also minimize the vectors that an attacker can use to get information from or access to the server.

◆ **Simple configurations:** The simpler the configuration, the more easily you can monitor for changes in the service or its setup. Simple configurations are also easier to replicate in the event of a dead disk.

◆ **Ease of monitoring:** This works two ways. First, you know what systems should be showing certain kinds of server activity, so if your Web server suddenly stops accepting port 80 connections, you know something is wrong. Second, you know what systems should *not* be generating service traffic, so if a telnet server suddenly appears on a machine that isn't supposed to run one, you know you have a different problem.

◆ **Ease of maintenance:** As far as maintenance goes, you now only have one server to patch when you uncover, say, a new `ftp` vulnerability or exploit. You, the admin, are also freed from having to update many systems when a new version of your `ftp` program is released.

 Remember, simplicity leads to security. Upfront investment in design and installation should pay off in simplicity of maintenance and upkeep.

Also consider the improvements that a dedicated service model can bring to your site's robustness. Replicating a server for transparent fail-over capability is much easier when the configs are simple and you only have one service to worry about. This way, you can have a whole bank of identical machines, allowing you to do load balancing, mirroring, and fail-over in a high availability environment. If one machine in the bank fails, the others will take up the slack while you cobble it back together. And if you need to expand a service, you can easily add one more dedicated server, identical to the others, to the bank.

Of course, if you want to have a robust and resilient environment, you need to plan on having replacement hardware available. People often overlook this aspect of server security, but they shouldn't. You can either maintain a cache of spare parts (of all kinds) or have a really good hardware maintenance contract that specifies a turnaround time measured in hours, not days or weeks.

Spares can be hot, warm, or cold, depending on the amount of effort you want to frontload (and how much maintenance you can reasonably manage):

◆ *Hot* spares are fully operational twins of the production server, ready to be dropped in at a moment's notice.

◆ *Warm* spares are usually standby systems with all the necessary hardware and software installed, but without the main server's current data.

◆ *Cold* spares are components sitting on a shelf. They're easier to collect and cheaper to maintain, but they also take the longest to get up to production capability.

Make sure that you know where the spares of each type are and how to deploy them quickly in an emergency. When the lights are out and the waters are rising isn't the time to wonder, "Now where did I leave that spare disk?" In fact, recovery time – anything from simple maintenance procedures (where the main concern is how fast you can reboot), to an electrical surge or outage, to a direct meteor strike (where the main question is where off-site do we have spares and backups) – is always significant in security. Here's the general rule: Given a bad event at time X, how long until you can get back to your pre-X state?

Reality comes and tramples these tidy models when dealing with smaller shops, small offices, or home-office environments, which can't always afford to have many spares or to divide up services one to a machine. For service distribution at a small site, you have to come up with your own best-fit design, but the guiding principles are the same. Keep your configurations and service models as simple as possible, and try to have dedicated systems for your most utterly critical and sensitive services – the things that may break or that would create havoc if they did. What rates as most important varies between sites, but examples include user home directories, the backend database server for your Web site if you're in e-commerce, or your DNS if you're running an ISP.

Although we can't determine what would definitely be best for your site, we can describe the following service groupings that we've seen work pretty well in a number of environments:

◆ **Place Web services on a dedicated box, or at worst, pair them with** `ftp`: Multi-purpose machines that run Web services are just cruisin' for a bruisin'. Additionally, you can have some serious performance issues. Popular Web sites get thousands of hits per hour, and their Web server daemons have a huge overhead that eats up system resources, leaving no ability to run another major service with decent performance.

◆ **Consider having dedicated servers for each of the following if your site handles a high volume of mail – incoming mail, outgoing mail, local-only mail, POP, and IMAP:** If you don't have much e-mail traffic, then go ahead and host all mail services on one server, possibly even pairing them up with home directory service (especially if you deliver mail to home directories instead of to `/var/mail`). You may even consider pairing mail and information services (such as NIS or LDAP), but again, the question is one of scale.

◆ **Provide centralized home directories and other file services with their own dedicated servers:** If you're sharing several files across the network – whether with NFS or SAMBA or some other solution – chances are that having the server run both efficiently and consistently is fairly important. Getting file-sharing to work well is tricky enough without having any other high-overhead services muddying the waters.

◆ **Pair DNS servers with time services at the most:** Otherwise, don't mess around with this critical piece of infrastructure. Too much in your organization will break if your DNS servers ever fall down!

While you're thinking about what servers to deploy, take a second to consider your clients. If you have to support client workstations, especially in a lab or cube-farm environment, then the ideal (and simple!) thing to do is have them be cookie-cutter copies, identical in most every respect. To facilitate this, you may want to maintain a Kickstart server with client images and configs. That way, if you need to replace a faulty machine, add a new system to the collective, or even double the size of a work lab, you're ready to roll in the minimum amount of time.

Now, an important word about backups and backup servers, both of which are absolutely key in securing a server. No matter how destructively an attacker assaults your system, you can recover – if you have good, recent backups. Think of backups as both disaster insurance and your chance at the ultimate win. As such, backups probably merit their own dedicated server and off-site media storage arrangements. You can take it from here for your own site's design.

Okay, so what's wrong with a scenario in which four major services (ftp, telnet, mail, and Web) are being offered from the same server? They should be broken out onto multiple servers, if at all possible. If not, then they should be segregated into chroot()ed jails so they don't interact.

Even if the attacker can't get local login access to the server, he can use a port scanner such as nmap to get this information, which suggests that he should be doing the same thing periodically. Then you can look to secure the services (or remove extraneous ones).

As far as the black-hat nmap-er goes, wouldn't you like to know when he's scanning you and then foil his dastardly plans? Running a lightweight NIDS, such as Snort, on the server can give you early warning of incoming scans. Chapter 18 tells you how to set up a system like this. Of course, you don't just want to find out that the attacker has walked off with your information, you also want to keep as much information from him as possible.

 You can actually set up a local firewall (see Chapter 4) to *blackhole,* or mysteriously drop connections that just don't smell right.

And just in case your attacker gets past your firewall, make sure that you have a file integrity checker, such as Tripwire or AIDE, which regularly scans the system looking for altered files. Things don't seem very simple or minimized when you're looking at Tripwire's configs or Snort's rulesets, but you get a big-win payoff at the end. The learning and setup curve all becomes worthwhile as soon as you get your first detect.

Summary

This chapter provided you with a better understanding of threats to security. It then went on to explain the importance of go beyond patches in order to guard against modern security exploits. You then learned how to identify your attackers. After that, you were advised to think about attacks in order to understand them as fully as possible. The final step was to consider a defense.

Chapter 16

Introducing Secure System Administration

IN THIS CHAPTER

- ◆ The Sysadmin and the Security Officer

- ◆ Auto-updating, Patching, and Caveats

- ◆ Minimizing, Standardizing, and Simplifying

- ◆ Monitoring and Secure Remote Administration

IN THE LAST CHAPTER, we began by asking what threat you were trying to defend your server against. In this chapter, you'll find out that you, the sysadmin, are one of the biggest threats your system faces. Think about it. You have root and other awesome powers, so you're the most likely candidate for inadvertently giving privilege away, or — really embarrassing, yet so easy to do — failing to secure the system and its secrets. The old saying, "loose lips sink ships," still holds. We just have more technologically advanced ways to trip ourselves up now.

Luckily, this chapter gives you ways to avoid the pitfalls that lie in wait for you so that you can try to benefit from others' mistakes before you make your own! By the way, we're discussing basic server security separately from secure system administration because you can apply secure sysadmin practices to all types of systems — servers, clients, workstations, kiosks, networks, offices, and so on. The principles in this chapter will stand you in good stead no matter what you're trying to admin.

Sysadmin and the Security Officer

Your site's security officers and your site's sysadmins will have different priorities for how the system should be set up, run, and used. If you're both the sysadmin and the security officer, well, welcome to the wonderful world of schizophrenia.

Think of a balance scale with usability on one side (for the sysadmin and the users) and security on the other (for the security officer and the other curmudgeons). The perfect balance above never *really* happens. Ultimate usability really means no security — hey, everybody gets root! Ultimate security means that the machine is off the network, unplugged, put in a deep hole, and then covered with quick-dry cement. And, that deep hole needs to be located in a scorpion- and queen-snake infested area, preferably near an active volcano. Anyway, you get the idea.

The balance commonly swings in favor of usability, though not to the exclusion of security. The concept of secure system administration takes you toward a usable system that can still deflect (or deter and detect) intruders. Although secure sysadmin is more of a mindset than anything else, you can do a bunch of practical things that, in the end, should make everyone but the hacker pretty happy. The first of the bunch is auto-updating, updating, and patching.

Auto-Updating, Patching, and Caveats

Although patching alone can't prevent security compromises, as mentioned in Chapter 15, you still must apply security fixes, or patches, to your systems! Applying fixes is your first, best, but hopefully not only, line of defense against malicious attackers.

Now, before we get ahead of ourselves, let's talk about the terminology, *patching*. When you look at the Red Hat Errata page, you won't find any mention of patches. Instead, you'll find *updates*. Updates are fully-contained replacement packages for the ones that came with your Red Hat operating system. Whereas most vendors' patches contain only one or two replacement files, a Red Hat update contains every file in the original package, with one or more changes. The terminology reflects this re-packaging, but what changes you're getting is a more subtle question.

The update contains either a fixed (patched) version of the files in the previous package or it simply contains the newest version of the affected software. For example, an update to wu-ftpd-2.4.0, contained in wu-ftpd-2.4.0-1.0.i386.rpm might be a patch applied to wu-ftpd-2.4.0, in which case it will be called wu-ftpd-2.4.0-1.1.i386.rpm. It might instead be an update to wu-ftpd-2.4.1, in which case it will be called wu-ftpd-2.4.1-1.0.i386.rpm.

To make this more clear, we'll generally talk about "applying security fixes" or "updating your binary packages" to make the discussion appropriately general. The former will include source-level patches, which are thankfully less necessary in most applications, along with binary package updates. The latter phrase is our attempt to encompass the terms "update," "patch," "hotfix," and "upgrade," which are each used by different vendors to describe their binary package fixing or replacement method. Now, let's get back to our discussion by first examining kernel security fixes.

Remember, we told you how to find vendor or author security fixes for your Operating System, kernel, and various software applications, mostly via Web sites. Because kernel security fixes are a vital part of secure system administration, also take a look at Red Hat's *Upgrading the Linux Kernel How-To* at www.redhat.com/support/resources/howto/kernel-upgrade/kernel-upgrade.html.

You can also find mailing lists and BBS-like "forums" devoted to the pursuit of more secure apps and systems on which to run them. Use these tools to keep current with what's going on in the wild, wacky world of highly specific technology.

Red Hat offers a number of forums:

- **Red Hat's Support Homepage:** `www.redhat.com/apps/support/`

- **Red Hat's Support Forums page:** `www.redhat.com/support/forums`

- **Red Hat's free mailing lists** (Web page sign-up interface and list archives): `www.redhat.com/mailing-lists/`

Security Focus hosts a wide variety of security-oriented free mailing lists:

- **List of lists:** `http://online.securityfocus.com/archive`

- **Subscription instructions:** `http://online.securityfocus.com/cgi-bin/sfonline/subscribe.pl`

- **BugTraq:** "BugTraq is a full disclosure moderated mailing list for the *detailed* discussion and announcement of computer security vulnerabilities: what they are, how to exploit them, and how to fix them." `http://online.securityfocus.com/archive/1`

The most important of these has to be BugTraq, which almost always provides the very first notice that we ever get of security vulnerabilities in our software. If you can't keep up with that mailing list, Red Hat's errata page (`www.redhat.com/errata`) provides a slower, but much lower volume (read: more manageable), source for vulnerability information. That errata page also provides security alerts, bugfixes, and enhancements for Red Hat.

When you get notice of new security fixes, you may be tempted to apply it to all the machines immediately, but doing so isn't advisable if you're administering a whole site. That statement can be pretty frustrating, especially after we've convinced you that you must apply fixes, and now we're telling you to wait. We do want you to apply those fixes as soon as possible, but doing so isn't as simple as you may think.

See, your server, as well as the rest of your environment (whether you have control over it or not), is a complex system, and complex systems have complex interactions. Changing the littlest thing can set off an enormous chain reaction of badness – kind of like being caught in an avalanche. In short, even a binary package update that's been thoroughly tested by the vendor may still have problems in your environment because of your particular software and settings mix.

Here's a real-world example involving one of the toughest cases out there: applying multiple source-level patches to a kernel. In this case, a poor system was running both the Andrew File System (AFS; see `www-2.cs.cmu.edu/afs/andrew.cmu.edu/usr/shadow/www/afs.html`) and Mosix (cluster-enabling software; see `www.mosix.cs.huji.ac.il/`). Both of these require Linux kernel modifications to work, usually through source-level patches. According to the sysadmin who had to roll out both products on one system across an independent lab, he negotiated a kind of precarious truce among the three contenders (kernel, AFS, and Mosix). So when the next round of security-related kernel updates came out, he had an important – and potentially resume-generating – choice to make. Should he roll out the patches or not? If so, how? Clearly, something was going to break once the bits got flying. What did he do? His solution to the problem was the one we're about to recommend to you now: maintain separate development and production environments.

By the way, we mentioned that this case was ugly. It's ugly partly because the sysadmin had to apply source-level patches to a kernel. The vendor-supplied kernel already has a number of source-level patches chosen by the vendor for maximum hardware support, performance and features, which complicates things greatly. See, the patches you want to apply to make Mosix work are generated against Linux's kernel usually, so they may not even work with the vendor kernel. Be extremely conservative before trying to apply any source-level patches to a vendor kernel. We'd even suggest researching whether your vendor has a supported method for handling that software (Mosix, in this case) before patching their kernel.

Production and Development Environments

In an ideal world, maintaining separate production and development environments means that you create and regularly update an exact duplicate of your frontline, production environment. The production systems are the ones where e-commerce actually happens, logins are hosted, news is spooled, and the Web sites are served. You definitely don't want to try out potentially show-stopping security fixes and other tweaks on these systems! Try out the fixes on less critical systems first. Think about using a *development environment*, a near-real-life simulator, by mirroring your production stuff onto a separate system, or group of systems.

Reproducing an entire environment means that you need to duplicate every-thing, in the closest manner possible. You need to have the same components, number of systems, size and type of disks, everything, which costs more than the loose change under the seat cushions. Whether you go to this extreme depends on whether you have the free capital to do so and whether making it happen is impor-tant enough to your company. For instance, if you're a multinational bank that loses millions of dollars per second of downtime, then a mirror-duplicate environ-ment is no great shakes. In fact, you can't really afford not to have it. The majority of system administrators won't have this luxury; however, you may be able to beg, borrow, or scrounge enough to have a small-scale version of your most important machines and services.

You may even be able to have identical-hardware versions of those important machines, especially in a shop that does its own application development. To help

Scheduled downtime? We don't need it.

You really do need scheduled downtime. Being polite to the users and to the boss is essential to job security, satisfaction, and positive karma. If you don't get your downtime approved ahead of time and announce it to your users well in advance, well, don't blame us if you come back as a squashy bug.

Your downtime will almost never be as routine or as simple as you may think. Be prepared for the worst (and be very pleasantly surprised if it doesn't happen!). Anticipate the worst-case scenario for your downtime and estimate how much time you'll need to deal with the fallout. Then present management with a figure 2 to 2½ times longer. Always pad your estimate (remember how Scotty got to be the Miracle Working Engineer?). Completing the task earlier is great, but finishing late may only earn you a pink slip.

pitch this case to management, remember this: not only does a development environment allow you to fully test new software, security fixes, and other things in a non-disastrous way, but you can also use the development systems as drop-in replacements, often called 'cold swaps,' if anything ever blows up on the production systems Remember, showing management how something is dual-purposed and actually saves money is always a step in the right direction (for example, getting your way).

Setting up a true development environment is hard work, but the payoff is so big that it's worth almost any amount of effort you have to frontload to make it work. Once your mini-development environment is in place, you're ready to let it earn its keep! Here are the possible outcomes:

◆ Case 1: Nothing bad happened! Now you have two questions left to answer. Is your development environment close enough to your production environment that you're pretty sure that nothing explosively bad will happen out there, too? And what is the best, most efficient way of getting this security fix out to all affected machines? (We address this question later in this chapter in the section "Autoupdates and Caveats.")

◆ Case 2: You had a minor glitch. You're either going to have to somehow correct the problem on your own (possibly with the aid of late-night caffeine or sugar) or you have to get a hold of the vendor and get them to correct it. At that point, you're back to Case 1.

◆ Case 3: There was brimstone, fire, and much wailing and gnashing of teeth. In short, it didn't work, it isn't going to work, and it may be time to tell management that this security fix is a no-go. The happiest possible outcome here is that the fix addresses something that you don't use in your environment (you've turned off, don't ever plan to use, or something like that).

> Otherwise, you need to find a different work-around. Can you do any-
> thing else to better protect the server, or can you turn off the vulnerable
> bits without destroying your company, career, or application?

This is why they say sysadmin is not for the faint of heart!

But wait, there's more. Suppose you had a Case 1 situation, but then suddenly have a blowout on the production system. It's a good thing that you scheduled plenty of downtime to allow for just this kind of emergency! (Which leads you to the next sidebar . . .)

So things have gone very wrong. Now what? Well, if you have a complete development environment, you may be able to drop in the doppelganger of the particular server in trouble. If not, things get tougher. See, RPM doesn't yet have support "update rollback," so going back to the previous release of an RPM can be difficult. You achieve something like rollback on an RPM based system by updating the original RPM over the replacement, like so:

```
rpm -Uvh -replacepkgs <original-rpm(s)>
```

In essence, you personally become the entire rollback system. This means that it's quite important to keep the original copies of any packages that you update, since you'll need them to apply if you have to rollback/update backwards.

If the fix was a source-code patch, you can generally back out the patch with the "-R" argument to the patch command. (See the following page at linuxdoc.org for more info: http://tldp.org/HOWTO/Kernel-HOWTO-6.html#ss6.2.) Finally, on other devices and legacy Unix systems, the package update mechanism may have integrated rollback, which is probably the easiest method. The application on those devices and systems saves a copy of your old files and can easily bring your system back to the previous state in a fairly deterministic way. In any case, going back is difficult – it's probably best to try to avoid having to pull a security fix back out on a production system. Nicely, these kinds of crises don't happen too often anymore.

Auto-updating, Caveats, and a Red Hat Solution

You may remember from the Chapter 15 that some packages can automatically update themselves from the Net. Although this is great for keeping current, it's not so great for secure deployment. Anytime a process has enough privilege to actually update your system, it has enough to totally frag your system, too – especially if the process can make kernel-level mods. Whenever you give away any kind of control over your system, you're that much closer to giving away all control over your system. You want to reduce your exposure – not boost it – which means that you don't want automated update processes on your system. If you must try auto-updating, then only do so on your development environment.

Manual updating, on the other hand, isn't going to complete the entire task done in five minutes. (You may have heard the saying, "Stable, secure, fast – pick two.")

If security fixes are so good, why are they so much trouble?

When security fixes go wrong, they tend to really go wrong. These days, however, they very rarely do go wrong, so most fixes aren't as much trouble as they seem. In fact, many fixes are seamlessly transparent to everyone (except maybe the person who installed them).

Problems arise when you have specialized pieces for your particular puzzle. For instance, everyone can pretty much agree on how a typical Red Hat 8.0 distro should look. But after you add a specialized kernel mod or piece of software to the mix, nobody can really say what it should look like. In that case, it works or it doesn't work. Basically, if you run an app or make a mod, you're on your own, so be careful.

For most sites, getting reliable updates out onto stable systems is far more important than pushing out immediate fixes that may or may not trash the system.

Wherever you fall on the auto versus manual update question, Red Hat does have some very nice solutions. Red Hat Network, a for-pay service that's free on a single machine, can help ease the process. It can automatically apply updates on systems where you feel comfortable letting this go less-supervised. It can also automatically generate a list of updates that must be applied, while leaving the sysadmin to apply the updates by hand. In either case, it's a pretty decent tool – it even confirms PGP/GPG signatures on any rpms before installing them! There's even an enterprise-class version called Red Hat Network Satellite that can help people who have airgaps or tight proxies between their networks and the Internet. We found this product to have every feature we had coded into our own small-enterprise package update solutions in the past.

The principle strength of automating any part of the process is that your systems get updated more uniformly and more often. We see too many compromised systems that would have been safe if they'd just had the latest fixes to not mention this benefit! So, while you should still be cautious with any automated update solution on production systems, this one is definitely worth checking out.

As with most things in system administration, your mileage may vary – yet another reason why system administration is more of an art than a science.

Minimizing, Standardizing, and Simplifying

As with any other art form, there are many different schools of thought on how to improve the sysadmin's end product. One fine arts paradigm that was very much in favor in the 90's was *minimalism*. Strange as it may seem, minimalism is an excellent approach for intelligent, secure server administration, too. Ironically, it is not enough by itself, but works best as part of a perpetual three-pronged server support process of minimizing, standardizing, and simplifying.

Embracing minimization

Minimization isn't just for waistlines and servers anymore. You can apply this principle equally well across your whole environment. Put simply, minimization means if you don't need a particular service or component, don't keep it. You can use two approaches to achieve the minimalist state:

- ◆ **The Way of the Sysadmin:** The Way of the Sysadmin starts at a default, known configuration and then weeds out extraneous services and processes. In firewall design, this approach is called *default allow.*

- ◆ **The Way of the Security Officer:** The Way of the Security Officer starts with everything turned off (yeah, except the power) and then adds services or components only as needed. In firewall design, this approach is *default deny.*

Think of the two approaches as though you're going grocery shopping. On the one hand, you can wander the aisles, hoping to end up with what you need (and nothing you don't). On the other, you can make out a shopping list ahead of time so that you're sure of the final outcome.

Okay, so we pretty obviously lean towards the Security Officer's shopping-list approach. Forgetting things is so easy, especially in a time-crunch situation. If you have a punch list ready to go, then you don't have to think as much on the fly. And removing human judgment – and associated human error – from the equation is the stuff of success stories. When you know that it absolutely must be right the first time around, you want to have a setup that a trained chimp could get right (or, more importantly, couldn't get wrong).

Another guiding principle is to front-load your work wherever possible. It's almost always worth the effort. Sure, getting all the little fiddly bits right to begin with is time-consuming, and shutting everything off and slowly adding back just what you need – you'd be surprised at all the hidden dependencies you can run into – can be a painful process. But while other sites' servers go up in flames and melt into puddles of bubbling slag, you can sit smugly comfortable in the knowledge that your Web server wasn't running `telnetd`, so it wasn't vulnerable to the most recent and deadly attack. Remember, minimization leads to security and is (almost) always worth it.

Here's another nifty benefit of minimization: If you don't install something, then you don't have to configure it. We intentionally said "install" rather than "turn on." Any service installed on your system may become available at some point in the future, whether you actually mean for it to, or not. And if a service daemon has any chance of just flicking on somehow, then you'd better make it as secure as possible. Otherwise, you may be the one with the slagheap that once was your server.

Configure 'Em! Configure 'Em All!

Once excess packages are removed, make sure to update and secure those services and other programs that you actually want to have on your system. Here's another axiom for you: *Never* leave installs in their default state. This means *all* installs, even seemingly minor or "unimportant ones." Applications are practically never configured just the way you want them to be and secure by default, right out of the box. At the very least, you need to check things out before letting them run amok on your system.

If you don't need it and you find it on your system, get rid of it! You can take care of an oversight at install time later, but remember to update your setup parameters for the next system. Aside from the obvious security threats a derelict install presents, by the time you do decide to turn it on, new versions, security updates, and other goodies will probably have been released for it. There's just no substitute for a nice, fresh RPM.

You can avoid the horrible and tedious outcome of sitting and configuring the same service for similar machines by hand by using standardization and automation. Why Bother Standardizing?

Remember the amazing virtues and goodness of simplicity? Standardized simplicity is even better! The original VW Beetle, circa 1950, was nothing more than an engine with four wheels and a shell that you could sit in – the simplest imaginable car design that could still manage to work. The Beetles had sparse moving parts – just one single engine suspended in a vast, empty space – provided a limited number of points of failure. The car's straightforward design (you could see all the engine's parts and actually get to them, too) prevented many complicated problems from arising and allowed quick fixes at curbside.

Standardization also makes a much easier task of deploying the same kind of hardware on your systems and network. If a bunch of computers are doing essentially the same thing, you can order the platforms "in bulk" and then deploy the same software configurations on all of them. With sufficient standardization, you may only need to configure one computer and then copy its image to all the others. At the very least you can keep the standard configs in a centralized repository, ready to deploy (either by hand or automated distribution). The same is true for package updates, as well. In a well-standardized environment, you can automate many of your administrative tasks and take full advantage of tools such as `cfengine` (see `www.cfengine.org`), which keeps your site's configuration files synchronized to a set of standards.

Standardized simplicity really comprises two ideas. You can standardize by applying the same pointlessly bizarre and unworkable configuration on all your systems, which we don't recommend. Simple is good, but simple may also mean a great deal of work up-front. (This should all start to sound very familiar . . . front-loading work is also a good thing.) You should finalize all major standards before you start to deploy them. Don't decide on centralized account management with Network Information Services (NIS) or a Lightweight Directory Access Protocol (LDAP) backend and then create a few /etc/passwd entries on one or two of your systems! If you need to support accounts that only exist on one particular system, make sure that your central account management scheme can handle that — and learn how it will handle that — before rolling it out.

If you're working for someone else, make sure that you take her needs into account in your setup. You don't want to have someone creating those /etc/passwd entries in the last paragraph because the boss wanted them now, you were in the bathroom, and no one else knew your system. Make sure that you have everything documented and try to take the possible needs of your organization into account. (In this case, a script that allows anyone with privileges to create accounts your makes going to the bathroom safe again.)

Whole books have been written on good automation and centralization tools. Any real discussion goes beyond the scope of this chapter, but we'd be wrong to not at least mention them:

◆ **rdist** (www.rdist.org): This tool was one of the earliest alternatives to just copying files around manually. With this tool, you would create a central repository tree and push out updates based on a central control file. The homepage says, "RDist is an open source program to maintain identical copies of files over multiple hosts. It preserves the owner, group, mode, and mtime of files if possible and can update programs that are executing." Better still, newer versions of rdist use SSH, Secure Shell, in place of rsh, remote shell, to transmit data across the network.

◆ **rsync** (www.rsync.org): This tool was the next best thing down the line after rdist. It was faster, smarter, and capable of handling incremental file transfers.

◆ **cfengine** (www.cfengine.org): Written by Mark Burgess, this tool is our favorite, especially for maintaining a consistent, large environment. This configuration management engine can not only copy files and perform incremental transfers, but it can also actually edit the files you want modified! cfengine can also manage processes and directory structures, not just regular files.

Of course, you need to realize that all these tools are just automated ways to implement and distribute your existing configs. They don't actually configure things for you, tweak settings, or anything like that. If you have bad configs, they'll be merrily propagated throughout your environment, so careful planning still has no substitute!

The Three Cardinal Virtues

So far, we've discussed three cardinal virtues here:

◆ **Minimization:** Also known as *parsimony*, this principle says don't do anything that isn't necessary to provide the services you must provide. Also, don't do anything in two places when just one is sufficient. With regard to security, this practice lowers your risk of having a vulnerable component.

◆ **Standardization:** As far as possible, only invent the wheel once and then keep re-using it. Figure out what all your systems can have in common and stick to that standard. Even dedicated hosts, such as fileservers, can use the standard partitioning scheme and directory configuration common to all your servers, possibly adjusted to allow for the server's extra disk space.

◆ **Simplicity:** KIS — Keep It Simple — is the fundamental rule of all good engineering. Simple is easier to support, to explain, and to augment. It's also much more secure, in that more complex systems often have interactive effects that aren't well understood.

When the rules are in conflict, simplicity is the trump. For instance, minimization may mean putting each service on a dedicated server (minimizing services per server), or it may imply minimizing the number of servers and having one big honking machine serve everything. Which is simpler, though? Which strategy has fewer moving parts to grind against each other? If an FTP server, running only FTP, breaks down, you don't need to worry about whether the last Web server package update was the cause. This strategy makes things easier and more secure by reducing the number of places where subsystems can interfere with each other. Simplicity is security's friend. If it's a contest between you and the bad guys to see who can unravel a complicated mess first, you lose. The bad guys outnumber you, they have much more time than you do and, at least some of them know more than you do.

Standardization seems to suggest that each system should offer the same set of services that all the others do. You can have all of your machines running both a Web server and an ftp server, but doing so conflicts with the other two principles. Both minimization and simplicity discourage this unnecessary and mostly purposeless redundancy.

Monitoring and Secure Remote Administration

Now that you've deployed your secure configurations, don't mess things up by giving away the root password. Most systems want to run `telnetd` in their default configurations. Don't install a system without turning this off in `/etc/inetd.conf` or `/etc/xinetd.d/`. If you have firewalls, block port `23/tcp`. If you have a metal ruler, smack anyone you see typing "telnet." The next two paragraphs discuss why.

The biggest advantage that SSH has over telnet is that SSH communications are encrypted, while telnet communications are in plaintext. Therefore, anyone who

Selling Security Measures

The little trick that SSH does of redirecting X applications automatically saves some users the typing they normally do to set the DISPLAY variable. Given that it acts like telnet otherwise, this little plus will have them flocking to SSH. It's nice when you can get added convenience and increased security at the same time.

Unfortunately, security measures are rarely convenient. Expiring passwords every thirty days and requiring new, unused ones, for instance, sounds like a great security measure, but it'll really upset your users. In one case, users in just that situation spent hours experimenting to find out just how many expired passwords the system really remembers. It turned out to be twelve, so these users developed systems like pass1, pass2, pass3, . . . ,pass12, pass1, . . . to avoid any hassle. Of course, this practice made their passwords even weaker than they would have been otherwise, defeating the purpose of the measure.

The moral is that the harder you pour on inconvenient security measures, the harder some of the people you are pouring on will work to circumvent them. At that point you have developed the same relationship with your users that you have with attackers. Both groups are spending significant amounts of time trying to get around your security measures.

Rather than avoiding inconvenience to your users (or yourself), at absolutely *any* price, you need to integrate your security strategy with the workings of the organization that's using your computer. Pick your battles and explain your reasons for changing or setting new site policy. These explanations can be extremely powerful!

Always remember that users aren't stupid — they just sometimes need you to tell them, show them, or both. (Make sure to get authorization before performing this demonstration!) Finally, remember that if you just build bigger and bigger walls on your own, people will start going around them (Remember the Maginot Line . . . ?). Always design and educate well, so people are able to do their jobs without unwittingly sabotaging yours.

can control a machine on any of the intervening networks between the telnet client and server can steal all of the passwords used. Actually, they can watch the entire session and possibly even take it over. This sort of usurpation even works on switched networks, though the switches make things tougher. If you want to understand why, go to www.google.com and search for "ettercap" or "dsniff."

Even though you may feel reasonably sure that no evil force will plant a sniffer on any of your networks, you can get burned when you or one of your users connects in from outside. Any outside connection goes through any number of potentially dangerous places on its way to you.

SSH actually works pretty much like telnet when all you need is a telnet replacement. It also does some "black magic" to allow you to forward any X-application interaction through the encrypted tunnel. This black magic includes creating a virtual X server on the client machine, setting the DISPLAY variable to that server, and then redirecting all communications to that server back to your X server, across the network. If you didn't understand that last sentence, don't worry – X seems virtually like magic when you first start working with Unix/Linux.

SSH has some other good tricks, too. You can use the RSA-challenge option to perform secure login and data transfer between systems. Basically, you can type a single pass-phrase (for a private key) on your primary management system once each day and then be granted access on all systems where you've placed the public key for the rest of the day. This neat feature makes administration much easier.

Here's another trick. If you put the private key without a pass-phrase in a secure account, you can write scripts that automate file transfer over a secure channel. Be careful when using this feature, though. During penetration tests, a machine that has non-pass-phrased keys is always easy to compromise, and they in turn let you into other machines that you may have been unable to compromise on your own.

SSH version 2 even has an SFTP utility, providing a secure replacement for good ol' ftp. You can actually get an entire book on SSH, but you can make your environment much easier to run just by spending an hour reading the SSH man page. Actually, the article "Stupid, stupid protocols: telnet, FTP, rsh/rcp/rlogin," at `www.bastille-linux.org/jay/stupid-protocols.html`, explains how you can use ssh for single-signon and authenticated automation.

Central Management Systems

Okay, you're at a conference on the other coast – you know, the one on the other side of the country from your computers. You're a good admin, so you're going to log in and do a little maintenance from the hotel. Of course, you didn't know what IP you'd be using, so you configured SSH to accept logins from anywhere before you left. In fact, you may have done that when you configured your systems in the first place.

Consider using a *bastion login host*. A bastion host is one that's exposed to the big, bad Internet while other hosts are not. You can reach the other hosts from the outside only *through* the bastion host. Of course, you must harden the bastion host to within an inch of its life, but you end up with a single system on which to spend most of your hardening work. A bastion host means that you take reasonable security measures for most of your systems, and obsessive, paranoid ones for the bastion.

So, only *one* system accepts SSH logins from outside the network. From there, you log into one or more of the protected systems. Remember also that the bastion host should be minimized and simplified. Ideally, it should only be running SSH.

Setting up a console server may be an interesting approach. You can buy a console server (expensive) or build one (expensive parts). Rather than hook monitors to each of your systems, you hook the systems up to ports in a specialized card on the console server. Each system's console is now accessible through X Windows. You can actually install a new operating system in your machines over the Internet if that suits your fancy. Of course, you really want to secure this server.

Now, once that server's built, one of the chief purposes will be monitoring the status of your systems both while at home/work and while away.

Status Monitoring

Here's another aspect of the sysadmin's job that could be a book all on its own — keeping an eye on your system (two eyes, as often as you can spare them). When you ask yourself who may be watching your system, you had best be at the top of the list! Again, it's a matter of who knows more about your system, the attackers or the defenders.

If you want full accountability, look into *process accounting*, which logs every single process that gets started on the system. Every command that someone types is logged, though the command-line arguments aren't. So, you'll see commands typed, such as ettercap or attack, but not the arguments, which may include the targets. Still, process accounting can be useful on a bastion host. For less complex endeavors, you may just write a quick monitoring shell script that is periodically run from cron. What you need to monitor varies from machine to machine as much as from site to site, but, of course, some pretty standard things are useful to know.

Use top to report on the five or so biggest CPU hogs. You'd be amazed at how much CPU time a SPAM-bot can suck down. Even a simple top command makes for a nice early-warning system, especially when teamed up with uptime. A derivative of w, uptime is chock-full of information: It gives the current clock time and date, the elapsed time since last bootup, the current number of logged-in users, and the system's load averages for the past 1, 5, and 15 minutes (see the uptime man page for more details). Use df to report on disk space usage; use vmstat to find out whether you're having to dip heavily into swap space; and, use grep on the system logs to check on recent su and sudo attempts. By the way, if you're not familiar with *sudo*, it's worth checking out via Google. Basically, it allows you to give one or more users root access for particular commands without having to give away the root password. Those users must type their own password, though, keeping someone who steals a user's console from using root privileges easily. Considered a system administration's best practice, sudo configuration is definitely worth checking out.

You may also want to look at a few other things: failed login attempts, user login patterns, and related deviations and oddities. If a user logs in at her desktop workstation every workday from 9 am through 6 pm, and never any other time, and you suddenly notice quite a bit of login activity to her account (or machine) at around 4 am, originating from an ISP in Howondaland, well, you know something is probably wrong. Something's really wrong — and this is always amusing — when the foreign login is happening at the same time the user is logged in locally.

Have you noticed how much of this monitoring and status assessment depends on good logs? In fact, most system processes are written with the express intention that they put out updates and status messages to the main system logs. Certainly all of your medium- to long-term pattern analysis depends heavily on complete logs. Check out Chapter 19 for more info on configuring system logging, monitoring arriving log messages in near-real-time, and other post-event analysis.

Summary

Check the Best Practices from Chapter 15 and apply them across other system types. These include using standardized configurations for better security and easier system management. These standardized configurations are often those that you choose while doing post-installation hardening on each system type. (We'll examine this more in the next chapter.)

As we've discussed, it's also quite important to apply all security fixes to your operating system components. This should include not only the applications, but also the kernel as necessary. Remember, updating or patching the kernel is tricky – you should follow Red Hat's instructions very carefully there. To find out what security fixes to apply, watch the updates mailing list, or at least Red Hat's "errata" page. To keep up with problems that don't yet have package updates, from learning temporary workarounds to the effect they're having on the Internet community, watch community mailing lists like BugTraq.

Finally, remember to do everything you can to minimize and simplify your systems and the programs running on them. Read on to the next chapter to see these practices in action.

Chapter 17

Hardening the System

IN THIS CHAPTER

◆ Understanding system hardening

◆ Hardening the system manually

◆ Hardening the system automatically with Bastille Linux

IN THIS CHAPTER, you'll learn how locking down, or hardening, a system can greatly decrease your system's chances of getting successfully taken over by crackers. You'll learn how to harden a system manually and be introduced to Bastille Linux, an extremely popular system hardening program.

Understanding System Hardening

You harden a system, or "lock it down," to increase its resistance to cracking. System hardening involves changing the operating system's configuration in a way that makes it much harder to compromise. When you harden a system, you're trying to do two things:

◆ **Reduce the system's exposure to attack:** In this case, you're trying to stop an attacker from finding and exploiting a vulnerable program by reducing both the number of programs that an attacker can access and the amount of access that an attacker has to those programs.

◆ **Reduce the effect of such an attack:** Here, you're trying to confine a successful attacker's effect on the system as much as possible, usually by placing restrictions on any target program's ability to influence the system.

Before we discuss these two areas, you must understand one simple thing: Attackers break into systems by exploiting bugs. Attackers gain privilege by getting a program on the computer to do something that its creator didn't intend it to do. And not every bug is a simple programming mistake, such as a buffer overflow — many exploitable bugs are design-related. For example, an attacker may exploit the Web server by getting it to give him the system's password file. The Web server wasn't originally intended to serve files outside of the special Web directory, but perhaps the programmer failed to check for " . . / " entries in the URL it serves.

These bugs crop up in software all the time. System administrators generally aren't in a position to influence the program creators enough to eliminate future bugs. However, you can try to configure the software so that an attacker has more difficulty turning these bugs into illegitimate access on your systems. The rest of this chapter explores how to do that sort of configuration, both manually and by using a hardening program, such as Bastille Linux. To explore this topic in extreme depth is beyond the scope of this book, so we're only going to introduce it here. For a more comprehensive treatment, consider the book *Locking Down Linux the Bastille Way* by Jay Beale.

We're going to explain the following methods to harden systems:

♦ **Stopping or removing unnecessary programs:** At some point, one of your programs will become vulnerable. If the program is deactivated, or better yet removed, then an attacker can't exploit it to gain access. You really won't know which ones will become vulnerable until said vulnerabilities are announced publicly. In the meantime, we try to deactivate every unnecessary privileged program. The ones that have privilege are the real risk, since they can give that privilege away. Privilege might mean "runs as root," but might also be "is accessible via the network."

♦ **Removing accounts:** Most Unix systems ship with a number of unused accounts. If you know which ones you're not going to use on your system, you can remove them. Doing so reduces the number of accounts that an attacker can try to take over in his quest for access.

♦ **Decreasing each account's privilege:** Anything you can do to decrease an attacker's access after he gets on the system is useful. You might make directories non-world-writeable or deactivate the Set-UID bits on programs. We'll explore this topic in greater detail when we talk about Bastille Linux in the last section of this chapter.

♦ **Reducing the attacker's access to each privileged program:** If an attacker can't use the exploitable functionality in a vulnerable program, then he can't exploit that program. For instance, if your Apache Web server has a vulnerable CGI script, but you've deactivated CGI execution, an attacker can't exploit the hole because he can't even run the script!

♦ **Reducing each program's privilege level, if possible:** Because an attacker may actually find some vulnerable program and be able to exploit the vulnerability, you need to concentrate on what to do once he gains access. If the program runs as root with no other containment, the attacker will probably have free run of the box. On the other hand, if the program runs as a user with virtually no privilege, chrooted (locked) into a jail directory, he'll have a great deal of trouble turning that access into root.

♦ **Educating the users:** You probably thought we wouldn't mention this option! Actually, your users can break a system or site's security, purely out of ignorance, more effectively than any cracker. For example, one of the first rules of firewall management is, "Don't make the firewall too restrictive or else your users will buy dial-up, DSL, or VPN solutions to work around it." Unless your users know why they can't do something, they'll usually work to defeat the restriction, especially if the restriction is preventing them from easily doing their jobs! Always make sure to communicate with and educate your users so that they can help your security, rather than hinder it.

Okay, so now you know the theory. The rest of the chapter actually helps you do the work of hardening your systems.

Hardening the system manually

This section shows you how to manually harden the system against attack. Because we're just able to offer an introduction to the topic, we're only covering the first major part of system hardening against Red Hat 7.x – 8.y, though it should be useful for most any Linux distribution. This information should still make your system a good deal harder to break into, as you gain a huge amount of benefit by giving an attacker fewer programs to attack.

Stopping or removing unnecessary programs

Remember, an attacker compromises a system by exploiting a security bug, or vulnerability, in one of the system's programs. It stands to reason, and to experience, that the fewer programs that are present, the lower the probability that an attacker can find a vulnerable one to exploit. For instance, some of the major vulnerabilities from 1999–2001 were in the BIND DNS server and in the WU-FTPd FTP server. If each of these had been turned off or removed from a given system, that system had a much, much lower chance of being randomly cracked or compromised. So, the first step in hardening a system is to deactivate as many of the system-level programs as possible.

For a program to be useful to an attacker it has to have more privilege than the attacker already has. If the attacker can already run commands on the system as the user juan, then he'll want to have some kind of access as a system user, such as sys or root. If the attacker can't run commands on the system yet, then "more privilege" means the ability to run commands on the system as some user. So, which programs do you target? You first want to remove all unnecessary network-attached programs, lessening the odds that the attacker can get any privilege on the system remotely. Next, try to remove privileged programs on the system, which decreases the odds that the attacker can escalate privilege from one level of access to another.

Start by getting a list of all programs listening on the network. The netstat command can output all kinds of information about the machine's networking stack. For a list of all programs listening on TCP ports, pass it the arguments vat for a verbose listing of all TCP connections:

```
# netstat -vat
Active Internet connections (servers and established)
Proto Recv-Q Send-Q Local Address          Foreign Address      State
tcp      0      0 *:1024                  *:*                  LISTEN
tcp      0      0 localhost.localdom:1025 *:*                  LISTEN
tcp      0      0 *:sunrpc                *:*                  LISTEN
tcp      0      0 *:ssh                   *:*                  LISTEN
tcp      0      0 localhost.localdom:smtp *:*                  LISTEN
```

By examining the fourth column, you can see which ports the operating system is listening on. You can track down what programs are actually listening on via the *lsof* command. For instance, to find out what is listening on port 1024:

```
[root@localhost root]# lsof -i tcp:1024
COMMAND    PID USER    FD    TYPE DEVICE SIZE NODE NAME
rpc.statd 665 root     6u   IPv4   1033      TCP *:1024 (LISTEN)
```

As you can see, the first column shows that the rpc.statd program is listening on that port. At this point, you need to track down what that program is so you can decide whether it has any right to be running on this machine. *Note:* Doing so is doubly important, because the rpc.statd program has been the source of a few major security remote-root vulnerabilities, such as the one described at http://online.securityfocus.com/bid/1480, which allowed attackers and worms to get root on a huge number of Linux/Unix machines. If you aren't familiar with rpc.statd, the best resources for more information are as follows:

◆ The man pages, which you access with the man command.

◆ Google (www.google.com).

◆ Other, possibly more experienced, system administrators.

We recommend that you try the man page first:

```
[root@localhost root]# man rpc.statd
rpc.statd(8)                                            rpc.statd(8)

NAME
       rpc.statd - NSM status monitor

SYNOPSIS
       /sbin/rpc.statd [-F] [-d] [-?] [-n  name ] [-o  port ] [-p
       port ] [-V]

DESCRIPTION
       The rpc.statd server implements the   NSM   (Network   Status
       Monitor) RPC protocol.  This service is somewhat misnamed,
```

> since it doesn't actually provide active monitoring as one
> might suspect; instead, NSM implements a reboot notifica-
> tion service. It is used by the NFS file locking service,
> rpc.lockd, to implement lock recovery when the NFS server
> machine crashes and reboots.

rpc.statd implements an NFS (Network File System) status protocol so that NFS clients know when their NFS servers are rebooting or are down. As the man page goes on to say, each NFS client or server needs rpc.statd running.

If your machine isn't an NFS client or server, then you can safely turn this script off. You start all the programs that are automatically running on the system either by the system boot's startup scripts or by facilities, such as cron and at (which start given programs at given times). You only need to be concerned with the former type here. So, to deactivate rpc.statd, simply find its startup script and turn it off.

 You can actually use rpm to determine which package owns the file, and then list the package's contents to find the init script. You can even just delete the package. On the other hand, we're trying to give you skills you can reuse on other Linux distributions — and even other Unixes — so this book takes the standard approach.

Before you can find and deactivate rpc.statd's boot script, you need to understand the Unix boot process.

Recapping the Linux startup process

When a computer first starts, it starts a boot loader, which loads the operating system's kernel into memory. That kernel is responsible for starting the operating system's remaining components, from the system logging daemon to the remote login daemon (sshd) to the graphical display subsystem. The kernel doesn't actually run all of these programs itself; rather, it runs the very first program that starts, init, which starts everything else.

init basically runs two scripts: rc.sysinit and rc. In Unix, rc (short for *run commands*) forms the main system start scripts. rc.sysinit performs many small, one-time tasks, such as loading necessary kernel modules, activating swap space (such as virtual memory), and mounting all main partitions. It starts no persistent programs. rc, on the other hand, starts all of the system daemons. By the way, a *daemon,* (pronounced "day-mon" or "dee-mon,") is a persistent program that serves some operating system function. The system starts them at boot.

rc knows, which programs to start because init passes a special parameter called a *runlevel,* to rc. For instance, if the run-level is 3, init runs the following command:

/etc/rc.d/rc 3

init gets this parameter from its configuration file, /etc/inittab, unless the system is being rebooted, halted, or being manually placed in a different run-level. Single-user maintenance mode is one such run-level, known as runlevel 1 or s on some systems. Runlevel 0 corresponds to the system that's being powered down, while runlevel 6 corresponds to a reboot. On Red Hat Linux systems, the default run-level is usually 3 or 5. To learn more about the default runlevel, take a look at /etc/inittab.

Here's the start of a default Red Hat 7.3 /etc/inittab. (Don't worry if you're not using 7.3 – at the time of this writing, this file hadn't changed much in over three years.)

```
#
# inittab       This file describes how the INIT process should set up
#               the system in a certain run-level.
#
# Author:       Miquel van Smoorenburg, <miquels@drinkel.nl.mugnet.org>
#               Modified for RHS Linux by Marc Ewing and Donnie Barnes
#

# Default runlevel. The runlevels used by RHS are:
#   0 - halt (Do NOT set initdefault to this)
#   1 - Single user mode
#   2 - Multiuser, without NFS (The same as 3, if you do not have networking)
#   3 - Full multiuser mode
#   4 - unused
#   5 - X11
#   6 - reboot (Do NOT set initdefault to this)
#
id:3:initdefault:

# System initialization.
si::sysinit:/etc/rc.d/rc.sysinit

l0:0:wait:/etc/rc.d/rc 0
l1:1:wait:/etc/rc.d/rc 1
l2:2:wait:/etc/rc.d/rc 2
l3:3:wait:/etc/rc.d/rc 3
```

The first uncommented line, labeled initdefault, tells you that this system's default run-level is 3. If your system's inittab doesn't have this value, it probably indicates runlevel 5. The primary difference is that in runlevel 5, the system brings up a graphical login screen; in `runlevel 3`, the login screen is on a text console, leaving the user to start X if she needs it.

Anyway, our system starts in `runlevel 3`. `init` will run `rc`, passing it 3 as an argument. `rc` then looks in the directory `/etc/rc3.d/`, where it finds the following:

```
[root@localhost init.d]# ls -l /etc/rc3.d/
total 0
lrwxrwxrwx    1 root      root        14 Apr 22 05:12 K05innd -> ../init.d/innd
lrwxrwxrwx    1 root      root        15 Apr 22 05:22 K15httpd ->
../init.d/httpd
lrwxrwxrwx    1 root      root        20 Apr 22 05:39 K15postgresql ->
/init.d/postgresql
lrwxrwxrwx    1 root      root        13 Apr 22 05:34 K20nfs -> ../init.d/nfs
lrwxrwxrwx    1 root      root        15 Apr 22 05:41 K25squid ->
../init.d/squid
lrwxrwxrwx    1 root      root        19 Apr 22 05:38 K34yppasswdd ->
../init.d/yppasswdd
lrwxrwxrwx    1 root      root        13 Apr 22 05:20 K35smb -> ../init.d/smb
lrwxrwxrwx    1 root      root        19 Apr 22 05:38 K35vncserver ->
../init.d/vncserver
lrwxrwxrwx    1 root      root        18 Apr 22 05:42 K45arpwatch ->
../init.d/arpwatch
lrwxrwxrwx    1 root      root        15 Apr 22 05:15 K45named ->
../init.d/named
lrwxrwxrwx    1 root      root        15 Apr 22 05:35 K46radvd ->
../init.d/radvd
lrwxrwxrwx    1 root      root        15 Apr 22 04:49 K50snmpd ->
../init.d/snmpd
lrwxrwxrwx    1 root      root        13 Apr 22 05:41 K50tux -> ../init.d/tux
lrwxrwxrwx    1 root      root        16 Apr 22 05:35 K65identd ->
../init.d/identd
lrwxrwxrwx    1 root      root        17 Apr 22 05:40 K70bcm5820 ->
../init.d/bcm5820
lrwxrwxrwx    1 root      root        14 Apr 22 05:07 K74ntpd -> ../init.d/ntpd
lrwxrwxrwx    1 root      root        16 Apr 22 05:38 K74ypserv ->
../init.d/ypserv
lrwxrwxrwx    1 root      root        16 Apr 22 05:38 K74ypxfrd ->
../init.d/ypxfrd
lrwxrwxrwx    1 root      root        15 Apr 22 05:01 S05kudzu ->
../init.d/kudzu
lrwxrwxrwx    1 root      root        18 Apr 22 05:14 S08ipchains ->
../init.d/ipchains
lrwxrwxrwx    1 root      root        18 Apr 22 05:19 S08iptables ->
../init.d/iptables
lrwxrwxrwx    1 root      root        14 Apr 22 05:14 S09isdn -> ../init.d/isdn
```

```
lrwxrwxrwx    1 root    root    17 Apr 22 05:13 S10network ->
../init.d/network
lrwxrwxrwx    1 root    root    16 Apr 22 05:08 S12syslog ->
../init.d/syslog
lrwxrwxrwx    1 root    root    17 Apr 22 05:13 S13portmap ->
../init.d/portmap
lrwxrwxrwx    1 root    root    17 Apr 22 05:34 S14nfslock ->
../init.d/nfslock
lrwxrwxrwx    1 root    root    18 Apr 22 04:56 S17keytable ->
../init.d/keytable
lrwxrwxrwx    1 root    root    16 Apr 22 05:13 S20random ->
../init.d/random
lrwxrwxrwx    1 root    root    15 Apr 22 05:13 S25netfs ->
../init.d/netfs
lrwxrwxrwx    1 root    root    14 Apr 22 05:22 S26apmd -> ../init.d/apmd
lrwxrwxrwx    1 root    root    16 Apr 22 05:34 S28autofs ->
../init.d/autofs
lrwxrwxrwx    1 root    root    14 Apr 22 05:15 S55sshd -> ../init.d/sshd
lrwxrwxrwx    1 root    root    20 Apr 22 05:13 S56rawdevices ->
../init.d/rawdevices
lrwxrwxrwx    1 root    root    16 Apr 22 05:13 S56xinetd ->
../init.d/xinetd
lrwxrwxrwx    1 root    root    13 Apr 22 05:06 S60lpd -> ../init.d/lpd
lrwxrwxrwx    1 root    root    18 Apr 22 05:12 S80sendmail ->
../init.d/sendmail
lrwxrwxrwx    1 root    root    13 Apr 22 05:00 S85gpm -> ../init.d/gpm
lrwxrwxrwx    1 root    root    15 Apr 22 05:14 S90crond ->
../init.d/crond
lrwxrwxrwx    1 root    root    13 Apr 22 04:51 S90xfs -> ../init.d/xfs
lrwxrwxrwx    1 root    root    17 Apr 22 05:22 S95anacron ->
../init.d/anacron
lrwxrwxrwx    1 root    root    15 Apr 22 05:20 S97rhnsd ->
../init.d/rhnsd
lrwxrwxrwx    1 root    root    11 Apr 22 05:13 S99local -> ../rc.local
```

So what is all this? Well, you find a number of symbolic links from /etc/rc3.d/ to scripts of about the same name in /etc/init.d. For instance:

```
lrwxrwxrwx    1 root    root    17 Apr 22 05:34 S14nfslock ->
../init.d/nfslock
```

Actually, the similarity follows this pattern: The symbolic link in the rc3.d directory starts with an "S" or a "K," then has two digits, and ends in the name of the script to which it links. (In this case, S14nfslock links to the nfslock script in /etc/init.d.) The "S" stands for "Start;" the "K" stands for "Kill." When rc receives the `runlevel 3`, it moves into `/etc/rc3.d` and executes each "K" script with the parameter `stop`. It then executes each "S" script with the parameter `start`. The numbers define an ordering, so scripts that depend on each other can be run in the right order. For instance, `S10network` starts the network before `S80sendmail` starts the network-dependent `sendmail` program. Here's a list of commands that rc will run:

```
K05innd stop
K15httpd stop
K15postgresql stop
K20nfs stop
K25squid stop
K34yppasswdd stop
K35smb stop
K35vncserver stop
K45arpwatch stop
K45named stop
K46radvd stop
K50snmpd stop
K50tux stop
K65identd stop
K70bcm5820 stop
K74ntpd stop
K74ypserv stop
K74ypxfrd stop
S05kudzu start
S08ipchains start
S08iptables start
S09isdn start
S10network start
S12syslog start
S13portmap start
S14nfslock start
S17keytable start
S20random start
S25netfs start
S26apmd start
S28autofs start
S55sshd start
S56rawdevices start
S56xinetd start
S60lpd start
S80sendmail start
S85gpm start
S90crond start
```

```
S90xfs start
S95anacron start
S95atd start
S97rhnsd start
S99local start
```

The S and K files are symbolic links so that the scripts only have to be written once, rather than copied into each appropriate runlevel.

This system is the SysV boot system, in use by most Linux distributions, along with Solaris and several other major Unices. Believe it or not, it was chosen over the simpler-looking BSD boot system for ease-of-use. This system may seem strange, but it'll soon become second nature to you. Once you get over the learning curve that you're currently sailing up, life gets much easier.

Traditionally, you stop a service from starting by renaming (or even deleting) its S script. Remember, rc starts all the scripts that begin with a capital "S," so you can deactivate S14nfslock by renaming it s14nfslock. Renaming this link is typically better than deleting it because deletion makes remembering the ordering number (14) more difficult if you want to reactivate later.

Red Hat actually has a tool, called chkconfig, that makes this process easier. chkconfig can manage all of these S and K scripts for you, deleting S scripts when you want to turn things off and adding S scripts when you want to turn things on. It figures out the ordering number by looking at a special comment section at the start of the script, such as this one for nfslock:

```
# nfslock      This shell script takes care of starting and stopping
#              the NFS file locking service.
#
# chkconfig: 345 14 86
# description: NFS is a popular protocol for file sharing across
```

The numbers next to the chkconfig line tell chkconfig what run-levels the script should start in by default, what the S number should be, and what the K number should be, respectively. You can turn off the nfslock script with the following code:

```
# chkconfig nfslock off
```
which deletes the S script and produces a K script for nfslock in /etc/rc3.d:

```
[root@localhost rc3.d]# ls -l *nfslock
lrwxrwxrwx 1 root root 17 Jun  2 11:38 K86nfslock -> ../init.d/nfslock
```

and turns it back on like this:

```
# chkconfig nfslock on
```

which deletes the K script and produces a new S script:

```
[root@localhost rc3.d]# ls -l *nfslock
lrwxrwxrwx 1 root root 17 Jun  2 11:39 S14nfslock -> ../init.d/nfslock
```

Returning to the network daemon audit

To deactivate rpc.statd, you still need to find out which script actually started it. You have two good options for finding this information. Remember that rpc.statd is NFS-related, which clues you in to checking the nfs and nfslock scripts. Barring that, you fall back on Yankee ingenuity and use grep to search all the /etc/rc3.d/ scripts for mention of rpc.statd:

```
[root@localhost rc3.d]# grep rpc.statd S*
S14nfslock:[ -x /sbin/rpc.statd ] || exit 0
S14nfslock:      daemon rpc.statd
S14nfslock:      killproc rpc.statd
S14nfslock:      status rpc.statd
S14nfslock:      /sbin/pidof rpc.statd >/dev/null 2>&1; STATD="$?"
```

Both methods show you that S14nfslock, a symbolic link to /etc/init.d/nfs-lock, is the culprit. Read this script, and you'll realize that you only need it if this system is an NFS client. It isn't, so you can turn this off for the next boot:

```
# chkconfig nfslock off
```

To stop this service immediately, you can run the script with the stop parameter, the same way that rc does:

```
# /etc/rc3.d/S14nfslock stop
```

Now you need to confirm that no program is listening on that port (TCP 1024) anymore:

```
[root@localhost rc3.d]# netstat -vat
Active Internet connections (servers and established)
Proto Recv-Q Send-Q Local Address           Foreign Address         State
tcp        0      0 localhost.localdom:1025 *:*                     LISTEN
tcp        0      0 *:sunrpc                *:*                     LISTEN
tcp        0      0 *:ssh                   *:*                     LISTEN
tcp        0      0 localhost.localdom:smtp *:*                     LISTEN
```

The rest of the audit is pretty easy. Once you learn how to track down and deactivate one network daemon, the rest work just the same. Let's keep going.

Now look at another open port, the one labeled sunrpc. Although the fact that this label isn't a port number per se may seem strange, this symbolic representation is one with which most system commands are totally comfortable. Each time a system needs to translate from port number to port name, it just looks up the translation in the /etc/services file. In this case, grep shows the following:

```
[root@localhost rc3.d]# grep sunrpc /etc/services
sunrpc          111/tcp          portmapper      # RPC 4.0 portmapper TCP
sunrpc          111/udp          portmapper      # RPC 4.0 portmapper UDP
```

According to the services file, TCP port 111 is called sunrpc. We're going to use the symbolic name for now just to increase your comfort level with it. You can find out what program is listening on that port by using lsof:

```
[root@localhost rc3.d]# lsof -i tcp:sunrpc
COMMAND PID USER    FD    TYPE DEVICE SIZE NODE NAME
portmap 637 root    4u   IPv4    968       TCP *:sunrpc (LISTEN)
```

So, the program that you need to investigate is portmap. The man page doesn't make this program's purpose obvious if you've never heard of Remote Procedure Call (RPC) programs. Honestly, some man pages only function well as references. A Google search (www.google.com) is useful here, probably with search terms like "portmap remote procedure call."

What you end up learning from Google is that portmap, called rpcbind on some other Unices, basically provides a necessary go-between service for RPC-based programs. On Linux, the primary RPC programs are NFS, which we've discussed, and NIS (Network Information Service), which is used to run a large collection of machines that all allow a user to login with the same name and password. If you're not using NIS or NFS, then deactivating portmap on a Linux system is generally safe. You can deactivate the portmap start script by using chkconfig as follows:

```
# chkconfig portmap off
# /etc/init.d/portmap stop
```

If you remember, S13portmap is just a link to /etc/init.d/portmap, so using /etc/init.d/portmap instead of /etc/rc3.d/S13portmap is basically the same thing. We use the one in /etc/init.d so that we don't have to look up the one in /etc/rc3.d/, numbers and all. Confirm that the port is no longer open and see what's left by using the following:

```
[root@localhost rc3.d]# netstat -vat
Active Internet connections (servers and established)
Proto Recv-Q Send-Q Local Address            Foreign Address         State
tcp        0      0 localhost.localdom:1025  *:*                     LISTEN
tcp        0      0 *:ssh                     *:*                     LISTEN
tcp        0      0 localhost.localdom:smtp  *:*                     LISTEN
```

Look at that ssh port. We always like to leave remote login available on our machines — even workstations sometimes. Make sure that the sshd program is really the one listening, like so:

```
[root@localhost rc3.d]# lsof -i tcp:ssh
COMMAND    PID USER    FD    TYPE DEVICE SIZE NODE NAME
sshd       843 root    3u   IPv4   1390       TCP *:ssh (LISTEN)
```

Well, the situation seems safe, since we see the ssh daemon program, sshd, is listening on that port.. You may investigate further by making sure that root, with a parent process of init, started process 843. Next, we'll look at the open smtp port.

Simple Mail Transfer Protocol (SMTP) is the dominant way that mail moves from one mail server to another. You can see that sendmail is the program listening on this port by using lsof:

```
COMMAND   PID USER    FD    TYPE DEVICE SIZE NODE NAME
sendmail 918 root    4u   IPv4   1504       TCP localhost.localdomain:smtp
(LISTEN)
```

Now you need to decide whether you'd like sendmail to listen on this machine. sendmail is a mail transfer agent (MTA), which you use to send or receive mail from one mail server to another. Whatever servers receive mail for your domain need to have an MTA. If you use POP or IMAP to read your mail, then a machine different from the one that operates your e-mail client actually receives the mail for the domain. Now, what about sending mail back out? Well, POP and IMAP clients are typically configured to speak SMTP to your organization's or ISP's mailserver, which then forwards the mail off the machine. In this case, you definitely don't need a mail server on your personal machine.

So, what if you don't read your mail via POP or IMAP? Though less common nowadays, many Unix users still read their mail by SSH-ing to their mail server and reading their mail with a text e-mail client, such as pine or mutt. These users don't need a mailserver on their workstations, but they do need a mailserver running on the system on which they read their mail.

The only other reason that you install sendmail on a workstation is so that the parts of the system that want to send alerts and notifications by e-mail can do so. Nicely, this functionality doesn't require that sendmail continually run in network daemon mode. Basically, whenever mutt, pine, or even mail/mailx need to send an e-mail, they start their own copy of sendmail and talk to it over a pipe. This sendmail either delivers the mail locally or talks to an MTA on a remote machine. If it fails to successfully send the mail, it'll add the mail to the queue to resend later.

Actually, you can run sendmail not as a network daemon, but instead in *queue cleanup mode* where sendmail runs every 15 minutes, or perhaps every hour, to resend any unsuccessfully sent e-mail. Traditionally, you deactivate sendmail's rc script, and then add sendmail -q to root's crontab file. Red Hat, offers a slightly easier approach: just change the DAEMON line in /etc/sysconfig/sendmail from

DAEMON=YES to DAEMON=NO. Whichever solution you choose, make the change in /etc/sysconfig/sendmail and then restart sendmail as follows:

```
[root@localhost rc3.d]# /etc/init.d/sendmail stop
Shutting down sendmail:                                  [  OK  ]
[root@localhost rc3.d]# /etc/init.d/sendmail start
Starting sendmail:                                       [  OK  ]
```

Using netstat to make sure that the change took place, you see one less open port:

```
[root@localhost rc3.d]# netstat -vat
Active Internet connections (servers and established)
Proto Recv-Q Send-Q Local Address           Foreign Address         State
tcp        0      0 localhost.localdom:1025 *:*                     LISTEN
tcp        0      0 *:ssh                   *:*                     LISTEN
```

Finally, take a look at TCP port 1025, which involves xinetd, as you see here:

```
[root@localhost root]# lsof -i tcp:1025
COMMAND PID USER   FD   TYPE DEVICE SIZE NODE NAME
xinetd  876 root    5u  IPv4   1416      TCP localhost.localdomain:1025
(LISTEN)
```

xinetd is a replacement for the original InterNET superserver Daemon (inetd). Each of these was created to allow the operating system to listen on a number of ports without having to have a separate program running (taking up memory and system resources) for each open port. inetd/ and /or xinetd starts up listening to a number of ports — when it receives a connection on a given port, it runs an instance of the program that can answer that connection. Particular network daemons, such as POP, IMAP, telnet, and FTP, use this method.

xinetd's configuration file, /etc/xinetd.conf, tells xinetd which ports to listen on, as well as which programs to start when it gets connections on those ports, by directing it to a number of single-port configuration files in /etc/xinetd.d/. Each file in /etc/xinet.d/ represents a particular network service. Here's an example for the WU-FTPD FTP daemon, in the file /etc/xinetd.d/wu-ftpd:

```
# default: on
# description: The wu-ftpd FTP server serves FTP connections. It uses \
#       normal, unencrypted usernames and passwords for authentication.
service ftp
{
        socket_type             = stream
        wait                    = no
        user                    = root
```

```
server                   = /usr/sbin/in.ftpd
server_args              = -l -a
log_on_success          += DURATION
nice                     = 10
disable                  = yes
}
```

Each line gives xinetd some specific information:

◆ The `service` line lists the port number, usually by the name used in /etc/services.

◆ The `server` and `server_args` lines tell `xinetd` which program to run, and with what arguments.

◆ The `socket_type` line tells `xinetd` to listen on TCP (stream) or UDP (datagram) ports.

◆ The `disable` line tells `xinetd` not to actually run this service, thus providing a non-destructive method for deactivating network services.

◆ The `user` line tells `xinetd`, a root-level process, what user to start the server as.

In this case, the file tells `xinetd` to listen to the FTP port and to run

```
/usr/sbin/in.ftpd -l -a
```

as root whenever it receives a connection. The `disable` line is also telling `xinetd` to ignore that command, so it'll never listen on that port, which is okay.

So, what about port 1025? Which file in /etc/xinetd.d/ is telling `xinetd` to listen on that port? If you do hunting around, you'll notice that you don't find any file that tells you about port 1025. You will notice, though, that the /etc/xinetd.d/sgi_fam file is the only file that doesn't have a `disable` line present. Here's that file:

```
# default: on
# description: FAM is a file monitoring daemon. It can \
# be used to get reports when files change.
service sgi_fam
{
        type            = RPC UNLISTED
        socket_type     = stream
        user            = root
        group           = nobody
        server          = /usr/bin/fam
        wait            = yes
```

```
protocol      = tcp
rpc_version   = 2
rpc_number    = 391002
bind          = 127.0.0.1
}
```

This file tells you, through the `rpc_version` and `rpc_number` lines, that the FAM (file alteration monitor) daemon is an RPC service, which is the reason for the non-deterministic port number. At this point, you need to decide whether or not you need this. If you do, then you not only need to leave this file alone, but you also need to reactivate `portmap`, because all RPC programs need `portmap` running to find each other.

FAM is a file monitoring daemon that programs can use to keep track of when files change, without having to poll the filesystem directly. The documentation isn't too clear about when you need FAM, but a Google (www.google.com) search shows that FAM is useful when running NFS. The Enlightenment window manager, the KDE desktop, and the Gnome desktop also use FAM. If you're not using one of these, then turning off FAM is probably OK. We're going to assume that you aren't using one of these, so we can show you how you reconfigure `xinetd`.

First, you want to tell `xinetd` not to run this service anymore by inserting a `disable = yes` line anywhere between the {}'s, say right after the `bind = 127.0.0.1` line. To review how this deactivation process works, look at the preceding WU-FTPd example.

Second, restart `xinetd`:

```
# /etc/init.d/xinetd stop
# /etc/init.d/xinetd start
```

Actually, you can tell `xinetd` to just re-read its configuration file, deactivating any newly-inactive ports just by passing it a HUP (hang up) signal with the kill or killall command:

```
# killall -HUP xinetd
```

Because every `xinetd` configuration file is now set with `disable=yes`, you can go further by deactivating the `xinetd` start script, too:

```
# chkconfig xinetd off
```

With that step complete, you're ready to get an updated list of open TCP ports:

```
[root@localhost xinetd.d]# netstat -vat
Active Internet connections (servers and established)
Proto Recv-Q Send-Q Local Address          Foreign Address
State
```

```
tcp        0      0 *:ssh                    *:*
LISTEN
```

Only one TCP port is open now — pretty sweet! You've greatly lessened the possible vectors for attack.

Conclude your network daemon audit by looking at the UDP ports. To get a list of all of the programs listening on UDP ports, change the t to a u.

```
[root@localhost xinetd.d]# netstat -vau
Active Internet connections (servers and established)
Proto Recv-Q Send-Q Local Address          Foreign Address
State
udp    12152      0 *:bootpc                 *:*
```

A couple more UDP ports were open before, but turning off the start scripts during the TCP part of this audit got them. Here was the UDP output before you started pruning:

```
root@localhost root]# netstat -vau
Active Internet connections (servers and established)
Proto Recv-Q Send-Q Local Address          Foreign Address        State
udp        0      0 *:1024                   *:*
udp        0      0 *:bootpc                 *:*
udp        0      0 *:sunrpc                 *:*
```

By the way, notice that we're using "-vau" now instead of "-vat." The "u" signifies UDP, while the "t" signified TCP.

Deactivating the nfslock script removed UDP port 1024 and deactivating the portmap script removed port sunrpc, which leaves only port bootpc. Use lsof to track down the program listening on this port:

```
[root@localhost xinetd.d]# lsof -i udp:bootpc
COMMAND PID USER    FD    TYPE DEVICE SIZE NODE NAME
dhcpcd  510 root    4u    IPv4    813      UDP *:bootpc
```

the lsof command showed that dhcpcd is listening on that port. Consulting the man page for dhcpcd as follows

```
DESCRIPTION
        dhcpcd is an implementation of the DHCP  client  specified
        in  RFC2131  (when -r option is not specified) and RFC1541
        (when -r option is specified).
```

reveals that *dhcpcd* is the Dynamic Host Configuration Protocol (DHCP), client daemon. It runs on a client so that said client can request an IP address, DNS servers, hostname, and other networking information from a server on the network. You use this daemon for checking out a dynamic IP address from a central DHCPd server, and it's totally necessary in a dynamic IP environment. This kind of setup is becoming extremely common in the modern enterprise, as it eases an organization's administration of the IP address space. Because the host you're hardening is in such an environment, leave the DHCP client daemon active.

Now, you're ready to look at the remaining S scripts in /etc/rc3.d, just to see what's still on:

```
[root@localhost rc3.d]# ls S*
S05kudzu      S10network    S25netfs      S56rawdevices  S90crond    S97rhnsd
S08ipchains   S12syslog     S26apmd       S60lpd         S90xfs      S99local
S08iptables   S17keytable   S28autofs     S80sendmail    S95anacron
S09isdn       S20random     S55sshd       S85gpm         S95atd
```

You need to run through each of these, deciding which scripts to leave active. For the sake of brevity, we're just going to discuss each of the scripts, rather than going through the discovery process. By the way, remember that these scripts are symbolic links to the real scripts in /etc/init.d. We'll start with S05kudzu.

S05KUDZU

This script runs the kudzu hardware detection (and configuration) tool. Kudzu runs on each boot and looks for new hardware. If kudzu finds new hardware, it allows the sysadmin to configure said hardware. Because kudzu is totally non-persistent, it doesn't provide much opportunity for an attack, making it pretty inoffensive. Leaving it on is fairly safe. In fact, we can only think of one way to abuse this S script.

If kudzu detects changed hardware when it starts up, it allows you to configure that hardware. Because it doesn't *authenticate* (request a password of) the user who it helps to configure the new device, kudzu does leave a slight avenue for attack. Only the overly paranoid raise this issue, but we'll address it anyway. Basically, if this machine is a highly-controlled server that will have infrequent hardware swap-outs, and then only made by a system administrator, then you should probably turn kudzu off. You can still see its benefits by running kudzu whenever you add new hardware. On the other hand, if this machine is a laptop, you may choose to leave kudzu on to account for frequent hardware swaps. (Actually, though, in our experience, kudzu isn't all that useful on laptops.) For the sake of minimalism and paranoia, you may decide to turn kudzu off, especially if several other people have access to your machine: There's no hard recommendation here. That's the point of individualized system hardening. For each system, in its own environment and with its own purpose, you will make different decisions.

```
# chkconfig kudzu off
```

The next two scripts are ipchains and iptables.

IPCHAINS AND IPTABLES

These scripts load up any saved firewall rules that you may have. Given this positive security function and the fact that they're non-persistent, you should definitely leave these scripts active. If you know that you're using `iptables`, you can safely remove the `ipchains` script, and vice versa. For instance:

```
# chkconfig ipchains off
```

By the way, you can learn more about these two firewalling technologies and what makes them different in these articles:

- Using Linux 2.4 Firewalling – Building a Firewall with Netfilter

  www.bastille-linux.org/jay/building-firewall.html

- Linux Gets Stateful Firewalling – Introducing Netfilter

  www.bastille-linux.org/jay/introducing-netfilter.html

- Firewall Configuration Prerequisites

  www.bastille-linux.org/jay/firewall-prereqs.html

The next script is called `isdn`. If an isdn card is configured (determined by the presence and contents of /etc/sysconfig/isdncard), it activates the `isdn` script. If you're not using ISDN for your Internet connection, go ahead and turn it off. You'll have fewer S scripts to investigate the next time you do this audit:

```
# chkconfig isdn off
```

By the way, you may notice that you're only setting these scripts to not run at the next boot. You don't need to run them with the `stop` argument either, because each of them is a non-persistent program, meaning there's no program to kill!

The next script is `network`.

NETWORK

This script starts up whatever networking has been configured and quietly exits. If this machine isn't going to be on a network, you can deactivate this script. Otherwise, please do leave it on. The next script is `syslog`.

SYSLOG

This script runs the `syslogd` system logging daemon. Definitely leave this script on! System logs are often the very first line of defense when you're responding to an attack. They frequently show you how you're being attacked, and they help you respond to the attack more readily. You do have to read them, of course, or at least have an automated tool, such as swatch (www.stanford.edu/~atkins/swatch/) or logsurfer (www.cert.dfn.de/eng/logsurf/), reading them for you and alerting you to possible hacking activity.

KEYTABLE

The keytable script is another non-persistent one that loads the current keyboard configuration for the country the system's configured for and exits. You can and should leave it on.

RANDOM

The next script, random, is also non-persistent. It stores and reloads the random number generator's "seed" value. The seed value is used to keep the random number generator more random. This one is also quite safe and recommended.

NETFS

The netfs script mounts any network-mounted filesystems at boot. If you're not using NFS, Samba (for Windows file sharing), or NCP (for Novell Netware), turning this off is totally safe. If you are using one of these, you should probably leave this active. Because the script just runs mount commands and exits, you don't have a program to kill. Remove the S (start) scripts with chkconfig:

```
# chkconfig netfs off
```

APMD

The next script, apmd, is responsible for starting the Advanced Power Management Daemon, apmd. This program basically watches the system's battery, if one exists, for low-power states and then alerts and/or runs commands at those states. It's useful for shutting down a notebook on low power. The program is also useful if you have an uninterruptible power supply (UPS) that can tell your operating system when the batteries are running out, allowing the system to power down naturally. If your machine doesn't fit either of those two descriptions, deactivating this script is totally safe:

```
# chkconfig apmd off
# /etc/init.d/apmd stop
```

AUTOFS

The script, autofs, is responsible for running the automount program and otherwise starting the Linux partition automounter. The automounter can mount network drives on demand. If you're not using this functionality, you can turn this program off with complete safety:

```
# chkconfig autofs off
# /etc/init.d/autofs stop
```

SSHD

The next script is sshd. This program allows secure remote login to this system. Generally, you want to keep this script active. If this machine is a workstation for which you don't need remote login, though, you can deactivate sshd by using the following commands:

```
# chkconfig sshd off
# /etc/init.d/sshd stop
```

For purposes of our example network, we're going to leave this script running. The next script is rawdevices.

RAWDEVICES

This program isn't configured with any data by default and, as such, doesn't do anything but exit quietly. If you have an application that uses raw-device support, such as Oracle, you may need it. You can determine your need in the same way that the script does, by looking at /etc/sysconfig/rawdevices. If this file is nothing but comments, as it is by default, feel free to deactivate the script. By the way, this script is non-persistent, so you only need to chkconfig it off:

```
# chkconfig rawdevices off
```

LPD

The next script, lpd, runs the printer daemon. If your machine has a printer attached to it, lpd is necessary. You also need lpd if your machine needs to allow its applications to print via it to another Unix machine with a printer. If your machine is a stand-alone Web server that won't be printing anything, you can safely deactivate lpd:

```
# chkconfig lpd off
# /etc/init.d/lpd stop
```

We discussed the next script, sendmail, in the previous section. If you decided to turn off network daemon mode, then you took one of two approaches. You could have changed the DAEMON line in /etc/sysconfig/sendmail to read DAEMON=no. The other approach is to deactivate the start script and then add a sendmail -q line to root's crontab file, using the crontab command. For the purposes of this example, we've chosen the former method, so we're leaving the start script alone.

GPM

The script, gpm, runs the console (text) mode mouse support daemon of the same name. This program lets you do things, such as cut-and-paste in text mode by using the mouse. Most people don't use this functionality any more; rather, they run text windows in graphics mode, cutting-and-pasting via X's built-in functionality. We recommend turning this script off on all systems, unless you actually use text mode frequently on one of them. gpm has had a few security vulnerabilities in the past, stemming from the fact that it lets you map actual commands to button presses, which unfortunately, grant an attacker root privileges. Use the following commands to turn off this script:

```
# chkconfig gpmd off
# /etc/init.d/gpm stop
```

The next script is crond.

CROND

The cron daemon runs programs automatically at later times. You usually use this script when you want a program to run at a set interval, such as every morning at 2 a.m., or every hour on the hour. Red Hat Linux already makes extensive use of this script, even if you don't. Look in the /etc/crontab file, and you'll see that the file defines a number of scripts in /etc/cron.hourly/, /etc/cron.daily/, /etc/cron.weekly/, and /etc/cron.monthly/ that perform basic automated system functions. Leave this script turned on.

The next script, xfs, starts the X Windows Font Server. This server, which by default doesn't listen on the network, provides the system's X server with access to fonts. If you're using graphical mode on this system, this script is quite necessary. You usually do need this script, but if you're only SSH-ing to the system and possibly running X programs on it, you don't. In the case of our dedicated Web server, we don't need it:

```
# chkconfig xfs off
# /etc/init.d/xfs stop
```

ANACRON

The next script, anacron, was written to bring cron functionality to systems such as laptops and home machines, which spend more of their late nights turned off than on. A cron job that runs at one a.m. every morning isn't very useful on a machine that's always turned off at one a.m. anacron changes the paradigm by allowing the administrator to set a frequency with which a job runs. If anacron starts up at boot and realizes that a job should have been done last night while the system was turned off, it runs that job. If you have a laptop, definitely leave this script on. If you're on an always-on workstation or server, you can safely deactivate anacron:

```
# chkconfig anacron off
# /etc/init.d/anacron stop
```

ATD

With three scripts left, the next is `atd`. This daemon supports "at" functionality, as in "run this program at four hours from now." Like `cron`, it lets a user run commands automatically at a later time. Unlike `cron`, it's not designed for periodic execution. `atd` used to have a number of security problems, but they seem to have been cleared up. Watch for a while—if you and your users don't seem to be using the functionality, turn it off. If you have an older system and want to know how long it's been since someone's used this facility, you can just `stat` its binary, `/usr/bin/at`:

```
[root@localhost rc3.d]# stat /usr/bin/at
  File: "/usr/bin/at"
  Size: 37528          Blocks: 80         IO Block: -4612009962040717312
Regular File
Device: 801h/2049d     Inode: 17073       Links: 1
Access: (4755/-rwsr-xr-x)  Uid: (    0/    root)  Gid: (    0/    root)
Access: Thu Jan 17 12:34:41 2002
Modify: Thu Jan 17 12:34:41 2002
Change: Mon Apr 22 05:08:45 2002
```

Check the `Access` time. If no one has used `at` for six months, turning it off is probably safe.

RHNSD

The next script is called `rhnsd`, which stands for the Red Hat Network Service Daemon. This program talks to the registration-based Red Hat Network and alerts you to the need for various updates/patches, security and otherwise, applying updates/patches automatically if you've requested. Use of this sort of commercial service is best decided on a site-by-site basis, based on questions of cost and control. Really, it's a strong solution. If you're ready for some automation, this might be exactly what you need. There's even an enterprise-class version of this, with additional management and bandwidth conservation features for large organizations. If you choose not to register and use it, though, make sure that you come up with a monthly/weekly patching solution. Modern operating systems end up with a large number of security vulnerabilities, often discovered while the first batch of CDs are being burned. Although system hardening often prevents an attacker from using these vulnerabilities to exploit your system, fixing them is still important.

LOCAL

The last script, `local`, is actually non-optional. Your small, site-specific "run me last" startup commands are supposed to go here. Leave this script active, but audit the contents periodically.

Okay, you've audited all, and deactivated many, of the SysV startup scripts. Here's how our example system turned out:

```
[root@localhost rc3.d]# ls S*
S08iptables  S12syslog    S20random   S56rawdevices  S90crond  S97rhnsd
S10network   S17keytable  S55sshd     S80sendmail    S95atd    S99local
```

Much less should be running on the system now. Here's what the example system's process list looks like:

```
[root@localhost root]# ps -ef
UID        PID  PPID  C STIME TTY       TIME CMD
root         1     0  0 05:03 ?     00:00:06 init
root         2     1  0 05:03 ?     00:00:00 [keventd]
root         3     1  0 05:03 ?     00:00:00 [kapmd]
root         4     1  0 05:03 ?     00:00:00 [ksoftirqd_CPU0]
root         5     1  0 05:03 ?     00:00:03 [kswapd]
root         6     1  0 05:03 ?     00:00:00 [bdflush]
root         7     1  0 05:03 ?     00:00:01 [kupdated]
root         8     1  0 05:03 ?     00:00:00 [mdrecoveryd]
root        16     1  0 05:03 ?     00:00:04 [kjournald]
root        95     1  0 05:03 ?     00:00:00 [khubd]
root       612     1  0 05:05 ?     00:00:02 syslogd -m 0
root       617     1  0 05:05 ?     00:00:00 klogd -x
root       843     1  0 05:05 ?     00:00:01 /usr/sbin/sshd
root       955     1  0 05:05 ?     00:00:00 crond
daemon    1083     1  0 05:05 ?     00:00:00 /usr/sbin/atd
root      1092     1  0 05:05 ?     00:00:00 login -- root
root      1093     1  0 05:05 ?     00:00:00 /sbin/mingetty tty2
root      1094     1  0 05:05 tty3  00:00:00 /sbin/mingetty tty3
root      1095     1  0 05:05 tty4  00:00:00 /sbin/mingetty tty4
root      1096     1  0 05:05 tty5  00:00:00 /sbin/mingetty tty5
root      1097     1  0 05:05 tty6  00:00:00 /sbin/mingetty tty6
root     10692     1  0 12:58 ?     00:00:00 /usr/sbin/sendmail -q1h
root     11666 11664  1 20:09 pts/0 00:00:00 -bash
root     11719 11666  0 20:09 pts/0 00:00:00 ps -ef
```

Compared to the system before we started the process, not much is here, given that everything in square brackets is a kernel process and all the mingetty processes are just console login prompts. You've made a tremendous cut in the cracker's set of possible attack vectors, making a break in much more difficult.

You can go much further with scripts, but that's another whole book! The next section introduces you to an automated solution, Bastille Linux, which can do some of this system hardening work for you.

Hardening the system automatically with Bastille Linux

You're probably starting to realize that system hardening can be fairly time-intensive and complicated. Before you get discouraged, realize that the tip-of-the-iceberg work that's in the first section of this chapter can be very effective.

An automated solution can do a great deal of this work very quickly. It also scales better, doing the work more quickly and consistently than a team of system administrators can. On the other hand, armed with enough information, you can do a great deal more for your system. Remember, you're much smarter than a computer!

Bastille Linux was designed to try to give you as close a solution as you can get to doing it yourself. At the time of this chapter's creation, Bastille runs on Red Hat Linux, Mandrake Linux, Debian, SuSE and Turbolinux, along with HP-UX.

A development team led by this chapter's author, Jay Beale, is working to port Bastille to more platforms and to add new steps to it.

When you run Bastille, it asks you a number of questions about how you're using the system. As you've seen, hardening a system must be greatly tailored to the system's purpose and site's general practice. To help you make as informed a decision as possible and to educate you about the measures it's taking, Bastille includes a paragraph or two with each question. In fact, many people have said that Bastille's explanations are a fairly useful training tool. Figure 17-1 shows what you see as a user.

So, Bastille's able to automate a number of hardening steps. The remainder of this section lists a paragraph on each major hardening method that Bastille uses, from the boot security measures to the daemon configuration steps. These are broken up into modules, roughly by topic.

Account Security module

This module works to protect user accounts from being stolen. It also takes measures to minimize the damage that an attacker can do if he or she steals an ordinary user account. Its actions include implementing password aging, so that old unused accounts are locked, raising the chances that an account's owner will notice the account theft and alert the sysadmin. This module also deactivates the flawed IP-based authentication r-tools, such as `rlogin` and `rsh`, which have been a major source of account theft over the years. It restricts `cron` usage to a more limited group of users and also disallows direct root logins. A root user has to login as another user first, and then `su` (switch user) to root. Consequently, someone who steals the root password must steal another account first, which foils many an attack.

Boot Security module

This module works to protect the boot process. As shown in the article "Anyone with a Screwdriver Can Break In," available via `www.bastille-linux.org/jay/anyone-with-a-screwdriver.html`, the Red Hat boot process is fairly easy to circumvent to get root. In all fairness to Red Hat, the same is true of most operating systems. Bastille can put passwords on the boot loader, either LILO (LInux LOader) or grub (GRand Unified Boot loader), and password protects single-user mode. The article cited above can tell you about some of the other measures available to you when you do tighten the boot process manually.

Configure Miscellaneous PAM Settings module

This module configures the pluggable authentication modules (PAM) security settings. Don't be fooled by PAM's name — a number of security settings have nothing to do with authentication. Bastille uses the PAM configuration files to set resource limits so that a single user can't launch a resource starvation Denial of Service (DoS) attack. It limits the number of processes per user, which blocks fork bombs, where an attacker creates a program that keeps splitting itself off into new programs, which do the same until there's no room for any new programs to execute. This module also fixes the maximum core dump size at 0. There are two reasons for this latter measure:

It stops an attacker from eating up disk space with core dumps.

Attackers frequently grab passwords out of the core dumps by causing a program that's loaded in user passwords to crash, stealing the passwords. Some of this system hardening stuff gets pretty subtle!

Deactivate Miscellaneous Daemons module

This module does much of the boot script audit that we just finished. Table 17-1 lists the programs the module deactivates.

TABLE 17-1 MISCELLANEOUS DAEMONS

Script	Program	Purpose	Advanced Power Management Daemon	Scheduled command execution
nfs	rpc.mountd,	NFS main	rpc.nfsd	daemon
nfs	lock	rpc.statd, rpc.lockd	NFS support programs	

Script	Program	Purpose	Advanced Power Management Daemon	Scheduled command execution
gated	gated	Better Unix routing daemon		
routed	routed	Unix routing daemon		
smb	smbd, nmbd	SAMBA Windows file/print sharing		
snmpd	snmpd	Simple Network Management Protocol		
ypbind	ypbind	NIS client system		
ypserv	ypserv	NIS server system		

Disable User Tools module

This module disables any compilers on the system. A standard attacker methodology includes bringing a toolkit to the target system, compiling the tools on said system. Disabling the compiler helps slow down the attacker. Like all of the other steps in Bastille, this one is only taken if the sysadmin chooses it.

File Permissions module

This module sets better permissions around the entire filesystem. Its most critical component, though, is a Set-UID audit. As shown in the article, "Shredding Access in the Name of Security: the Set-UID audit," available via www.bastille-linux.org/jay/suid-audit.html, a Set-UID audit can be the most powerful measure you can take to halt an attacker's escalation of privilege on the system. It's bad enough if an attacker can get access as the Web server user (apache) — it's much worse if he can use a vulnerable Set-UID program to turn this access into root!

Logging module

Recall that logging is often your first, best alert to an attack on your system. You also have better luck tracking the attacker's activities if she doesn't successfully erase your logs.

   This module adds better logging to a Red Hat system. It logs all kernel messages and high-severity events to separate log files, helping you to find the critical alerts among the noise. It also logs all logins to a loginlog file, which can help create a good audit trail when you're trying to track down what accounts were being used during an incident. Additionally, the module sends logs to an extra console screen so that you can easily watch them in real-time. Finally, it optionally configures the machine to log to a central logserver, which can be extremely helpful, both for event correlation and in keeping a safe copy off the machine should an attacker delete the logs on her target right after gaining access.

Printing module

This module just deactivates the printer daemon, if possible.

Secure inetd/xinetd module

This module audits inetd or xinetd, deactivating network services that aren't necessary. Although Red Hat 7.3 doesn't have much to turn off in its default configuration, the earlier Red Hat distributions had a great deal more listening in the default install. The most important measure in this chapter's audit was definitely the deactivation of telnet and FTP. Because these protocols are both cleartext (don't involve any data encryption, such that they're easy to eavesdrop on), an attacker can steal passwords or even take over interactive sessions outright. Most FTP servers still present extreme problems, as they develop major security holes every year or so.

tmpdir Protection module

This module, created by Pete Watkins, protects users from /tmp directory exploits, a class of exploit which uses the fact that most programs write temporary files to the /tmp directory, where other users can read, or even possibly intercept, them. Bastille's tmpdir program gives every user a special temporary directory to which the other users don't have access. Doing so prevents data interception (spying), along with a number of race condition attacks, where an attacker steals your data or privileges by waiting for you to start accessing your data, then swipes your access before you can make use of it.

The next four modules are for major server applications: Apache (Web), BIND (DNS), FTP, and sendmail (E-mail). Deactivating every network service on a machine would be nice, but the computer wouldn't be very useful. You may not be able to deactivate a server, but you can still configure it for better security by trying to reduce both the number of ways that an attacker can access or attack the program and the privilege she'd get if successful.

Apache module

This module deactivates parts of Apache's functionality that you aren't using. If you're using Apache solely as a Web developer's test machine, then Apache stops listening to the network card. If you aren't using any CGI scripts, Bastille deactivates CGI execution entirely. Actually, this one step can prevent the vast majority of all Web server exploitations – most of them rely on a badly coded CGI script. You can often thwart the remaining threats by turning off server side includes (SSI), index generation, and symbolic link following, all special features of a Web server. Bastille does all these things.

BIND (DNS) module

For a couple of years, the Berkeley Internet Name Daemon (BIND), produced some of the most widespread remote root grabs available for Unix. Bastille wasn't able to stop the vulnerability from being exploited, but it was quite effective in locking the attacker in a "chroot prison" directory, so that she couldn't use the system for anything or compromise any data. It still performs this function, forcing BIND to run as a non-root user while locked in a specially-constructed chroot directory.

You can do even more than Bastille does, because you have an understanding of your site's needs that only a human can. You can read more about these measures in the article "Attacking and Defending DNS," available at www.bastille-linux. org/jay/defending-dns.html.

FTP module

FTP servers have two primary modes:

♦ **Real mode:** Allows normal users on the system to remotely transfer files to and from their accounts. This mode has two flaws: It allows passwords to travel in cleartext, and it's vulnerable to session hijacking. For these reasons, FTP is no longer in use at security-conscious sites, having been replaced by SSH's sftp.

♦ **Anonymous mode:** Allows a site to give away files easily. This mode still suffers from hijacking problems, but those aren't really a concern with public data. Further, most every FTP daemon for Unix has had multiple security holes.

Bastille tries to better your odds by either deactivating the FTP server altogether, (after teaching you why you should) or at least turning off either one of the two modes.

sendmail (E-Mail) module

Bastille offers to, as we did in the previous section, stop sendmail's network daemon mode on a host, running it in queue cleanup mode instead. This measure drastically reduces the risk from a remote attacker, though it doesn't help you against an attacker already on the box.

This module also shuts down the EXPN (expand alias) and VRFY (verify user existence) commands, which an external attacker can use to get account names. An attacker will use these commands either to build spam lists or to profile a target site.

The last two modules are both network-level defenses: a firewall and a port scan detector.

Firewall module

This module, also created by Pete Watkins, creates a personal (single machine) firewall or a single-network firewall. The latter case is excellent for small offices or even for a single machine that needs to share its Internet connection with a few other computers. This module can be time-intensive, but it builds a very strong firewall tuned to the individual or to the site.

Port Scan Attack Detector (PSAD) module

Bastille's newest module, at the time of this writing, is the Port Scan Attack Detector (PSAD). Written by Mike Rash, it's a successor and competitor to PortSentry. It watches the firewall logs and tries to determine whether the system is being port scanned. This firewall log monitoring can be quite useful because it lets you know when you're being probed and possibly attacked.

Summary

This chapter gives you some introductory instructions on how to harden a system. Before you're tempted to procrastinate, let us share a statistic with you. The HoneyNet (http://project.honeynet.org) project found that the average – note, that's average – life span of a non-hardened, non-patched/updated Red Hat 6.2 box, from the point it was connected to the Internet to the time it was randomly cracked, was about 72 hours. The shortest time they found for a human attacker was 15 minutes. The shortest time they found for an automated attacker (a worm) was 92 seconds. Although things have improved since then, a huge number of machines are cracked randomly every day. You need to harden your systems as soon as possible!

Chapter 18

Introducing Simple Intrusion Detection Systems

IN THIS CHAPTER

◆ Examining network versus host-based intrusion detection

◆ Defining the scope of responsibility

◆ Reviewing useful network concepts

◆ Devising a defensive network configuration

◆ Designing an ID strategy

◆ Setting the rules

◆ Presenting our example NIDS – Snort.

THIS CHAPTER DISCUSSES NETWORK-BASED IDS. An IDS doesn't know what an intruder is, let alone how to detect one. It detects events and conditions that are associated with hostile activity on your computer or your network. So, someone — namely you – has to decide what kind of things are associated with intrusions and then make sure that the IDS is looking for them.

Actually, most IDS come with several default conditions that experience has associated with Bad Things Happening, but even so, new Bad Things Happen every day and someone has to keep your IDS updated. Also, as you'll see later, you'll want the IDS to watch some things specific to your setup, and many of the conditions that the IDS vendor bundles may not apply to you.

Examining Network vs. Host-Based Intrusion Detection

Many strange and bad people are out there looking at your computer. You may have met some of them already, peering through the screen from directories where they've moved in and replaced your system utilities with ones they find more comfortable.

The burglar alarm business booms when the burglars are busy. So the burglar alarms of networked computers, Intrusion Detection Systems (IDS), are hot sellers now. Many marketers push them the way they push firewalls – as though they were a "magic bullet" you can use to stop the bad guys. Just in case you believe marketers, we'll state again for the record that there *are* no magic bullets. Really. Trust us.

Understand, we're not coming down on firewalls or IDS here. You need firewalls and IDS to have a good security design. You also don't get much advantage from a firewall or IDS unless you think carefully about what it can do and how it fits into your particular network and/or system setup. This chapter discusses the real idea behind IDS, and gives you enough background to start playing with a very nice – free – NIDS called Snort. By the way, NIDS and HIDS stand for Network Intrusion Detection System and Host Intrusion Detection System, respectively.

Network-based IDS generally watch network traffic and look for attacks. Host-based IDS generally run on the system that's being watched and tend to look for unauthorized access attempts or even just strange system/user behavior. The advantage of the network approach is that it scales a whole lot better and is much, much simpler. As a result, most people think of Network-based IDS when you say "IDS."

Theoretically, the host-based approach has the capacity to be much more accurate, with fewer false positives, but implementations of strange-behavior HIDS are rare. The most popular implementation of Host-based IDS is file integrity checking, where the program tracks important files on your system and looks for changes, reasoning that an attacker will generally change the contents of critical configuration files in the process of obtaining or maintaining illegitimate access.

In the next section we will approach NIDS as part of an overall security design, beginning with determining the role that we expect NIDS to play.

Defining the Scope of Responsibility

Okay, you're going to set up a NIDS, which, as you already know, involves some pre-setup thinking and planning. Before you start concentrating on the exciting, geeky stuff, such as network attacks, you need to answer a couple of issues that are so obvious you may not even think of them. Without the answers, though, nothing else you do will make any sense. These issues are addressed in the following sections.

Your responsibilities

The universe may be big and scary, but the entire universe isn't your problem. This part of the book is about security, so you need to know what you're responsible for protecting.

The more you look at any computer – on its own or in a network – the more you see that it needs to be guarded, watched, or both! People examining network traffic for the first time are amazed at the volume of transactions taking place. You get the same effect the first time someone looks at the log on a central loghost. Determining the implications of each bit of traffic and each record in the logs is the easy part of a big job. The real work comes in trying to figure out what each thing means in relation to all the other things that are happening, especially when you can always get more information and potential vulnerabilities are always being discovered.

If you're going to maintain control, you have to set limits from the start. You need to know what your security systems need to do, and what your security systems can do before you can think about how to set them up. In all these cases, you have to think about what you must protect and make that the scope of your security requirements:

◆ **Running a system for an employer:** Do you work for someone? What have you been hired to do? The answer to this question should be in writing, such as in a contract. What are you responsible for protecting? These things form the scope of your responsibilities. Any NIDS (or other) strategy you design must address the security of everything within your scope. If your strategies happen to benefit others, fine, but you need to keep your plans focused if you're going to accomplish anything.

◆ **Running a system for your own business:** If you're running the system for your own business, then what does your business need from the system? If you're doing Web hosting, you don't need to run an Internet Relay Chat server (especially not on the same system!). After you know what your business needs, you know what you have to protect. Simply, you have to protect your business' ability to do what your business needs to do. This guideline generally translates directly into protecting specific systems, or even specific functions of a system.

◆ **Running a server for your own use:** Finally, you may be running a server for personal use or for a group of friends. "Fun," they call it. In that instance, you want to protect the system's ability to provide fun for you and your friends.

Obviously, you want to watch anything that directly involves the servers (or at least the services on the servers) within your scope. You may want to watch other things as well. For instance, you can watch just the network traffic directed to the servers in your scope. If some strange traffic gets reported on one or two of them, though, you may have trouble determining whether you caught a reconnaissance probe or a burp from some faulty network equipment in the south of France. However, if you're watching all the traffic on your network, and see that more than three out of four hosts got the same traffic – in order of ascending addresses to boot – you can be pretty sure that you've seen a probe. Network equipment burps are rarely so well organized.

Now that you know what you're protecting, you have to consider what you want to watch in order to gather the information you need to protect it. You need to define the scope of your security monitoring.

What is it you do, again . . . ?

If you can't figure out your job responsibilities from your job description or contract, get them in writing. System administrators are in a position to get blamed for all sorts of things. Computer security people are even more so! Make sure that everyone agrees — on paper — about what you must do.

The monitoring scope can justifiably include the entire Internet, every host on the Internet, and even every power grid potentially connected to yours. Okay, you don't have access to all that, so concentrate on the access you do have, which is all the network traffic that goes by your host (whether or not the traffic is going to that host). You have access to all the logs your processes can generate (unfortunately, not all processes that can log will do so by default). Do you have substantial information? Probably. Do you have enough information? No. You never have enough. Is the amount you have reasonable in terms of your resources and other things you have to do? Up to you. We can't tell you what your monitoring scope should be, but if you're going to make this work, we can tell you that the scope of monitoring must include what's in the scope of requirements.

Responsibility equals authority

In the preceding sections, we've assumed without saying that you're actually in a position to take security measures on the servers for which you're responsible. In other words, no one will hold you responsible for things out of your control. In a rational world, we wouldn't need to state this assumption at all. In this world, though, we thought it was a good idea to point it out. If you ever think that something is important to your server security, but can't get the authority to make it happen, put the problem in writing immediately.

A Memo of Understanding (MOU) is this great business tool that you can actually use for clarification; for now, however, think of it as a polite way to cover your heiny against someone else's bad decision. Here's an example of an MOU:

From: Me

To: The boss and the boss's boss

Subject: Memo of Understanding

This MOU is intended to document the results of the meeting of 30 February 2002, regarding security measures on the primary database server. After considering the recommendation from the security officer (see previous memo dated 31 November 2001) that a non-blank root password be used on this system, the copy editors determined that the extra complications this measure would introduce into the user authentication process outweighed the advantages of improved security.

And so forth . . .

Notice that the MOU refers to a previous memo. If you're working for someone other than yourself, then leave a paper trail (or at least an e-mail trail) for everything important to your job. If you're working for yourself, you should do the same, if only to make sure that you remember what you've said.

Before we define our NIDS further, we will review some fundamental concepts of networking. Readers with a strong grasp in the TCP/IP protocol may want to skim the next section.

Reviewing Useful Network Concepts

This chapter is about setting up an IDS, particularly a NIDS, and more particularly, Snort. We've agreed that figuring out what's important to know about what's happening on your network is your responsibility. In order to do *that*, you need to have some idea of the kinds of things that go on over a network. If you already have a grip on the TCP/IP protocol and the kind of probes and attacks that your system may see from the network, then this section is review. If not, this section is a very small step towards the very thick books you're going to get to know if you keep working with NIDS.

TCP/IP is the standard protocol family used over the Internet (in fact, IP stands for "Internet Protocol"). Think of a network protocol as a language that network devices use to talk over the wires (or fiber, 2.4GHz transmissions, and so on). Your network may carry other types of traffic, too, especially if you share it with Microsoft Windows platforms. In fact, if you're running SAMBA to talk to Windows systems, then you're using another protocol yourself. We're not going to worry about that here. This chapter focuses on the TCP/IP protocol, since that protocol defines Internet communication.

Packets

The first thing you need to know is that information sent over networks is broken into chunks rather than squirted like a stream. This way, multiple transactions get a bit of the network almost all of the time. One of your *packets* goes through, then one of mine, then one of hers, and then it's your turn again . . . Actually, most of this activity goes on between your keystrokes and while you stare at Web pages.

Your data is sent in chunks "packaged" in front and back with the necessary information for navigation and delivery over the Internet. The exact type of packaging varies depending on things such as the transmitted data's purpose and the kind of delivery service you want to use.

An IDS such as Snort works by looking at the packaging information on the packet as well as the data inside. In fact, you can get quite a bit of information from the packaging alone! Most firewalls work by looking at only the packaging. Many of the things you'll be looking for will involve "bad packaging" as the basis of a threat, no matter what information is (or isn't) in the package.

ENCAPSULATION

Look more closely at this packaging, and you'll find that the data you want to transmit doesn't just get put in one package; rather, it's tucked inside a package that's inside another package that's inside another package, and so forth – usually four or so layers deep. The packaging is like a set of nested envelopes, each with just part of the information needed to deliver the ultimate message inside all of them. This nesting of delivery information is part of the communications strategy called *encapsulation*. You need this sort of traveling strategy because the trip is complicated, and you don't want to use more than you need to at each step. Remember that the trip goes from a particular process on one particular host on one particular network, to some other process probably on another host on, quite possibly, another network.

The packet may pass through several networks on its way. The outer envelope always has the information needed to get to the next network on the trip. Once there, the router strips off the outer envelope and slaps on a new one with the information on how to get to the next network. Successive layers of inner envelopes contain increasingly detailed information about which host on the Internet and which process on that host are the packet's final destination. They also contain varying types of information about the message's priority and assorted other items that help get the message delivered safely.

DELIVERY OVERHEAD: CONNECTION-ORIENTED VS. CONNECTIONLESS

In network communications, applying the procedures that a high-reliability communications system uses to assure successful communication is called establishing a connection. Low-reliability delivery systems in which the message is tossed out and its arrival is never confirmed are called *connectionless*. High-reliability systems are called *connection-oriented*. TCP/IP offers a connectionless protocol called UDP (User Datagram Protocol) and a connection-oriented protocol called TCP (Transmission Control Protocol).

IP addresses

Each network interface on the Internet has a unique IP address. Assuming that your server has only one network card, then your server has a unique IP address. At home, your ISP normally assigns you this address. At work, the address probably comes from the network administrator.

 If you've set up a NAT (Network Address Translator) and are using your own network addresses, you either know enough to skip this section entirely or are setting yourself up for a world of trouble and should call someone who will help you if you give them money.

The address is written as four numbers, each number in the range from 0 through 254, like this: 192.168.1.4. Not all numbers are possible addresses, but you don't need to worry about that because you're not handing them out.

Any network packets aimed specifically at your server will show your IP address as their *Destination IP*. Any packets coming from your server will show your IP address as their *Source IP*. The same holds true for packets to and from any other hosts whose traffic you can monitor from your server. You can tell your NIDS to be interested in specific Source and Destination IP addresses (either on their own or in combination). Those specs tell your NIDS which "conversations" between hosts to watch.

DYNAMIC ADDRESSES

An IP address configured permanently into a host[6] is called a *static* address. Many organizations have gone to a different system in which a host requests and is assigned an IP address from a pool of available addresses at boot time. (The Dynamic Host Configuration Protocol, or DHCP, facilitates this system of dynamic addresses.) This practice can complicate the configuration of a NIDS, because the IPs of the host or hosts that the NIDS is watching keep on changing.

DNS

Most people aren't very good at remembering quartets of numbers between 1 and 254 inclusive (though if you keep working with NIDS you'll get much better at it.) People prefer to remember names, such as "Jenny," "Fred," and "www.yahoo.com". The DNS (Domain Name System) is a way to associate IP addresses with names and to make the names on each DNS server on the Internet available to all the others. This way, each local organization can maintain the list of names of the hosts it has on the Internet.

When your host is given another host's name, it'll usually ask a DNS server to provide the corresponding IP address so that it can send data there. Note that this request, in itself, is a network transaction that takes place before the transaction you requested. If you have a program that displays IP information by name as well as number (many NIDS do – Snort does not), then frequent DNS requests may slow down the generation of the display. We recommend that you disable DNS lookups where possible in both application and system commands until you know for sure that you need them.

ROUTERS

In general, your communications (as packets) pass through a number of devices called *routers* or *gateways* to get from their source host to the destination host. A router basically passes packets from one network to another. Within a medium size organization, an internal communication usually passes through one to four of these devices. An external communication generally passes through 10-20 such routers.

We frequently refer to "your network" as opposed to "other networks." Advancing network technology has made the boundaries of your network a little

Play nice with the other admins in the sandbox!

You may have noticed that much of what you need to get on the network and what should stay there comes from your network administrator. In fact, one of the best time investments you can make is getting to know your netadmin and how she works. If you're serious about NIDS, keeping up with improvements and changes in the network that other people may not even notice is even more important. The netadmin has this information because she's the one who made it happen!

If something goes wrong, don't start insulting your netadmin's competence. You need to work with this person in order to get your job done. Remember that the netadmin probably thinks about you the way you think about your users.

fuzzier than they used to be, but we can still safely say that the border router marks a definite point beyond which you are outside any of your home networks.

A border router is the last thing between your site and the Internet. Now, routers generally have two or more network interfaces, each one part of a different network. If a packet can reach another host without going through your border router, that destination host is on your network. Some years ago, you could monitor any packet that came through the border router onto your network, even if it was destined for another host. On many networks with either old or inexpensive equipment, you still can.

Switched networks are increasingly common, however. On these networks, the only packets that reach your network interface are those that are specifically sent there. Traffic that is neither to nor from your host never goes by your interface. If you really want to know what is going on elsewhere on the network, your network administrator may be able to arrange a connection to a *spanning port*, a special device that allows an attached interface to monitor all the traffic to and from a set of hosts on the switch. For instance, if you detect hostile traffic on a subnet that appears to come from outside your network, but the traffic is not detected at the border router, then you have strong evidence that a compromised system inside your network is spoofing IP source addresses.

SUBNETS (CIDR NOTATION)

The term *subnet* gets fuzzy on a close look. A subnet is still a network. Calling it a subnet just means that you're thinking about it as part of a larger network. A network is usually broken into subnets with routers or switches, so the comments in the previous section, "Routers," apply to subnets.

You need to know two important things about a subnet:

◆ The range of IP addresses that can be on it.

◆ The IP address of the router that the hosts in the subnet need to use to communicate outside the subnet: This information is especially critical if one of those hosts is your server!

Subnet ranges are typically described by using CIDR notation. CIDR stands for "Classless Inter-Domain Routing." If CIDR notation describes a subnet as 192.168.249.42/23, it means that the IP range consists of all the addresses whose first 23 bits in binary representation match those of the binary representation of 192.168.249.42. The subnet, 192.168.249.42, is represented as follows in binary notation:

```
11000000 10101000 11111001 00101010
```

So any IP address with the same first 23 bits is part of the subnet. Then the address range is

```
11000000 10101000 11111000 00000000
```

through

```
11000000 10101000 11111001 11111111
```

or

```
192.168.248.0
```

through

```
192.168.249.255
```

Similarly, 192.168.249.42/29 denotes the range from 192.168.249.40 through 192.168.249.47.

Ports

Unique IP addresses are the framework that enables packets to be delivered to the right Internet host. Communication doesn't really take place between hosts, though, but between two processes that — in this case — run on different hosts. Delivering a packet to a host isn't enough; the packet must ultimately be delivered to a process that can make sense of it.

Any host process that communicates over the network is assigned a unique port number in the range 1-65535. Any packet delivered to the host with a Destination Port matching the process' port number is delivered to that process. Not surprisingly, any packet transmitted by that process uses that same port number as its Source Port.

Earlier, we mentioned the UDP and TCP delivery options. These options are so different that two processes can use the same port number as long as one is using TCP and the other is using UDP. In fact, TCP and UDP instances of the same port number are treated as two, distinct ports. The former are described as `<number>/tcp` and the latter as `<number>/udp`.

By convention, the port numbers from 1 to 1024 are permanently assigned to specific Internet services. For instance, the `sendmail` process is always assigned port 25/tcp, Web processes are found at port 80/tcp, DNS service processes at port 53/udp and 53/tcp (which one is used depends on just what you're requesting from DNS), and so forth.

PROCESSES, SOCKETS, AND BINDING

In the preceding section, we told you that the `sendmail` process is always assigned to port 25/tcp, meaning that the `sendmail` process must wait at port 25/tcp listening for incoming connections. To do so, sendmail issues a special command called `bind`. `bind` requests that port 25/tcp be associated with the sendmail process even though no connection is active. The process then enters the LISTENING state, a state in which it is prepared to accept connections, until a connection is initiated or the process releases the port and shuts down.

The Linux operating system, like other Unices, likes to treat everything as a file. To establish itself at a port, a process first requests a *socket* from Linux. A socket is, in essence, one side of a communications connection. Linux returns a file descriptor, which the process can use to access network communications as a file with some specialized configuration options. The process then calls `bind` to request that a specific port be associated with the socket.

·You can even monitor the presence of a process listening for a connection request from outside the host offering the service. When a host offers a service on port 25/tcp, port 25 is said to be *open*. Because this port is dedicated to `sendmail` by convention, `sendmail` is assumed to be the process listening at that port. If a connection actually occurs, `sendmail` normally sends a text string along the connection announcing its version and other pertinent information (sometimes, too much!).

You can learn much more from within the host. The command `netstat -apn` displays the status of all active sockets, including those that are in LISTENING state. The `-a` option causes netstat to include LISTENING ports, the `-p` option displays the PID (Process IDentifier) and name of the process bound to the socket and the `-n` option disables DNS name lookup (as we recommended earlier).

Following is a sample output excerpt of a `netstat -apn` call:

```
% netstat -apn | more
Active Internet connections (servers and established)
Proto Recv-Q Send-Q Local Address         Foreign Address
State        PID/Program name
tcp       0      0 0.0.0.0:32768         0.0.0.0:*
LISTEN       495/rpc.statd
tcp       0      0 0.0.0.0:514           0.0.0.0:*
LISTEN       619/xinetd
tcp       0      0 0.0.0.0:5666          0.0.0.0:*
LISTEN       619/xinetd
tcp       0      0 0.0.0.0:6019          0.0.0.0:*
```

```
LISTEN      2955/sshd
tcp      0      0 0.0.0.0:6020        0.0.0.0:*
LISTEN      31991/sshd
tcp      0      0 0.0.0.0:6021        0.0.0.0:*
LISTEN      13355/sshd
tcp      0      0 0.0.0.0:645         0.0.0.0:*
LISTEN      464/ypbind
tcp      0      0 0.0.0.0:111         0.0.0.0:*
LISTEN      449/portmap
tcp      0      0 0.0.0.0:21          0.0.0.0:*
LISTEN      619/xinetd
tcp      0      0 0.0.0.0:22          0.0.0.0:*
LISTEN      629/sshd
tcp      0      0 0.0.0.0:23          0.0.0.0:*
LISTEN      619/xinetd
tcp      0      0 0.0.0.0:6010        0.0.0.0:*
LISTEN      7840/sshd
tcp      0      0 0.0.0.0:6011        0.0.0.0:*
LISTEN      10507/sshd
tcp      0      0 0.0.0.0:6012        0.0.0.0:*
LISTEN      32054/sshd
tcp      0      0 0.0.0.0:6013        0.0.0.0:*
LISTEN      9281/sshd
tcp      0      0 0.0.0.0:6014        0.0.0.0:*
LISTEN      10437/sshd
tcp      0      0 0.0.0.0:6015        0.0.0.0:*
LISTEN      492/sshd
tcp      0      0 10.100.60.38:6011   10.100.60.38:54804
ESTABLISHED 10507/sshd
tcp      0      0 10.100.60.38:6011   10.100.60.38:54800
ESTABLISHED 10507/sshd
tcp      0      0 10.100.60.38:23     10.100.202.234:2253
ESTABLISHED 29887/in.telnetd: r
tcp      0     52 10.100.60.38:22     10.100.82.66:1030
ESTABLISHED 6338/sshd
tcp      0      0 10.100.60.38:22     10.100.99.81:50237
ESTABLISHED 10437/sshd
tcp      0      0 10.100.60.38:22     10.100.179.83:1511
ESTABLISHED 3015/sshd
tcp      0      0 10.100.60.38:23     10.100.100.220:2115
ESTABLISHED 4001/in.telnetd: ec
tcp      0      0 10.100.60.38:23     10.100.110.70:35857
ESTABLISHED 17750/in.telnetd: u
tcp      0      0 10.100.60.38:23     131.118.161.29:41387
ESTABLISHED 9512/in.telnetd: la
```

```
tcp         0      0 10.100.60.38:6020      10.100.60.38:47910
ESTABLISHED 31991/sshd
tcp         0      0 10.100.60.38:23        10.100.110.76:1034
ESTABLISHED 14735/in.telnetd: e
tcp         0      0 10.100.60.38:22        68.50.77.205:1082
ESTABLISHED 28390/sshd
```

Note that LISTENING processes are listed with IP 0.0.0.0. Some systems have several IP addresses. All systems have at least two, their assigned address and the "loopback" address 127.0.0.1. The IP 0.0.0.0 is interpreted as referring to *all* addresses of a system. Thus, for instance, there is an sshd process listening on port 22/tcp at both 10.100.60.38 and 127.0.0.1 (and at any other addresses the system might be assigned).

LSOF

Another utility, lsof, displays even more information. In general, lsof <file-name> displays the processes that are currently accessing the given file. The -i option restricts the display to processes associated with sockets. You have to run lsof as root to get all this information:

```
% lsof -i tcp | more
COMMAND     PID USER FD    TYPE   DEVICE SIZE NODE NAME
sshd       7313 root  4u IPv4 64526277      TCP me.my.org:ssh->ppp-
199.dialup.com:1975 (ESTABLISHED)
xinetd     7334 root  3u IPv4     2590      TCP *:ftp (LISTEN)
xinetd     7334 root  4u IPv4     2591      TCP *:nrpe (LISTEN)
xinetd     7334 root  7u IPv4     2593      TCP *:shell (LISTEN)
xinetd     7334 root  9u IPv4     2595      TCP *:telnet (LISTEN)
xinetd     7334 root 10u IPv4 64526304      TCP me.my.org:ftp->ppp-
191.dialup.com:2501 (ESTABLISHED)
xinetd     7334 root 11u IPv4 64526305      TCP m.my.org:54740-
>ftp.my.org:ftp (ESTABLISHED)
in.telnet 7475 root  0u IPv4 63969514      TCP m.my.org:telnet-
>pc.cb.net:1964 (ESTABLISHED)
in.telnet 7475 root  1u IPv4 63969514      TCP m.my.org:telnet-
>pc.cb.net:1964 (ESTABLISHED)
in.telnet 7475 root  2u IPv4 63969514      TCP m.my.org:telnet-
>pc.cb.net:1964 (ESTABLISHED)
sshd       7840 root  4u IPv4 63970291      TCP m.my.org:ssh-
>pc.nasa.gov:37606 (ESTABLISHED)
```

The output of lsof displays each socket as a file, including the name of the process using that socket, the process id of that process, and the owner of that process. This can be very useful in tracking down the origin and originator of a network connection that you aren't expecting to see and can't easily explain.

ICMP

ICMP (Internet Control Message Protocol) consists of packets representing a relatively small number of network management and control messages. Many of the messages tell you that something isn't going to work and why. For instance, if you send a packet to a system that's non-existent, the router on the subnet where it would be may send you a type 3 (Destination Unreachable), code 1 (Host Unreachable) ICMP packet.

The most widely recognized implementation of ICMP is the `ping` command, which sends a type 8 (Echo Request) ICMP message and receives (or doesn't receive) a type 0 (Echo Reply) ICMP message in response.

UDP

Recall that UDP (User Datagram Protocol) supports connectionless communication in the TCP/IP protocol suite. You often use UDP for communications that you wouldn't normally expect to pass through many (if any) routers. In other words, you use UDP for services, such as NFS, that you expect to find on your local network servers.

Because UDP is connectionless, its packet header is relatively simple. For our purposes here, assume that it carries only the source and destination IP addresses and the source and destination ports.

TCP

TCP is the connection-oriented side of TCP/IP. The packet header carries a good deal of information that the TCP/IP protocol uses to make sure that each packet arrives successfully and that the communication is successfully reconstructed from the bits carried in the packets. TCP helps make sure that all the packets are reconstructed in the proper order, even if they didn't arrive in such. (Since two packets can take a different path through the Internet, they can easily arrive out of order.) TCP also makes sure that the packet data's integrity has been preserved and that each and every packet in a communication arrives properly. It can, and does, even request that particular packets in a session be resent. These procedures, ensuring that data is properly delivered, are characteristic of a "connection-oriented" protocol. In fact, TCP connections start with the exchange of some dataless packets with nothing but headers simply to establish the communication and agree to necessary parameters.

Not surprisingly, you use TCP in applications that are normally expected to communicate over long (in network terms) distances, such as ftp and SSH.

TCP is a *stateful* protocol. With UDP, you send a packet and that's that. The protocol keeps no record of the transmission because a connectionless protocol isn't worried about whether or not the packet arrives. When TCP sends a packet, it needs to know whether the packet arrived at the other end. Thus, TCP must remember that the packet went out so that the packet can be checked off after its receipt has been acknowledged.

Such a memory is called the *state*. In this case, after sending the packet, TCP enters an "awaiting receipt" state. After confirming safe arrival, TCP enters a "not awaiting receipt" state. In fact, TCP has multiple states that it uses to fine-tune the reliable transmission of data.

SYN, ACK, FIN

You want to watch the *flag bits* – bits that are set or unset to help maintain the state of both ends of the communication – in TCP headers. Flag bits are defined by their position in the header. This section looks at the SYN, ACK, and FIN flags.

The SYN flag is set in a packet that initiates a communications session. The SYN flag means roughly "I would like to talk to you." The ACK flag is set to show that a packet contains information that acknowledges receipt of a previous packet. Take it to mean: "I heard you."

To start a session, host A sends a packet consisting only of headers to host B. Only the SYN bit will be set. Host B then sends a packet to host A that serves two functions (called *piggybacking*). This packet confirms receipt of the first packet and so has its ACK bit set. It also signals to A that it's ready to start up its end of a conversation by setting the SYN bit as well.

On receiving this packet, host A sends a packet to host B acknowledging receipt and having the ACK bit set. Note that the SYN bit is not set in this third packet. Both hosts have already indicated that they want to talk and don't need to do so again.

 This exchange of SYN, SYN-ACK, and ACK packets is called the *triple handshake* or *three-way handshake of the TCP connection*.

When host A has nothing more to say, it sends a packet to host B with the FIN bit set. An ACK bit is set as well to acknowledge the last packet received. Host B acknowledges with an ACK packet. TCP recognizes that host A may be finished talking, but host B may still have more to say. The connection at this point is called *half-closed* and stays that way until host B sends a FIN-ACK packet to host A, and host A responds with an ACK packet.

We offered these procedures to illustrate some aspects of TCP communication, and to give you something to tell the NIDS to find.

SEQ/ACK NUMBERS

Sequence (SEQ) and Acknowledgement (ACK) numbering can get pretty hairy. Put simply, host A makes sure that its packets get to host B by numbering them sequentially. When host B gets a packet, the actual proof of receipt (whose presence is indicated by the ACK bit) is the *acknowledgment number* – the packet's sequence number plus one. So, in host B's next packet, the host sets the acknowledgement number to the last packet it received.

Host B is doing the same thing with the packets it sends. Each side of the communication chooses its initial sequence number independently, so host B normally starts with different sequence numbers than host A. Well-implemented communications protocols use the most random numbers available for their initial sequence numbers.

Probes and threats

Now that we have some grounding in the principles of the TCP/IP protocol suite, we will look at some of the ways that an attacker can use those principles. Broadly speaking, hostile actions can be classified as either *probes* or *threats*.

A probe refers to an attempt to learn more about your system without doing any damage to it. In fact, most probes try to have as little effect as possible in order to avoid detection. A threat is anything with the potential to compromise or damage your system.

SYN AND SYNFIN PROBES

SYN probes are very common. They exploit the triple-handshake protocol. Remember that host A sends a SYN packet and host B responds with a SYN-ACK packet? Suppose that host A doesn't complete the handshake at that point. Eventually host B will time out and go back to waiting for the next SYN packet. Host A, however, has learned that the port on host B where the SYN packet went to is open.

If host A sends a SYN packet to each of the ports below 1024, it will catalog the common services that host B is offering. Host A gets this data from the way in which host B replies. Rather than complete the handshake, though, host A sends a packet with the "reset" flag activated to kill the connection. During this process, the originating host is collecting a good sample of initial sequence numbers and can determine how random they are. Because none of the triple-handshakes are ever completed, most of the services on host B never log a connection from host A.

A SYNFIN probe takes advantage of a deeper loophole in the established TCP protocol. The protocol as originally conceived and established never considered the possibility of "impossible" flag bit combinations. A packet that has both a SYN bit ("I want to initiate a communications session") and a FIN bit ("I want to close this communications session") set is meaningless. Since no standard method for dealing with meaningless packets exists, the way that host B responds on receiving them depends on how the networking part of that particular operating system was written. One thing that most – if not all – Unices have in common is that open ports respond to SYNFIN packets differently than closed ports. The way that host B responds says a great deal about the operating system, possibly even its release number and patch level, as well as which ports are open.

DOS ATTACKS

A DoS (Denial of Service) attack is not in itself an attempt to break in to your host, but rather, an attempt to render some service your host offers unavailable.

Sometimes a DoS attack crashes the host itself. The simplest DoS attacks are "flood" attacks, which create more traffic than the service – or that entire host – can handle. "Mail bombing" a mailserver is an example.

SYN flooding is a slightly more sophisticated DoS flood attack. In the preceding section we described how you can use SYN packets to probe the open ports on a system without establishing a connection. (The target ports would respond with a SYN-ACK packet and then eventually time out and stop waiting for the final ACK.) Now suppose host A sends thousands of SYN packets to host B, and keeps on sending them in waves. Eventually, all of host B's networking resources will be tied up waiting for final ACK packets, and host B will be effectively isolated from the Internet – though there won't be any actual connections.

We talk about another type of DoS attack in the section, "Buffer Overflow Attacks."

EXPLOIT ATTACKS

People, not machines, write code – even Linux is written by humans. Humans have this annoying trait of being inconsistent and occasionally making mistakes in design or implementation, the unfortunate price of creative, organic brains. When someone else can manipulate one of these mistakes to cause the system to do something not intended by the code's author or the system's owner, you have a security vulnerability.

Here's just one example of a design bug. Some early versions of `sendmail` had a `wizard` command. If you connected to `sendmail` through the mail port (`25/tcp`) and typed WIZ, `sendmail` would respond, "Pass, O Mighty Wizard" and give you root access. Although the WIZ feature initiated a simple debugging mode, it sure as heck wasn't a good idea. Knowledge of the word WIZ wasn't hard to come by, especially because anyone could read the source code to `sendmail`. Suffice to say that modern versions of `sendmail` no longer offer this feature.

BUFFER OVERFLOW ATTACKS

When you type a small amount of information into a program, the program often temporarily stores the information in memory. For instance, when you log in to a host, the login program stores your userid at least until you type in your password for authentication. So, a program uses memory other than what is needed to store its code and initial data. No real shock, right?

But how much memory does it need for new information? Your userid may be only 8 bytes long, your password almost certainly less than 15 bytes. A carefully written login may allocate, say, 30 bytes of memory for each in order to make sure that you have enough room. What happens if you type a 31-byte string in for the userid? Well-written code counts the bytes as they're stored in memory and refuses to accept that last byte until the buffer has been cleared. An amazing amount of code is not well written.

When you enter more data into a program than it has allocated memory, and the program keeps accepting it, the data starts to overwrite other areas of memory. This trespass beyond the limits of allocated data storage is called a *buffer overflow*. If the program accepting the data is running under root, then it can overwrite any part of memory. A simple buffer overflow can overwrite the operating system, crashing or hanging the entire system. A sophisticated buffer overflow has just the right data to replace part of the operating system and allow an attacker to take over as root. The former case is a type of DoS attack; the latter is a successful exploit.

APPLICATION-BASED ATTACKS

So far we haven't considered the data that these packets are delivering. That's why we have the packets, after all. The data may be a message going to the mail server, or a URL going to a Web server, or almost anything going to a network application.

The `httpd` and `sshd` daemons are subject to exploit attacks, the same as the network communications software.

A badly configured Web server will allow a URL with lots of `../../..` entries to access directories above the `wwwroot` www root until it finds `../../etc/passwd`. Recently, a subtle buffer overflow exploit of `sshd` was discovered. Almost immediately, root exploits for Linux became available. Linux users are still recovering from that one.

You can't detect these attacks by looking at packet headers, because the attacks themselves are in the data that the packets deliver.

Devising a Defensive Network Configuration

Before setting up a NIDS, you need to know how the network is configured. This section looks at some of the strategies you can use to set up a relatively secure network.

Router filtering and firewalls

You know that routers are the "gates" to the network. Many routers allow you to block certain types of packets from entering or leaving the network. For instance, if you know that a specific host has been causing trouble, you can tell the router to refuse to pass any packet with that host's source IP. If only one host needs protection, the router can stop packets with the source IP of the bad host and the destination IP of the host needing protection. If you want to protect certain services, you can block specific destination ports.

A *firewall* is a device designed to allow and block packets according to a more complex set of rules than a router can handle quickly. A sophisticated firewall can even block SYN probes and floods by preserving state. For instance, the firewall can negotiate a connection to a host outside the network on behalf of a host inside the network, negotiate another connection with the internal host, and then simply pipe data between the two connections. Of course, the firewall still gets hit with the SYN flood attack, but now you only have to put extraordinary resources in the firewall, rather than in all your servers.

Ingress/egress filtering

We're imploring you to put these two rules on your router, your firewall, or whatever you have at the edge of your network. Suppose your network consists of all IP addresses of the form `10.20.400.xxx`, or `10.20.400.1/24`.

   ◆ **Rule 1:** On the outside, block all incoming packets with IP in the range `10.20.400/24`. This is your *ingress filter*.

   ◆ **Rule 2:** On the inside, block all outgoing packets with IP not in the range `10.20.400/24`. This is your *egress filter*.

Ingress filters protect you from packets that pretend to come from hosts inside your network but actually come from the outside. Egress filters protect everyone else from packets that any of your hosts may send pretending to be from someone else's network.

The value of ingress filtering is obvious. The value of egress filtering becomes obvious when `men.in.black.mil` painstakingly traces the NFS exploit through various ISP's back to your network, and General Warbutton calls up at three a.m. asking for an explanation and your spleen on a stick, not in that order. Trust us. Put the egress filter in, too.

DMZ

This term has gotten a little fuzzy. It actually stands for "De-Militarized Zone". In our context, it usually refers to a part of your network between the router and the firewall, or between two firewalls. The idea is that most of your network is behind the firewall, protected from or even inaccessible to the outside world. You interact through a few very well-secured hosts between the router and the firewall (in the DMZ), which are the only systems allowed to communicate freely with those behind the firewall.

Bastion Hosts

Bastion Hosts go along with the idea of a DMZ. If you want to provide a secure Web server, then one strategy is to configure a host that offers nothing but Web service and in which you invest considerable effort in patching and hardening. That server becomes your Bastion Web Host and will probably sit in the DMZ. Bastion Hosts aren't a bad strategy, even without a DMZ.

Dedicated servers

Establishing dedicated servers is a management as well as a security strategy. The idea is that your ftp servers offer nothing but ftp, your login servers offer nothing but SSH, your mailservers run nothing but `sendmail`, and so forth.

From a management point of view, if you get an ftp patch, you know exactly which hosts need to get it. You also don't worry about the patch's interaction with, say, `httpd`.

From a security point of view, you know which hosts may be vulnerable to an ftp exploit. More importantly, you know which servers can't possibly be vulnerable to an ftp exploit, because they aren't running ftp unless they're part of your ftp server group. Moreover, you can configure your router or firewall to refuse to pass packets when the destination IP belongs to a host that isn't offering the service that goes with the destination port. In other words, if the destination IP belongs to a mailserver, there's no reason to pass a packet to that server's port 21 (ftp).

Of course, blocking packets to ports that you know won't be open anyway — the "*belt-and-suspenders*" approach — may seem redundant. It is. You never really know how many precautions to take in this world. Would you rather take too many or too few?

Now we have designed defenses to secure our systems. In the next section, we will install a "burglar alarm" in case, in spite of our best efforts, those defenses are breached.

Designing an ID Strategy

Okay, the hosts are allocated to their services, the bastions are hardened, and the firewall rules are in place. Now you're ready to set up the NIDS. Remember "Defining the Scope of Responsibility" earlier in this chapter?

Ask the question again: What are you actually responsible for? Whether it's a subnet, a specific host, or even a particular service at a particular port on a particular host, you want to keep your security plans focused on what you're expected to protect.

An NIDS watching a host can be on that host or somewhere else as long as it can see all traffic to and from the host. Locating the NIDS on the host to be guarded is the simplest approach,, and it ensures that the NIDS sees all appropriate traffic.

Locating the NIDS in a different host, however, offers the following advantages:

◆ Whatever processing is associated with operating the NIDS won't impact the host that you're trying to protect. Otherwise, a flood of strange packets may make your NIDS go wild crunching statistics, making pie charts, and so on. Eventually the host you're guarding can't do anything but watch packets go by — something to keep in mind if you use a busy NIDS.

◆ If the system you're guarding is compromised and the NIDS is on it, then the NIDS may get shut down or, even worse, modified to generate only "happy" reports.

In general, we feel that the best place for a NIDS is just inside the innermost router or firewall with respect to whatever you're guarding. If you only have one

NIDS, it should be watching whatever makes it through the nearest gate. If you have two NIDS, or one with two sensors, consider watching just outside the same gate to see the traffic that arrives and leaves. That way you know what people are trying to do and whether the gate continues to do its job correctly.

Obviously, you watch all traffic to and from any host you need to protect, which is where the scope of responsibility comes in. Your scope of monitoring, on the other hand, should really include just about everything that it can. A SYN packet at your port 21/tcp may be a mistake. A SYN packet at every port 21 on the network (even to hosts that don't exist) is a hostile probe.

Also, even if you aren't responsible for every system on the network, you certainly want to know whether one of them looks compromised. That system may then start watching *your* traffic. After you decide where the NIDS will go, you need to decide what it's going to look for.

Setting the Rules

This section discusses the following factors that you should keep in mind:

- ◆ Intrusion detectors don't detect intrusions
- ◆ Positive specifications – things that are bad
- ◆ Negative specifications – things that are not good
- ◆ Heuristic anomaly detection – The Holy Grail

Intrusion detectors don't detect intrusions

Yeah, we said this already. We're saying it again. It's important. Intrusion detection was probably just the best term that the vendors could agree on or the simplest that customers could understand. At best, IDS detect attacks, rather than successful intrusions. At worst, IDS detect traffic thought to be related to an attack. Most IDS just check packet data and headers against a block of "signatures" of known attacks and report matches. Always keep this fact in mind when reading your IDS output.

Positive specifications – things that are bad

You know that some packets are trouble. Any TCP packet with SYN and FIN set is bad news. If a SYN packet contains data, something is rotten in Netland. SSH packets with /bin/sh or known binary shellcode in the data are usually looking to overflow buffers. (On the false positive side, there is some random chance that the encrypted data stream will look like shellcode.)

So, positive specifications work in this way: When you're looking at a line of people for one who seems suspicious, start by comparing them to wanted posters. Anyone wanted for felonies in six or more states looks suspicious by definition.

Negative specifications — things that are not good

You've accounted for the easy stuff; the stuff you know is bad. Now you get creative and think about things that may be okay in general but have no place on your network:

- Is your host offering telnet? If not, then don't allow any packet to port 23/tcp on your host.

- Is your firewall blocking access to port 25/tcp except at the mailserver? Then anything directed to that port on any other system indicates a problem.

- Do you encourage people to trade warez and MP3s with their buds from your NFS server? No? Then what's all that traffic between that server and port 6667 on irc.copyright.violation.net?

- Are you a completely Linux-based organization? Why, then, do you have so much NetBIOS (Windows filesharing, and so on) traffic?

These are negative specifications. To find them, you create a detailed picture of what's supposed to be happening on this network and then start looking for everything else.

Heuristic anomaly detection — The Holy Grail

We've already said that you should watch your network for things that shouldn't be there. Some things, though, only become obvious over time. Like Uncle Floyd, who always logs off at 4:30 p.m. on Tuesdays so he can hit the "double wings and an extra roll for $1.59 deal" before it's over at 5:00. You don't have any way to recognize this pattern until you've been watching the network closely for a long time.

"So gee," you're thinking, "if I could write a NIDS that saw these patterns and then created new rules to watch for sudden changes, people would think I'm clever and get excited!" Well, the idea isn't bad, but only one package is known to make this idea work effectively in almost any environment, and you carry it behind your eyes and between your ears. Use that package! Watch the network traffic occasionally. See how it tallies with your system logs. Get used to the patterns and, if possible, figure out ways for your NIDS to monitor them and tell you when they change.

By the way, if you do manage to automate this whole thing and need an agent, we're available.

In the next section, we will take a look at a do-it-yourself NIDS built around *Snort.*

Our Example NIDS – Snort

Snort is as flexible, as simple, and as versatile as you care to make it. It's small in memory requirements and in processing impact. It's free. Can't beat that with a stick.

If you like building from source, go to: `www.snort.org/dl` for the latest version.

Description and History (current version: 1.8.6)

Snort snuffled onto the world scene through a paper presented at LISA (Large Installation System Administration) in November 1999. Marty Roesch had responded to the need for a NIDS more useful than `tcpdump`, but smaller and cheaper than anything else. Since then, Snort has grown increasingly flexible without gaining much overhead in installation, configuration, and operation. Although Snort has a wide array of features, you can use it in its simplest configurations after perusing the README file for a few minutes. Marty went on to found a company, called Sourcefire, to develop and sell high-end solutions around Snort. Although most of us can easily use Snort as it is, a large enterprise's needs are definitely different; commercial companies, such as Sourcefire, meet those needs.

Overview of Snort Function (selected command-line options)

Snort has an impressive array of command-line options. We'll look at the ones you really need to use to get Snort up and running for you.

Snort can watch packets at a network interface or it can read them from a raw dump file. You want it to watch the network. The command-line option `-i <interface>` directs Snort to capture packets from the indicated interface device. For you, this interface is probably `eth0`. If you aren't sure, the command `netstat -in` lists your interface devices.

You can send Snort output to a logging directory. By default, Snort tries to organize packet data in a structure of subdirectories in the logging directory, in which the subdirectories are IP addresses and contain file names after source ports, destination ports, and protocols. Unless you're running Snort on a honeypot, in which case you probably want the level of detail afforded by this subdirectory structure, suppress this behavior with the `-N` option.

Snort's processing can also produce alerts based on specific evaluation rules that you specify, which is what you want to do in your NIDS. By default, alerts go into a file in the logging directory. By further default, that directory is `/var/log/snort`. The `-l <logdir>` option directs logs to directory `logdir`. The `-s` option directs alerts to `/var/log/secure`.

One or more files contain the rules used in processing. You can use an instruction within a "root" rules file to include other rules files, making the rules easy to organize into separate files. The command line argument `-c <rulesfile>` directs Snort to the "root" rules file.

We recommend that Snort run on a directory structure with a "root" directory containing the following subdirectories:

- ◆ `./logs`: Containing alerts in a file `alert`,

- ◆ `./rules`: Containing the all rules files, including the `root` file,

and the file

- ◆ `Snort_Command`: Containing the full command line you use to run Snort on your system.

The command

```
snort -i eth0 -N -l ./logs -c ./rules/rules_root
```

starts Snort sniffing at `eth0`, using rules in the `./rules` directory and logging to the file named `alert` in the `./logs` directory.

If you want a full listing of command-line options, type **snort –h**.

PROCESSING: RULES AND MORE RULES

There is an excellent tutorial on Snort rules at `www.snort.org/docs/writing_rules`. The actual document is titled "Snort User's Manual." We won't try to improve on it here, but we will go over a few simple rules, modified from the rules in the Snort distribution, to get you started writing your own.

Here's an example:

```
alert tcp $EXTERNAL_NET any -> $HOME_NET any (msg:"SCAN SYN
FIN";flags:SF;)
```

This rule generates an alert on detecting a SYNFIN packet. You define the variables $EXTERNAL_NET and $HOME_NET in the `rules` files by using CIDR notation.

The first keyword indicates that this rule is an *alert* rule, which is the simplest type of rule for your configuration. The second field indicates the protocol you're interested in. Then you have a statement of the form:

```
<source ip> <source port> -> <destination ip> <destination port>
```

An alternate form triggers an alert for a packet going in either direction:

```
< ip> < port> <> < ip> < port>
```

The rest of the rule (in parentheses) follows the format:

```
option:argument;[option:argument;]
```

The option `msg` sets the message that will appear in the `alert` file when this rule is triggered. (The message will accompany a time stamp, source and destination IP and ports, and other information about the packet.)

The option `flags` specifies that the alert be triggered for packets with only the SYN and FIN flags set.

Note one more thing in that signature rule: the `$HOME_NET` and `$EXTERNAL_NET` variables. Snort, along with any other NIDS, works best when tailored at least a little bit to your environment. Setting these variables in Snort's configuration file will help you detect attacks against you and ignore false positives, such as data from your own DNS servers.

Here's an example:

```
alert ip $EXTERNAL_NET any -> $HOME_NET any (msg:"SHELLCODE linux shellcode";
content:"|90 90 90 e8 c0 ff ff ff|/bin/sh";)
```

The `content` option in this rule looks at the data that a packet carries to see whether it matches the argument string. The numbers between the vertical bars are hexadecimal numbers, each pair of which represents a data byte. The `/bin/sh` is intended as literal text. This rule is searching for a match to a known Linux root exploit. Notice also that an IP packet, which includes both TCP and UDP, triggers this rule .

Now you're ready to try one for your network. Suppose you're running ftp on `10.20.400.15` and nowhere else. You shouldn't have any ftp traffic other than to and from that server, so you can add the following rule:

```
alert tcp any any -> !10.20.400.15 21 (msg:"Suspicious FTP packet";)
```

We slipped one in here. Notice the `!` before the FTP server's IP address. This specifies "any IP that is NOT 10.20.400.15." The "!" symbol is very handy for the negative specs we discussed earlier. If the FTP server is dedicated (serving only FTP), you can also add the following:

```
alert tcp any any -> 10.20.400.15 !21 (msg:"Possible probe of FTP
server";)
```

Again, remember the benefits of the simplicity. Single-purpose machines make intrusion/attack detection that much easier!

PLUG-INS: PRE- AND POST-PROCESSING (EXAMPLE: PORTSCAN)

Snort is designed to accept pre-programmed plug-ins that process packet information going into Snort or coming out of it. You specify them in the rules files, along with most other things Snortish; their invocation is described in the file `snort.conf` that comes in the Snort distribution.

We recommend the portscan plug-in in particular. It simply identifies certain types of packets going to multiple ports in a short time (you can define how many packets and how short a time) and logs what it detects in a file that you specify. You may want to put that file in the `./logs` directory, or create a separate `./scans` directory. Neatness counts.

Summary

In this chapter, we considered NIDS as an integrated part of an overall defense strategy. Before NIDS was even considered, we examined the isolation of services on dedicated hosts, the configuration of firewalls, and the use of bastion hosts in a DMZ. The NIDS was then considered in terms of its scope in the network design, which helped to determine its location. Both scope and location came into play in determining the rules used by the NIDS in monitoring the network traffic. You will not get the full benefit of a NIDS, a firewall, or any other network security device if you treat it as a "magic box" that will solve all of your problems. You will get the most mileage out of all the separate components of your security plan if each one augments the function of the others.

We've walked — well, skipped lightly — through the process of designing a security strategy to include a NIDS. Part of the goal was to introduce you to Snort so that you can find out for yourself what kinds of threats and probes are carried over your network every day. The other goal was to get you to think about security as a design of interlocking parts, network access controls, dedicated server hosts, and NIDS. We'd like to say that your having fun was also a goal, but if you are having fun, it's because you've put this book down and are configuring your NIDS already, not because you're reading this. So, go enjoy Snort!

Chapter 19

Log Monitoring and Incident Response

IN THIS CHAPTER

◆ Reading your system logs

◆ Logging

◆ Performing selector actions

◆ Using logs

◆ Managing event responses

THIS CHAPTER LOOKS AT LOGGING, particularly system logging. We'll discuss the ways that you can configure logging to best collect the information you need, and we'll suggest some relatively painless ways to extract that same information later.

While logging follows patching as the second most boring area of host security, it's also quite important. Your logs are often your first, and sometimes only, sign of an intrusion. The critical hacker-catching logs might come from your system, your router, your firewall, your IDS, or any combination of those. This means that it's critically important that you get and read or skim logs on all of these.

Reading Your System Logs

People are attracted to Unix system administration for various reasons. For some, it's the satisfaction of making a complex system work in coordination with other such systems and with the needs of the users. For others, it's the delusion of divine power coming from the exercise of root privileges. Of course, there's also something to be said for a job in which your supervisor probably can't tell what you are doing, or even whether or not you're working at all. Rarely, though, does anyone suggest that she became a sysadmin out of a desire to review logs daily. Novice sysadmins will agree that they should review logs much as they agree that they should visit the dentist. The task has to be done and they'll do it Real Soon Now. . . .

In a day full of urgent requests involving researching this or reconfiguring that, reviewing logs can seem to be, at best, a pointless indulgence. Fight that feeling. Your logs are often your best and only friends. Think about it. System and application logs are where your server records what it's doing and what is happening to it. If a user logs in after a two-week vacation only to find his NFS-mounted home directory gone, you can try to find and remount it. If you'd looked at the logs of the NFS server and client before, though, you would probably have known not only when the filesystem first dismounted (or failed to mount), but also why it did so and how to keep it from doing that again.

You can use logs to infer things that are happening elsewhere, too. Say you're running a Web server for your own business, and you rolled out a big promotional campaign last week. The promotion details are on a page called `big_promo.html` on your server. The counter you put on this page has reported about 100 hits a day. That number isn't bad, but if your frozen-potato-on-a-stick snack idea is going to take off, you need more exposure.

If you were watching your Web logs, you would've seen the thousands of 404 records reporting failed requests for the page `big_promo.html` and realized that an important hyperlink to your page was messed up somewhere. A simple fix, and by now you could've shipped so many potatoes that the fast food sellers would have to ask, "You want Brussels sprouts with that?"

Looking at your logs may appear boring, but doing so can save you a great deal of future work. Fixing a problem right at the start is always easier than scrambling two weeks later, when things have blown up, people are breathing down your neck for a solution, and you're desperately trying to leave for the weekend. Remember the Principle of Enlightened Self-Interest: It is better to take care of things proactively, *before* they turn into problems, while they are still minor and easy to vanquish. Doing so will not only make your life easier, but will help other admins who work with you. You will therefore have made life better for all, improved your karma, and come out looking like a hero. Bottom line: reading your logs more often than you visit the dentist is clearly a good idea.

Logging

So, now that we all agree that logging is important, we need to figure out what "logging" really means.

Well, *logging* is the process of information gathering and storage. You can use several methods to get information about and from your system. Very much like people, systems will happily chatter on forever to anyone who shows even the slightest interest. Of course the world does harbor some very Bad People, and your poor defenseless systems shouldn't talk to them, but we'll find out more about that later.

For the purpose of this discussion, you can divide logging into three different categories:

◆ Application logging

◆ System logging

◆ Hybrid logging

You're almost certainly going to have to configure and maintain logs from each category at one time or another, so we're going to touch on all three.

Application logging

Now, most Unix apps and services are specifically designed to give you as much information as you want (and probably even more). Just give the high sign, and they're ready and willing to babble. The upside to application logging is that it can give you a very detailed picture of an application's state at any given time. This is also the downside.

"Wait a second!" you say. "What's wrong with huge amounts of detail?" Well, we'll let you in on a trade secret (no secret decoder ring required): Too much *undifferentiated* information can be as bad as too little highly specific information. In other words, if you've got loads — say, multiple Gigs worth — of plaintext log data, you just aren't going to be able to sift through it all (at least, not by hand). Even automated tools take a long time to crunch that much input. It'd be like looking for a particular needle in a needle factory! The trick is to weed out the useless "cruft" before the machine stores it.

The good news is that trimming down what you're logging isn't too difficult. The bad news is that:

◆ **Toning down the logging level sometimes causes you to lose events that you really needed to know about:** For example, ssh lets you set the logging verbosity so high that you can track when a remote user sneezes. Most people don't want nor need nearly this much information. Lower the level too much, though, and you'll only get messages such as `sshd started`, `sshd restarted`, and maybe a few others. This chary reporting is probably a bit too tight-lipped.

◆ **Becoming familiar enough with the application to know what sort of log messages and log volume is normal for that particular application takes time.**

◆ **Reducing applies to everything:** You have to go through the reduction process for every app, service, or other log generator, so expect a learning curve with every new application or service you deploy. (Sometimes even new versions of the same application will change enough that you have to start from scratch).

Open Source and freeware applications usually allow you to specify where you want to store output logs. Occasionally you'll have to actually compile the value in, so be sure to know where you plan to keep logs of various types.

One of the best-known — but sometimes forgotten — application log types is the Web server log. A well-configured Web log can, whatever the server type is, record scads of information about incoming requests: originating IP, request type, success/failure, timestamp, and so on.

System logging

Application logs are great for telling you about the generating application's state, but are pretty much blind to what's going on elsewhere in or on the system. The kind of nitty-gritty view you want now comes from system logging. The most obvious place to start is with the big process at the top of the food chain: the kernel. The kernel has the power; it *is* the technology — you just have to figure out how much of the truth you can handle. True to the philosophy of Unix, though, the kernel doesn't do all the work. Instead, it hands off status observations and error messages to a distinct logging process.

Every Unix system ships with some form of the original BSD logger, `syslog`, a friendly little program that takes incoming status messages, massages them into a standardized format, and drops them into the system log file. `syslog` is so friendly because it'll take input from pretty much any process on the system. You can write an app that sends messages to the system logger, and it'll accept them happily.

Have you noticed how everything good seems to have a dark side, too? Having one process act as the gateway for all this information is undeniably convenient. Trouble is, if the gateway process isn't choosy, then you may end up with nicely formatted trash instead of useful data.

If a bad guy knows that you're running vanilla `syslog`, he knows that he can get hordes of messages sent to it (whether by writing a program to generate them or tickling other processes to make them spew). You can bet that in the resulting message storm a single line about naughty activity will either go unnoticed or won't get permanently logged at all ("`syslog is currently busy; please try again, later`").

Of course, intelligent versions of `syslog` aggregate output messages, so if your log shows something like the following:

```
May 11 13:57:31 last message repeated 4 times
```

Then you know that you should check the previous log entry to see what's happened five times now. This kind of aggregation simplifies the logs and helps defeat the cracker's scatter-chaff distraction.

In an effort to produce something a little more robust and secure, the developer community created `syslog-ng`, `nsyslog`, `msyslog`, `mtsyslog`, and many other friends. For a complete list, go to `www.counterpane.com/log-analysis.html #replacements`.

Unfortunately, we only really have space to discuss one system-logging program, so we're going to go with the one bundled in standard with Red Hat. The daemon is called **syslogd**, but don't be fooled — it's more! The logging subsystem is more correctly called `sysklogd` and actually combines the functionality of the standard-model system logger `syslogd` with the low-level kernel logger `klogd`.

But before diving into the drowning pool of `syslog`, we need to talk about the third category of logging.

Hybrid logging

There's no real industry-standard term for this kind of logging, but we call it "hybrid logging" because these apps can log to the system log, their own logs, or both. Writing a message to multiple files, probably by different mechanisms, obviously "costs" more, so you're probably wondering where the advantage is.

Well, take the belt-and-suspenders approach—keep redundant logs because you never know when one may be corrupted, deleted, or otherwise tampered with. Of course, if one log is missing incriminating evidence and the other isn't, you may start to wonder whether something funky is happening.

Related, but separate, is the concept of simplicity. Having everything go to the system log is a good idea for putting events into their proper context, but isolating only the messages from a specific app becomes harder. With hybrid logging, you can tell the app to log to the system log and to its own application log. The simplicity comes from being able to check whichever log has the type of information that you want.

Of course, you can always set up your own in-house scripts or programs to use `syslog` and/or a private logging scheme. Just check the local `man` or `info` pages for the syntax and pertinent numeric codes.

One of the better-known, hybrid-enabled software packages is `sudo`. If you don't already know and use `sudo`, here's a little info about it:

"Sudo (superuser do) allows a system administrator to give certain users (or groups of users) the ability to run some (or all) commands as root or another user while logging the commands and arguments." See `www.courtesan.com/sudo/index.html`.

Snort is another favorite that takes the hybrid approach. It has a pretty involved logging system of its own, but is happy to use whatever system logger you point it at (exclusively or in tandem). Snort is also an interesting example because the logs changed format from version 1.7 to 1.8. Nicely, though, you can set a backwards-compatibility flag to get the log format with which you may already be familiar. This backwards compatibility offers you a smooth transition, but many other software writers pull a paradigm shift without a clutch, so watch out!

 See Chapter 18 for a discussion of Snort.

Syslog

So, we promised to tell you more about syslog. By now, hopefully, you're wondering how syslog works behind all the smoke and mirrors—especially since we're going to tell you anyway. Syslog uses your basic client-server architecture; syslogd hangs out in the process table until some process steps up for attention. syslogd is obviously the server, so all the other processes — some of them daemons in their own right — are the clients in this transaction. That client and server can run on the same system — heck, the X Windows system has been doing it for years! — is important to grok.

The `syslog` program handles message processing differently than many other servers do. Think of `syslog` less like a trapdoor — where the first matching rule drops you out of processing — and more like a gauntlet, where you get hit by every matching rule, not just the first one. With a sufficiently complex configuration file — `/etc/syslog.conf` — you can store a log message eight to ten times.

Now, what about that configuration file? When you first look at `/etc/syslog.conf`, it seems pretty complex, but you'll catch on quickly — after all, you're strong, good-looking, and definitely above average (You bought this book, didn't you? What more proof do you need, anyway?) The best way to understand the syntax is to look at some examples, once you know what you're looking at. Every entry in the `config` file has the following format:

> facility.priority   destination
> (Selector)   (Action)

Let's consider what these mean.

Performing Selector Actions

Note that whitespace separates entry elements. In this case "whitespace" can be tabs, spaces, or a combination thereof (this is important because older versions of syslog only understood tab-delimited configuration files).

So, what exactly are all these mysterious entry elements? The short answer is that they're ways to label inbound messages and outbound destinations. Compliance with these standards isn't enforced (or even enforceable, really), but it is a Really Good Idea.

Selector fields, facilities, and priorities

The syslog.conf entry's Selector field is made up of facilities and priorities. *Facilities* tell which subsystem generated the message — cron, `mail`, `news`, or possibly some other `daemon` without a more specific facility name. You can even assign up to eight locally defined facilities — for home-brew scripts and such — by using `local0` through `local7`. Here's a list of those facilities:

- ◆ auth
- ◆ authpriv
- ◆ cron
- ◆ daemon
- ◆ kern

◆ lpr

◆ mail

◆ mark

◆ news

◆ syslog

◆ user

◆ uucp

◆ local0 – local7

◆ * (wildcard meaning "all facilities")

 The mark facility is for internal use by syslog only, so don't plan on using it anywhere else.

Priorities tell you how important the message is (or how important the program sending the message thinks it is). Remember, one process' disaster is another's minor glitch. The priorities in the Table 19-1 are listed in ascending order of severity. The less severe a log message (the lowest being debug), the more frequent and chatty the messages will be. The priories that syslog uses are as follows:

1. debug

2. info

3. notice

4. warning

5. err

6. crit

7. alert

8. emerg

9. * (wildcard meaning 'all priorties')

Remember, if you configure syslog to store all messages (in a given facility) at a one priority level, it will also store all messages at higher priorities in the same place. So, *facility.priority* means "all messages in facility *facility* at priority *priority* or higher."

The Selector field syntax is `facility.priority.` (note that a ".") joins the two.) Now, rather than make you specify every priority that you're interested in, the clever BSD folks set up the syntax so you can simply specify the lowest severity of message you're willing to accept; then, you'll see everything from that priority and up through `emerg`. The folks writing Red Hat's version of `syslog` thought this control wasn't fine enough, so they added Optional Priority Modifiers, which are used pretty much the way you'd guess. If you use `=warning`, for example, you'll only see warning-level messages. And if you say `!=warning`, you'll see all priorities of messages *except* for warning.

The action portion of the entry specifies the location of the various log files you're using, and how the outbound message should get there.

Destinations

Messages are typically redirected into local log files, but they can also be sent to other local and remote destinations. Even more usefully, log messages can have multiple destinations. For example, you can log everything to one file (`/var/log/messages` is the standard) and then *also* send particular messages to carefully selected files. Many admins like to have a critical log file so they can tell at a glance what high-priority, but non-fatal, errors have been cropping up. Along these same lines, admins also tend to send messages to separate files for their most important facilities. One favorite is to send all kernel messages to someplace such as `/var/log/kernel`.

Log messages don't have to go to files (or just to files). You can send messages to local files, the local console, local named pipes, local users, and even remote systems. Now you're probably thinking, "Yeah, but why?!" Well, think back to what we said before about hybrid logging. You want to scatter copies of logs around so that if you lose one, another one containing the same information is out there. Most crackers aren't swift enough, or even empowered enough, to get all of them. Redundancy, robustness, paranoia: All of these are perfectly valid reasons.

Here's a list of the different types of available destinations.

♦ Full path to a file

♦ Full path to a named pipe

♦ Full path to a named tty

♦ Full path to the console device

♦ Name of a remote machine (this must be preceeded by the @ sign)

♦ List of local usernames

♦ (wildcard meaning 'all users logged in')

Also consider that you have to deal with a notification speed differential. Messages written to a superuser's `tty/login` session may get noticed more quickly than messages simply added to an already bloated system log file. And if you have folks who are paid to watch the system consoles (help desk, operators, and so forth), then you can bet that a message sent to `/dev/console` is likely to get noticed in a hurry. You can't start handling the crisis until you know about it, so quick response is a good thing. Then again, messages slide off those consoles fast, so you probably want them written to files, too. Honestly, logging to several different places is a very useful thing to do.

Referring back to the columns for a second—did you notice the various wild-cards? They're actually pretty intuitive - for instance, * means "everything in the category." The keyword `none` is like an inverse * — it means "nothing in the category."

The Action redirectors let `syslog` know when messages are supposed to go somewhere other than a regular file or console. In particular, @ precedes the name of a remote loghost. By the way, in case it's at all unclear, we think that having local logs and a central loghost is a really good idea.

We're not going to rehash the `man` page here, but definitely check it out for yourself. It has some very useful examples of the various fun and games you can have with `config` file syntax. Here are some examples we thought would be useful to you just to get a feel for how the facilities, priorities and destinations combine.

- ◆ Store all kernel messages in their own file:
  - `kern.*/var/adm/kern.log`
- ◆ Store all non-kernel messages of priority "warning" and higher locally:
  - `.warning; kern.none/var/adm/messages`
- ◆ Send all non-debug-level messages to remote loghost (shown two ways):
  - `.!debug@loghost`
  - `.info@loghost`

Once all your syntax is straight, but before you start funneling huge volumes of text into various collection areas, you will want to consider what you want these logs for. How you will use them can also have some bearing on how you structure their collection and management. It's time to consider using logs.

Using Logs

After you decide how and where to collect your logs, you need to decide what you're going to do with them. You have two choices: You can look at them directly by using simple tools to parse out the records of interest, or you can use utilities to examine the logs and even make simple decisions about how to handle various conditions that logs may report. This section looks at the first choice—more-or-less direct examination of the logs themselves.

Direct examination

Direct examination provides the least return for the greatest effort, making it the most inefficient way to scrutinize logs. If you really want to know what something looks like, you have to see it, so we recommend that you practice direct examination for at least 20 minutes, two or three times a week. Bad as it is, direct examination is the only way to confirm that the record formats aren't changing, that new applications aren't starting to log, and that standard messages from an application haven't changed. Although such aberrations are unlikely to happen at any given moment, we can almost guarantee that all of these things will happen to you eventually — perhaps because of a patch or an upgrade.

Log parsing tools

Looking at an entire log file at one time makes analysis a difficult task, which is why we recommend only occasional direct inspections. Even in a casual examination of logs, you need to find ways to either select the records of interest to you — or at least to filter out those that you know you don't want to look at.

System logs begin with a standard format that you can exploit to filter certain types of records into or out of your consideration. A process produces a system log record when it sends a message to the syslogd daemon. The daemon prefixes the message with a header consisting of the following:

```
Month Day Timestamp System Process_Name [Process_ID]:
```

Here's a list of what each field of the message means, respectively:

- Month: A three-letter abbreviation for the month.
- Day: The day of the month.
- Timestamp: Has the format hours:minutes:seconds with hours ranging from 0 through 23 inclusive.
- System: The name of the system from which the log record was generated.
- Process_Name: The name of the process (sshd, for example) that generated the message to the syslogd daemon.
- [Process_ID]: The ID of the process that generated the message.

As an example, take the following:

```
May  3 10:18:38 treetop.example.com ftpd[2433031]: User bleak timed
out after 900 seconds at Fri May  3 10:18:38 2002
```

The ftpd process with Process ID 2433031 on the system treetop.example.com sent the message User bleak timed out after 900 seconds at Fri May 3 10:18:38 2002 to syslogd. The message was received for logging at 10:18:38 on May 3. Notice that the message itself contains a timestamp, which the ftpd process generated. This isn't always the case. In fact, there is no standard for a log message's content at all; rather, the content is left to the programmer who enters the logging call into the process's source code.

Note also that the timestamps match, suggesting that the systems involved in generating and accepting logs are well-synchronized. Time coordination is very important in log analysis, so you need to become familiar with the configuration and use of ntpd. While we don't discuss it here, ntpd is fairly easy to deploy. You might want to start by reading the homepage www.eecis.udel.edu/~ntp.

egrep — fast and dirty

Without getting into the horrifying details of regular expressions, this section presents a tool that you can use to parse out log records quickly based on the message headers.

You know egrep, right? If you've used it for a week, you probably can't survive without it. I know dozens of people who have gotten (or written) egrep ports for non-Unix operating systems just so they need never be without it. egrep basically works like grep, passing you lines that match a given pattern, but egrep is slightly more powerful, because it can search for regeps, or regular expressions.

We're using a specialized kind of wildcard notation with egrep to pick out headers with certain information. Table 19-1 shows you how to interpret the strange notation inside the double quotes in the command.

TABLE 19-1 REGULAR EXPRESSION SYMBOLS

Symbol	Characters	Meaning
[^]*	left-square, caret, space, right-square, asterisk	All characters until you hit a space (Note the space after the caret.)
*	space, asterisk	One or more spaces until we hit a non-space character (Note the space before the asterisk.)
.*	period, asterisk	All remaining characters in the record (Note the period before the asterisk.)

The line

```
"[^ ]* *[^ ]* *[^ ]* *pinoak.*"
```

means

```
any field, space, any field, space, any field, space, pinoak, the
rest of the string
```

The regular expression matches a log record's Month, Day, and Timestamp fields, whatever their contents. It matches any System field beginning with pinoak. It matches the rest of the record, whatever it may contain.

Briefly, the regex picks out any record generated by the system pinoak. (We're assuming that you don't have other systems named pinoakjr, pinoak3, pinoakjoe, and so forth. Here it is in action:

```
% egrep "[^ ]* *[^ ]* *[^ ]* *pinoak.*" /var/log/messages.6
May  4 01:41:32 pinoak.example.com ipop3d[2552111]: port 110 service
init from 68.55.33.151
May  4 01:41:33 pinoak.example.com ipop3d[2552111]: Login
user=thirmble host=some.cable.modem.net [68.55.33.151] nmsgs=0/0
May  4 01:41:36 pinoak.example.com ipop3d[2552111]: Logout
user=thirmble host=some.cable.modem.net [68.55.33.151] nmsgs=0
ndele=0
May  4 01:41:36 pinoak.example.com sendmail[2762482]:
g445eewT2968157: to=<events@pinoak.example.com>, delay=00:00:56,
xdelay=00:00:56, mailer=local, pri=151144, dsn=5.0.0, stat=Can't
create output
May  4 01:41:36 pinoak.example.com sendmail[2762482]:
g445eewT2968157: g445fawT2762482: DSN: Can't create output
May  4 01:41:38 pinoak.example.com sendmail[2921148]:
g445egwT2934992: to=<gall@pinoak.example.com>, delay=00:00:56,
xdelay=00:00:56, mailer=local, pri=139354, dsn=2.0.0, stat=Sent
May  4 01:41:38 pinoak.example.com sendmail[3000315]:
g445fcwT3000315:
from=<Online#3.13436.85-1IzD_vBcokGY.1.b@newsletter.online.com>,
size=2353, class=0, nrcpts=1,
msgid=<4275762.1020490878254.JavaMail.root@abv-sfo1-ac-agent9>,
bodytype=7BIT, proto=ESMTP, daemon=MTA, relay=sugarmaple.example.com
[130.85.6.40]
May  4 01:41:38 sugarmaple.example.com sendmail[19834]: [ID 801593
mail.info] g445fTaE019819: to=squirk@research.example.com,
delay=00:00:05, xdelay=00:00:00, mailer=esmtp, pri=32367,
relay=pinoak.example.com. [130.85.6.7], dsn=2.0.0, stat=Sent
(g445fcwT3000315 Message accepted for delivery)
May  4 01:41:39 pinoak.example.com sendmail[3055915]:
g445fcwT3000315: to=<squirk@pinoak.example.com>, delay=00:00:01,
xdelay=00:00:01, mailer=local, pri=32368, dsn=2.0.0, stat=Sent
```

From there, you can examine all the logs referencing pinoak. Regular expressions are definitely one of the most useful tools you'll ever find in Linux. Using egrep to find the useful parts of our logs makes diagnosing problems so much easier!

Report generation

When you find yourself looking for the same things in your logs for two or three days running, consider setting up a simple cron job to run a script that generates the report and mails it to you each morning. This morning read can save you from major catastrophes by showing you where problems are brewing before they grow scary.

Of course, you want to decide what interests you before you set up your system to deliver it over your first coffee of the day. You may want to watch certain systems, the activity of certain processes (such as ftpd, sshd, and telnetd), or even activity under specific user accounts (which means parsing the messages).

The following sections discuss how to select reports based on the following criteria:

◆ Applications

◆ System name and application

◆ Messages

Finally, it provides an example of performing more advanced techniques using Perl.

SELECTION ON APPLICATION
The following command returns records of all sshd activity in your log file:

.

.

.

```
% egrep "[^ ]* *[^ ]* *[^ ]* *[^ ]* *sshd.*" /var/syslog/messages.6
May  4 07:52:12 redmaple1.example.com sshd[240]: [ID 363151
local1.info] log: Generating new 768 bit RSA key.
May  4 07:52:16 redmaple1.example.com sshd[240]: [ID 363151
local1.info] log: RSA key generation complete.
May  4 07:54:14 blackbirch.example.com sshd[285]: [ID 363151
local1.info] log: Generating new 768 bit RSA key.
May  4 07:54:18 blackbirch.example.com sshd[285]: [ID 363151
local1.info] log: RSA key generation complete.
May  4 07:55:27 pinoak.example.com sshd[348]: [ID 363151
local1.info] log: Generating new 768 bit RSA key.
May  4 07:55:30 pinoak.example.com sshd[348]: [ID 363151
local1.info] log: RSA key generation complete.
May  4 07:56:55 beech1.example.com sshd[629]: log: Generating new
```

```
768 bit RSA key.
May   4 07:56:56 beech1.example.com sshd[629]: log: RSA key
generation complete.
May   4 07:57:18 beech3.example.com sshd[8251]: log: Connection from
192.168.231.34 port 4797
May   4 07:57:24 beech3.example.com sshd[8251]: log: Password
authentication for araim1 accepted.
May   4 07:57:24 beech3.example.com sshd[8253]: bad pwd
May   4 07:57:49 monitor.example.com sshd[20178]: log: Connection
from 192.168.253.14 port 41507
May   4 07:57:49 monitor.example.com sshd[20178]: fatal: Connection
closed by remote host.
May   4 07:58:25 blackoak.example.com sshd[26381]: [ID 363151
local1.info] log: Connection from 192.168.253.14 port 41541
May   4 07:58:25 blackoak.example.com sshd[26381]: [ID 593182
local1.info] fatal: Connection closed by remote host.
May   4 07:58:47 sugarmaple.example.com sshd[12763]: [ID 363151
local1.info] log: Connection from 192.168.253.14 port 41559
May   4 07:58:47 sugarmaple.example.com sshd[12763]: [ID 593182
local1.info] fatal: Connection closed by remote host.
May   4 08:01:06 beech1.example.com sshd[19928]: log: Connection from
192.168.253.14 port 41607
May   4 08:01:06 beech1.example.com sshd[19928]: fatal: Connection
closed by remote host.
May   4 08:01:43 whitebirch.example.com sshd[3056939]: log:
Connection from 68.55.201.203 port 1032
May   4 08:01:52 whitebirch.example.com sshd[3056939]: log: Password
authentication for kpensy1 accepted.
May   4 08:01:58 beech3.example.com sshd[611]: log: Generating new
768 bit RSA key.
May   4 08:01:58 beech3.example.com sshd[611]: log: RSA key
generation complete.
```

.

.

.

SELECTION ON SYSTEM NAME AND APPLICATION

This command selects records of ftpd activity on the system beech.example.com:

.

.

.

```
%egrep "[^ ]* *[^ ]* *[^ ]* *beech.* *ftpd.*" /var/syslog/messages.6
May   4 17:01:27 beech.example.com ftpd[2921446]: connect from
104.balt.east.verizon.net
```

```
May  4 17:01:28 beech.example.com ftpd[2921446]: login from
104.balt.east.verizon.net as skeen
May  4 17:53:27 beech.example.com ftpd[2983174]: connect
from.dialup.mindspring.com
May  4 17:53:34 beech.example.com ftpd[2983174]: login from
dialup.mindspring.com as bloov
May  4 17:56:20 beech.example.com ftpd[3072765]: connect from
192.168.98.232
May  4 17:56:21 beech.example.com ftpd[3072765]: login from
192.168.98.232 as hoinkle
May  4 17:57:13 beech.example.com ftpd[3045771]: connect from
dialup.mindspring.com
May  4 17:57:19 beech.example.com ftpd[3045771]: login from
dialup.mindspring.com as bloov
May  4 17:58:00 beech.example.com ftpd[3037935]: connect from
education.example.com
May  4 17:58:08 beech.example.com ftpd[3037935]: login from
education.example.com as hoinkle
May  4 17:59:35 beech.example.com ftpd[3085005]: connect from
192.168.98.232
May  4 17:59:36 beech.example.com ftpd[3085005]: login from
192.168.98.232 as hoinkle
May  4 18:42:05 beech.example.com ftpd[3087448]: connect from
thoon.example.com
May  4 18:42:10 beech.example.com ftpd[3087448]: login from
thoon.example.com as freen
May  4 19:00:12 beech.example.com ftpd[3124962]: connect from
pcp345590pcs.comcast.net
May  4 19:00:13 beech.example.com ftpd[3124962]: login from
pcp345590pcs.comcast.net as glornk
May  4 19:30:51 beech.example.com ftpd[3031610]: connect from ppp-
050.dialup.example.com
May  4 19:30:54 beech.example.com ftpd[3031610]: login from ppp-
050.dialup.example.com as twee
May  4 20:14:52 beech.example.com ftpd[3090028]: connect from ppp-
239.dialup.example.com
May  4 20:14:53 beech.example.com ftpd[3090028]: login from ppp-
239.dialup.example.com as norg
May  4 20:15:26 beech.example.com ftpd[2860271]: connect from ppp-
239.dialup.example.com
May  4 20:15:26 beech.example.com ftpd[2860271]: login from ppp-
239.dialup.example.com as norg
May  4 20:26:51 beech.example.com ftpd[2974611]: connect from ppp-
98-111.dialup.example.com
May  4 20:26:52 beech.example.com ftpd[2974611]: login from ppp-
```

98-111.dialup.example.com as mleenplik
May 4 20:43:14 beech.example.com ftpd[2974611]: User mleenplik
timed out after 900 seconds at Sat May 4 20:43:14 2002

.

.

.

SELECTION ON MESSAGE

Most of the time, you'll really want to select on the message contents. The following egrep command retrieves all records regarding activity involving the user
account vroont:

```
% egrep "[^ ]* *[^ ]* *[^ ]* *[^ ]* *[^ ]:.*vroont.*"
/var/syslog/messages.3
May  7 12:04:22 redmaple.example.com sshd[3385918]: log: Password
authentication for vroont accepted.
May  7 12:04:36 redmaple.example.com sudo:  vroont : TTY=ttyq71 ;
PWD=/users/s/b/vroont/home ; USER=root ; COMMAND=/usr/local/bin/bash
May  7 18:30:58 blackoak3.example.com sshd[15901]: log: Password
authentication for vroont accepted.
May  7 19:38:07 blackoak3.example.com sshd[21873]: log: Password
authentication for vroont accepted.
May  7 19:42:09 kerberos.example.com fakeka[178]: authenticate:
vroont.top from 192.168.60.39
May  7 19:42:09 kerberos.example.com fakeka[178]: getticket:
vroont.top from 192.168.60.39 for afs.
May  7 20:35:13 blackoak3.example.com sudo:  vroont : TTY=pts/67 ;
PWD=/users/root ; USER=root ; COMMAND=/bin/bash
May  7 20:46:31 blackoak2.example.com sshd[30092]: log: Kerberos
authentication accepted vroont@EXAMPLE.COM for login to account
vroont from blackoak3.example.com
May  7 20:46:57 blackoak2.example.com sudo:  vroont : TTY=pts/70 ;
PWD=/afs/example.com/users/s/b/vroont/home ; USER=root ;
COMMAND=/bin/bash
May  7 20:49:33 blackoak1.example.com sshd[2308]: log: Kerberos
authentication accepted vroont@EXAMPLE.COM for login to account
vroont from blackoak3.example.com
May  7 20:49:50 blackoak1.example.com sudo:  vroont : TTY=pts/90 ;
PWD=/afs/example.com/users/s/b/vroont/home ; USER=root ;
COMMAND=/bin/bash
May  7 20:56:32 hickory1.example.com sshd[13373]: [ID 363151
local1.info] log: Kerberos authentication accepted
vroont@EXAMPLE.COM for login to account vroont from
blackoak3.example.com
```

MORE ADVANCED TECHNIQUES — USING PERL

There are some things you can't do well by using Unix shell commands. Nice report formats, in particular, don't come easily. If you don't yet know a good scripting language, learn one — and make it Perl. (Even those who prefer some other language will justify their choice through comparisons with Perl.) Perl is easy to learn and if you spend some time learning the language, you can learn to write some really sophisticated applications. One of the first applications that Perl was used for is parsing text reports. Actually, that application motivated Perl's name: Practical Extraction and Reporting Language.

Log monitoring tools

In addition to what you may set up yourself, other log-monitoring tools are publicly available; you can also configure these tools to respond to defined conditions in various ways. LogWatch, which comes with the Red Hat 7.3 distribution, is one example.

 Red Hat version 7.2 comes with LogWatch version 2.1.1, which has a race condition security problem, allowing a local user to access root. A fix appeared in version 2.5, so the problem is solved in LogWatch version 2.6.2, which comes with Red Hat version 7.3.

If you want to update your version of LogWatch, you can get the latest version on the Web at `www.logwatch.org/tabs/download`. We recommend that you download this version no matter what version of Red Hat you're using to make sure that your version is up-to-date.

Although you can reconfigure LogWatch after installation, the program is really meant to be used pretty much as is. LogWatch has a variety of command-line options, which you can use to configure its behavior and output.

These options (from the LogWatch `man` page) include the following:

- `--detail`: Defines the level of detail in the report.

- `--logfile log-file-group`: Determines which logs LogWatch processes.

- `--service service-name`: Sets which services (login, pam, identd) that Logwatch analyzes.

- `--print`: Directs output to STDOUT.

- `--mailto address`: Directs output to be mailed to indicated address.

- `--archives`: Searches archived logs.

- `--usage` and `-help`: Displays usage information.

You can also use the `-range` option to specify a time range for reporting. We recommend against its use as of the current version, as it's currently in the BUGS section of the LogWatch man page. In any case, LogWatch is well-suited for daily summaries. If anything interesting appears, use the techniques discussed earlier to examine your logs directly. In the next section, we will discuss what to do when you discover that you actually *do* have a problem.

Managing Event Responses

After going through all the work of configuring your logs and the daily drudgery of reading the reports, what do you do when you discover that something is actually happening? In some cases, the answer is a no-brainer. If you're accumulating SCSI access errors from a disk, then you need to replace that disk. If a user keeps logging in successfully but can't access her home directory, you need to double-check the permissions, ownership, and existence of that directory.

Suppose, though, that the boss has been logging in every night around 2 a.m. — from Brazil. If he's also been showing up in his office each morning, then someone else is very likely accessing his account. Alternatively, you may see a great deal of `ftp` traffic between a workstation in the accounting department and an IP belonging to a competing company. Is someone in accounting passing along financial information to a competitor? You may also detect odd log records from your Web server, which turn out to match the signature of a new exploit, just publicized that morning. (Good thing you subscribe to BugTraq at `http://online.security focus.com/cgi-bin/sfonline/subscribe.pl`!)

Panic is bad, think ahead

You may be faced with a quick decision (now is a good time to resist the temptation to bolt for the nearest door). For instance, if your Web server is now a haven for hundreds of script kiddies, common sense directs that you shut it down right away. You certainly wonder what the boss's reaction will be to the news that he's sharing his e-mail with a twelve-year-old in Rio. Marketing, however, may have a very different idea. If you use that server to take customer orders, shutting it down will cause copious fallout. You also may be personally reluctant to "rat out" a co-employee who is doing something inappropriate with system resources.

Thinking ahead means policy

Here's the problem. You shouldn't be trying to make these sorts of decisions after you detect a problem. Whether you have your own business or work for someone else's dime, you need to get agreement on the correct course of action before trouble hits. You won't be able to anticipate every eventuality, but try to parse it into broad categories of potential problems. Always include the "unknown" category, which should at least contain instructions on who you inform. Most of the hard decisions involve trade-offs that go outside the responsibility of most sysadmins. Get the people who should make the decisions to agree to some course of action.

Oh, yeah. Any policy of this type should include language that requires the sysadmins to report any suspicious activity (even if that activity is unrelated to the specific problem you're troubleshooting). The language should also include a "Don't shoot the messenger" rule.

Summary

The point of this chapter is that logging and examining logs – while banal and laborious – is one of the most effective measures available in maintaining the security of a system. However, you can use automated reporting to reduce the drudgery drastically. Always remember that log monitoring must be done. After a short time, you will find that you gain a much deeper understanding of your system and how it is used than you would have had otherwise. That understanding tends to be extremely valuable when you're able to head off major disasters while they're still in their infancy.

Appendix A

What's Stored at www.wiley.com?

Wiley provides several software packages and custom scripts. You can find the items at http://www.wiley.com/compbooks/sery:

- ◆ Automated, network-based backups configurations
- ◆ DNS configurations
- ◆ Dynamic IP (DHCP) allocation configurations
- ◆ E-mail server configurations
- ◆ Firewall configuration
- ◆ Icecast/IceS configuration
- ◆ Internet dialup connectivity

Backup Download Content

Download AMANDA client and server configuration files.

Dialup Download Content

Download sample diald and PPP scripts

DNS Download Content

Download the sample DNS configuration and zone files

DCHP Download Content

Download the sample DHCP configuration file

E-Mail Download Content

Sample sendmail.mc M4 scripts are provided for the internal and external sendmail servers (Chivas and Atlas, respectively).

- ◆ Chivas (private network) sendmail.mc M4, mailtertable and other scripts
- ◆ Atlas (DMZ) sendmail.mc M4, mailtertable and other scripts

Firewall Download Content

The following files are available for download:

- ◆ Simple firewall/iptables script (fw.simpl)
- ◆ Advanced firewall/iptables script (fw.full)
- ◆ Firewall reset script (fw.reset)

Kickstart Download Content

The following Kickstart files are available for download:

- ◆ Sample Atlas kickstart (ks.cfg) configuration
- ◆ Sample Chivas kickstart (ks.cfg) configuration

Icecast/IceS Download Content

Here you may download the necessary configuration files for creating a streaming media server.

- ◆ Icecast and Ices version 1 sample configuration files
- ◆ Icecast and Ices version 2 sample configuration files

Appendix B

Configuring a Dial-up Internet Connection

YOU DON'T NEED HIGH–SPEED TECHNOLOGY to connect your private network to the Internet. Old technology – 1990's vintage! – gives a small network Internet functionality. The speed is slow by today's standards, of course, but at least you'll have connectivity. This appendix describes how to use a modem and Point-to-Point Protocol (PPP) to make the connection.

Locating Your Modem

Go ahead and make my day by installing your modem. Follow the instructions that come with the modem, if available. After you insert your modem into your motherboard, or connect it with a serial cable, you have to tell Linux where to find it; that means setting a device file that points to the serial port to which the modem is connected. The following two sections describe how to find a modem by using Microsoft Windows or Red Hat Linux utilities.

 Avoid using WinModems, which are modems designed for Microsoft Windows computers only. They're cheaper than regular modems because they're lazy (or smart, depending on how you look at it) and depend on the Windows operating system to do much of their work for them. Linux drivers are only now beginning to appear for such modems.

Using Red Hat Linux utilities

You can only connect your modem to one of four serial ports available on your PC. Armed with that fact, you should always be able to locate a hiding modem. External modems are generally connected to port /dev/ttyS0 or /dev/ttyS1. (Configuring a modem as /dev/ttyS2 or /dev/ttyS3 is possible, but uncommon). If you have an internal modem, then it can be any one of the tty devices.

During the boot process, the Red Hat Linux kudzu system attempts to locate new devices. This system is quite good at detecting equipment, such as PCI modems.

When you first install either an external or internal modem, kudzu should be able to find it during the boot process. When it prompts you to configure the device, let it do so, and make a note of what device it's attached to.

If kudzu is unable to find your modem, then finding it by the process of elimination — a crude, but effective method — isn't unreasonable.

If you have an external modem, then you can send information to it and look for the light emitting diodes (LEDs) to light up. Login as `root` and open a terminal session. Run the following command (the characters in the echo statement are arbitrary and just used to get the LEDs to light up):

```
echo "asdfasdfasdfasdf" > /dev/ttyS0
```

This simple command sends a text string to the first serial port and if connected, the LEDs should light up in a short burst. If they don't, then try sending the string to /dev/ttyS1, /dev/ttyS2, and finally /dev/ttyS3.

If you have an internal modem, life is a bit harder because you won't have a visual response. You can, however, use the modem's speaker to provide an audio response. Enter the following command:

```
echo "atdt5555309" > /dev/ttyS0
```

If you hear the modem pick up and dial, then you've won the game of hide-and-go-seek. Send the following command to the modem to kill the connection:

```
echo "atz" > /dev/ttyS0
```

If that doesn't work, then use the dial-up program DIP. Type in **dip -t**; the DIP program starts with a `DIP>` prompt. Enter the following commands from the `DIP>` prompt:

```
DIP>port ttyS0
DIP>dial 555-5309
```

Many experienced computer nerds use pppd instead of DIP when setting up their modem. However, pppd is fairly difficult to use because you have to set up supporting scripts and/or use many different options. We use DIP, on the other hand, because you can use it interactively, a great advantage when experimenting or troubleshooting modems.

If the modem picks up and dials, then you've won. Yeah! (Press the Return key immediately to kill the connection.) If not, then after a time, DIP returns to the prompt. You must quit DIP and then restart in order to try ports ttyS1, ttyS2, and finally ttyS3.

 You can also use the Linux boot log system dmesg to locate an internal modem. Use the command dmesg | grep -i modem. If it produces output, then that information should contain the device file to which your modem is attached.

Making the Internet connection

After you obtain an ISP account and locate your modem, you need to tell the Red Hat Linux how to establish a PPP connection. To do so, you must do the following:

1. Execute the PPP program.

2. Dial your modem to connect to your ISP.

3. Make the connection.

4. Negotiate the speed at which the mutual modems will talk.

5. Log on to the ISP's system, giving your username and password.

6. Start the PPP services on either end, creating an Internet Protocol (IP) to flow over the serial line.

SETTING UP YOUR ISP (PPP) CONNECTION

To set up your dial-up PPP connection to your ISP, follow these steps to get into the network configuration window:

1. Log in as root and start linuxconf from a terminal session:

   ```
   linuxconf
   ```

   You may have to manually install linuxconf. To do so, log in as root, mount a Red Hat Linux distribution CD-ROM, and run the following command:

   ```
   rpm -ivh /mnt/cdrom/dialup/linuxconf*
   ```

2. Click on the Config@->Networking@->PPP/SLIP/PLIP option, and the PPP/Slip/Plip menu appears.

3. Click Add, and then Accept. The new window opens.

4. Enter your ISP's phone number.

5. Select the modem port.

6. Enter your ISP user name.

7. Enter your ISP user name password. A sample screen is shown in
Figure 6-3.

8. Click on Customize. A more detailed display of your PPP configuration
appears. Click on any of the tabs to see more information. You shouldn't
have to modify any more settings, but you can if you like.

9. Click on Connect. Your modem dials your ISP, connects, and negotiates
the login process. After you're logged in, your Red Hat Linux box is connected to the Internet.

10. Save your PPP configuration by clicking on Accept, and then clicking on
Quit.

11. Click on Quit, in the lower left hand of the screen. In a few seconds the
screen changes; click on the Activate the changes button in the middle of
the screen. linuxconf exits.

Your settings are saved and ready for use.

ACTIVATING THE CONNECTION

You can use linuxconf to turn your PPP connection on again, as described in Step
9 of the section "Setting up your PPP (ISP) connection."

You can also login as a regular user. Open a terminal emulator shell by clicking
the terminal icon on the Gnome menu bar. From the terminal emulator, type the
following at the command line:

```
ifup ppp0
```

You should first hear a dial tone as your modem picks up the line, followed by
your modem dialing the number. After a ring or two, you hear a scratchy, squawk-
ing sound and then silence.

After a few seconds, networking is working, and your computer is connected to
the Internet. To test that everything is okay, type the following at the command:

```
ping www.swcp.com
```

If you get a message saying that the system is not found, wait a minute more
and try again. Eventually, you should receive a message, talking about how many
milliseconds a round-trip message takes. Congratulations, your networking is
working.

To turn off networking, simply type the following:

```
ifdown ppp0
```

You have now set up the hardware and software to connect your system to the Internet.

AUTOMATING YOUR INTERNET CONNECTION WITH dIALD

Red Hat Linux supplies a simple and effective way to connect to the Internet via its linuxconf system, described in the previous section. This process is a good one, but another system – diald – automates the entire process. diald monitors your computer for any communication going to the Internet. When it sees a packet destined for the outside world, it dials your ISP and negotiates a PPP connection.

We provide the diald package at http://www.wiley.com/compbooks/sery. The following instructions describe how to install and configure the diald package:

1. Log in as root.

2. Mount the companion CD-ROM and install the PPP package:

   ```
   rpm -ivh /mnt/cdrom/dialup/ppp*.rpm
   ```

3. Install the diald package by entering the following command:

   ```
   rpm -ivh /mnt/cdorm/dialup/diald*.rpm
   ```

4. A sample connect script containing the information that diald needs to connect to your ISP is provided at our Web site. diald expects to find the script in the */etc/diald* directory, so copy it there:

   ```
   cp /mnt/cdrom/dialup/connect /etc/diald
   ```

5. The connect script uses example parameters, so you must modify it to match your own ISP's configuration. The essential parameters are the phone number, user name, user password, and prompt. Pay particular attention to the PROMPT option. If your expected value doesn't match with the actual one, then your connection may fail. Your ISP doesn't necessarily supply this information, so you may need to ask for it explicitly; you can also use the DIP program to login and record the information directly. The following list shows the sample connect script:

   ```
   # The initialization string for your modem
   MODEM_INIT="ATZ&C1&D2%C0"
   # The phone number to dial
   PHONE_NUMBER="555-5309"
   # The chat sequence to recognize that the remote system
   # is asking for your user name.
   USER_CHAT_SEQ="ogin:"

   # The string to send in response to the request for your user
   name.
   USER_NAME="Piwantppp"
   ```

```
# The chat sequence to recognize that the remote system
# is asking for your password.
PASSWD_CHAT_SEQ="word:"

# The string to send in response to the request for your
password.
PASSWORD="freewayscarsandtrucks"
# The prompt the remote system will give once you are logged
in
# If you do not define this then the script will assume that
# there is no command to be issued to start up the remote
protocol.
PROMPT="PPP session"
```

6. You must also configure the `diald.conf` script to work with your ISP. That file contains the rules about how `diald` will operate. The standard `diald` expects to find this file in the */etc* directory, so copy it there:

```
cp /mnt/cdrom/dialup/diald.conf      /etc
```

7. Modify the `/etc/diald.conf` script to match your own computer and ISP's configuration. Following is the sample script, which should work without modification:

```
fifo /etc/diald/diald.ctl
mode ppp
connect "sh /etc/diald/connect"
device /dev/modem
speed 115200
modem
lock
crtscts
local 127.0.0.2
remote 127.0.0.3
dynamic
defaultroute
pppd-options asyncmap 0
include /usr/lib/diald/standard.filter
####The following lines activate the firewall described later
in this chapter. ####ip-up /usr/local/etc/ipchains.rules
####ip-down /usr/local/etc/ipchains.reset
```

8. Create a link to your modem port. For instance, if the port is port /dev/ttyS1, then enter the following command:

```
ln -s /dev/ttyS1 /dev/modem
```

9. Finally, if you wish `diald` to start every time you reboot, you need to copy its startup script to the */etc/rc.d/init.d* directory and create a link to it in the startup run-level directories. (Otherwise, simply enter `diald` to start the system manually.)

```
ln -s /etc/rc.d/init.d/diald /etc/rc.d/rc3.d/S91diald
ln -s /etc/rc.d/init.d/diald /etc/rc.d/rc5.d/S91diald
```

10. The default `/etc/rc.d/init.d/diald` startup script expects to see the `diald.conf` script in the */etc/diald* directory. You should see the following line in the script:

```
[ -f /etc/diald/diald.conf ] || exit 0
```

However, the `diald` program itself expects to see the */etc/diald.conf* file. Change the script to reflect that difference:

```
[ -f /etc/diald.conf ] || exit 0
```

11. Start `diald` by running its startup script:

```
/etc/rc.d/init.d/diald start
```

12. Run the **ps x | grep diald** command and the `diald` daemon process should display in a manner similar to the following:

```
324 ?          S        0:07 diald
```

The `diald` program runs in the background as a daemon. The SLIP device is, in general, the default route to the external Internet. When packets destined for an outside network appear on the SLIP device, `diald` starts up the chat script that dials the modem and negotiates the login process with the remote server. The `diald` daemon can set up either a SLIP or a PPP connection, but is most often used with PPP.

`diald` gives your network a functional, effectively continuous Internet connection. Of course, you do have to accept a latency between the time the packets are generated and when they finally get delivered, but you don't have to deal with manually making the Internet connection.

The diald daemon is responsible for setting up your default route — the route that handles all packets that can't be routed explicitly. Using the default route option is a good idea if your LAN has no other Internet connections. (This is why we recommended that you leave the default route blank during the network configuration in Chapter 1.) As a general rule, you probably want any packets not intended for your network going to the Internet. (If you have other Internet connections, you know what's what anyway.)

Nothing happens until a packet hits the default route. Try using a network program, such as Telnet, to access an outside machine — that is, one not on your LAN. Your ISP login computer is a safe bet. If you're running X, open another terminal window or go to an alternate screen and run the `ps/grep` command again. As shown in the resulting output, `diald` spawns a chat script to dial the modem and log in to your ISP's PPP server:

```
1030  ?  S    0:00 diald
1045  ?  S    0:00 sh /etc/ppp/connect
1049  ?  S    0:00 chat -r /var/log/connect REPORT CONNECT TIMEOUT 45 ABORT NO
```

The modem fires up and dials your ISP. After establishing a connection, it feeds your login name and password, and your connection is established. To see that the `pppd` daemon is running, run the following command:

```
ps -x | grep ppp
```

You see the `pppd` daemon as shown in the following line (note that the line is cut short):

```
1132  S0 S    0:00 /usr/sbin/pppd -detach modem crtscts mtu 1500 mru 1500 asyn
```

MODIFYING THE FIREWALL SCRIPTS FOR A DIAL-UP CONNECTION

You must make two changes to the firewall scripts described in Chapter 4 at `http://www.wiley.com/compbooks/sery` to work with the dial-up connection we describe in this appendix.

- ◆ Change the Internet/ISP network connection — `eth1` in our examples — to the PPP device.

- ◆ Use the iptables Masquerade table instead of Source NAT: Most ISPs provide dynamic IP addresses for dial-up connections and the appropriate iptables mode is Masquerade.

The following listing shows the first firewall scripts with the appropriate changes:

```
iptables --flush
iptables --flush -t nat
iptables --policy INPUT   DROP
iptables --policy OUTPUT  DROP
iptables --policy FORWARD DROP
iptables -A OUTPUT -j ACCEPT -o lo
iptables -A INPUT  -j ACCEPT -i lo
```

```
iptables -A OUTPUT -j ACCEPT -o eth1 -p tcp -m state --state ESTABLISHED,NEW
iptables -A INPUT -i eth0 -p -s $PRIV -j ACCEPT
iptables -A INPUT -i ppp0 -p -m state --state ESTABLISHED,RELATED -j ACCEPT
iptables -A FORWARD -i eth0 -j ACCEPT
iptables -A FORWARD -i ppp0 -m state -state ESTABLISHED,RELATED -j ACCEPT
iptables -A POSTROUTING -t nat -o ppp0 -j MASQUERADE
```

Appendix C

Automating Your Server Configuration

THIS APPENDIX DESCRIBES how to use Red Hat's Kickstart installation method and create your own Red Hat Package Manager (RPM) packages. Red Hat designed the system to help automate the installation of its Linux distribution. Automatic installation provides a power tool to the Linux administrator by reducing the labor involved in building Red Hat Linux installations and increasing a Red Hat Linux computer's security (by insuring the exact system configuration and package selection).

You can control a Red Hat Linux installation via the Kickstart system. Kickstart controls the following systems:

◆ Language

◆ Network configuration

◆ Keyboard

◆ Linux loader (LILO)

◆ Disk partitions

◆ Mouse selection (not used here)

◆ X Window System configuration (not used here)

Note that we use non-graphical Red Hat Linux servers in this book and, thus, do not install the X Window System. The final two bullet items are superfluous to our needs.

Performing a Kickstart Installation

Kickstart can use a local CD-ROM, a local hard drive, NFS, FTP, or HTTP to perform a Red Hat Linux installation. Kickstart uses the `ks.cfg` configuration file, which can be located on a local boot drive or the local network.

Typically, the `ks.cfg` file is stored on a bootable MS-DOS diskette. Otherwise, your computer must be able to boot off the network and find the configuration via the network. The network-based process is more difficult to perform and we concentrate on using a floppy diskette-based system in this appendix.

Using Kickstart over a network

Network-based Kickstart installations are more difficult to implement than the floppy-based ones. However, network-based Kickstart installations offer advantages. Once configured, a network-based system offers better automation features than the floppy method. Rather than building different floppies for different installation options, the process is made easier when using a network.

You need a BOOTP or DHCP server on your private network to perform a network-based Kickstart installation. The BOOTP or DHCP server provides the installation client with its IP address so that it can communicate on the network; network connectivity is, of course, essential if the computer is to receive the Kickstart configuration. Please see Appendix D for instructions on configuring a DHCP server.

The Kickstart client needs to NFS mount the directory on the Kickstart server that contains the *ks.cfg* file. For instance, following is the default DHCP server configured by Red Hat Linux:

```
filename "/usr/new-machine/kickstart/";
next-server blarg.redhat.com;
```

The server `blarg.redhat.com` contains the directory `/usr/new-machine/kickstart` where the Kickstart configuration file is stored. The client mounts that directory and proceeds to download and use the *ks.cfg* file. Once loaded, the client installs the Red Hat packages specified from the server's configuration file.

For more information about performing network-based Kickstart installations, please consult the documents in the Kickstart directory stored at `http://www.wiley.com/compbooks/sery`.

Creating a Kickstart Configuration File

A simple-text file, the Kickstart file contains a list of the elements, identified by a key word, used to create a Red Hat Linux computer. Some elements are optional, others are required. You can omit optional elements from the *ks.cfg* file; however, you must manually enter the omitted information during the installation process.

The elements have the following form:

```
<command section> <any combination of %pre, %post, %packages> <installclass>
```

Comments are allowed. Each comment line must begin with the pound — # — sign.

Kickstart can control upgrades. Please consult the Kickstart documentation for information about performing upgrades.

The Kickstart file is divided into three sections:

◆ Commands

◆ Package list

◆ Scripts

The Kickstart file has the following form, an order you must maintain:

```
<kickstart commands>
%packages
<package list>
%post
<post script>
```

The following listing shows the beginning of a sample *ks.cfg* file, based on the server chivas we used in this book:

```
lang en_US

#network --bootproto static --ip 10.0.0.1 --netmask 255.255.255.0 --gateway 10.0
.0.254

cdrom

device ethernet ne2k-pci

keyboard "us"

zerombr yes
clearpart --linux
part swap --size 94
part /home --size 8014
install

mouse genericps/2

timezone America/Denver

...
```

Creating a Kickstart Boot Floppy Diskette

This section describes how to make a Kickstart configuration file based on the current Red Hat Linux computer. We use the server chivas — a server used throughout this book — in this example, and we assume that the Kickstart file is stored on an MS-DOS formatted floppy diskette.

The following instructions take you through the process of creating the diskette and then starting the Red Hat installation process:

1. Install the non-graphical Kickstart configuration package:

   ```
   rpm -ivh /mnt/cdrom/kickstart/mkkickstart*rpm
   ```

2. If necessary, install the boot disk configuration package, too:

   ```
   rpm -ivh /mnt/cdrom/kickstart/mkbootdisk*rpm
   ```

3. Create the Kickstart configuration file (based on the computer from which you run the command):

   ```
   mkkickstart > ks.cfg
   ```

4. Edit the file to automate the network configuration, changing the following lines:

   ```
   #network --bootproto static --ip 10.0.0.1 --netmask
   255.255.255.0 --gateway 10.0
   .0.254
   ```

   to

   ```
   network --bootproto static --ip 192.168.1.250 --netmask
   255.255.255.0 --gateway 192.168.1.254
   ```

   Note that we removed the pound sign — # @m so the line is no longer treated as a comment. The IP addresses have been changed to match the ones we use in this book's examples.

5. If you don't have an MS-DOS formatted floppy, then create one as follows:

   ```
   fdformat /dev/fd1H1440
   ```

6. Create a boot disk:.

   ```
   mkbootdisk 2.4-2.2
   ```

   The command requires that you supply the version of the kernel that you want to use on the floppy diskette. In this case, we use the default version for 7.1. Use the command **uname -a** to find the running version.

7. Copy the *ks.cfg* file to the floppy diskette:

```
mcopy ks.cfg a:
```

Once the file has been copied to the floppy, you can begin a Kickstart installation.

The next section describes using Kickstart to install Red Hat Linux.

Performing a Kickstart Installation

You need to boot from the Red Hat Linux boot disk to begin a Kickstart installation, and you need to pass the Kickstart parameters from the LILO prompt. The following instructions describe the process:

1. Insert the Linux boot disk containing the *ks.cfg* file into the floppy drive.

2. Insert a Red Hat Linux distribution disk in the CD-ROM drive.

3. Turn the power on. The following LILO prompt is displayed when the kernel has loaded from the floppy:

```
boot:
```

4. Specify the Kickstart boot from the floppy by entering the following line at the `boot:` prompt:

```
linux ks=floppy
```

5. The Kickstart process begins; you're prompted for any information that hasn't been included in the *ks.cfg* file.

 Alternatively, you can place the *ks.cfg* file on a Linux file system. The format for this method is `ks=file:/<file>`. For instance, if the Kickstart file is on the `hda7:/var/kickstart` partition, then the syntax is `ks=hda7:/var/kickstart/ks.cfg`.

Creating Custom RPMs

The RPM greatly simplifies the process of installing, deleting, and maintaining Linux software. RPM allows you to create packages containing specialized configurations, as well as just software, so you can use RPM to create custom packages of your own design, too.

You can use a custom RPM package to automate and systematize your server configuration, and then use the Kickstart system to install such packages, further automating your server configuration. This section describes in cookbook form how to create a custom RPM package. The package described here configures the private network sendmail server, which we described in Chapter 11.

Introducing the RPM package layout

`www.redhat.com/support/books/max-rpm/max-rpm-html/ch-rpm-basics.html`
An RPM package has three inputs:

◆ **Sources:** The location of the software included in the package. The location should be of the unmodified sources – the location of the pristine source is essential in order to establish a known starting point.

◆ **Patches:** Since the pristine software is given as the starting point, all changes must be implemented from patches.

◆ **Spec File:** This file contains all the information about how to build the package. The spec file defines which files the package includes and where you should install them.

The spec file is composed of the following sections:

- **Preamble:** This information, which displays when you use the RPM manager query option, identifies information, such as the version number.

- **Prep:** Consisting of either a shell script or RPM macros, this section contains the information that's used to start the RPM build process.

- **Build:** This section consists of a shell script that's used to execute the commands necessary to build the package.

- **Install:** This section contains another shell script that's used to install the package's individual pieces.

- **Install and Uninstall Scripts:** This section includes the commands and scripts that the target system uses to install or remove the package. You run these scripts either pre-installation or post-installation.

- **Verify Script:** You use this script to verify the package contents beyond what the RPM program is able to do on its own.

- **Clean:** You use this optional script to clean up after the build beyond what RPM is able to do itself.

- **File List:** The list of files comprising the package, as well as any macros used to control file attributes during the installation, are stored here. No package build can occur without this list.

Building an example RPM package

You can use the following script (called `chivas_mail.pre`) to create an RPM package that builds an */etc/sendmail.cf* file for our example mail server, `chivas`:

```
#
# Example spec file for Red Hat Linux Internet Server
# example mail server
# Summary: Private network - paunchy.net - mail server
# configuration file
Name: chivas
Version: 0.1
Release: 1
Copyright: GPL
Group: bogus/misc
Source: ftp://ftp.mylinuxbooks.com/pub/email/chivas.tgz
URL: http://www.mylinuxbooks.com/rhlis/email/chivas.html
Distribution: test
Vendor: Paunchy Heavy Industries, Ltd
Packager: paunchy the demi dog <pdog@mylinuxbooks.com>
Summary: The private network M4 file and the Makefile to build it
%description
Build an M4 macro to create a private network sendmail.cf

%prep

%build
m4 $RPM_SOURCES_DIR/sendmail.mc > /tmp/sendmail.cf

%install
mv -f $RPM_BUILD_DIR/sendmail.cf > /etc
/etc/rc.d/init.d/sendmail restart

%files
/etc/mail/sendmail.mc
/etc/mail/Makefile
/etc/mail/access
/etc/mail/domaintable
/etc/mail/virtusertable
/etc/mail/mailertable
```

The following instructions describe how to use the script to create the package:

1. Log in as `root`.

2. Copy the M4 script from Chapter 11 into the */usr/src/redhat/SOURCES* directory. The script is reprinted here for your convenience:

```
divert(-1)
dnl This is the sendmail macro config file. If you make
changes to this file,
dnl you need the sendmail-cf rpm installed and then have to
generate a
dnl new /etc/sendmail.cf by running the following command:
dnl
dnl          m4 /etc/mail/sendmail.mc > /etc/sendmail.cf
dnl
include(`/usr/share/sendmail-cf/m4/cf.m4')
VERSIONID(`linux setup for Red Hat Linux')dnl
OSTYPE(`linux')
define(`confDEF_USER_ID',``8:12'')dnl

define(`confPRIVACY_FLAGS',
`authwarnings,novrfy,noexpn,restrictqrun')
define(`confMAX_HOP',`25')
define(`confMIME_FORMAT_ERRORS',`False')

FEATURE(`promiscuous_relay')
FEATURE(`accept_unqualified_senders')
FEATURE(`use_cw_file')

MASQUERADE_AS(paunchy.net)
FEATURE(`mailertable',`hash -o /etc/mail/mailertable')

MAILER(smtp)dnl
MAILER(procmail)dnl
```

3. Copy the `Makefile, access, domaintable, mailertable, virtusertable,` and `trusted-users` files from /etc/mail into the /usr/src/redhat/ SOURCES directory, too.

4. Build the RPM package:

```
rpm -qa chivas_mail.pre
```

5. Install the package, and you've created the customized sendmail configuration.

You now can automatically construct the private network sendmail server we describe in Chapter 10. You can also use the RPM system to customize any other of your configurations. This method greatly simplifies the job of designing and creating servers.

Appendix D

Using DHCP

THE EXAMPLE NETWORKS WE USE in this book use static IP addresses, which is reasonable for small to medium-sized networks where your workstations are stationary. However, if you use laptops, or if you tend to move your computers around, then you may want to use dynamic IP addresses.

You can use the Dynamic Host Configuration Protocol (DHCP) to assign IP addresses to any or all of the computers on your network. This appendix describes a simple DHCP example where mobile Windows and Linux computers use a portion of the 192.168.1.0 subnet.

Installing dhcpd

You have to install the DHCP on a server, as shown in the following steps (using `chivas` as the example server):

1. Login to `chivas` as `root`.

2. Mount a Red Hat Linux CD-ROM.

3. Install the DHCP server:

   ```
   rpm -ivh /mnt/cdrom/utilities/dhcpd*
   ```

4. Create the */etc/dhcpd.conf* file and enter the following information:

   ```
   option routers 192.168.1.254;
   shared-network PAUNCHY.NET {
           subnet 192.168.1.0 netmask 255.255.255.0 {
              range 192.168.1.40 192.168.1.50;
           }
        }
   ```

   The first section describes the range of IP addresses, within the class C subnet 192.168.1.0, that the DHCP clients are going to use.

5. Create the */etc/dhcpd.leases* file:

   ```
   touch /etc/dhcpd.leases
   ```

   You don't need to put anything into this file. The dhcpd daemon dynamically puts information here about the computers that are getting their IP addresses from DHCP. Not surprisingly, those addresses are called *leases*.

513

6. Start the dhcpd server:

```
/etc/rc.d/init.d/dhcpd start
```

Your dhcpd server chivas is now ready for Windows and Linux computers to get their IP addresses and routing information.

Configuring a Red Hat Linux Workstation to Use DHCP

You only need to modify the /etc/sysconfig/network-scripts/ifcfg-eth0 file to make a Linux box look to the dhcpd server for its network configuration. The file should look as follows:

```
DEVICE=eth0
BOOTPROTO=dhcp
ONBOOT=yes
Tip
```

You can also use linuxconf to modify your Ethernet NIC. Open up the network host configuration window and click on the DHCP radio button.

The next time that you boot your Linux computer, or restart the /etc/rc.d/init.d/network script, you'll obtain the IP address, netmask, broadcast address, and routing information from the dhcpd server.

 If you manually modify the ifcfg-eth0 file, you don't need to remove the static IP information. By modifying the PROTOCOL parameter to use DHCP, your system will ignore the static information and pick up its parameters dynamically. However, your computer will revert to using the static parameters if the DHCP service is unavailable.

Configuring Windows As a DHCP Client

Setting up a Microsoft Windows computer to use DHCP is very simple:

1. Log into your Windows computer. (NT systems require you to login as the administrator).

2. Open the Network Configuration dialog box:

   Start ➪ Control Panel ➪ Network

3. Open the TCP/IP properties dialog box.

4. Click on the IP Address tab.

5. Click on the Obtain an IP address dynamically radio button.

6. Click on OK.

7. Click on the OK button in the Network dialog box.

8. Click OK when asked if you want to restart you computer.

9. When your Windows computer restarts, it'll be assigned an IP address between 192.168.1.40 and 192.168.1.50; the address will be 192.168.1.40 the first time that you use this system. You can prove this to yourself by looking at the /etc/dhcpd.aliases file and/or pinging the 192.168.1.40 address.

Your Windows computer will now obtain its address from the DHCP server on your network. For instance, you can now use your laptop on both your home and work network (if they both use DHCP) without reconfiguring it each time.

Index

Symbols & Numbers

continued

continued

continued